Occupational Licensure and Regulation

A Conference Sponsored by the
American Enterprise Institute for Public Policy Research

Occupational Licensure and Regulation

Edited by Simon Rottenberg

American Enterprise Institute for Public Policy Research
Washington and London

Library of Congress Cataloging in Publication Data

Main entry under title:

Occupational licensure and regulation.

(AEI symposia ; 80F)
1. Occupations—Law and legislation—United States.—
Congresses. 2. Occupations—Licenses—United States.—
Congresses. I. Rottenberg, Simon. II. Series:
American Enterprise Institute for Public Policy
Research. AEI symposia ; 80F.
KF2900.A75023   344.73'017   80–23205
ISBN 0–8447–2192–1
ISBN 0–8447–2193–X (pbk.)

AEI Symposia 80-F

Printed in the United States of America

Contents

PART THREE

PART FOUR

PART FIVE

PART SIX

PART SEVEN

Contributors

Lee Benham
Center for the Study of American Business, Washington University

Bryan L. Boulier
Office of Population Research, Princeton University

Kenneth W. Clarkson
Law and Economics Center, University of Miami

William S. Comanor
Department of Economics, University of California at Santa Barbara

Stuart Dorsey
College of Business, Western Illinois University

Robert G. Evans
Department of Economics, University of British Columbia

Richard B. Freeman
Department of Economics, Harvard University

Mark F. Grady
College of Law, University of Iowa

George A. Hay
Cornell University Law School

Donald R. House
Resources Research Corporation

Keith B. Leffler
Department of Economics, University of Washington

Hayne E. Leland
Graduate School of Business, University of California at Berkeley

Janice F. Madden
Regional Science Department, University of Pennsylvania

Donald L. Martin
National Economic Research Associates, Inc.

Alex R. Maurizi
Maurizi Associates, Inc.

Jack A. Meyer
American Enterprise Institute

Timothy J. Muris
Law and Economics Center, University of Miami

B. Peter Pashigan
Graduate School of Business, University of Chicago

Michael Pertschuk
Federal Trade Commission

Robert B. Reich
Federal Trade Commission

Simon Rottenberg
University of Massachusetts

Peter Schuck
Yale Law School

Benjamin Shimberg
Educational Testing Service

George J. Stigler
Charles R. Walgreen Foundation for the Study of American
Institutions, University of Chicago

Michael J. Trebilcock
Faculty of Law, University of Toronto

Carolyn J. Tuohy
Department of Political Economy and School of Health
Administration, University of Toronto

William D. White
Department of Economics, University of Illinois at Chicago Circle

Walter E. Williams
Department of Economics, George Mason University

Alan D. Wolfson
Department of Political Economy and School of Health
Administration, University of Toronto

*This conference was held
at the Mayflower Hotel in Washington, D.C.,
February 22–29, 1979*

Foreword

"Competition of ideas is fundamental to a free society." That is the motto at the American Enterprise Institute, and it is not simply a plea for space in a world already crowded with policy analysts, academic specialists, and government experts of one sort or another. Although AEI itself does not take any official positions on public policy questions, over the years we have sponsored a considerable amount of research exploring the advantages of increasing competition in the economy and illustrating the advantage of competition of ideas.

One of the things that those carrying out the research have reported, in case after case, is that competition encourages innovation and experimentation (with ultimate benefits in price and quality for the consumer), while regulation that limits competition chokes off incentives for improvement and experimentation. After a number of disillusioning experiences with government regulatory schemes over the last decades, educated opinion is now much less inclined to welcome government planning and control than it used to be. We would like to think that some of the careful scholarship we have sponsored over the years has contributed to a full discussion of this subject.

A conference on occupational licensing and regulation, however, differs in one essential respect from a conference on, say, transportation regulation. We are not dealing with a control scheme put together or extended from its previous scope in quick response to a passing crisis. While state regulation of certain professions *does* seem to have increased in recent years, regulation of professions like law or medicine can be traced back to the guild system of the Middle Ages, or even before. When Robin Hood was regulating transportation in Sherwood Forest (somewhat irregularly), professional groups were regulating themselves under royal charter in the towns of England.

Of course, licensure increases costs and is thus a kind of tax on society, but in the words of Oliver Wendell Holmes, inscribed beneath the pediment of the Internal Revenue Service building, "Taxes are what we pay for a civilized society." So it may be here, as with other taxes, that there really is no way to avoid *some* of the costs and inconveniences of licensure in public health, safety, and justice. Licensure may be part of the price we pay for civilized society.

Nonetheless, there remain important questions about the proper scope and shape of professional self-regulation. How much choice should be left to the consumer, and how can he or she be taught to purchase professional services wisely? Should the consumer be permitted to choose practitioners of less than best quality, if the only alternative is to have professional services priced altogether beyond his or her range? How can we balance the need to maintain professional standards against the dangers of monopoly pricing? There may be no single or easy answer to any of these questions, but they are still questions that should be asked.

Many of the participants in this AEI Conference on Occupational Licensure have extensive practical experience in this area, and they know that close study and careful thought are required to improve on present practices. They know also, as we do, that the proper relation between scholars and practitioners in public policy debates is not for scholars to preach the latest academic gospel to a passive congregation of practitioners. It is for scholars and practitioners together to attack the problems, with scholarly discipline and practical knowledge. And if we can stimulate additional inquiries into this important subject, we will have furthered our aims in particular and the aims of public policy research in general.

WILLIAM J. BAROODY, JR.
President
American Enterprise Institute
for Public Policy Research

Introduction

Simon Rottenberg

Occupational licensure can be approached within a framework of basic economics. The people of every country produce and consume diverse commodities and services. This mixed bag—the economy's output—is produced by combining the services of labor with other factors of production. These services of labor appear in varied forms; some involve more—and some less—energy, skill, intellect, and risk. The different tasks that are performed by those who render labor services and the different properties of those tasks are many and varied. People specialize in rendering labor services; each person who works performs a set of tasks that constitutes a very small portion of all the tasks done by all the people of the community. Since there is specialization of labor but less specialization in consumption, exchange occurs. Each person exchanges part of the product of his or her own specialized services for the products of others who also are specialized in the services they offer.

Invention, innovation, discovery, resource exhaustion, changes in the age composition of the population, and other such phenomena cause the composite set of tasks carried out by a country's people to be changed over time in sum and in the way they are arranged. That is to say, these variables affect the way in which all tasks are subdivided into subsets of tasks performed by an individual specialized worker. At any given time, however, some structure of task distribution occurs in society, and we have adopted the convention of calling each small set of tasks done by a homogeneous class of workers an occupation. The actual number of such occupations in any country will depend on the degree of diversity of the output of the country and on the degree of specialization in work.

In the United States, most occupations can be freely entered. An individual desiring to enter need only invest in acquiring the skills necessary to perform the tasks of the occupation, offer his services in the market at the market price, and diffuse information among prospective purchasers that his services are available on those terms. When exchange occurs, it is consensual. Both sellers and buyers of the proffered services are unconstrained; neither is compelled to transact or to refrain from transacting. Since exchange, when it occurs, is consensual, both sellers and buyers are made better off for having made the exchange.

Some occupations are, however, licensed. In those cases, entry into an occupation cannot occur except with the permission of the state, and sellers and buyers cannot transact an exchange of the relevant services of the occupation unless the state has given its permission. There are said to be some eight hundred occupations licensed by at least one state in the United States. They include some learned professions (medicine and the law, for example) and some occupations requiring less time to learn (such as barbering) that are licensed in all states and other occupations that are licensed in only a smaller number of states. Some, indeed, are licensed in only a single state. Walter Gellhorn has reported that "in many parts of this country today aspiring bee keepers, embalmers, lightning rod salesmen, septic tank cleaners, taxidermists, and tree surgeons must obtain official approval before seeking the public's patronage."[1] To this list one might add tattooers, tourist guides, rainmakers, horse hunters, transporters of horses, cotton classers, threshers, textbook salesmen, and cosmeticians, all of which are licensed occupations in at least one state. Moreover, in addition to occupational licensing by states, some occupations require licenses issued by the federal government, and others require licenses issued by municipal authorities. The freedom of entry into occupations is additionally diminished indirectly by the licensing of businesses (interstate trucking), activities (the grazing of livestock on public lands, the storage of acids), and physical assets (air pollution control equipment, aircraft engines).

Occupational licensing appears in state statutes in three forms. In the strongest and most authentic form, the statutes define the tasks and functions of the occupation, prescribe that these tasks and functions may not be legally performed except by those upon whom the state has conferred a license, and describe the procedures for the acquisition of a license—which are, usually, the passing of an examination by those who are qualified by statute to be admitted to the examination and who petition for the right to be examined. In a weaker form, the statutes permit any person to offer his services in an occupation and permit the tasks of the occupation to be done by anyone, but they prescribe that only those who have qualified by examination may use the title of the occupation when services are offered to the public. These are sometimes called "title-protection" statutes. In a still weaker form, the statutes permit any person to offer services and to perform the relevant tasks,

---

[1] Walter Gellhorn, "The Abuse of Occupational Licensing," *University of Chicago Law Review,* vol. 44, no. 1 (Fall 1976), p. 6.

but the state administers an examination periodically and certifies those who have passed. This is sometimes called "certification."

Of greatest interest here are the implications of the strongest of these forms because it is in that form that occupational licensing is an instrument of public policy by which the state most clearly constrains entry into the licensed occupations. These strong occupational licensing statutes provide that only licensed persons may practice the relevant profession or trade and that, to secure a license, applicants must usually fulfill criteria of schooling, experience, and examination of competence. The licensing statutes generally define the behavior or the activities that only licensed persons may engage in. Persons not licensed may not legally engage in these activities. Thus, licensed persons "monopolize" the statutorily prescribed activities. Sometimes these defined activities encompass a broad area of tasks and cover many important activities; sometimes the definition of those activities that may by undertaken only by licensed persons is narrow, encompassing only few and trivial tasks.

Given the strength of the constraints on entry into the occupations imposed by licensing requirements regarding schooling, experience, and examination, the monopoly effects of a licensing statute will be powerful or weak, depending on the breadth or narrowness of the activities that may be legally performed only by licensed persons.

Licensing imposes higher costs of entry into the occupation than would exist if the occupation were not licensed. The stronger the constraints on entry and the more restrictive the requirements for procuring a license, the larger are the incremental costs of entry into the occupation imposed by licensing. If entry costs into an occupation are raised, the quantity of services produced in that occupation will diminish, and the price of the services will rise. The size of these output and price effects will depend on how good the available substitutes are. The more imperfect the substitutes, the larger will be the effect on prices and the smaller the effect on output; conversely, of course, the better the substitutes for the services of the licensed occupation, the smaller will be the effect on price and the larger the effect on output.

Entry costs imposed by licensing may be considered an entry fee paid by new entrants to the occupation to buy the right to acquire income in the practice of the licensed trade. Or they may be considered a tax on entry into the occupation. In the end, after market adjustments have had time to work themselves out, the incremental licensing costs of entry will really be borne jointly by buyers and sellers of the relevant services. The more imperfect the substitutes for the services produced in the licensed occupation, the larger the fraction of the incremental costs borne by buyers.

Sometimes the effects of an increase in the entry costs for new

3

entrants can be achieved without additional legislation by the exercise of discretion by license examining boards. Examining boards are almost invariably heavily composed of incumbent practitioners in the relevant profession—the nominal defense for which is that practitioners are most knowledgeable about the profession. Practitioners on examining boards can, however, administer the licensing law in ways that advance their interests at the expense of others (such as consumers of the services of the relevant profession, those who aspire to enter the profession, or employers of those in the relevant profession). Thus examining boards can strengthen constraints on entry into licensed occupations by manipulating the examination pass rates. If the boards desire to reduce the number of new entrants at any time, they can raise the standards for passing the examination. Thus they will achieve the same purpose as an amendment to the licensing law imposing stronger constraints on entry (more schooling, or experience, or a higher age to qualify for taking the licensing examination).

For a given licensed occupation, there will be variance among states in the quality of schooling and experience required before a candidate may present himself or herself for examination, and there will be variance among states in pass rates on the license examination. Similarly, for a given licensed occupation and a given state, there will be variance in examination pass rates from one period of time to another. Thus, in some states and at some times, the constraints on entry into a licensed occupation will be stronger or more restrictive than in other states or at other times.

For some occupations, having a license in one state suffices to permit practice of the profession in some other states; for others, having a license in one state suffices to secure a license, without examination, in some other states; in still others, having a license in one state is *not* sufficient to secure a license in other states or to engage in professional practice in other states. In other words, there is variance in reciprocity rules among licensed occupations. In the absence of reciprocity, a practitioner must qualify for examination, pass the exmination, and secure a license in each state in which he or she practices his profession. This diminishes the interstate movement of professionals and impedes the adjustment of the supply of professional services to changes in the interstate structure of the demand for those services.

When campaigns are mounted to have what has been an unlicensed occupation licensed by a state, they are usually organized by incumbent practitioners in the occupation. Statutes that first provide for the licensing of occupations commonly contain what have come to be called "grandfather clauses," which provide that persons practicing the relevant occupation at the time of the initial enactment of the licensing statute shall be licensed without examination. Current practitioners are thus not required to establish their competence by examination, nor are they necessarily required to fulfill the statute's prescriptions on schooling and experience. It is sometimes said that grandfather clauses are placed in licensing statutes because incumbent practitioners have established their competence by their survival in practice, but it seems clear that their main purpose is to ensure enactment of the licensing statute. Legislatures are not likely to accept a licensing arrangement for an occupation if incumbents make known their opposition to it, and incumbents are likely to oppose, and make known their opposition, if the law threatens their livelihoods and their survival in the occupation.

When licensing laws contain grandfather clauses, the additional costs of entry into the occupation imposed by the laws fall only upon new entrants. Since the cost of entry is then higher for new entrants than it was for those engaged in the practice of the profession at the time the law was enacted, the *net* earnings from the profession are higher for those practicing before the law was passed than for new entrants. When a licensing law thus imposes additional costs of entry upon new entrants to a profession, this produces a monopoly return for the current practitioners: what economists call an economic rent. In general, the size of this monopoly return will depend on the size of the entry costs imposed by the licensing law. New entrants do not get a monopoly return. The licensing law will secure higher earnings for them, but it also imposes upon them higher entry costs. If the market functions well, incrementally higher earnings will be just sufficient to compensate new entrants for higher entry costs. Adjusted for entry costs, earnings will be the same in licensed professions as in similar, unlicensed professions.

In addition to campaigns for the licensing of still unlicensed occupations, campaigns are also mounted for additional legislation affecting already licensed occupations; those campaigns are also frequently coupled with grandfather clauses. Such campaigns propose, for example, raising standards for (cost of) entry into the licensed occupations, extending the definitions of professional practice requiring license, striking down exemptions that permit some professional practice to be done by unlicensed persons, and so on.

When campaigns are conducted to secure the initial passage of a licensing statute for an occupation that is still unlicensed, or to secure stronger constraints on entry into a licensed occupation, or to strike down exemptions that permit unlicensed persons to practice a profession in some defined circumstances, or to broaden the definition of professional practice that can be carried out only by licensed persons, it is almost invariably true that the campaigners will assert that the legislation they are promoting will serve the public interest. Licensing (or the strengthening or extension of licensing), they say, will assure the public that the quality of the service or products they buy will be of higher and thus acceptable quality because incompetents who have not passed muster and exhibited their competence by successful performance on an examination are excluded from offering their services in the relevant occupation. The public safety, they say, is served by licensing because those offering unsafe service and products are excluded from performing in the relevant profession. Consumers are thus assured that only people of certified competence will make their services legally available.

It is of some interest, however, that consumers rarely engage in campaigns to have occupations licensed, but incumbent practitioners in an occupation often do engage in such campaigns. If the purpose of licensing were to improve the quality of service, one would expect licensing campaigns to be promoted by consumers, who might be the beneficiaries. If we observe that licensing is systematically promoted by practitioners, we might reasonably suspect that it is the interests of the practitioners that are advanced by licensing legislation.

It is, in fact, not unambiguously clear that occupational licensing improves the quality of service and product or that it promotes safety. Licensing, by making entry into an occupation more costly, increases the price of service rendered in the occupation and diminishes the numbers employed in the occupation. As a result, some consumers resort to do-it-yourself methods, and this sometimes results in lower-quality work and less safety than would occur if there were no licensing. In addition, if some consumers are moved from lower-quality to higher-quality consumption as a result of licensing, they will do so at increased expense. The increment of their expenditure for this service will be taken from other things that they might have purchased and, all things considered, they may be made worse off by the enactment of a licensing law. They may, in the economists' jargon, be forced to lower indifference curves. (These ambiguous quality effects of licensing are reinforced by license examinations that test for knowledge and skills sometimes irrelevant to the successful performance of the task of the trade.)

It is sometimes said that the state must act as the agent of consumers and prevent the practice of professions and trades by incompetents in those cases in which information is not symmetrically distributed in markets, in other words, in markets in which sellers know more about the quality of the products and services they offer for sale than do the buyers. In such markets the forces of competition will, we are told, ineluctably lead to the survival only of firms offering commodities of the lowest quality produced at the lowest cost.

In the real world, sellers are specialized producers, and consuming buyers are (generally) nonspecialized households. Producers sell a small number of different commodities; households buy a large number of them. In these conditions of differential intensities of specialization, information appears to be asymmetrically distributed in almost all markets. Sellers would appear systematically to know more about product qualities than buyers generally. Thus, in this argument, we should expect to find only lowest-quality models of commodities offered everywhere, but this is not what we do find. In unregulated markets in which commodities and services may be offered without constraints on entry and without the enforcement of standards of quality by the state, we observe arrays of models offered for sale; competition does not foreclose the entry of high-quality commodities and services. It is clearly apparent to the most casual observer that relatively high-quality goods and services are available (at relatively high prices) in markets for food, clothing, shelter, transportation, education, health care, recreation, and so on.

How can observed experience be reconciled with theoretical expectation? Probably market processes operate in such a way that the assumption of informational asymmetry is rarely fulfilled. Nonspecialized buyers turn out to be not so ignorant of the qualitative properties of commodities and services as they seem to be. They seek out informational surrogates that serve them well. They acquire information by repeatedly purchasing certain commodities; for infrequently purchased commodities, they are informed by the experience of kinfolk, friends, and neighbors. Sellers of complex commodities have market incentives to inform buyers of the qualities of products and services they themselves offer and of those offered by their competitors. Buyers are further informed by inference by the length of life of firms making offers, because it is reasonable to assume that firms with a long life have survived the consensual judgment of the market about the quality of the commodities they offer for sale; shops with professional staffs of buyers serve as surrogate information agents of consumers; and tort law that imposes liability on producers and sellers to "make whole" those whom they harm gives sellers incentives to produce goods and services of a quality that does not fall below some given standard.

It does not appear that competitive markets in the real world serve consumers as badly as the informational asymmetry model suggests they do. Therefore, it does not follow that apparent informational asymmetry should be optimally adjusted for by state enforcement of standards of quality and competence, as through the enactment of occupational licensing statutes.

There is a fairly substantial literature on the economics of occupational licensing, most of which appears in the professional economic journals. The consensus of that literature can be summarized in the following statements:

- Occupational licensing is primarily promoted by practitioners of the occupation rather than by consumers of its services. Licensing primarily serves the interests of practitioners rather than the interests of consumers.

- The public-interest defenses for occupational licensing are of questionable merit.

- Whether licensing of occupations results in improvement in the quality of service offered is debatable. It is not certain that quality of service is improved if a license is required for the performance of an occupation.

- Certification provides consumers with information by telling them that all who are certified in an occupation are qualified in the sense that they have successfully passed the certification examination; but certification does not permit the use of the law to constrain entry into an occupation for purposes that serve the interests of practitioners rather than consumers.

- The licensing of occupations tends to dampen the rate of innovation in the licensed occupations.

- The administration of licensing laws is carried out in ways that reduce the dissemination of information.

- The licensing of occupations permits the definition and enforcement of anticompetitive practices in the delivery of services.

- Licensing has the effect of increasing earnings in the licensed occupations.

- The enforcement of the monopoly right of licensed persons to practice a licensed occupation is frequently undertaken by private professional associations of licensed practitioners who use agencies of the state as instruments of enforcement.

- Examining boards in licensed occupations are frequently composed of licensed persons in the relevant occupation and only infrequently include representatives of consumers of the services of the occupation.

- Examining boards are able to control the rate of entry into a licensed occupation by manipulating the "pass rate" of those taking the license examination. The pass rate will be sometimes high or low, depending on the state of earnings and employment of those already in the licensed occupation. The manipulation of the pass rate is evidence that examining boards administer licensing legislation primarily to protect incumbent licensed practitioners in the licensed occupations.

- When practitioners in an occupation promote the licensing of that occupation, they frequently permit incumbent practitioners to continue to practice in the occupation without being required to pass a competence examination. Incumbents who are thus "grandfathered in" will earn a monopoly return in the practice of the occupation.

- Occupation licensing checks entry into occupations by imposing additional costs of entry.

- Practitioners in a licensed occupation are given an advantage if the standards and costs of entry are made higher than they were when current practitioners entered the relevant occupation. Practitioners have an incentive to promote continuously higher standards and cost of entry into licensed occupations.

- The licensing of occupations inhibits the movement of practitioners among the states, because the possession of a license in one state does not necessarily qualify a person to practice in another state. Therefore, licensing checks the rate at which the allocation of services in licensed occupations among the states can adjust to changes in the locational distribution of the demand for the services of those occupations.

- The licensing of an occupation reduces the number who practice that occupation. Those who are excluded make their way into other occupations; they are less productive in those second-best occupations than they would be in the licensed occupation from which they are excluded.

The papers of this volume, which were prepared for a Conference on Occupational Licensure and Regulation in Washington, D.C., in February 1979, contain findings that sometimes confirm, sometimes question, and sometimes modify the prior consensus of professional judgment on occupational licensing. They constitute an interesting and important contribution to the literature.

The papers discuss explanations for the existence of occupational licensing, the nature and consequences of the forms of social organization implied by licensure, and the history of constraints on entry into occupations. They treat the distribution of the licensing phenomenon among occupations and seek to explain why some, but not all, occupations are licensed and the principles that influence the social decision on which of them will be licensed.

They analyze some of the effects of licensing in some particular occupational contexts: California contractors, registered nurses, and dentists.

These occupational reviews suggest that the licensing of an occupation need not improve the quality of services rendered in it and may increase the price of services in it; that incumbents in an occupation, rather than consumers of their services, may be the main protagonists for the licensing of their occupation and might be mainly moved in this activity by the desire to reduce the competition for their services of persons in related, but less-skilled, occupations; that sometimes the effects of licensing on earnings in the licensed occupation are not clear-cut; and that licensing limits the movement of licensed practitioners among states, influences the geographical distribution of licensed professional services, and diminishes both consumer and producer benefits generated by professional service.

The papers examine the administration of the law on occupational regulation. One scrutinizes the activities of the Federal Trade Commission in the occupational regulation field, and another reviews the prospective effects on occupational licensing of the sunset legislation adopted by many state legislatures to review periodically and systematically the continuing desirability of public programs and laws. Both papers are, for different reasons, doubtful that the administration of the law in these respects will have a large influence on the quantity of occupational regulation that occurs in the American economy.

The papers also treat the effects of licensing on the employment of blacks, the interstate mobility of members of the licensed occupations, the theoretical principles of professional regulation, the forms of regulation that are open to choice, and the characteristics of market failure, including informational asymmetry that, it is suggested, produce warrants for occupational regulation. All are critically examined by discussants whose comments appear in the volume.

The volume concludes with two conference luncheon addresses by Michael Pertschuk, chairman of the Federal Trade Commission, and George J. Stigler, Charles R. Walgreen Distinguished Service Professor and director, Center for the Study of the Economy and the State, at the University of Chicago.

Part
One

The Demand for
Occupational Licensure

Lee Benham

The regulation of occupations has a long tradition. Until the eighteenth century, the usual form of association among workers was the guild, which had striking similarities to the modern licensed occupation.[1] Guilds have been traced from the tenth century in London and the eleventh century in western Europe. The impulse to regulate occupations through licensure or its equivalent has been widespread, and the resulting associations have shown strong survival traits. In this regard the nineteenth century, which saw a decline in guild influence, appears to have been an anomaly. During the present century, the United States appears to be reverting to the norm.

Licensed occupations have deeper historical roots and probably stronger survival traits than many of our present-day institutions—including the limited liability stock company—and because licensing sometimes significantly alters the character of economic activity, it would seem reasonable that we should have an explanation for the existence of this form of regulation and the nature and consequences of the resulting organizations.

Economic theory concerning occupational licensure is limited, and a better general understanding of the phenomenon is essential if we are to explain the common characteristics of licensed occupations, the conditions that appear to affect their growth, and their consequences. This paper does not provide such a theory but has the modest objective of describing some characteristics that such a theory would illuminate.

We can begin by asking what it is that makes guild regulation or the licensure process attractive to the members of an occupation. The existence or prospect of gain is a facile but unilluminating answer. The

I thank Alexandra Benham for extensive comments and for furnishing some of the source material and Mark Moran for research assistance. Financial support for this project was provided in part by the Center for the Study of American Business, Washington University, St. Louis.
[1] The guilds in India were hereditary and may have been precursors of the caste system. See E. H. Phelps-Brown, *The Economics of Labor* (New Haven: Yale University Press, 1962), p. 29. Also George Unwin, *The Gilds and Companies of London* (London: Methuen, 1908), pp. 1–14.

question is, What forms do the gains take, and what are their magnitudes?

Licensed occupations or guilds are characterized by controls over entry. We expect that entry barriers will create windfall gains (rents), that these prospective rents provide an important impetus for licensure, and that the threat of loss of rents is a major reason why removal of licensure is so strongly resisted by members of a licensed occupation. Economists have given considerable attention to the impact of licensure on barriers to entry but, as will be noted later, the rents thus calculated in the economic literature are likely to be an incomplete measure of the benefits received. In particular, one benefit of licensure not generally captured in conventional rate-of-return calculations is that of increased security.

We expect that individuals will purchase insurance policies to reduce risks. Given that many individuals have a substantial long-term undiversified investment in their education and training—their human capital—we should not be surprised at the existence of a strong underlying demand for human capital or "career" insurance. There are, however, serious constraints on the extent to which an individual can insure or diversify to reduce risks. As training becomes longer and more specialized, diversification becomes more difficult. The transactions costs of shifting careers are likely to be high. Insurance policies to hedge against a fall in career earnings are limited to a few areas (life and health insurance, for example) while unemployment insurance and welfare payments provide some coverage. Beyond these and the element of insurance provided in long-term employment contracts,[2] it is only the unusual individual who can hedge by selling interest in his or her future earnings: a few athletes and executives can do so.

One way individuals hedge is by supporting institutional arrangements that serve some of the same functions as insurance. These institutional arrangements include licensing of occupations or the establishment of guilds that protect their members from the consequences of market competition, whether between members and outsiders or among the members themselves. The idea that the demand for security is a principal reason for many of our labor market institutions is hardly new. Back in 1928, Selig Perlman argued the point very effectively in his *A Theory of the Labor Movement*.[3] What has not been done is to examine

---

[2] This may be one reason why occupations characterized by large employers are less frequently licensed. The usual argument is that the employers can effectively resist licensure.

[3] Selig Perlman, *A Theory of the Labor Movement* (1928; reprint ed., New York: Augustus Kelley, 1949).

systematically the implications of this idea for the character of regulations associated with occupational licensure.

If members or potential members of an occupation have an underlying demand for higher earnings and for security, we expect the quantity observed of such "services" to be a function of the strength of demand and the costs associated with supplying them. A variety of "firms" supply such services: unions, political parties, corporations, voluntary professional associations, licensed occupations, and guilds. To understand the role licensure plays in the supply of rents and security, some discussion of the ways in which these "firms" provide these services appears warranted.[4]

That licensed occupations regulate entry and attempt to maintain and expand their jurisdiction is not surprising. Both activities have obvious consequences for the earnings of their members. In addition to regulating the competition from outsiders, many licensed groups regulate the competition among members through restrictions on the production process. The reasons for this internal regulation are not self-evident in terms of simple rent-seeking behavior. These restrictions on the production process often appear to be remarkably inefficient methods of restricting output and increasing members' income. Some examples will illustrate these types of restraints.

Among the early guild records were discussions of the "stint" rolls, which limited the quantity of input one could buy and the quantity of output one could sell. For example, the Merchant Adventurers, originating in the fourteenth century, stated that:

> Upon complaint made by the yong men, that some great traders doe buy up such quantities of Clothes weekly, that the yong men cannot get Cloth for their money. It was ordered that whosoever shall hereafter shipp more than *his respective Stint*, he shall pay doble imposicions and doble imprest for all that he shall soe Shipp.[5]

It is not surprising that the number of apprentices a member of a craft guild could hire was limited, given that apprentices would soon be competitors, but there were also limits placed on the number of journeymen one could hire. Competition was not limited solely by the regulation of firm size and constraints on firm sales. Attempts to solicit consumers or to advertise were also restricted. For example, the Merchant Adventurers stated:

---

[4] It can be argued that the term "rent" should include all the benefits accruing from licensure. Virtually no attention has been given in empirical work to insurance benefits, however.

[5] W. E. Lingelback, *The Merchant Adventurers of England: Their Laws and Ordinances* (New York: Lenox Hill, 1971; reprinted from New York: Burt Franklin, 1902), p. 135.

[N]o persons shall stand watchinge at the Corners on the ends of streets or at other mens Pack houses [places of business] or at the house or place where anie Clothe merchant or draper ys lodged, nor seeinge anie such in the Street shall run or ffollow after hym with intent to Entyce or lead hym to his packhouse, upon pain of fyve pounds ster.[6]

Most modern licensed occupations similarly attempt to regulate competition among members. Advertising and soliciting of business are continuing areas of concern.[7] The conditions under which a licensed member can be employed are frequently constrained.[8] In general, the role of the entrepreneur who seeks to introduce technological or managerial innovations is restricted whether or not the entrepreneur is within the occupation.[9]

Licensing provides security in another form. The enforcement of admissions standards or performance standards generally varies with the state of employment of those holding licenses. When some are unemployed or underemployed at the "fair wage," there is a much greater likelihood of an organizational effort to limit new entrants and to enforce the codes more strictly. This, of course, is hardly unique to licensed occupations; unions and nation-states are commonly observed to behave differently when members or citizens are employed than when they are not. When members are unemployed, stricter restrictions are sought. Licensing appears to provide some hedge against downside risks because of the "firm's" willingness or ability to reduce competition differentially when conditions are bad.[10]

To say that licensing exists because it provides rents and security is not very illuminating, however, since all individuals presumably prefer

---

[6] Ibid., p. 91.

[7] Lee Benham and Alexandra Benham, "Regulating through the Professions: A Perspective on Information Control," *Journal of Law and Economics*, vol. 18, no. 2 (October 1975), pp. 421–48.

[8] "The bar . . . would be degraded if even its humblest member became subject to the order of a money making corporation." *In re* Cooperative Law Co., 198 N.Y. 479, 92 N.E. 14, 16 (1910). See People v. John H. Woodbury Dermatological Institute, 1922 N.Y. 454, 85 N.E. 697 (1908) for a discussion of the limits placed on the corporate practice of medicine.

[9] "Existing task delegation regulations in most states—by precluding certain cost-effective input substitution possibilities—significantly contract the productivity potential of dentists. . . . A model practice in the least restrictive state (Kentucky) generates about 86 percent more output and 186 percent more net revenue than one in the more restrictive state (North Dakota)." Joseph Lipscomb, "Legal Restrictions on Input Substitution in Production: The Case of General Dentistry," Institution of Policy Sciences and Public Affairs, Duke University, February 1977.

[10] This behavior appears anomalous, inasmuch as it implies that a gain forgone is different from a loss incurred. Lower costs to the organization of imposing the additional restrictions when members are unemployed offer one possible explanation.

more of these to less. The question is why some groups are more successful than others at obtaining the licensure control necessary to provide these services. One reason appears to be an ability to persuade the larger society.

Licensed occupations place great emphasis on convincing the larger society of the benefits associated with their licensure, undertaking a wide range of activities and expending substantial resources to persuade their own members and the public at large of their legitimacy. Indeed, in this regard, a common activity in twentieth-century America has been the cultivation of the public perception of "market failures" or externalities. Almost all licensed occupations have claimed they will successfully cope with undesirable market failures. Frequently there has been little or no evidence in support of the proposition that such externalities exist or that the proposed solution will improve the situation. The absence of systematic evidence in support of such claims has, however, never appeared to act as a deterrent. Presumably the groups making such claims are not doing so solely for their own edification: the claims appear to be important, perhaps even essential, to survival.

Economists have rarely given any systematic attention to this issue, generally viewing such "educational" efforts as merely self-serving and largely irrelevant. However, this attitude ignores the substantial resources directed to this activity and their effect on the terms under which competition is carried out, on the nature of property rights, and on transactions costs. Our perception of the existence of externalities and their importance is significantly influenced by the efforts of these groups. Douglass North has defined the public good as "nothing more or less than the comprehensive system of cognition and moral beliefs called ideology. Political and judicial conceptions of 'the public good' have obviously changed in the past century."[11] The efforts of the licensed occupations have substantially contributed to the formation of and changes in our notion of the public good.

Resources expended to this end consist not only of those used in public proclamations of the "good" forthcoming from stricter regulation and the "bad" forthcoming otherwise but also of the investments in training programs to educate new members into understanding the public benefits provided and their role in communicating those benefits to the public. It should come as no surprise that much of the research undertaken within the occupation is focused on the services that can be provided by members and discovering further serious consequences of relaxing controls. If influencing the definition of the public good is as

---

[11] Douglass North, "Structure and Performance: The Task of Economic History," *Journal of Economic Literature*, vol. 16 (September 1978), p. 973.

important to the success of occupational licensure as I am suggesting, then the efforts expended to this end are no surprise. That the emphasis on public benefit expressed by these groups is not simply an artifact of current times can be illustrated by the petitions of the English guilds. Even when the petitioners were proposing purchase of a guild monopoly from the sovereign, they emphasized the public's benefits along with the sovereign's. A typical example is the Petition of the Brick and Tile Makers of London in 1634:

> For the making of bricks and tiles being a matter of great consequence and the commonwealth much suffering by reason of the badness of stuffs now usually made which causeth men to build houses upon leases in slight and dangerous manner. And raiseth much the rents of houses and breedeth many other enormities. For remedy whereof and for prevention of the daily destruction of timber which will cause the decay of shipping within your Majesty's kingdoms, your Majesty's first petitioners offering to your Majesty 4d. for every thousand of bricks and tiles which shall be made and sold; and we your now petitioners do willingly offer 6d. for every thousand shall be made and sold, as said is, which truly may be given without wronging the subject or damaging the makers.
>
> . . . And for the speedy furtherance of a good yearly revenue to your Majesty (seeing that there is neither law nor reason to the contrary) that your Majesty would be graciously pleased to cause [to] give order to your Attorney-General for the drawing up of a corporation about the City of London and 20 miles compass thereof. . . .
>
> And we (as by duty bound) shall ever pray for your Majesty's long life and most happy reign.[12]

The Goldsmiths' Complaints against the Aliens in 1622 express great concern that

> "said aliens and strangers . . . make and sell many deceitful jewels, pearls, counterfeit stones, and other goldsmith's wares of gold and silver to the great deceit of the nobility and people of this kingdom."[13]

In more recent times the argument of public benefit has continued, with particular emphasis on public health. One example is that of an 1895 legal case in New York in which a master plumber named Nechameus argued that he was unable to get a license because of his race and religion and because he did not belong to an association of master

---

[12] Joan Thirsk and J. P. Cooper, eds., *Seventeenth Century Economic Documents* (Oxford: Clarendon Press, 1972), pp. 236–37.
[13] Ibid., pp. 716–17.

plumbers. The court found the law fully justified for reasons of public health.[14]

In 1901, S. J. Errington, at a banquet of Local 14 of the Barbers' Union in Fort Wayne, Indiana, complained indignantly of eight-week barber courses that produced a flood of new barbers who "cut prices" and were "unable to tell the difference between a filthy disease and a pimple." The remedy he proposed was licensing laws. "It takes legislation to protect us from scab prices, pestilence and disease."[15]

Obtaining licensure and successfully protecting the occupation's jurisdiction require more than a proclamation of doing good, however, at least most of the time.[16] They require an ability to mobilize resources to lobby in the political arena and to defend against attacks by other groups. In this connection, there are several free-rider problems with which a successful guild must deal. First, members of the group benefit as a result of efforts by the group, but individually they have little incentive to contribute time or money. Dues or tie-in purchase arrangements for occupationally related activities are common methods of raising revenue. The requirement that members hold a license, the issuance of which is controlled by representatives of the occupation, obviously reduces the costs of dealing with this form of free-rider problem.

A second free-rider problem arises because of the intimate connection between the necessary public support for licensure and an occupation's claims of enhancing the public welfare. If licensing is a response to alleged market failures, the occupation is under some constraint to do more than simply restrict entry and go about business as usual. The implicit quid pro quo is that undesirable market failures will be constrained and uncertainties concerning quality of service will be reduced. Thus individual members of the occupation who deviate from publicly approved norms or codes of conduct are viewed by others in the occupation as harming not only themselves and their customers but the occupation at large. To control this problem, occupations usually seek to set standards of training, and they bring sanctions against those who deviate from the occupationally acceptable forms of behavior.

---

[14] Lawrence Friedman, "Freedom of Contract and Occupational Licensing 1890–1910: A Legal and Social Study," *California Law Review*, vol. 53, p. 521.

[15] *Barbers' Journal* 34 (1901), cited in Friedman, "Freedom of Contract," p. 500.

[16] When the horseshoers of Illinois sought a law to regulate their practice in 1901, they were aware of the need for some defense on grounds of public health and welfare. They argued that the law was connected with the health of horses, a veterinary surgeon was put on the board, and apprentices were required to attend a series of lectures on the anatomy of horses' feet. The horseshoers' physical contact with horses gave some plausibility to the argument, but a court decision in 1904 limited public health considerations to human beings: the court argued that, at worst, bad horseshoeing might produce an occasional corn or pain. An Illinois Horseshoeing Act was finally passed in 1915. See Friedman, "Freedom of Contract," p. 518.

A third free-rider problem arises because members' support for a given licensing arrangement depends in part on the distribution of earnings within the occupation. If competition among members is so keen that rents are eliminated for a significant proportion of the members, those members have little reason to support the overall objectives of the occupation, to contribute time and money, or to oppose the formation of new rival groups. If an occupation is to be able to mobilize its members politically over time, it will need to offer benefits to most of them. This point may appear obvious, but its implication for the character of the regulation of competition among members is perhaps less so. Were no constraints placed on the activities members could undertake once licensed, the more enterprising members would be unconstrained in the forms of innovation they could introduce. Whether technical or organizational, such innovations generally tend to increase output and to substitute the labor or less-skilled unlicensed workers for that of licensed practitioners. Successful entrepreneurs of this type within the occupation would do very well for themselves, but in the process many other members would be made worse off. Thus the integrity of the organization as a whole—particularly as a political entity—would be threatened by excessive competition among members.

To obtain licensing initially generally requires a significant effort with little prospect for the individuals involved of capturing more than a tiny fraction of the rents generated. Apparently there are other rewards because there have been many aspirants.[17] A certain amount of political power accrues to the heads of newly licensed occupations, and the leader who initially obtains licensing for the occupation is generally revered thereafter as a kind of patron saint of the occupation.

This characterization of the behavior of licensed occupations has implications for the ways in which rents are created and dissipated. Even those observers most sympathetic to licensure expect some rents

---

[17] One example of a pioneer in "professionalizing" undertakers was Hudson Sampson. He demanded a law "regulating the care and burial of the dead the same as there is for the practice of medicine." He designed "the artifacts of a professional funeral [including] a special eight poster, oval-decked funeral car [and] a magnificent hand-carved wooden draped hearse." Friedman, "Freedom of Contract," p. 50.

Charles Prentice, the founder of organized optometry in the United States, launched his crusade upon receiving a letter from Henry Noyes, a New York physician who complained that Prentice was accepting a fee for examination. According to Noyes, Prentice was only supposed to sell glasses. Prentice responded that despite his own training in optics and his publication on ophthalmic lenses, the local oculists were not sending enough prescriptions for him to operate successfully as an optician. Prentice then continued, "You must admit that, with my scientific training and sense of justice, I could hardly be expected to starve, merely in deference to the opinions of these scientific men, oculists, who remain wholly indifferent to my welfare, while lending their undivided support to my less worthy competitors." Monroe Hirsch and Ralph Wick, The Optometric Profession (Philadelphia: Chilton Book Co., 1968), p. 132.

to be created in the process, but economists on the whole have generally found relatively moderate rents when they have calculated rates of return to new entrants in the occupation.[18] In my view, it is an error to conclude from these estimates that the distortion caused by licensure is low. The creation of rents through licensure results in competition for those rents. We should therefore expect that over time this competition will dissipate the rents[19] and that new entrants will receive a normal rate of return.[20]

Any systematic deviation from normal returns would thus be more likely to reflect incomplete accounting of either costs or returns than rents. It is therefore difficult to ascertain whether or not rents to new entrants exist. Moreover, even if such calculations could be made with reasonable precision, the magnitude of the estimates would be an extremely unreliable measure of the overall distortion introduced by licensure. This is so for the reasons discussed. The nature of the production process is in many cases significantly altered as a consequence of licensure, and there is no reason why these distortions should be reflected (except perhaps temporarily) in the rents received by members. This line of argument, though pessimistic about the usefulness of direct calculation of rents, does suggest we can learn by examining more closely the forms in which the rents are dissipated.

One of the most common ways of dissipating rents is by lengthening training programs. From the "firm's" standpoint, this method has the advantage that it can be rationalized on grounds of raising quality. The longer and more specialized training in turn increases the professional character of graduates, who then better understand and can better articulate the public benefits provided and who also are more aware of the close relationship between their own fortunes and those of the "firm." To neglect the impact of licensing control over length of training can lead to serious errors in assessing the impact of licensure.

Consider, for example, optometry. When optometry was first licensed in 1901, it was possible to train for optometry in a two-week course. Since then the length of training has increased approximately one year per decade. The current training period of eight years consti-

---

[18] "Any reasonable objective of physicians colluding via the American Medical Association (AMA) should include the promotion of rents to currently practicing physicians. Therefore, the essential test of the success of the AMA in controlling supply is to examine the returns to physician training." Keith B. Leffler, "Physician Licensure: Competition and Monopoly in American Medicine," *Journal of Law and Economics*, vol. 21 (April 1978), p. 166. Leffler also has a discussion of other estimates for physicians.

[19] See Richard A. Posner, "The Social Costs of Monopoly and Regulation," *Journal of Political Economy*, vol. 83, no. 4 (August 1975), p. 807.

[20] See Gordon Tullock, "The Transitory Gains Gap," *Bell Journal of Economics and Management Science*, vol. 6, no. 2 (Autumn 1975), p. 671.

tutes a 15,600 percent increase across this seventy-eight-year period.[21] If the number of applications is any indication, some rents currently remain. There are now approximately ten "qualified" applicants for each position available.[22]

How do members of an occupation take advantage of increased demand for admission? Some argue that this competition is used to select higher-quality applicants, but there is little direct evidence to support this proposition. On the other hand, there is unambiguous evidence that some nonperformance criteria are used in selecting applicants.[23] An example from veterinary medicine will illustrate this point. The College of Veterinary Medicine at the University of Missouri at Columbia states, "The University of Missouri does not discriminate on the basis of race, color, religion, marital status, sex, national origin or age."[24] Directly above this statement are data on state and school of origin for students admitted in 1976. The data show that of the seventy-six applicants admitted, seventy-one came from Missouri, including fifty-one from the University of Missouri system, of whom forty-six were from the University of Missouri at Columbia. It cannot be argued that this selection criterion is designed to ensure the most qualified veterinarians. Among state veterinary schools, the University of Missouri is comparatively generous in admitting out-of-state students. Illinois, Florida, Tennessee, and Texas A&M admitted no out-of-state students during the same period. Most out-of-state residents in state veterinarian schools appear to be admitted under an arrangement through which states without such schools buy a certain number of

---

[21] "Optometry in 1960 was the third most rapidly advancing profession in income. Although it has a long way to go to equal the medical and dental professions, it seems to be well on its way; there are enough optometrists who are on equal footing economically with other professional men to influence attitudes in most communities." Hirsch and Wick, *The Optometric Profession*, p. 237.

[22] Students may be admitted to the four-year optometric training program after only two years of undergraduate work, but the proportion with four years of undergraduate or preoptometric training is now over 60 percent and increasing. Department of Higher Education, State of Missouri, *Proposal: A Regional School of Optometry*, December 1, 1977, p. 8.

[23] One study of foreign medical graduates concluded that "variables unrelated to competence, namely state and visa-citizenship status, are important determinants of medical licensure in the United States. The pattern is quite clear: (1) the closer the FMG [Foreign Medical Graduate] is to U.S. citizenship, the greater the probability of being licensed; (2) in certain states (e.g., Florida and Missouri) FMG & USMG [U.S. Medical Graduates] licensing rates are similar. In other states (e.g., New Jersey and West Virginia) USMG licensing rates are far higher than FMG rates; (3) this pattern holds irrespective of the physician's country of medical education." Arlene Goldblatt, Louis Goodman, Stephen Mick, and Rosemary Stevens, "Licensure, Competence and Manpower Distribution," Yale University Institute for Social and Policy Analysis, Working Paper W4–37.

[24] College of Veterinary Medicine, University of Missouri-Columbia, "Summary Profile of Class of 1982," Fall 1979.

positions in other states' schools. Students from states lacking both veterinarian schools and buy-in arrangements elsewhere are unlikely to become veterinarians. It is noteworthy that in 1976 the only private veterinarian school, at Tuskegee, took less than 35 percent of its students from Georgia. The remainder were distributed across many states and also included the only four foreign students admitted to U.S. veterinary schools in that year. This pattern is characteristic of many licensed occupations in which training is subsidized by the state. One of the reasons given for such policies by state schools is that they are designed to increase the number of members of an occupation working in the state, so as to reduce the "shortages." The evidence supporting this argument is weak.

To examine directly the issue of the impact of school location on the number of veterinarians practicing within the state, the following equation was estimated across the fifty states for 1977:[25]

Veterinarians per 1,000 people $= 0.6536$
$$+ \; 0.2636 \text{ cattle per capita}$$
$$(3.8)$$
$$+ \; 0.2244 \text{ sheep per capita}$$
$$(1.4)$$
$$+ \; 0.4246 \text{ hogs per capita}$$
$$(4.0)$$
$$+ \; 0.000077 \text{ income}$$
$$(1.07)$$
$$+ \; 0.2017 \text{ veterinarian school in state}$$
$$(1.64)$$

($R^2 = 0.73$; t-statistics in parentheses)

The presence of schools within the state does not have a significant effect on the number of veterinarians per capita in the state.

My own view is that the windfall gains captured by some entrants provide a powerful impetus for having positions available for state residents. The dramatically reduced opportunity for entry into the most highly remunerated occupations, such as medicine and dentistry, because of the absence of a state school is not viewed favorably by voters. From this viewpoint, it is largely irrelevant whether or not the construction of a school actually leads to a net increase in the number of graduates practicing in the state. The number of home-grown members will increase, and some of these home-state members will capture windfalls. This can be viewed as a type of expensive lottery run by the state, which

---

[25] This equation is missing a key set of variables that we were unable to locate: the number of dogs and cats per capita.

permits a few local college students to win a valuable admission to a profession.

The same process of escalating educational standards is at work even when no formal education is required for entry. Stuart Dorsey has shown in his study of cosmetologists (hairdressers) that the licensing examination favors those with more education. Estimating the rates of return to education in this case provides virtually no useful information concerning the distortion introduced by the licensing process. Dorsey documents the distributive impact of this licensing process, indicating that minority candidates and those with less education or less formal training in cosmetology are disadvantaged.[26]

As this discussion makes clear, it is my view that economists have concentrated excessively on the direct effects of barriers to entry and too little on such issues as restrictions on innovation, excessive training requirements, and politically generated demand for services supplied by the occupation. Licensing can be viewed as a type of innovation that permits new forms of economic organization to evolve. The nature of competition is fundamentally altered by the licensing process. An understanding of the causes and consequences of licensure and the resulting organizational structures should be an objective of research. This task is difficult because our theory of institutional change is very limited and most of our standard analytical tools have been developed to examine economic behavior when institutions are defined to facilitate efficient market exchange.[27]

We are most unlikely to succeed in understanding these organizations if we limit ourselves to what Hirshleifer has called "constitutional economics." He places conventional market analysis within the following hierarchy:

> On the strictest, most constrained, level is "constitutional economics"—market economics. The "constitutional politics" game is at a higher level, as it can be played to change the rules or conditions of market rivalry, for example by redistributing wealth. But constitutional politics is itself limited by accepted man-made constraints in the form of initial distributions of legitimate power. The highest and biggest game of all is *non-constitutional* politics (or, better perhaps, *meta-constitutional* politics). The biggest game of social interaction is subject only to the laws of nature. There are no property rights, and the ultimate arbiter is the physical force of individuals or of the coalitions they can form.[28]

---

[26] Stuart Dorsey, "The Occupational Licensing Queue," *Journal of Human Resources*, vol. 15, no. 3 (Summer 1980), p. 424.

[27] See North, *Structure and Performance*, p. 968.

The form of competition in which licensed occupations appear to invest their most substantial resources and to engage most effectively lies in the realm of constitutional politics—in defining and changing the rules and conditions of market rivalry. This competition warrants our attention.

---

[28] Jack Hirshleifer, "Comment," *Journal of Law and Economics*, vol. 19, no. 2 (August 1976), p. 244.

The Impact of Regulation on Quality: The Case of California Contractors

Alex R. Maurizi

The principal rationale for licensing occupations is the protection of the public health and safety. It is said that consumers sometimes face difficulty in making rational choices because they lack information on the quality of available goods or services before purchase. If it is difficult for the consumer to recover damages suffered at the hands of a "low-quality" practitioner or if the damages are irreparable, avoiding these damages is said to be worth the higher prices that accompany the licensing that prevents these transactions from occurring. The objective of occupational licensing is to raise the average level of quality by eliminating the low-cost, low-quality providers. Average prices increase, but the resulting higher quality is said to be worth this cost.

Maintaining minimum standards of competence may be difficult, however. Some consumers will actually want lower-priced, lower-quality service. Lower-quality practitioners will supply this service if they have the opportunity. These transactions can take place illegally if enforcement is lax or the penalty for such illegal transactions is low in relation to the possible gain. More important, perhaps, the low-quality suppliers may attempt to circumvent the minimum-quality standards in quite legal ways. If the minimum standards can be circumvented, consumers will be receiving the same quality service as they would if there were no licensing, but they will be paying higher prices because of the entry restriction and the costs of circumvention. In this event, consumers would be better off without licensing.

Economists have long been concerned about the impact of licensing provisions on prices, but it is only recently that they have become concerned about the lower quality of service that may result from licensing. Studies by Sidney Carroll and Robert Gaston[1] and Roger Feld-

The author wishes to thank Joseph Hight and Sandra Benham for their helpful comments on an earlier draft.

[1] Sidney Carroll and Robert Gaston, "Occupational Licensing," unpublished paper (Knoxville, Tenn.: University of Tennessee, October 31, 1977), and "The Quality of Legal Services: Peer Review, Insurance & Disciplinary Evidence," unpublished paper (Knoxville, Tenn.: University of Tennessee, 1978).

man and James Begun[2] are examples of this growing concern. As a result of investigations such as these and a recent study by Benjamin Shimberg,[3] a number of states have begun to consider alternatives to the traditional methods of licensing professions and occupations. California,[4] Michigan,[5] Washington,[6] and Wisconsin[7] have conducted studies to determine if the public interest could be better served in alternative ways.

Because so little investigation of quality impact has been done, that is what this study focuses on. It examines data on consumer complaints before one regulatory board—the Contractors' State License Board in California. Although the investigation reaches no definite conclusions, its results do suggest that minimum competency standards for licensing contractors are being circumvented. The policy implications of this finding are discussed later.

Consumer Complaints: An Indicator of Low-Quality Service

It should be noted at the outset that we are examining voiced complaints emanating largely from consumers but that consumer dissatisfaction does not always manifest itself in voiced complaints. Consumers may simply seek another provider of the good or service at the next time of purchase. This alternative is more likely the more frequent the purchase, the less expensive it is, the smaller the proportion of the consumer's income devoted to it, and the less serious the damage resulting from poor quality. The purchase of haircuts is an excellent case in point, in which the typical consumer is unlikely to voice a formal complaint about poor quality. The purchase of a contractor's services, on the other hand, is just the opposite. Consumers' purchase of a contractor's services is infrequent at best, is expensive, costs a sizable portion of the typical consumer's income, and can produce serious and long-lasting damages if the services are of poor quality.

The increased likelihood that consumers will voice complaints if

[2] Roger Feldman and James Begun, "The Effects of Advertising—Lessons from Optometry," *Journal of Human Resources*, vol. 13, supplement (1978), pp. 247–62.

[3] Benjamin Shimberg, *Improving Occupational Regulation* (Princeton, N.J.: Educational Testing Service, 1976).

[4] California State Department of Consumer Affairs, *Regulatory Review Task Force Report* (Sacramento, Calif., May 31, 1978).

[5] Michigan House of Representatives, *Final Report of the Special Committee to Investigate the Department of Licensing & Regulation* (Lansing, Mich., February 1977).

[6] Washington House of Representatives Commerce Committee, *Licensure: Professions & Occupations* (Olympia, Wash., January 1977).

[7] Wisconsin Legislative Council Staff, *Regulation and Licensing: An Overview* (Madison, Wis., July 1976).

they receive poor-quality work from a contractor does not, by itself, mean that an increase in the frequency of poor-quality work will produce an equivalent increase in the number of voiced complaints. If the licensing board has a history of rejecting justifiable consumer complaints or of failing to rectify them, consumers will in many cases fail to voice them. Moreover, if consumers who want to voice formal complaints face considerable difficulties in doing so, they will be dissuaded from that course of action. There could be few office locations to which consumers could go to voice complaints, for example, or the forms and instructions for filing a complaint could be long and involved and difficult to understand. A recent survey by the Field Research Corporation revealed that 95 percent of the 12.7 million California adults used the services of a licensee in 1977 and between 4.7 million and 6.7 million were dissatisfied with the services. Only half of the dissatisfied consumers complained; one-third of those who did not complain felt that by doing so they would accomplish nothing.[8] Some of these factors are measurable, of course, and data are available for some of them. To the extent possible, these factors will be incorporated in the analysis. But it must be admitted that investigation into the tendency of consumers to voice complaints and into the meaning of this behavior is in its infancy.

Nevertheless, it seems safe to ascribe importance to the frequency of consumer complaints. In a report by another California agency, the California Department of Consumer Affairs was criticized because "little or no use is made of complaint data."[9] The director of the Consumer Affairs Department responded that he and his staff were serious about using complaints to determine the nature of consumer problems.[10]

The California Contractors' State License Board, in particular, has been criticized for its handling of consumer complaints. As of October 1978, the board had a backlog of nearly 35,000 unprocessed complaints against contractors.[11] The chief executive officer of the board became "part of a major war in the Brown Administration, the legislature and among industry representatives over the efficiency and integrity of the Board."[12] As a result, the officer was ousted from his position.[13] At the same time, the board passed a consumer disclosure motion that would allow a consumer to look at complaints filed against a contractor pro-

---

[8] Jim Lewis, "Report Critical of Regulatory Boards," *Sacramento Bee* (June 2, 1978).

[9] Jim Lewis, "Audit Attacks Consumer Affairs Unit," *Sacramento Bee* (October 19, 1978).

[10] Ibid.

[11] Jim Lewis, "Contractor Registrar Faces Scathing Report," *Sacramento Bee* (October 27, 1978).

[12] Jim Lewis, "Contractor Licensing Board May Fire Aide," *Sacramento Bee* (October 24, 1978).

[13] "Registrar of Board Ousted," *Sacramento Bee* (December 12, 1978).

vided there had been at least four during the preceding eighteen months.[14] This decision was later rescinded, however.[15] A legislative subcommittee expressed its displeasure with the board in May 1979 and augmented the board's budget for the purpose of adding staff to reduce the backlog of complaints.[16] A report by the auditor general indicated that the backlog of consumer complaints was due to "poor management, a lack of production goals, and other weaknesses . . . in the Board's automated system."[17]

It seems evident from these events that there is widespread acceptance of the notion that consumer complaints provide an indication of consumer dissatisfaction and that the greater the number of complaints per licensed contractor, the lower the contractor's quality of work performed is likely to be. Our analysis rests on these basic notions. Since most consumer complaints about price are dismissed by the board as being out of its jurisdiction (complaints that the actual price is higher than the contract price are within that jurisdiction, but complaints about the contract price itself are not), consumers really cannot usefully complain about high prices. This means they are more likely to complain about the quality of work done.

Factors Affecting Quality of Service

Let us suppose there is a negative relationship between the number of practitioners and the average quality of service provided—that is, the fewer the number, the higher the quality of their service. Establishing a minimum-competency standard for licensing reduces the number of practitioners by eliminating those who cannot meet the standards. Let us suppose further that the average quality of existing practitioners is above the minimum—in other words, that the licensing process allows fewer practitioners to enter than actually meet the minimum-quality standards. It has been found, for example, that individuals with little education who meet minimum proficiency standards often fail to obtain a license because they fail the written portion of the exam.[18] Under these circumstances, for a given number of licensees, the average quality

[14] Ibid.

[15] Jim Lewis, "Contractors' Board Rescinds Small Claims Court Policy," *Sacramento Bee* (May 19, 1979).

[16] Jim Lewis, "Assembly Panel Criticizes Contractors' License Board," *Sacramento Bee* (May 9, 1979).

[17] Jim Lewis, "Pile of Gripes, Disclosure Policy Battle Burden Board," *Sacramento Bee* (May 3, 1979).

[18] Stuart Dorsey, "The Occupational Licensing Queue," *Journal of Human Resources*, vol. 15, no. 3 (Summer 1980), pp.424–34.

of those providing services will fall more (though remaining above the minimum) the greater the increase in that number. Clearly, the extent of decline in quality associated with 1,000 more licensees will be less if there are already 100,000 licensees than if there are only 10,000. A more accurate indicator of the extent of decline in quality than the number of new licensees would be the proportionate change represented by the number of new licensees. We thus expect a positive relationship between the proportionate change in the number of practitioners and the frequency of consumer complaints.

The number of offices to which the consumer can bring his complaint will also affect the frequency of complaints. Members of the board staff indicated that the opening of a district or branch office was usually followed by a substantial increase in the number of complaints received. They attributed this to the fact that many consumers were made aware that they could file their complaints nearby and began to do so. In other words, the costs of filing had been reduced. The numbers of districts and branch offices and the sum of the two have been chosen as three different ways of increasing the extent of consumer access to a local office.

Our initial investigation attempts to explain the frequency of consumer complaints to the contractors' board in terms of these two independent variables: the annual proportionate increase in the number of licensees and the growth in the number of board offices throughout the state.

The Data

The California Contractors' State License Board recently began to maintain a computerized monthly file of all consumer complaints. This file is intended to make it easy for the board to retrieve information on complaints once they have been recorded. Since 1954 the board has maintained a record of complaints on an annual basis, and there are annual data available on the number of applicants, applicants rejected, individuals examined, individuals passed, and licensees. Our analysis is based on the annual data from 1954 to 1975. Table 1 presents the historical data for these years.

The first column presents the ratio of complaints to licensees, what we term the complaint frequency. It should be noted that in calculating the complaint frequency, we have adjusted the data to extract only complaints by consumers about licensees. The great bulk—86 to 90 percent—of complaints to the board are, however, from consumers; most of the others are from applicants and licensees themselves. Annual complaint data were adjusted to remove these complaints from appli-

TABLE 1

HISTORICAL DATA FOR THE CALIFORNIA CONTRACTORS' BOARD

Year	Ratio of Complaints to Licensees	Proportionate Annual Increase in Number of Licensees	District Offices	Branch Offices	District plus Branch Offices
1954	0.071	0.051	5	4	9
1955	0.080	0.052	5	4	9
1956	0.080	0.044	5	4	9
1957	0.078	0.045	5	4	9
1958	0.077	0.047	5	4	9
1959	0.080	0.051	5	4	9
1960	0.074	0.046	5	4	9
1961	0.069	0.045	5	4	9
1962	0.081	0.044	8	12	20
1963	0.089	0.047	8	13	21
1964	0.084	0.047	8	13	21
1965	0.101	0.038	11	14	25
1966	0.102	0.026	11	15	26
1967	0.097	0.023	11	15	26
1968	0.111	0.025	11	15	26
1969	0.111	0.032	11	15	26
1970	0.109	0.035	12	13	25
1971	0.127	0.044	13	13	26
1972	0.148	0.055	13	13	26
1973	0.154	0.066	13	16	29
1974	0.153	0.077	15	14	29
1975	0.137	0.093	15	14	29

SOURCE. See text above.

cants and licensees and to account for differences between annual and fiscal year data. Roughly 50 percent of consumer complaints concern willful disregard of plans or specifications; others concern abandonment of a project without cause, willful violation of building laws, failure to complete the project for the contracted price, and willful project delay causing material injury.

Empirical Results

The initial regression results are presented in table 2. Since we have used three alternative measures for the number of board offices, we present a separate regression equation for each measure. The propor-

TABLE 2

REGRESSION RESULTS FOR CALIFORNIA CONTRACTORS' COMPLAINT
FREQUENCY, 1954–1975

Equation	R^2	$D\text{-}W$
(1) $COMP = \quad 0.024 + 0.368\ (INC) + 0.007\ (OFD)$ $\qquad\qquad (3.20) \quad (2.71) \qquad\qquad (10.81)$	0.89	0.97
(2) $COMP = \quad 0.020 + 0.808\ (INC) + 0.004\ (OFB)$ $\qquad\qquad (1.67) \quad (4.08) \qquad\quad (6.40)$	0.74	0.63
(3) $COMP = \quad 0.020 + 0.633\ (INC) + 0.003\ (OFS)$ $\qquad\qquad (2.03) \quad (3.84) \qquad\quad (8.24)$	0.82	0.69

NOTE: $COMP$ = complaint frequency; INC = increase in stock of licensees; OFD = number of district offices; OFB = number of branch offices; OFS = number of district plus branch offices; t-statistics in parentheses.

tionate annual increase in the number of licensees is positively and significantly related to the frequency of complaints in each of the three equations. The number of district offices is positively and significantly related to the frequency of complaints in equation (1); the number of branch offices is positively and significantly related in equation (2); and the sum of the number of district and branch offices is positively and significantly related in equation (3). The coefficient of determination (R^2) is 0.89, 0.74, and 0.82 in these three equations, respectively, indicating that these two variables have substantial explanatory power. However, the Durbin-Watson statistic in each case (0.97, 0.63, and 0.69, respectively) indicates the presence of serial correlation—that is, the disturbance terms are not serially independent. This results in "tracking" of the disturbance term; the value for the disturbance term in one year will tend to be high whenever its value in the previous year is high. Tracking of the disturbance term over time causes underestimation of the sampling variances of the regression coefficients.[19] Statistically significant results can be obtained when there is no significant relation present.

The presence of serial correlation suggests the addition of other variables to explain the upward trend in complaint frequency. For several reasons, it seemed advisable to add a variable for the increase in the number of contractor license exam schools from zero in 1964 to thirty-six in 1970 and fifty-seven in 1975.

---

[19] See Jack Johnston, *Econometric Methods* (New York: McGraw-Hill, 1972), pp. 243–49, and Ronald Wonnacott and Thomas Wonnacott, *Econometrics* (New York: John Wiley, 1970), pp. 136–45.

The contractors' license exam changed little from 1964 to 1975. Half of the exam, dealing with contract and lien law, did not change at all over this period; the other half, designed for people with four years' experience, did not change from 1972 to 1975. In the eleven years from 1964 to 1975, there was a dramatic increase in the number of schools offering courses designed to enable those enrolled to pass the contractors' license exam. It is alleged that the course of study in these schools consists of taking a license exam essentially identical with that given by the board and then receiving extensive tutoring for the questions answered incorrectly. The schools would have been able to obtain copies of all the exam questions merely by paying people to take the exam for the purpose of remembering the questions. There is some evidence to indicate that knowledge of the content of the exams was widespread. During a meeting of the California Contractors' State License Board on August 26, 1977, a publication of the California Contractors' License Service was discussed by the board. Emblazoned on the cover of this publication were the words "Exclusive Release Contractors' Examination." Testimony before the board at this meeting revealed that the information in the publication was compiled over a period of ten or eleven years; the examination reproduced in the back of the book contained questions and answers and was reputed by Mr. Hostler, the board chairman, to be an exact copy of the license exam. Mr. Sanchez, a representative of the California Contractors' License Service, testified that the information for the publication was compiled as follows: former students of license exam schools who "have taken the exam at one point or another have returned to us and have given us information."[20]

Accordingly, a variable indicating the number of schools offering courses in how to pass the contractors' license exam has been entered into the analysis in the hopes of explaining some of the upward trend in the number of complaints per licensee. The regression results indicate that this variable is positively and significantly related to the number of complaints per licensee, as would be expected (see table 3).

The greater the number of schools and course offerings, the greater the number of complaints per licensee. In addition, all three of the variables measuring accessibility to the board remain significantly related, each positively. These variables explain the historical data quite well. Finally, in each case the proportionate annual increase in the number of licensees is positively and significantly related to the com-

---

[20] Minutes of Special Meeting of Contractors' State License Board, August 26, 1977, at the Airportec Inn, Irvine, California, transcribed by L. R. Linn and Associates, Certified Shorthand Reporters, pp. 87–88.

TABLE 3

REGRESSION RESULTS FOR CALIFORNIA CONTRACTORS' COMPLAINT
FREQUENCY, 1954–1975

Equation	R^2	$D\text{-}W$
(1) $COMP = 0.045 + 0.267\ (INC) + 0.004\ (OFD) + 0.0006\ (SCH)$ (4.06) (2.07) (2.71) (2.37)	0.91	1.28
(2) $COMP = 0.053 + 0.351\ (INC) + 0.001\ (OFB) + 0.0009\ (SCH)$ (5.61) (2.39) (2.36) (5.64)	0.91	1.33
(3) $COMP = 0.050 + 0.334\ (INC) + 0.001\ (OFS) + 0.0008\ (SCH)$ (4.94) (2.40) (2.55) (4.21)	0.91	1.29

NOTE: $COMP$ = complaint frequency; INC = increase in stock of licensees; OFD = number of board district offices; OFB = number of board branch offices; OFS = number of district plus branch offices; SCH = number of contractor license exam schools; t-statistics in parentheses.

plaint frequency. The Durbin-Watson statistics of 1.28, 1.33, and 1.29, respectively, in the three equations no longer conclusively indicate that serial correlation is present. This strongly suggests that the introduction of the number of schools into the equation has accounted for the upward trend in complaint frequency since 1964.

Summary and Conclusions

The principal conclusions from this analysis are (1) that the growth in the number of district and branch offices of the board has made it easier for consumers to complain and explains part of the increase in the number of complaints per licensee that has occurred, (2) that the growth in the number of schools offering courses to help enrollees pass the contractors' license exam (together with the fact that the exam changed little from 1964 to 1975) explains the recent upward trend in the number of complaints per licensee, and (3) that the number of complaints per licensee has been greater the greater the percentage increase in the stock of licensees.

The appearance of contractor license exam schools has made it possible for lower-quality practitioners to circumvent the minimum-quality standards; they can learn how to pass the exam without learning the skills of a contractor. Evidence indicates that the emergence of these schools in rapidly increasing numbers explains the upward trend in complaint frequency since 1964. Thus, consumers may be receiving a quality of service quite similar to what would prevail in the absence of licensing, and they may be paying higher prices for that quality.

There is currently a provision that allows unlicensed contractors in California to perform contractor services so long as the value of these services does not exceed $250. It seems clear that consumers would be better off with a policy that considerably increased this dollar limit than with the policy that has been in effect. Some of the unlicensed contractors would no doubt have obtained a license by attending a license exam school and provided service of the same quality as they would without having a license. If able to do business without a license, these contractors could provide their services at a lower price than that charged by licensees. Consumers would end up paying less for the same services that would have been provided if these individuals had a license.

Of course, an alternative course of action for the Contractors' State License Board would be to alter the license exam more frequently and ensure that skills other than exam-taking skills would have to be demonstrated. This would make it more difficult for the exam schools to enable lower-quality providers to obtain a license. As long as an exam is required to obtain a license, however, there will be a market opportunity for firms that provide training in how to take the exam. Individuals purchasing this training will have a mechanism, in other words, for circumventing to some extent the minimum standards that licensing is supposed to guarantee.

This fundamental difficulty with ensuring quality by testing for it has recently become a major concern in connection with the scholastic aptitude test, the graduate record examination, the medical college admissions test, the dental aptitude test, the law school admissions test, the graduate management admissions test, the optometry college admissions test, and the veterinary aptitude test. There are test preparation courses, "cram" courses, for each of these tests. The largest course enrollment for such purposes is in bar review courses designed to help individuals pass state bar exams and become licensed attorneys. The operators of such courses state that the most important thing they teach is "testmanship"; the students learn "how to take the test, what kind of questions are usually asked, what kind of answers are customarily sought."[21]

Clearly, the market provides opportunities for individuals who wish to circumvent the minimum-quality standards that licensing is supposed to guarantee. This study suggests that lower-than-minimum-quality contractors do obtain licenses as a result and that consumers would be better off without licensing in this case.

---

[21] Edwin Kiester, "Cramming Your Way to Fortune's Door," *Parade* (May 6, 1979), p. 23.

Commentary

Walter E. Williams

Lee Benham's paper makes at least one important contribution to the discussion of occupational licensure, namely, that licensure is not new: it has a medieval forerunner or counterpart. This recognition, if widely published, ought to cause Americans just a bit of cognitive dissonance, given that the articulated values in our society are those of equality of opportunity.

Benham rightly criticizes the economic literature on the reasons licensure exists, pointing out that rent-seeking and security-seeking hypotheses are not very illuminating. But I find his argument, focusing on the ability of licensed occupations to persuade the larger society of the "benefits" of licensing, not very illuminating either. The reason is that several studies have shown that licensing (1) raises product or service prices, (2) has not coped with "market failures," and (3) has not raised product quality—indeed may even lower it if we are to believe the Carroll and Gaston study.[1] If we are to believe any of these studies, which show consumers bearing much of the burden of higher licensed-practitioner incomes, then what are we to assume about consumers ("the larger society") as voters?

If we assume that consumers are stupid, Benham's hypotheses will work. But any theory that requires the assumption of stupidity (and its equivalent, long-run ignorance) is not a very good theory. We are thus left with the question: If occupational licensure reduces the wealth of receivers of licensed services, why does the larger society permit an action contrary to its best interests? I doubt whether we can explain this outcome by invoking the *persuasive* powers of licensed groups.

Benham recognizes this problem, I believe, in his discussion of the weakness of economic theory in analyzing institutional change. I believe

---

[1] Sidney L. Carroll and Robert J. Gaston, "Occupational Licensing," unpublished report (University of Tennessee). The authors show a lower received quality resulting from the licensing of electricians.

we will be able to make definitive statements about occupational licensure only when we allow the incentive to license to enter our models endogenously. This is precisely the thrust of Professor Hirshleifer's lengthy statement pointing out that the constitutional rules under which we live have been rapidly eroding. I am not at all sure how we can accommodate institutional change in our economic models, but there does seem to be a fruitful line of research suggested by the coalition literature, namely, the phenomena of *narrow benefits* and dispersed costs of rule changes. Under this regime, practitioners find the payoffs of expending resources to restrict markets enormous in relation to the costs. The practitioners are a well-identified group; their free-rider policing costs are relatively low; and these two factors, in combination with others, make organization costs relatively low. On the other hand, consumers, precisely because they do not share the cost/benefit characteristics of producer organizations, individually or collectively, have little incentive to prevent the subversion of open markets.

On balance the Benham paper is interesting not only for giving us an historical insight into occupational licensure but for raising important questions for the economist studying market closure. Now all that remains is to find the answers.

The effect of occupational licensure and regulation on the quality of service received by consumers is at once an important area for consideration and one that presses hard at the state-of-the-art limitations of economics. Professor Maurizi, in his case study of California contractors, takes up the challenge.

Intuitively speaking, at least, there are several empirical proxies that might serve as quantifiable estimates of quality for such a study: (1) average length of queue; (2) substitutes for licensed services (including do-it-yourself, the use of illegal unlicensed practitioners, and not-do-it-at-all); (3) some quality attributes of the actual work; and (4) perhaps, as Maurizi suggests, the number of complaints.

The premise upon which Maurizi's study rests is that voiced complaints are inversely related to service quality. Conceptually, there are some problems with this premise, having to do with user expectations and changes in liability laws. That is, rising user expectations and institutional changes that raise the probability of complaints' being successful may give rise to an increased incidence of complaints independent of quality. What I have in mind here may be present in the medical profession. Over the last decades, we have observed increased malpractice suits, but from that observation alone I would hesitate to argue that the quality of medical services has declined during this period. An additional problem in using the frequency of complaints as an estimate of quality is that one wants to have a way to make sure that complaints

37

are not used to win from contractors concessions too costly to achieve through the market.[2]

In Maurizi's study complaint frequency is the dependent variable for which an explanation is sought, and this dependent variable, complaints per licensee, raises a question in my mind. Does it equate with complaints as a percentage of total contracting work done? If these two possible dependent variables differ, as I suspect they do, why was one chosen over the other? It may be that the choice was made because of the availability of data—which is a good reason. To the extent, however, that such data were available (which they appear to have been, at least for complaints caused by violation of building codes where the licensee had to get a building permit), the test should have been run against total contracts rather than per licensee. In that way one could determine whether there are any systematic errors involved in alternative definitions of the dependent variable. It appears that, for Maurizi's dependent variable to be a reliable estimate of the detection of changes in quality from licensure, complaints would have to be assumed equal from licensee to licensee.

Another part of the problem in this study is related to the variables that Professor Maurizi selects to explain complaint frequency. He finds that the number of schools and the increase in the stock of licensees are both positively related to the frequency of complaints. Here, I believe these variables introduce problems of multi-collinearity in his regression equations—that is, the number of contractor licensee schools and the stock of licensees may be systematically related to one another.

In general I find the conclusions of Maurizi's study persuasive to the extent that they are consistent with what would be an economist's theoretical predictions, but I think the evidence has been presented rather prematurely and is in need of much more work. At the minimum, if I were Maurizi, I would share the findings of the study with the attorney general of California—particularly those findings showing how prospective licensees obtain the state examination as part of the practice for the license examination.

Peter Schuck

The subject of professional licensure has long fascinated me. My first attempt to reform professional licensure was a lawsuit on behalf of my former employer, Consumers Union, against the American Bar Asso-

---

[2] In further development of the study, the author might attempt to classify complaints according to the demographic characteristics of the consumer. Do high-income people complain more? Are there systematic differences in complaint frequency when people receive their income in bond form as opposed to wage form?

ciation, challenging the profession's "ethical" restrictions on lawyer advertising. That effort, which was followed by similar lawsuits in many states, was *successful*, and many lawyers are now advertising. I am told that a recent review of experience with lawyer advertising published in the *New York Times*, however, suggests that a great deal of fraud has been alleged in connection with the lawyer advertising that my lawsuit helped to generate. This need not—and does not—suggest that the earlier ban on lawyer advertising was justified, even if the charges are true: the earlier system also imposed costs on consumers. It does suggest, however, that we should not permit our skepticism concerning the motivations and consequences of professional licensure to blind us to potential benefits. We ought to restrain some of our righteous indignation against what often appears to be purely self-interested, self-seeking, self-regulation and try instead to evaluate particular restrictions by studying their *effects* on competition and on other values. It should be the consequences of a particular restriction that informs our judgment, not the motives that led to its adoption.

My second effort in this area was a lawsuit filed in Virginia against the Board of Optometry, challenging the requirement under Virginia law that all members of the board be licensed optometrists, a relatively common provision. My argument essentially was that members of the general public possessed a Fourteenth Amendment right to be *considered* for appointment to such boards and could not be flatly excluded by state law. That lawsuit floundered on a procedural matter—a point worth mentioning for reasons I hope will be obvious. One of the arbitrary elements of self-regulation by the legal profession is a requirement by courts in particular states, including the *federal* courts in those states, that out-of-town lawyers may not appear before those courts alone but must be accompanied by local counsel. (Local lawyers generally demand payment for their services on behalf of the out-of-state lawyer.) So I obtained a local counsel in Virginia who was simply to file pleadings that I sent to him, receive papers filed by the court and opposing counsel, and appear in court with me.

The culmination came when I called to find out when a decision might be expected, only to learn that the court had already rendered a decision against my client (my local counsel had failed to inform me of that) and our time to appeal had expired. That, in essence, was the end of the lawsuit. One lesson I derived from this experience was that it is easier to attack licensure restrictions in other professions than to ensure that the restrictions imposed by one's own do ensure minimum levels of competence in one's colleagues. In short, there is plenty of work to be done in our own professional backyards.

Lee Benham reminds us not to be preoccupied with the rents that are supposed to flow from restrictions on occupational licensure. I would expand his caveat by suggesting that we also ought not to be preoccupied with the narrowly economic motivations of professional licensure. In support of my suggestion, I offer two data.

The first of these derive from my experience with the legal profession. The lawyers who most strenuously opposed—and continue to oppose—advertising by lawyers are precisely those who have the least to fear from advertising from an economic point of view. They tend to be the prominent corporate lawyers, the pillars of the bar in the large cities. They are the least likely to advertise or to be affected economically by advertising on the part of other lawyers.

A second datum is alluded to in a footnote in Dr. Benham's paper. The dental profession has tended to oppose very strenuously the use of what are called expanded duty dental auxiliaries (EDDAs), even though it has been shown in a number of studies that dentists can make a great deal more money by using such paraprofessionals. Moreover, there is no risk that the EDDAs will compete with dentists, for even where EDDAs are permitted to perform certain dental functions, those functions are limited. Nevertheless, even in those states, dentists have tended not to use EDDAs extensively, even though they could earn more by doing so.

The conclusion I draw from this—and it is a cautious and a narrow conclusion—is that much of the occupational licensure behavior of professions cannot be explained solely by the standard profit-maximizing model. The professions are clearly maximizing something, but it is not clear exactly what it is. Certainly, it is not simply income. I would offer two hypotheses based on my own observations and experience in this area.

The first is that licensed occupations tend to place a very high value on *status*, and status is usually elevated by professional licensure. There is, of course, no question that status is often highly correlated with income, but the pursuit of status is not purely a pursuit of income, and it is important to recognize—and attempt to understand—the broader motivation.

Second—and this is closely related to a point Dr. Benham makes— the licensed professions pursue *stability*, and stability, while related to competitive conditions within an industry and therefore to income, is not solely an income-related objective. Pursuit of stability is not simply a way of protecting profit margins. It is also a way of assuring licensed practitioners of the quiet life that monopolists are said to prefer, the quiet life that most of us in fact prefer. It is a way of ensuring that they can continue to do what they have always done in the way that they have always done it for the rest of their professional lives.

It would therefore be useful to study some of the noneconomic motives underlying licensure restrictions, motives only partially related to profit maximizing. They are probably more important than we have generally believed. A related area to which Dr. Benham alludes (neglected somewhat by research in this area) is the professions as *organizations*—that is, institutions with a life, an incentive structure, and a dynamic of their own, quite apart from the economic self-interest of their members. There is a large literature on organizations generally, but little of that literature has been directed at organizations controlling the licensure process.

I would suggest that the incentives driving professions *as organizations* may be as much status and stability as income. This would explain, to some extent, their frequent hostility to innovations, even those that would increase profits. In addition to the example of the dental profession, I would call attention to the past opposition of the American Bar Association to group legal services—not only because such practices affected its members' incomes but also because there is an image of legal practice that most practitioners of the bar share, which is challenged somewhat by the notion of group legal services with its assembly-line connotations. Lawyers do not like to think of themselves as performing tasks that can be performed in such a manner, whatever the reality may be.

This self-image also explains behavior by other professional organizations. The opposition of the American Medical Association to Medicare, for example, is something that cannot be explained on purely economic grounds. As we all know, the medical profession has prospered under Medicare, and there was always reason to believe that would be the case. Yet the medical profession continues to oppose restrictions on its professional independence that probably would not threaten the profession economically but would affect its self-image and sense of what the practice of medicine ought to be.

Finally, as Dr. Benham implies, a lot more study ought to be given to the free-rider problem—as it affects professional organizations. For example, the membership of the American Medical Association is now considerably less than 50 percent of the total members of the medical profession, providing quite a number of possible free riders.

I would make several observations about Professor Maurizi's methods. My experience in the consumer-protection field suggests several relevant questions. In fairness, he has recognized some of them in his paper, and it may be that, given the nature of reality, we cannot do much better than he has done. I refer to his use of the incidence of consumer complaints as a measure of quality.

He properly calls attention to the limitations of this measure, and

I share his concern. Many factors affect the number of consumer complaints and the likelihood of their being filed with a public agency. Consumer complaints, as several studies have indicated, tend to be filed by middle- and upper-income consumers who have the time, the sophistication, and the interest to prepare them. We know that when the availability of consumer remedies is advertised, there is a massive increase in the number of consumer complaints filed. If there is mass-media publicity concerning a particular consumer problem—the Firestone 500 is an example—consumer complaints rise steeply. According to an American Bar Association study, the mere mention of the existence of lawyer referral services had a dramatic and immediate effect on their use. In short, using the volume of consumer complaints to measure the competence of the providers of a service is of questionable value.

Professor Maurizi suggests that lower prices are likely to produce lower expectations from consumers and that the increase in the number of licensees will therefore lessen the number of complaints. If that is what he said, I would tend to disagree, although I doubt we have any empirical data to support the proposition one way or the other. I would, however, predict a priori that lower prices would produce lower quality without materially affecting consumer expectations. The expectations consumers tend to have about what they ought to be getting are probably, within a fairly broad range, quite independent of what they are paying for the product—however unreasonable that attitude on their part may be as a purely economic matter. Even though one generally gets what one pays for, most of us tend to lose sight of that fact when we are paying what we think is a large amount for a product or service.

One of the most disturbing effects of licensure at any level of competence—and Professor Maurizi mentions this—is that it eliminates trade-offs between quality and cost. That is, even if one were to find a minimally satisfactory level of competence we could largely agree upon, we would still be preventing consumers from making a quality-cost trade-off at a level below that, and we would be preventing them even when they simply did not have the money to spend for the higher, more satisfactory product or service. It ought to be emphasized that this is a troublesome and systematic consequence of professional licensure.

It is not surprising that Professor Maurizi found the licensure tests to be poorly correlated with competence. Indeed, I would be skeptical of any test purporting to measure the competence of a professional service: there would be no need for such a test unless that service were rendered in a market with great informational asymmetry between consumers and providers; even in such a market, one might doubt the benefits of such a test. It seems to me that the best assurance of competence in those areas where information is reasonably symmetrical is the old-fashioned grapevine. We should, as a policy matter, look for ways to institutionalize the grapevine and to build on the high quality of the information implicit in grapevines. Let me suggest one possibility. We could require by law—and though there is clearly a cost involved here, it might well be exceeded by the benefits—that providers of certain reasonably standardized services, such as TV repair, auto repair, perhaps contractors, and so forth, be required to include on their bills a detachable standardized form on which the consumer could evaluate the service received. That evaluation could then be submitted to a government agency, a local consumer organization, or professional licensing organization (assuming that the licensing organization had a somewhat different composition than it now has, a point I will address in a moment). The recipient agency could analyze and publish that information in an appropriate manner and with the appropriate caveats. This would not be a simple task. Nevertheless, the quality of the information would probably be somewhat higher than the quality of the information generated by the present licensing system, which, as Professor Maurizi points out, relies on testing that is likely to be deficient.

Another policy approach that should be considered—nothwithstanding the failure of my lawsuit to achieve that end—is reform of the composition of licensing boards. We should make sure that there are some disinterested members or at least members who have consumers'—not producers'—welfare in mind. I have no illusions about the ability of so-called public members to have much effect on the markets these boards regulate. Except when they are considering the most blatantly anticompetitive restrictions, they will have no particular knowledge of where consumers' interests lie; indeed, I would predict that they will tend to promote higher quality at the expense of reduced consumer choice for those with low incomes. Nevertheless, boards so constituted might at least be able to perform some of the grapevine-reinforcing or grapevine-institutionalizing functions I have described, as well as improve the functioning and legitimacy of the board in areas of professional discipline, consumer education, outreach, and the like, which depend on a broad consumer orientation and an ability to distance oneself from professional norms.

Part
Two

Mandatory Licensure of Registered Nurses: Introduction and Impact

William D. White

In recent years there has been increasing concern about the impact of occupational licensure laws on efficiency and career mobility in the U.S. economy. Officially, licensure laws are supposed to protect the public by maintaining the quality of services. But critics question whether their benefits are worth their costs. They also question whether such regulation is introduced to protect the public or the occupations.

Frequently debates center on the type of licensure law used. Licensure laws can be either voluntary or mandatory. Voluntary laws limit the use of an occupational title to licensed personnel. They certify that individuals who are permitted to use this title have met certain standards. For this reason they are often simply called "certification" laws. Voluntary laws are also sometimes referred to as "open" or "permissive" licensure laws because they permit unlicensed personnel to enter an occupation so long as they do not make use of the title reserved to those with licenses. Mandatory licensure laws not only restrict the use of occupational titles but also close occupations to unlicensed personnel. Under mandatory licensure not only must personnel be licensed to use a licensed title, but they must be licensed to practice the occupation at all.

Economists such as Milton Friedman have suggested that the government may perform a valuable function by certifying the quality of manpower through voluntary laws.[1] But they argue against mandatory licensure because it limits individual freedom of choice in the marketplace. Supporters of mandatory licensure argue that choices should not

NOTE: This research was partly supported by a grant from the University of Illinois and by Grant Number HS 03596 from the National Center for Health Studies, OASH. The views expressed in this chapter, however, are solely those of the author and do not necessarily reflect the position of the sponsoring institutions. I am grateful to Barry Chiswick, Joseph Persky, Harsh Thaker, Frances Waddle, and Gilbert F. White for their comments on earlier versions of this chapter and to Kemal Ider for research assistance. Any errors that remain are, of course, my own.
[1] Milton Friedman, *Capitalism and Freedom* (Chicago: University of Chicago Press, 1962), pp. 137–61.

always be left to the market. Meanwhile, institutionally oriented economists have sometimes questioned whether introducing mandatory licensure makes much difference in labor markets where voluntary licensure is already well established.[2]

In discussions of the process by which licensure is introduced, economists have noted that mandatory laws may be especially attractive to members of an occupation seeking their own gain because they force consumers to use licensed personnel whether they want to or not. Some critics of mandatory licensure even question the use of voluntary licensure on the grounds that the introduction of voluntary laws has often been followed historically by the introduction of mandatory ones.[3]

Despite the debate over the merits of voluntary and mandatory licensure, there have been few studies of what happens when there is a shift from voluntary to mandatory licensure or of the reasons this kind of shift has occurred. One of my objectives here is to help provide a better empirical basis for making policy decisions about licensure laws by investigating the economics of the introduction and impact of mandatory licensure of registered nurses (RNs).

RNs were selected for study for two reasons. First, they are of interest in their own right as one of the main groups of workers that is subject to mandatory licensure in the health industry. Second, because mandatory licensure for RNs has been introduced gradually over a long period, there is considerable economic information available on the group. The availability of information permits us to make cross-sectional comparisons of states with and without mandatory licensure at a series of points in time.

Most states introduced voluntary licensure laws for RNs during the early part of this century. They began to replace voluntary licensure laws with mandatory laws in the late 1930s, and today most states have mandatory laws. There are a number of economic studies on various aspects of the labor market for RNs since World War II, including those by Altman, Benham, and Yett.[4] These studies note that there are large

---

[2] For general discussions of occupational licensure, see also W. Gellhorn, *Individual Freedom and Government Restraints* (Baton Rouge: Louisiana State University Press, 1956); T. Moore, "The Purpose of Licensing," *Journal of Law and Economics*, vol. 4 (October 1961), pp. 93–117; and Simon Rottenberg, "The Economics of Occupational Licensure," in *Aspects of Labor Economics* (Princeton: Princeton University Press for National Bureau of Economic Research, 1962).

[3] See U.S. Department of Health, Education and Welfare, *Report on Licensure and Related Health Personnel Credentialing* (Washington, D.C., 1975), DHEW HSM 72–11.

[4] S. Altman, *Present and Future Supply of Registered Nurses* (Washington, D.C.: Department of Health, Education and Welfare, 1971), DHEW NIH 73–134; Lee Benham, "The Labor Market for Registered Nurses: A Three Equation Model," *Review of Economics and Statistics*, vol. 3 (August 1971), pp. 246–52; and D. Yett, *An Economic Analysis of the Nurse Shortage* (Lexington, Mass.: D.C. Heath, 1975).

regional variations in the number of RNs per capita and in the use of other types of nursing personnel. Altman and others suggest that these variations may be affected by legal restrictions, but the only study that specifically considers the impact of mandatory licensure is by Monheit.[5]

In his study Monheit seeks to estimate the effects of mandatory licensure on the relative wages and employment of RNs and practical nurses using cross-sectional state data. He concludes that mandatory licensure has had a positive impact on the wages and employment of RNs relative to those of practical nurses. He does not examine the direct impact of licensure on the absolute wages and employment of RNs, however, and this makes it difficult to make inferences about the impact of mandatory licensure on the welfare of this group.

Both Monheit and Stigler consider economic factors that may have affected the timing of the introduction of voluntary licensure of RNs.[6] But there have been no detailed studies of the introduction of mandatory licensure for this group, and I hope here to contribute to the understanding of licensure of nurses by considering two basic questions: First, why was there a shift in state laws from voluntary to mandatory licensure for RNs beginning in the late 1930s? Second, what has been the impact of this shift on their wages and employment? I will not attempt, however, to evaluate the effects of mandatory licensure on the quality of nursing services.

The paper is divided into five sections. The first section develops a model of the economic impact of mandatory licensure. The second provides some historical background on the development of nursing in the United States. The third examines the introduction of mandatory licensure laws, and the fourth considers their economic impact. The final section presents my conclusions.

The Model

We can examine the economic impact of replacing voluntary licensure with mandatory licensure by considering the following simple model.[7] Suppose that there is more than one type of labor used to produce

---

[5] Altman, *Present and Future Supply*; and A. Monheit, "An Economic Analysis of State Licensing of Nursing Labor" (Ph.D. diss., Department of Economics, City University of New York, 1975).

[6] Monheit, "Economic Analysis"; and George J. Stigler, "The Theory of Economic Regulation," *Bell Journal of Economics and Management Science*, vol. 1, no. 2 (Spring 1971), pp. 1–21.

[7] For a more detailed discussion, see William D. White, *Public Health and Private Gain: The Economics of Licensing Clinical Laboratory Personnel* (Chicago: Maaroufa Press, 1979).

output in an industry and that within limits it is technologically feasible to substitute different types of personnel (that is, labor) for each other in the production process. Assume that one type of labor—perhaps the most skilled group—is subject to voluntary licensure and that other types are not. Voluntary licensure will provide workers in the licensed group with a legal credential that they can use to identify themselves in the labor market. But no one will be legally required to purchase their services.

Mandatory licensure may force employers to substitute licensed personnel for unlicensed personnel in the production process to comply with the law. To the extent that licensure constraints are binding and substitution actually occurs, this will tend to increase the demand for licensed personnel at any given level of output. As a result, wages and employment in the licensed occupation will tend to rise. The size of the increase will depend on the elasticities of substitution between licensed personnel and other factors used in the production process, including capital and other types of workers, and the relative prices of the factors.

Changing factor proportions and substituting licensed for unlicensed personnel may not only increase the demand for licensed workers at any given level of output but also increase the price of final output. A rise in the price of final output may decrease final demand and therefore lower the derived demand for licensed personnel. As a result, wages and employment in the licensed occupation will tend to fall. The size of the decrease will depend on the price elasticity of final demand. Given that substitution and final price effects tend to offset each other, the net wage and employment impact of introducing mandatory licensure will be indeterminate.

This analysis assumes that licensure laws apply uniformly to an entire labor market. What if they apply only to a geographic subsection of this market? If the net effect of introducing mandatory licensure is to *increase* the derived demand for licensed personnel, then employment will tend to increase. This will tend to drive up wages and over the short run may result in wage differentials between areas with and without licensure. Over the long run, higher wages will attract workers from other areas, and this will tend to eliminate any wage differentials due to mandatory licensure *unless* there is friction in the labor market. Similarly, if derived demand *decreases*, employment will also decrease, but once again there will be no long-run differences in wages between areas *unless* there is friction in the labor market.

Advocates of mandatory licensure usually focus in public debates on quality effects. But critics note that the net impact of quality improvements on the welfare of consumers may not always be positive; the benefits of quality gains may be offset by increases in costs.

Whether or not mandatory licensure benefits consumers, however, it may still benefit members of licensed occupations. As noted earlier, the possibility of economic gain may provide an incentive for these groups to seek mandatory licensure regardless of the impact on the public.

Historical Background

During the last seventy-five years, there have been significant changes in the education and employment of nurses. This section briefly reviews developments in nursing since the turn of the century and argues that efforts to introduce voluntary and mandatory licensure for RNs have been closely related to changes in economic conditions in the profession.

Nursing began to develop as a profession during the late nineteenth century, when the first formal training programs for nurses were established. At the turn of the century, most graduates of professional nursing programs went into private-duty nursing, taking care of individual patients in their homes or in hospitals. Some nurses also found jobs in public health agencies or doctors' offices or as instructors in nursing schools. But jobs as staff nurses in hospitals were rare, because hospitals were setting up their own nursing schools and using students as an inexpensive source of labor. Between 1900 and 1926, the number of these schools shot up from 432 to 2,155, while a survey in 1924 showed that only slightly more than a quarter of the hospitals with schools employed any graduate nurses for general-duty nursing.[8]

In the market for private-duty nurses, graduates of hospital programs faced competition from untrained workers and graduates of commercial schools. Because most private patients tended to buy small quantities of nursing services irregularly and lacked the expertise to evaluate nursing personnel, there was a good deal of emphasis on formal credentials, and the private registries operated by hospitals played an important role in determining employment opportunities. There were still no legal constraints on any persons calling themselves trained nurses or using any other title they chose.

Many nurses felt that this lack of legal control over the use of the title trained (or professional) nurse was a serious problem. They were also concerned about the growth of training programs in hospitals and

---

[8] L. Flanagan, *One Strong Voice: The Story of the American Nurses' Association* (Kansas City: American Nurses' Association, 1976), p. 84; and "More General Staff Nurses," *American Journal of Nursing*, vol. 38, no. 2 (February 1938), pp. 186–90. The study cited here covered only nursing schools accredited by the National League of Nursing (NLN). Most hospital schools were accredited by this time, however, while the number of unaccredited schools employing graduate nurses was probably not very different.

hospital control of registries. Many nurses argued that hospital training programs put too much emphasis on work and too little emphasis on education and were creating an oversupply of nurses.[9] In some cases they also believed that the hospital registries gave hospitals undue control over the labor market.

The American Nurses' Association (ANA) and the National League of Nursing (NLN) launched a national campaign for voluntary licensure for nurses in 1900.[10] The basic goals of this campaign were (1) to establish legal credentials that graduate nurses could use to identify themselves in the labor market and (2) to establish control by nurses over access to credentials and use this control as a basis for setting standards for educational programs.

The campaign quickly led to the growth of state nurses' associations, which began to lobby actively for voluntary licensure. The first voluntary licensure laws were passed three years later in New Jersey, New York, and North Carolina (1903). As table 1 shows, by 1923 all the existing states had voluntary laws. These laws reserved the title "registered nurse," "professional nurse," or some similar designation for those satisfying licensure requirements, which usually involved passing an examination and graduating from a state-approved nursing program. In most states, nurses also succeeded in gaining control over the boards that administered licensure laws.[11] After World War I, RNs sought to use voluntary licensure laws as a basis for upgrading training programs. Ultimately, these efforts resulted in a series of reforms in nursing education in the 1930s.

Meanwhile, major changes were taking place in the labor market for nurses. During the 1930s the demand for private-duty nurses declined, while the number of nurses employed in hospitals began to increase rapidly. At the same time, many hospitals closed their nursing schools, and even those that still had schools started hiring graduate nurses to do general-duty nursing.[12]

Several factors seem important in explaining these changes in the

---

[9] Philip Kalisch and Beatrice Kalisch, *The Advance of American Nursing* (Boston: Little, Brown, 1978), chaps. 5, 6, and 7.

[10] At this time the ANA was actually known as the Nurses' Associated Alumnae, and the NLN was known as the National League for Nursing Education; their present names are used in this discussion to avoid confusion. The other main national nursing group in existence at this time was the National Organization for Public Health Nursing, which also supported voluntary licensure.

[11] Flanagan, *One Strong Voice*, pp. 43–45; M. Shannon, "Our First Four Licensure Laws," *American Journal of Nursing*, vol. 75, no. 8 (August 1975), pp. 1327–39.

[12] The proportion of hospitals with accredited nursing schools that did not employ any graduate general-duty nurses had fallen to 24 percent by 1934 and to 10 percent by 1937. See Flanagan, "More General Staff Nurses."

TABLE 1

Licensure Laws for Registered Nurses

State	Year Voluntary Licensure Passed	Year Mandatory Licensure Passed	Year Mandatory Licensure Effective
Alabama	1915	1966	1968
Alaska	1941	1957	1957
Arizona	1921	1952	1953
Arkansas	1913	1947	1947
California	1905	1939	1939
Colorado	1905	1957	1957
Connecticut	1905	1957	1957
Delaware	1909	1963	1963
District of Columbia	1907	—	—
Florida	1913	1951	1952
Georgia	1907	1975	1975
Hawaii	1917	1945	1945
Idaho	1911	1951	1951
Illinois	1907	1947	1952
Indiana	1905	—	—
Iowa	1907	1963	1963
Kansas	1913	1949	1951
Kentucky	1914	1966	1966
Louisiana	1912	1942	1942
Maine	1915	1959	1961
Maryland	1904	1967	1967
Massachusetts[a]	1910	—	—
Michigan	1909	1967	1967
Minnesota	1907	1959	1960
Mississippi	1914	1970	1970
Missouri	1909	1953	1953
Montana	1913	1953	1954
Nebraska	1909	1953	1953
Nevada	1923	1949	1949
New Hampshire	1907	1959	1959
New Jersey	1903	1955	1956
New Mexico	1923	1953	1953
New York	1903	1938	1949
North Carolina	1903	1965	1965
North Dakota	1915	1963	1963
Ohio	1915	1967	1968
Oklahoma	1909	—	—
Oregon	1911	1957	1957
Pennsylvania	1909	1951	1952

TABLE 1 (continued)

State	Year Voluntary Licensure Passed	Year Mandatory Licensure Passed	Year Mandatory Licensure Effective
Rhode Island	1912	1952	1952
South Carolina	1910	1969	1969
South Dakota	1917	1955	1955
Tennessee	1911	1967	1967
Texas	1909	—	—
Utah	1917	1963	1963
Vermont	1911	1962	1962
Virginia	1903	1970	1970
Washington	1909	1961	1961
West Virginia	1907	1965	1965
Wisconsin	1911	1955	1956
Wyoming	1909	1955	1955

[a] Massachusetts passed a new licensure law for nurses in 1957, which the state nursing association believed to be mandatory at the time. However, the law contains several major loopholes, and the state board of nursing and the state nurses' association now view the law as voluntary. (Telephone conversation, executive secretary, Massachusetts State Board of Registration in Nursing, Boston, Mass., December 15, 1978; issue also discussed in Monheit, "Economic Analysis.")

SOURCES: State codes and statute books; American Nurses' Association, *Facts about Nursing, 1974–75*; conversation with Frances Waddle, coordinator of ethical and legal aspects of nursing practice, American Nurses' Association, Kansas City, Mo., February 6, 1979.

market. On the demand side, changes in medical practice and the use of more sophisticated technology increased the demand for experienced nurses in hospitals. On the supply side, Altman argues that decreases in nurses' wages during the Great Depression made it cheaper for hospitals to hire graduate nurses as employees than to operate schools. Reforms in nursing education (which increased the amount of formal instruction student nurses received and reduced the amount of time they spent working in hospital wards) also probably tended to increase the costs of using nursing students in hospitals.

RNs were not the only kind of nursing personnel employed in hospitals during this period. Many hospitals also used lower-level personnel, such as attendants and orderlies, to help provide nursing services. As more RNs began to work for hospitals, they began to become increasingly concerned about establishing control not only over the use of titles through voluntary licensure but also over the practice of nursing as an occupation (which meant limiting competition from lower-level personnel). Their concern was probably partly a product of the high unemployment in nursing in the 1930s[13] and partly a result of studies showing that a large number of untrained personnel were being used to perform nursing duties in many areas. But RNs were also concerned about the development of formal educational programs for practical nurses, because these programs were beginning to offer hospitals an alternative source of trained nursing personnel.[14]

Some RNs argued that the best way to deal with the problem of competition from lower-level personnel was to exclude them from nursing activities. But others argued that this approach was politically unrealistic and that in any case there were important advantages to using subordinate personnel inasmuch as the presence of subordinates would upgrade the status of professional nurses.

Organized efforts to deal with the problem of competition from lower-level personnel began around 1930. At the state level, some of the more active state nurses' associations began to investigate mandatory licensure. At the national level, the ANA made its first effort at a formal definition of the practice of professional nursing in 1932, and in 1936 it joined with the NLN and the National Organization for Public Health Nursing to form a special joint committee on the problems of subordinate personnel.[15] By 1939 these groups had begun to evolve a general program to deal with the problem of competition from less-skilled workers based on licensure of "all those who nurse for hire."[16]

The basic goals of this program were (1) to provide formal recognition to practical nurses as part of the nursing team, (2) to establish control by RNs over the supervision and training of practical nurses through licensure and voluntary institutional arrangements, and (3) to use mandatory licensure of RNs and practical nurses to eliminate the

---

[13] Data on unemployment rates for nurses during this period are scarce, and those data that do exist are difficult to interpret because most graduate nurses worked as private-duty nurses and did not have any regular hours. The general consensus seems to be that private-duty nurses were already having difficulty obtaining employment in the late 1920s and that the Great Depression made a bad situation even worse. See Yett, *Economic Analysis*, p. 3.

[14] For examples of discussions of the use of untrained personnel, see E. Burgess, "A Good Nurse Practice Act: What Are the Essentials?" *American Journal of Nursing*, vol. 34, no. 4 (July 1934), pp. 651–56; or "New York's Legislative Struggle," *American Journal of Nursing*, vol. 37, no. 5 (May 1937), pp. 516–18. See D. Johnson, *History and Trends of Practical Nursing* (St. Louis: C. V. Mosby, 1966), for a history of educational programs for practical nurses.

[15] Flanagan, *One Strong Voice*, p. 91.

[16] "All Those Who Nurse for Hire," *American Journal of Nursing*, vol. 39, no. 3 (March 1939), pp. 275–77.

use of unlicensed lower-level personnel to perform bedside nursing duties.[17] However, nurses viewed licensure laws mainly as a way of setting minimum standards for personnel because they found that it was difficult to keep laws current with advances in nursing care. The ANA and other nursing groups also sought to establish national standards for good nursing care through such voluntary means as the hospital accreditation standards of the Joint Commission on Hospital Accreditation.[18]

World War II created an acute shortage of RNs and led to a sharp increase in the use of practical nurses and other personnel with less training, such as nurses' aides. After World War II, this "shortage" of registered nurses assumed chronic proportions,[19] while the use of less-skilled nursing personnel continued to grow. The policy of licensing "all those who nurse for hire" created growing opposition from hospital administrators and physicians, who argued they were already having difficulty staffing hospitals even without restrictive legislation.

In the postwar period, the ANA continued to support mandatory licensure of RNs. But in 1951 it moved away from trying to eliminate the use of other types of nursing personnel (other than licensed RNs and practical nurses) from bedside nursing duties—much to the relief of such groups as the American Hospital Association.[20]

Since World War II, there have been persistent regional differences

---

[17] Flanagan, *One Strong Voice*, pp. 110–12.

[18] For a discussion of legal standards versus private voluntary standards, see American Nurses' Association, *Legislation Manual for Committees on Legislation of State Nurses Associations* (New York: American Nurses' Association, 1959), p. 36. Private voluntary standards for nursing personnel appear in accreditation standards of the American College of Surgeons, which pioneered early hospital accreditation efforts, as early as 1940. (American College of Surgeons, *Manual of Hospital Standardization* [Chicago: American College of Surgeons, 1940]). After World War II, the American Hospital Association and the American Medical Association joined the American College of Surgeons and others to form the Joint Commission on Hospital Accreditation. Today the standards of the joint commission have additional force, inasmuch as hospitals must meet these or a similar set of government standards to quality for Medicare and Medicaid payments.

[19] Yett, in *Economic Analysis*, questions whether this has been a true shortage in the economic sense. Although the labor market for nurses has not cleared at existing wage rates since World War II, this may—he argues—be because hospitals have used their monopsony power to hold wages below the market clearing level, rather than because of a real shortage.

[20] The ANA platform for 1950 called for state licensure of all those who nurse for hire. (American Nurses' Association, *Proceedings of the House of Delegates, 37th Convention, 1950* [New York: American Nurses' Association, 1950]). In 1951, however, the ANA committee on legislation took the position that, at least for the time being, licensure should be mandatory only for registered nurses and not for practical nurses, permitting the use of unlicensed subordinate personnel. This position was eventually adopted by the ANA board. (Minutes of Meeting of ANA Board of Directors, September 15, 1951, mimeo, p. 12, exhibit II). The American Hospital Association applauded in an editorial ("Common Sense Prevails," *Hospitals*, vol. 26, no. 5 [May 1951], p. 72). In 1952 the

in the ratio of RNs to other types of nursing personnel in the United States. Altman suggests that these regional differences may be related to differences in relative wages between RNs and other personnel.[21] He notes that in the Northeast, where the wages of less-skilled personnel tend to be relatively high, relatively more RNs are used in hospitals. In contrast, in the South, where the wages of less-skilled workers tend to be relatively low, more less-skilled personnel such as practical nurses and nurses' aides are used.

The next section of this paper considers in detail the introduction of mandatory licensure laws for registered nurses. The following section seeks to use cross-sectional state data to estimate the impact of mandatory laws on the wages and employment of registered nurses.

The Introduction of Mandatory Licensure

The first attempt to introduce mandatory licensure for RNs began in New York in 1933 after nurses there became concerned about a report issued by the New York State Department of Education. This report showed that a large number of untrained workers were being used to provide nursing services despite voluntary licensure laws.[22] At first, efforts to introduce a compulsory law failed. But in 1938 the state nursing association succeeded in getting mandatory licensure for both registered and practical nurses on the grounds that everyone who provided nursing services should be regulated.[23]

RNs in California organized a campaign for mandatory licensure of RNs in 1938 and succeeded in obtaining it in 1939. Louisiana introduced a mandatory law for RNs in 1942. No other states followed the example of New York and California until the end of World War II, and existing licensure laws were amended in the face of wartime short-

---

ANA revised its platform and simply adopted the goal of "promoting state nursing practice laws which will protect the public and which will facilitate interstate registration or licensure of qualified professional and practical nurses." (American Nurses' Association, *Proceedings of the House of Delegates, 38th Convention, 1952* [New York: American Nurses' Association, 1952], vol. 1, p. 125.)

[21] Altman, *Present and Future Supply*, pp. 26–30.

[22] See Burgess, "New York's Legislative Struggle" and AJN, "All Those Who Nurse for Hire."

[23] When the New York act first passed, it was apparently interpreted to mean that everyone who provided direct services to patients, including orderlies, had to be licensed (J. Hayes, "New York's New Nursing Law," *Modern Hospital*, vol. 52, no. 4 [February 1939], pp. 69–70). This interpretation was not followed, however, when the law finally became effective in 1949.

ages of nurses,[24] but after the war efforts began anew.

By 1950 seven states and the territory of Hawaii had mandatory licensure. In 1960 there were thirty states with mandatory licensure laws for RNs. Most of these states were in the northeastern and western regions of the country; less than 20 percent of the states in the South had compulsory laws. During the 1960s, however, most of the southern states also introduced mandatory laws. At the time of this writing, only four states and the District of Columbia did not have mandatory licensure.

Who supported and who opposed the introduction of these laws? At the state level, campaigns to introduce mandatory licensure have consistently been led by state nurses' associations, following the pattern set in New York and California. Government agencies and citizen groups have sometimes lent support, but the leadership role seems uniformly to have belonged to registered nurses. At the national level, the ANA adopted its policy of licensure for "all who nurse for hire" shortly before the New York mandatory law was passed in 1938. Under this policy the ANA supported mandatory licensure of RNs and practical nurses. (Many of the states that subsequently introduced mandatory licensure for RNs also introduced voluntary or mandatory licensure for practical nurses.) But while the ANA supported mandatory licensure for RNs, it did not try to organize the kind of national campaign that had been organized for voluntary licensure at the turn of the century. Instead, it provided legislative assistance—eventually preparing a model bill in 1954—and left the initiative for introducing licensure to the state associations. Then in the late 1950s the ANA seems to have become concerned about the slow rate at which mandatory laws were being introduced in some areas of the country. In 1958 it passed resolutions encouraging state associations that had not already done so to begin looking into mandatory licensure,[25] which probably contributed to the rapid spread of mandatory licensure in the South in the 1960s.

The basic argument used by state and national nurses' groups has been that mandatory laws can prevent the serious harm that can result from using unqualified personnel and that the public needs to be protected accordingly, even if this involves abridging individual freedom and potentially increasing the cost of care. At the same time, nurses'

---

[24] Implementation of the New York law was initially delayed because of administrative problems. Then the law was amended because of the wartime emergency, and mandatory licensure did not become effective until 1949. The California law was suspended between 1942 and 1948. In Louisiana the state nursing board was permitted to license out-of-state graduate nurses without examination until 1950, although it is not clear whether the board actually did so.

[25] Flanagan, *One Strong Voice*, p. 217.

groups have also argued that registered nurses themselves need protection from "unfair competition" from less well trained-workers.[26]

Opposition to mandatory licensure has come from several quarters. Hospitals and physicians have sometimes opposed mandatory laws because they have feared that the laws would increase labor costs. Practical nurses have also opposed mandatory laws in some areas because they feared that it would reduce their employment opportunities. In the 1930s and 1940s, commercial nursing schools fought mandatory licensure because it threatened to destroy the market for their graduates.[27]

In more than one case, opposition from these sources has stalled campaigns to introduce new licensure laws. For example, RNs in Washington state attempted to introduce mandatory licensure in 1945, but their bill was defeated, apparently as a result of opposition from practical nurses.[28] RNs in the state did not succeed in getting a mandatory law passed until 1961.

Overall, this general discussion suggests that support for mandatory licensure has come mainly from the nursing occupation itself, while opposition has come mainly from hospitals and physicians concerned about the impact of mandatory laws on labor costs and from lower-level personnel. Stigler used regression analysis to consider the introduction of voluntary licensure laws for RNs in individual states by looking at the relationship between the year licensure was introduced in states and conditions in these states in some base year.[29] A similar approach would be to look at the relationship between conditions in individual states in some base year and the percentage of years when these states had mandatory licensure during some subsequent period, for example, the next twenty-five years.

Until 1950 data on employment patterns in nursing are limited. But we can use Stigler's general approach to consider the introduction of mandatory licensure after 1950. In the regression that follows, the dependent variable (*PYML*) is the percentage of years in which states without mandatory licensure for RNs in the continental United States

---

[26] For example, see editorials such as "Nurse Practice Acts," *American Journal of Nursing*, vol. 49, no. 4 (April 1949), pp. 197–99, and Burgess, "New York's Legislative Struggle."

[27] See "Nursing Legislation 1939: What State Nursing Associations Accomplished," *American Journal of Nursing*, vol. 39, no. 9 (September 1939), pp. 947–78; "Licensure for Those Who Nurse," *American Journal of Nursing*, vol. 50, no. 1 (January 1950), p. 43; L. Given, "Licensing for Nursing—Professional and Practical," *Nursing World*, vol. 125, no. 5 (May 1951), p. 186; and C. Ramsey, "As Association Works for Mandatory Licensure," *American Journal of Nursing*, vol. 58, no. 9 (September 1958), pp. 1267–69.

[28] "News Here and There," *American Journal of Nursing*, vol. 45, no. 4 (July 1945), p. 580.

[29] Stigler, "Theory of Economic Regulation."

in 1950 had mandatory laws in force between 1951 and 1976. The District of Columbia is included in this analysis, but Hawaii and Alaska are not. States that already had mandatory licensure in 1950 are excluded.

The independent variables in this regression are RN employment (*RNEMP*), female registered nurses per 100,000 population in states (in 1950), and *PRNH*, the percentage of nursing personnel in general hospitals who were RNs (in 1951). We hypothesize that the expected sign of *RNEMP* is positive because the more nurses that are employed in an area, the more votes they will have and the greater pressure they can bring on state legislators. The expected sign of *PRNH* is also positive for two reasons. First, in areas where the percentage of RNs is high, mandatory laws are less likely to have a large impact on labor costs, so that there is likely to be less resistance from hospitals and physicians. Second, the greater the percentage of RNs, the larger the size of this group relative to other nursing personnel who may oppose mandatory laws.[30] The results of this regression of *PYML* are:

$$PYML = 0.0328 - 0.0006 \ RNEMP + 1.5806 \ PRNH$$

$$(0.15) \qquad (-0.74) \qquad\qquad (2.26^*)$$

$$F(3,42) = 3.18 \qquad R^2 = 0.14$$

The bracketed figures are *t*-statistics. One asterisk (*) indicates significance at the 5 percent level. (That is, we are 95 percent confident that the coefficient is significantly different from zero.)

In this regression the coefficient of *RNEMP* is not significant. The coefficient of *PRNH* is significant at the 5 percent level. The size of this coefficient implies that a 1 percent increase in the proportion of registered nurses will result in an increase of slightly over 1.5 percent in the percentage of years with mandatory licensure. This result suggests that mandatory licensure came first in areas where there were relatively large numbers of RNs in hospitals (mandatory licensure thus being less likely to force changes in employment patterns). The low coefficient of determination (R^2) obtained in the regression, 0.14, is similar to the kind of results obtained by Stigler in his use of this type of model for a variety of occupations.[31] This suggests that political and economic

---

[30] Data for these variables were obtained from the U.S. Bureau of the Census, *U.S. Census of Population: Characteristics of the Population, 1950* (Washington, D.C., 1952); and U.S Public Health Service, Division of Nursing, *Source Book on Nursing Personnel*, DHEW HRA-75-43 (Washington, D.C., 1974).

[31] Stigler, "Theory of Economic Regulation."

factors we have not considered here may also be important (as, for example, geographic patterns in the diffusion of legislation).[32]

The Impact of Mandatory Licensure

In the theoretical model presented, the impact of mandatory licensure on the wages and employment of licensed personnel is indeterminate. It will depend not only on substitution effects but also on final price effects. There are several reasons for believing that negative final price effects—that is, the effect of higher wages for RNs on the demand for final output—are likely to be small. First, the demand for the final output they help to produce—health services—tends to be inelastic, not only because of the nature of this good but also because of insurance arrangements. Second, nursing services make up only a part of the cost of producing health services and are complements of a large range of other medical services. It seems reasonable to hypothesize that substitution effects—that is, the effect of licensure on the substitution of RNs for other types of personnel—will dominate final price effects and that mandatory licensure will have a nonnegative impact on the wages and employment of registered nurses.

The size of this impact will depend on the extent to which mandatory licensure laws impose binding constraints and the extent to which they are enforced. Since RNs seem to have sought mandatory laws primarily to control the use of lower-level personnel, we should expect these laws, if enforced, to have a significant positive impact on the wages and employment of the higher personnel. Mandatory laws seem likely to be enforced because RNs control nursing boards in most states and are in a good position to observe violations.

On the other hand, there sometimes seem to be problems in interpreting mandatory laws. There is also some question how zealous RNs have been in pushing for their enforcement. For example, in 1958 the ANA committee on legislation was sufficiently concerned about the matter to pass a resolution directing state nursing associations in areas with this type of regulation to look into the enforcement of mandatory laws.[33] Monheit suggests that registered nurses may be ambivalent about enforcement because, even though subordinate personnel are potential substitutes, their use tends to increase the status of RNs.[34]

---

[32] To take into account possible regional effects, this equation was also estimated with regional dummies for the Northeast, North-Central, South, and West. Including these dummies left the signs and magnitudes of the original dependent variables basically unchanged, while the R^2 of the regression increased to 0.35.

[33] Flanagan, *One Strong Voice*, p. 217.

[34] Monheit, *Economic Analysis*.

61

As we noted in the second section, there are large regional variations in the use of different types of nursing personnel in the United States, and these variations seem related to regional differences in the relative wages of RNs and other nursing personnel. In this section, I seek to test the hypothesis that mandatory licensure laws limit the substitution of other nursing personnel for RNs and that they have a positive impact on their wages and employment. My test uses cross-sectional data, a modified version of Lee Benham's model of the labor market for RNs, and regression analysis.[35]

As we discussed in the first section, there may not be significant wage differentials between areas with and without mandatory licensure if there is a smoothly functioning labor market. However, if licensure constraints are binding and our hypothesis is correct, we would still expect mandatory laws to have a positive impact.

The general model used by Benham was selected for our analysis because it permits us to look directly at possible effects on the wages and employment of registered nurses. Since the vast majority of RNs, about 98 percent, are female, Benham does not attempt to consider male nurses, and neither do we. In Benham's model of the labor market for female nurses, there are three structural equations: one demand equation and two supply equations. On the demand side, the basic argument is that the demand for RNs is a function of their own wage, of the cost of using substitute nursing personnel, and of the overall demand for health services. On the supply side, there is one equation for the stock of nurses and one for their labor force participation rate. (The stock of nurses multiplied by their participation rate is, by definition, equal to the number of nurses in the labor force.) The basic argument is that the stock of nurses is a function of their wage rate, their husbands' income, and educational opportunities in states and that the participation rate of nurses is a function of the first two variables again plus their family responsibilities. The model does not contain any licensure variables.

The primary effect of mandatory licensure is to impose constraints on the demand side of the market by forcing employers to use RNs. We can introduce mandatory licensure into Benham's model by adding dummies for mandatory laws to his demand equation.

Table 2 lists the variables used in this modified version of Benham's model. The demand equation (1) in this modified model is

$$RNWAGE = f(RNLFPR,^* \ RN\overset{-}{STOCK},^* \ AT\overset{+}{WAGE}, \ P\overset{+}{CY}, \qquad (1)$$
$$M\overset{+}{LIC}, \ ML\overset{-}{ICL5})$$

---

[35] Benham, "Labor Market for Registered Nurses."

TABLE 2

LIST OF VARIABLES USED IN THREE-EQUATION MODEL OF THE LABOR MARKET FOR REGISTERED NURSES

RNWAGE	= Median income of female RNs in the experienced civilian labor force in state
RNSTOCK	= Total female RNs per 100,000 population in state
RNLFPR	= Labor force participation rate of female RNs in state
RNEMP	= Female RNs employed per 100,000 population in state (*RNSTOCK* × *RNLFPR*)
PCY	= Per capita personal income in state
ATWAGE	= Median earnings of hospital and other institutional attendants in the experienced civilian labor force with known income in state
MHY	= Median income of male heads of families in state
CHILD	= Number of children under five years of age/number of women between ages of fifteen and forty-nine ever married in state
RNG	= Total graduations from schools of nursing in state ten years earlier per 100,000 current population in state
MLIC	= 1: State has mandatory licensure law in effect for RNs 0: State does not have mandatory licensure law in effect for RNs
MLIC5	= 1: State has mandatory licensure law for RNs that has been in effect for less than five years 0: State does not have mandatory licensure law for RNs that has been in effect for less than five years

Endogenous variables are noted with an asterisk (*), and expected signs are shown above each of the dependent variables. In the equation the median income of female RNs is used as a proxy for their wage rate. (*RNWAGE*). It is hypothesized in the equation that the wage rate of RNs is a negative function of both the endogenous variables in the equation, the RN labor force participation rate, *RNLFPR*, and the stock of RNs, *RNSTOCK*. By definition, the product of these two variables is equal to the total employment of RNs per 100,000 population, the variable *RNEMP* in table 2. Since a given percentage change in either *RNLFPR* or *RNSTOCK* should have the same effect on employment, the coefficients of these two variables are constrained to be equal in estimates of the equation.

Of the exogenous variables in the equation, the median income of hospital attendants, *ATWAGE*, is included as a proxy for the wage cost of substitute nursing personnel. Per capita income in states, *PCY*, is included as a proxy for the overall level of demand for health services.

The expected sign of both variables is positive. *MLIC* is a dummy for mandatory licensure. This dummy takes the value *one* for states with effective mandatory laws and *zero* for those without. The expected sign of this dummy is positive. The expected sign of the dummy for states that have had effective mandatory licensure laws for less than five years, *MLICL5*, is negative because it is expected that there may be a time lag before new laws become fully effective.

On the supply side of the model, Benham has one equation for the labor participation rate of registered nurses, *RNLFPR*, and one for the stock of these personnel, *RNSTOCK*. These equations are used here in their original form. The labor force participation rate equation (2) is

$$RNLFPR = f(RN\overset{+}{WAGE},^* \overset{-}{MHY}, \overset{-}{CHILD}) \tag{2}$$

This equation hypothesizes that the labor force participation rate of nurses will be a positive function of nurses' wages, *RNWAGE*, the endogenous variable in the equation. It is hypothesized that the participation rate will decrease with the income of the husbands of married nurses and the number of young children they have, where the income of male heads of households in states (*MHY*) and the number of children under five divided by the number of women between ages fifteen and forty-nine who have ever been married in states (*CHILD*) are used as proxies for these variables.

Benham seeks to explain the geographic distribution of nurses in the stock equation (3):

$$RNSTOCK = f(RN\overset{+}{WAGE},^* \overset{+}{MHY}, \overset{+}{RNG}) \tag{3}$$

This equation hypothesizes that the stock of nurses in a state will be a positive function of their wage rate, *RNWAGE*. Benham also argues that nurses will tend to be attracted to states where their husbands can find high wages or where they can find husbands with high incomes, with the income of male heads of households in states, *MHY*, included as a proxy for this variable. Finally, the number of graduates from nursing programs in the state ten years before, *RNG*, is included to provide a measure of the effects of local training programs, with the expected sign of this variable also positive.

These equations were estimated using three-stage least-squares and cross-sectional data on states in the continental United States, plus the District of Columbia, for three years: 1950, 1960, and 1970.[36] In 1950

---

[36] Following Benham ("Labor Market for Registered Nurses," p. 248), three-stage least-squares were used to estimate the model because they allow us to take into account the possibility of correlation between the disturbance terms of the different structural equations in the model. (See J. Kmenta, *Elements of Econometrics* [New York: Macmillan, 1971], pp. 573–78). Data for these estimates were obtained from the following sources: U.S. Bureau of the Census, *Statistical Abstract of the United States*, 1963, 1967, 1973

only one dummy for mandatory licensure is included, *MLIC*, because none of the existing laws had been in effect for more than five years. (In 1950 only two of the six states with effective mandatory licensure laws had had them for more than five years; in both of these states, laws had been subject to wartime amendments that prevented them from being fully implemented.) The anticipated size of the coefficient of the licensure dummy for 1950 in the structural equation in the model is small, because laws had not really had time to take effect.

In 1960 and 1970, both dummies for licensure are included. Since more states had had mandatory licensure for a longer period in 1960 than in 1950, it is hypothesized that the coefficient of the dummy for mandatory licensure, *MLIC*, should be relatively large in estimates for this year. In 1970 it seems possible that the coefficient of *MLIC* may be smaller, because only six areas in the sample did not have mandatory licensure and also because the amount of variation in wage and employment variables was somewhat lower than in 1950 and 1960.

The structural equations are estimated with all of the variables in log form except for the zero-one dummies for licensure. Placing the variables in log form has the advantage that the regression coefficients of these variables can be interpreted directly as elasticities. The results of our estimates of the structural equations of the model for 1950, 1960, and 1970, using three-stage least-squares, are reported in table 3.[37]

The results of these estimates are used in table 4 to solve for the endogenous variables in the model and to get reduced-form estimates of the endogenous variables in terms of the exogenous variables. In table 4 the endogenous variables are ln *RNWAGE*, ln *RNLFPR*, and ln *RNSTOCK*. We also solve for the effects of the exogenous variables on the employment of female registered nurses per 100,000 population, ln *RNEMP*.[38]

(Washington, D.C., 1963, 1967, 1973); U.S. Bureau of the Census, *U.S. Census of Population: Characteristics of the Population*, 1950, 1960, 1970 (Washington D.C., 1952, 1963, 1973); U.S. Department of Health, Education and Welfare, *Health Manpower Source Book*, section 2, section 2 revised, section 5, section 17 (Washington, D.C., 1953, 1966, 1954, 1963); and U.S. Public Health Service, Division of Nursing, *Source Book on Nursing Personnel*.

[37] Three-stage least-squares estimates were computed using a program written by Les Jennings and modified by Houston H. Stokes. (See Houston H. Stokes, "The B34S Data Analysis Program: A Short Writeup," University of Illinois at Chicago Circle College of Business Administration Working Paper 77–1, mimeo., 1977). *T*-statistics were computed following Kmenta, *Elements of Econometrics*. Note that the ratio of coefficients to their standard errors in a simultaneous equation model do not have a *t* distribution. But they do have distribution that is approximately normal, so that large *t* values can be taken as an approximate indication of statistical significance.

[38] By definition, the log of the product of two numbers is equal to the sum of their logs, and so ln *RNEMP* equals the sum of ln *RNLFPR* and ln *RMSTOCK*, and the reduced-form coefficients of ln *RNEMP* are simply equal to the sums of the reduced-form coefficients of ln *RNLFPR* and ln *RNSTOCK*.

TABLE 3
THREE-STAGE LEAST-SQUARES ESTIMATES OF THREE-EQUATION MODEL OF THE LABOR MARKET FOR REGISTERED NURSES WITH DUMMIES FOR MANDATORY LICENSURE: 1950, 1960, 1970

Regression	1950 Coefficient	1950 t-ratio	1960 Coefficient	1960 t-ratio	1970 Coefficient	1970 t-ratio	Expected Sign of Independent Variables
(1) ln RNWAGE							
Constant	3.1244	5.38	4.6864	6.17	4.0329	5.35	
ln RNSTOCK[a]	−0.3216	−4.34	−0.6720	−1.28	−0.3729	−2.34	−
ln RNLFPR[a]	−0.3216	−4.34	−0.6720	−1.28	−0.3729	−2.34	−
ln ATWAGE	0.2649	3.86	0.3854	2.79	0.1569	1.33	+
ln PCY	0.5821	5.46	0.5558	1.41	0.6705	3.72	+
MLIC	0.0543	1.88	−0.0124	−0.42	−0.0044	−0.13	+
MLIC5	—	—	−0.0280	−0.58	0.0505	1.58	−
(2) ln RNLFR							
Constant	0.3740	0.25	−1.8486	−2.00	−0.7992	−1.79	
ln RNWAGE	0.2126	0.87	0.5445	2.88	0.1984	1.97	+
ln MHY	−0.3336	−3.83	−0.3713	−4.49	−0.1330	−2.11	−
ln CHILD	−0.1807	−1.33	−0.2228	−2.13	0.1224	1.62	−
(3) ln RNSTOCK							
Constant	−19.7121	−3.11	−1.8000	−0.74	1.5581	0.75	
ln RNWAGE	2.4210	2.12	0.1667	0.40	−0.0930	−0.25	+
ln MHY	0.7451	1.77	0.7595	4.18	0.5973	2.58	+
ln RNG	0.3936	3.58	0.0846	3.05	0.1046	3.80	+

[a] The coefficients of RNSTOCK and RNLFPR are constrained to be equal in regression (1).

TABLE 4

THREE-STAGE LEAST-SQUARES REDUCED-FORM COEFFICIENTS FOR THREE-EQUATION MODEL OF LABOR MARKET FOR REGISTERED NURSES WITH DUMMIES FOR MANDATORY LICENSURE: 1950, 1960, 1970

Dependent Variable	ln ATWAGE	ln PCY	ln MHY	ln CHILD	ln RNG	MLIC	MLIC5	Constant
1950								
ln RNWAGE	0.1434	0.3151	−0.0716	0.0315	−0.0685	0.0294	—	5.0589
ln RNLFPR	0.0305	0.0670	−0.3489	−0.1741	−0.0146	0.0063	—	1.4493
ln RNSTOCK	0.3473	0.7630	0.5717	0.0762	0.2277	0.0712	—	7.4647
ln RNEMP	0.3778	0.8300	0.2228	−0.0979	0.2131	0.0775	—	−6.0154
1960								
ln RNWAGE	0.2607	0.3761	−0.1765	0.1013	−0.0385	−0.0084	−0.0190	4.8298
ln RNLFPR	0.1420	0.2048	−0.4675	−0.1677	−0.0210	−0.0046	−0.0103	0.7815
ln RNSTOCK	0.0435	0.0627	0.7301	0.0169	0.0782	−0.0014	−0.0032	−0.9949
ln RNEMP	0.1855	0.2675	0.2626	−0.1508	0.0572	−0.0060	−0.0135	−0.2134
1970								
ln RNWAGE	0.1536	0.6452	−0.1666	−0.0439	−0.0375	0.0042	0.0486	3.6081
ln RNLFPR	0.0305	0.1280	−0.1661	0.1137	−0.0074	−0.0008	0.0096	−0.0833
ln RNSTOCK	−0.0143	−0.0600	0.6127	0.0041	0.1081	0.0004	−0.0045	1.2227
ln RNEMP	0.0162	0.0680	0.4466	0.1178	0.1007	−0.0004	0.0051	1.1394

Overall, the results of our estimates are consistent with Benham's model. For the purpose of this paper, it is not necessary to consider the coefficients of all the individual variables. Our discussion here focuses on the dummies for mandatory licensure. It is interesting to note in the structural equations in table 3, however, that in 1970 the signs reverse for the coefficients of $CHILD$ in the labor force participation equation (2) and $RNWAGE$ in the stock equation (3). This suggests that changes may have taken place in the supply of RNs during the 1960s. Also note that the variable for attendants' wages, $ATWAGE$, has large positive coefficients and large t-statistics for 1950 and 1960 in equation (1) but that both the size of the coefficient of $ATWAGE$ and the size of the t-statistics decline in the 1970 estimates. The results for 1950 and 1960 tend to support the hypothesis that less-skilled nursing personnel are substitutes for RNs and that the level of substitution depends on relative wages. But the results for 1970 suggest that there was a decrease in the elasticity of substitution of other types of nursing personnel for RNs during the 1960s.

The results for 1950 suggest that mandatory licensure may have had a small positive impact on the wages and employment of registered nurses. In table 3, the dummy for states with mandatory licensure, $MLIC$, has a positive coefficient with a magnitude of 0.0543, suggesting that mandatory licensure increases wages by approximately 5 percent. The t-statistic for this coefficient is 1.88, which is fairly large by conventional standards. In table 4, the reduced-form coefficients of $MLIC$ for 1950 are all positive, and the presence of mandatory licensure is associated with a 2.9 percent increase in wages and a 7.75 percent increase in employment. However, these results are somewhat difficult to interpret because, as noted, most of the mandatory laws in force at this time were new and the older laws were subject to wartime waivers.

Results for 1960 and 1970, when more states had laws and had had them for longer periods, do not provide any evidence that mandatory licensure has a positive effect. In 1960 and 1970 the coefficient of $MLIC$ in table 3 reverses sign and becomes negative. The magnitude of this coefficient is small in both periods, -0.0124 in 1960 and -0.0044 in 1970, and the t-statistics are low. The reduced-form coefficients of $MLIC$ in table 4 are also negative and small for both the wages and employment in 1960 and 1970.

The dummy to adjust for states that has recently introduced mandatory licensure (and may thus not have had time for full implementation), $MLIC5$, has relatively small coefficients in the structural equations for both 1960 and 1970, and the t-statistics are low. In 1960 the coefficient of $MLIC5$ was -0.0280 with a t-statistic of -0.58. In 1970 this coefficient reversed sign and had a magnitude of 0.0505 and a *t*-statistic of 1.58. In the reduced-form coefficients in table 4, the dummy *MLIC5* is associated with a negative wage effect of -0.0190 in 1960 and a negative employment effect of -0.0135. In 1970, it is associated with a positive wage effect of 0.0486 and a positive employment effect of 0.0051. These results suggest that the wages and employment of RNs have been slightly lower in states that had recently introduced mandatory licensure than in states that had introduced it more than five years before 1960 and that in 1970, for the same comparison, wages and employment have been slightly higher.

One problem is that female RNs employed per 100,000 population, *RNEMP*, may not be a good measure of employment. The amount of hospital care received by the population, and therefore also possibly the demand for nurses, vary considerably among states. One alternative measure of employment is the number of RNs employed per 100 average patient-days in general hospitals, which are the main employers of nurses. To provide a crude check of these results, reduced-form employment equations were run for 1950 and 1960 using this as the dependent variable, using the same independent variables as in the equations above, and using ordinary least-squares. Dummies for licensure were not significant in either regression.[39] These results again suggest that mandatory licensure of RNs did not have any impact on employment of RNs.[40]

---

[39] Data on RNs engaged in bedside nursing activities per 100 average daily patients in general hospitals in 1951 were used for the dependent variable in the 1950 regression. Data for 1959 were used for the 1960 regression. The source of these data was the U.S. Public Health Service, Division of Nursing, *Source Book on Nursing Personnel*. Unfortunately, comparable data were not available for 1970.

[40] Even if mandatory licensure of registered nurses has not affected the employment of RNs, it may have affected the employment of other types of nursing personnel. One possible measure of the mix of nursing personnel is the percentage of total bedside nursing personnel per 100 average patient days who are RNs in general hospitals. Reduced-form equations were also run for 1950 and 1960 using this as the dependent variable, the same independent variables as in the modified Benham model, and ordinary least-squares. Data on the percentage of nurses who were RNs in 1951 were used for the 1950 regression and in 1959 for the 1960 regression. The source of these data was the U.S. Public Health Service, Division of Nursing, *Source Book on Nursing Personnel*. Dummies for licensure were not significant in either the 1950 or the 1960 regression. These results suggests that mandatory licensure of RNs did not have any impact on the use of other nursing personnel, at least in general hospitals. As noted earlier, Monheit ("Economic Analysis") found evidence that licensure laws affected the relative employment and wages of registered nurses and practical nurses in 1960. In this study he did not consider the use of other types of personnel, however, and the subject clearly needs further investigation. An appendix containing the results of these reduced-form estimates and estimates referred to in footnote 39 is available on request from the author.

Conclusions

The historical analysis in this paper suggests that mandatory licensure laws for RNs have been introduced mainly as a result of the nurses' efforts. RNs appear to have sought these laws as part of a more general effort to deal with the problems of competition from less-skilled personnel. These problems began to develop on a large scale for the first time in the 1920s and 1930s, as a result of a shift from private-duty nursing to general-duty nursing in hospitals, and they continue today. Opposition to mandatory licensure laws for nurses has come mainly from hospitals and physicians, who have been concerned about the impact of mandatory laws on labor costs, and from practical nurses, who have been concerned about the impact of laws on their employment opportunities. Resistance from hospital groups seems to have increased since World War II, a result of shortages of RNs at existing wage rates.

Our hypothesis was that mandatory laws would result in an increase in the wages and the employment of RNs. The cross-sectional studies of states with and without mandatory laws suggest that this type of regulation may have had a positive effect in 1950. But there is no evidence in these studies that mandatory laws had a positive impact on the wages or employment of RNs in 1960 (when we would have expected effects to be large) or in 1970.

On the assumption that these results are valid, they raise two questions. First, why did mandatory licensure laws for RNs not have any impact on the overall wages or employment of this group in 1960 or in 1970? Second, given this lack of impact, why did RNs continue to seek mandatory licensure laws throughout the 1950s and 1960s?

One possible explanation of the lack of impact is that the laws set minimum standards below the standards that nurses succeeded in setting through voluntary means (such as hospital accreditation standards). The existence of large regional variations in the use of practical nurses and other types of nursing personnel in 1960 and 1970 makes this view questionable, however. A second explanation is that RNs simply failed to achieve laws with binding constraints or failed to get the laws enforced.

In either case, the question remains why they continued to seek mandatory laws if these laws did not have any impact on overall wages or employment in their occupation. One reason may have been that mandatory laws have had effects not considered by this study. For example, they may have helped to establish RNs as the dominant group in nursing and reinforced their supervisory role over other personnel. Since the number of supervisory positions is small, this would not have a major impact on employment, but retaining supervisory positions for

RNs could have had an important impact on the status of the occupation. In addition, mandatory laws may have had effects on the quality of nursing care, which is not considered here, or on the type of lower-level nursing personnel employed in hospitals.

Another possibility is that RNs were not aware that mandatory licensure laws did not have any significant impact on their overall wages or employment. There do not seem to have been any detailed studies of the effects of mandatory licensure either on the quality of nursing care or on wages or employment during the 1950s or 1960s. In fact, there is very little discussion in nursing journals about the actual impact of mandatory laws.

On the other hand, discussions with RNs who are currently interested in issues involving licensure suggest that they do not believe mandatory laws have had a major impact on the use of nursing personnel.[41] It is possible that they may have been aware of the limitations of new mandatory laws introduced during the postwar period. But in the face of strong opposition from hospitals and physicians because of personnel shortages, they may have preferred weak mandatory laws to no laws at all, perhaps as a form of insurance against drastic change. The fact that the ANA moved away from its position of licensure for "all those who nurse for hire" after the nursing shortage that followed World War II tends to support this view. So does our finding in section three that, at least after 1950, mandatory laws tended to come first in states where they were likely to have the least impact, rather than in those where there was heavy use of less-skilled personnel as substitutes for RNs.

Even though mandatory licensure laws do not seem to have had any impact in 1960 or 1970, it is still possible that they could be important in the future. There are signs that the nursing "shortage" of the past thirty years may be easing. This could considerably improve the relative political bargaining position of RNs and allow them to push for a more rigorous interpretation of mandatory laws. Mandatory laws could also be important in blocking any attempt to use new technology and less-skilled personnel to replace RNs completely, although this is not currently an issue and does not seem likely to become one in the near future.[42]

At a more general level, the experiences of RNs with mandatory licensure suggest two conclusions. First, changes in labor market con-

---

[41] Conversation with Frances Waddle, coordinator of ethical and legal aspects of nursing practice, American Nurses' Association, Kansas City, Mo., February 6, 1979.

[42] At a general level, this type of issue has frequently been raised in discussions of institutional licensure in the health industry. (See U.S. Department of Health, Education and Welfare, *Report on Licensure*.)

ditions may play an important role in encouraging other occupations to press for mandatory licensure laws. Second, even if mandatory licensure laws are introduced as a result of the occupation's efforts, they may not have any direct economic impact.

An Empirical Examination of the Influence of Licensure and Licensure Reform on the Geographical Distribution of Dentists

Bryan L. Boulier

State licensing of occupations has long been criticized but has thus far resisted substantial reform. One reason for the successful resistance is that regulated professions dominate the regulatory process and exert considerable influence on reform measures. A second reason is that, with few exceptions, those who urge reform have been unable to demonstrate empirically the benefits of the changes proposed. The purpose of this paper is to measure the consequences of a specific reform proposal—a change in the system of dental licensure that would permit dentists once licensed in at least one state to migrate without restriction to other states. This proposal is called "nationwide reciprocity."

Three considerations prompt the evaluation of this proposal. First, there is concern that dental licensing boards have influenced the geographical distributions of dentists through their powers to limit the number of dentists who are permitted to practice in their jurisdictions and that "the shortage of dentists is accentuated by uneven distribution."[1] Second, nationwide reciprocity has considerable support among dentists, being favored by 68.0 percent of dentists responding to a 1972 survey conducted by the American Dental Association.[2] That dentists recognize their economic interest in the licensing process is demonstrated by the pattern of responses to the questionnaire: dentists residing

NOTE: I am grateful to Orley Ashenfelter, Eleanor Brown, Ray Fair, Jane Menken, Sam Peltzman, Michael Rothschild, and Dan Saks for their advice on earlier drafts of this paper and especially to Jack Wilson for many helpful comments. Programming assistance by Hannah Kaufman and research assistance by David Bloom and Debra Stempel are also gratefully acknowledged. Financial support for this research was received from the National Institutes of Health and a Ford Foundation grant to the Office of Population Research.

[1] National Advisory Commission on Health Manpower, *Report of the National Advisory Commission on Health Manpower* (Washington, D.C., 1969), p. 497.

[2] American Dental Association, Bureau of Economic Research and Statistics, "Survey of Attitudes on Dental Licensing Procedures," *Journal of the American Dental Association*, vol. 85 (December 1972), pp. 1269–1306.

in states with fees above the national average were less favorable toward nationwide reciprocity than dentists residing in states with below average fees, presumably because reciprocity would result in increased migration of dentists into states with fees above the average.[3] Third, the American Dental Association House of Delegates adopted a resolution in 1975 stating that the American Dental Association, "through its constituent societies, strongly encourages state boards of dentistry to establish criteria by which dentists could be licensed by credentials to permit the freedom of interstate movement while retaining those controls necessary to fulfill the public responsibilities of the respective state boards"[4] and adopted a resolution in 1978 calling for a study to determine the feasibility of estimating the potential impact of nationwide reciprocity on the redistribution of dentists.

In what follows, I describe briefly the dental licensing system, review past studies of licensure, and assemble evidence that suggests that the licensing process has affected the geographical distribution of dentists. I then present an estimate of the effect of nationwide reciprocity on the distribution of dentists, the price and aggregate quantity of dental services produced and consumed, consumer welfare, and dentists' incomes in 1967.

The Licensing System

All states have dental practice acts that establish licensing boards. In general, licensing boards are composed of practicing dentists, with members appointed by the governor of the state upon recommendation or nomination by the state dental society. The boards establish and administer regulations pertaining to the practice of dentistry within their states, including the examination of candidates for licensure. Regulations established by the boards are limited by state dental practice acts,

---

[3] Correlation of the percentage of dentists in favor of nationwide reciprocity in a state in 1972 with the average fee for a two-sided amalgam filling in that state in 1970 yields a correlation coefficient of -0.33, which is significantly less than zero at the 0.01 level (one-tail test). Opinion data are from the American Dental Association, Bureau of Economic Research and Statistics, "Survey of Attitudes on Dental Licensing Procedures"; fee data are from the American Dental Association, Bureau of Economic Research and Statistics, "National Dental Fee Survey, 1970," *Journal of the American Dental Association*, vol. 83 (July 1971), pp. 57–69.

[4] American Dental Association, "New Licensure Policy," *Journal of the American Dental Association*, vol. 91 (December 1975), p. 1105. For background on the 1975 resolution and reviews of ADA licensure policy, see American Dental Association, Commission on Licensure, "1975 Annual Report," *Journal of the American Dental Association*, vol. 91 (September 1975), pp. 567–92; and American Dental Association, "Review of Licensure Policy," *Journal of the American Dental Association*, vol. 95 (July 1977), pp. 133–66.

but legislatures normally depend on the boards for advice in drawing and amending these acts.

The requirements for licensure vary from state to state. All states require graduation from a dental school approved by the state board. For admission to the practice of dentistry in a state, a graduate of an approved school must take a licensing examination unless he is licensed elsewhere and there is a reciprocity agreement between the states. Licensure examinations consist of two parts: a written examination and a practical or clinical examination.

In 1928 the National Board of Dental Examiners was formed to write standardized examinations on the theory and science of dentistry. By 1967 forty-four states recognized the certificate of the national board; by 1976 that number had increased to forty-eight. The content of the practical or clinical examination varies by state but typically includes a set of prescribed operative procedures (gold inlay, gold foil, or amalgam restoration), prosthetics (for example, complete upper denture to final try-in, including preparation of a laboratory prescription), crown and bridge work, oral diagnosis and treatment planning, and surgery. In some cases, portions of the clinical examination are written. In 1976 five states had oral or written examinations on dental ethics or on state laws pertaining to dentistry, twenty-one states required candidates for licensure to bring their own patients to the examination, and the fee for examination ranged from $25 to $150.[5]

Beginning in 1969, the dental boards of Maine, Maryland, Massachusetts, New Hampshire, New York, Pennsylvania, and West Virginia agreed to conduct a standardized clinical examination in five cities with members of each board forming the examination committees. There was tacit agreement that presentation of the regional test certificate for the clinical examination and the National Board of Dental Examiners certificate by a candidate would qualify him for licensure in one of the participating states.[6] By 1976 fourteen states accepted certificates on clinical examinations from the North East Regional Board, eleven states from the Central Regional Dental Testing Service, and three from the Southern Regional Testing Agency.[7] Wisconsin accepted

---

[5] American Dental Association, Bureau of Economic Research and Statistics, *Facts about States for the Dentist Seeking a Location, 1976* (Chicago: American Dental Association, 1976), pp. 10–18.

[6] New York and Washington, D.C., conducted simultaneous examinations as early as 1966. The concept of regional boards was endorsed by the ADA House of Delegates in 1968.

[7] American Dental Association, Bureau of Economic Research and Statistics, *Facts about States, 1976*, p. 13.

examination results from the North East Regional Board and the Central Regional Dental Testing Service.

There has been considerable criticism of state board practical examinations.[8] The most common complaints are that the examinations include material irrelevant to good dental practice and that, because the examinations are subjectively graded, they can be used as a tool to discriminate against out-of-state applicants. The instructions to dentists applying for an Indiana license illustrate the point that "quality" as perceived by a state board may have little to do with conventional notions of fitness to practice dentistry:

1. An applicant may be called upon to perform, write or discuss any aspect of dentistry at the discretion of the examiners, and
2. Any applicants will be disqualified if their general appearance, attitude and housekeeping do not satisfy the professional standards of the Board. Neatness, correct spelling, legibility of writing, and good English will be considered in grading the manuscripts.[9]

Failure rates of out-of-state graduates are often higher than those of in-state graduates, although this can be a misleading indicator of board bias, because out-of-state applicants may not have the same qualifications as in-state applicants. Students who fail their in-state examinations or believe they will fail are more likely to apply in more than one state to increase their probability of being licensed to practice dentistry somewhere, and in-state schools may teach special skills required on the examination. Of course, to the extent that these special skills are unrelated or only marginally related to good dental practice, their presence on the licensing examination constitutes a subtle form of restriction against entry from out-of-state. On the 1970 licensing examinations, the failure rates of 1970 graduates for all states combined were 4 percent for applicants from in-state schools and 18 percent for applicants from out-of-state schools; the failure rates for applicants who graduated before 1970 from in-state and out-of-state schools were 8 percent and 26

---

[8] See the statement by the National Council for Improvement of Dental Licensure in U.S. Congress, Senate, Committee on Labor and Welfare, Subcommittee on Health, *Hearings before the Subcommittee on Labor and Public Welfare*, 92nd Congress, 1st session, 1971, pt. 7, pp. 1721–23; Mark Doktor, "The Irrelevance of Licensing Examinations," *Journal of the American College of Dentistry*, vol. 40 (April 1973), pp. 100–107; and Lawrence E. Shepard, "Licensing Restrictions and the Cost of Dental Care," *Journal of Law and Economics*, vol. 21 (April 1978), pp. 187–201.

[9] J. E. Regan, "State Dental Board Examination Changed," *Journal of the Indiana Dental Association*, vol. 49 (April 1970), pp. 140–43.

percent, respectively.[10] In California the failure rates of 1970 graduates on the 1970 examinations were 7 percent for applicants from in-state schools and 59 percent for applicants from out-of-state schools;[11] the corresponding failure rates for 1973 graduates on the 1973 licensing examination were 12 percent and 63 percent, respectively.[12]

In 1967 forty states and the District of Columbia had statutory provisions for recognition, by reciprocity or endorsement, of dental licenses issued in other states.[13] Typically, however, several qualifications had to be met before reciprocity was granted—several years of continuous practice, possibly a clinical or practical examination, and usually an agreement of reciprocity between the states. In spite of the large number of states with statutory provisions for reciprocity, there are even now only a few states with even limited agreements. In 1969 only seventeen states reported some form of reciprocity agreement.[14] As an example of the restrictiveness of some of these agreements, New Hampshire recognized licenses only from Alaska, and Alaska only from New Hampshire. In 1976 twenty-one states plus the District of Columbia reported such agreements.[15]

In addition to licensing dentists and dental hygienists, the state boards establish and administer regulations covering the operation of dental practices—for example, determining the duties that can be performed by auxiliaries, establishing requirements for license renewal, and setting restrictions against the corporate practice of dentistry and advertising. Boards are also disciplinary agents for violations of their own regulations and of state dental practice acts.

It is clear that state licensing boards have considerable ability to limit entry of dentists into their jurisdictions by deciding whether to establish reciprocity agreements, by conducting rigorous qualifying examinations and setting high passing standards, and by otherwise raising application costs. What remains to be seen is whether state licensing boards have had a measurable impact on the distribution of dentists among states.

---

[10] Calculated from data given in American Dental Association, Council on Dental Education, *Dental Licensure Examinations, 1970* (Chicago: American Dental Association, 1970).

[11] Ibid.

[12] American Dental Association, Council on Dental Education, *Dental Licensure Examinations, 1973* (Chicago: American Dental Association, 1973).

[13] National Advisory Commission on Health Manpower, *Report*, p. 502.

[14] American Dental Association, Bureau of Economic Research and Statistics, *Facts about States for the Dentist Seeking a Location, 1969* (Chicago: American Dental Association, 1969), p. 19.

[15] American Dental Association, Bureau of Economic Research and Statistics, *Facts about States, 1976*, p. 19.

Empirical Tests of the Effects of Licensure
on the Distribution of Dentists

Four important studies have attempted to measure the effects of the licensing of dentists on interstate markets for dental services: direct estimation of the influence of reciprocity on fees, dentists per capita, and net incomes of dentists by Lawrence Shepard; an analysis of licensure and the migration, location, and income of dentists and physicians by Lee Benham, Alex Maurizi, and Melvin Reder; a study of the migration of dentists by Alex Maurizi; and an article by Arlene Holen on the effects of professional licensing arrangements on interstate mobility of professionals (dentists, lawyers, and physicians).[16]

Shepard concluded that in 1970 the average price of services in states that had a reciprocity provision as part of their licensing regulations was nearly 15 percent lower than the average price of the same services in states without reciprocity.[17] As will be shown, however, the impact of reciprocity on prices implied by his econometric model of the dental care market is far smaller than he reports. The economic model consists of five equations:

(1) Dentists per capita – f(earnings, reciprocity, exogenous variables)
(2) Price $= f$(quantity of services demanded per capita, exogenous variables)
(3) Price $= f$(quantity of services supplied per capita, dentists per capita, reciprocity, exogenous variables)
(4) Earnings $= f$(dentists per capita, reciprocity, exogenous variables)
(5) Quantity demanded per capita $=$ quantity supplied per capita

where f means "function of." The model is estimated by two-stage least-squares regression using states in 1970 as observations. In the estimated equations, reciprocity is positively related to dentists per capita and negatively to price and net earnings.[18]

---

[16] Lawrence E. Shepard, "Licensing Restrictions and the Cost of Dental Care," *Journal of Law and Economics*, vol. 21 (April 1978), pp. 187–201; Lee Benham, Alex R. Maurizi, and Melvin W. Reder, "Migration, Location and Remuneration of Medical Personnel," *Review of Economics and Statistics*, vol. 50 (August 1968), pp. 332–47; Alex R. Maurizi, *Economic Essays on the Dental Profession* (Iowa City: College of Business Administration, University of Iowa, 1969); and Arlene S. Holen, "Effects of Professional Licensing Arrangements on Interstate Labor Mobility and Resource Allocation," *Journal of Political Economy*, vol. 73 (October 1965), pp. 492–98.

[17] Shepard, "Licensing Restrictions," p. 199.

[18] Ibid., table 4, p. 198.

To calculate the impact of reciprocity on price, Shepard adds the direct effect of reciprocity on price in the supply of services in equation (3) to the indirect effect resulting from the influence of reciprocity on the number of dentists per capita in equation (1) multiplied by the effect of a change in the number of dentists per capita on price in equation (3). This calculation is incomplete, however, because reciprocity also affects the earnings of dentists—equation (4)—thereby altering the supply of practitioners. To take into account all the direct and indirect impacts of reciprocity, one must solve all five equations simultaneously for price as a function of reciprocity and other exogenous variables. In this price equation, reciprocity reduces the fee index by only $0.16, less than 10 percent of the $1.87 figure reported by Shepard.[19]

While Shepard's model implies a negligible impact of reciprocity on dental prices, there is some reason to doubt the model's validity. In particular, the specification of the net earnings equation is theoretically inappropriate. By definition, net earnings equal gross receipts minus costs, and gross receipts per practitioner equal price times quantity supplied per practitioner. Price and quantity supplied are determined in the demand and supply of services equations, but their values in these equations are not reflected in the earnings equation. In addition, no economic rationale is offered for including the reciprocity variable in the earnings equation. Since Shepard's econometric model of the dental care market appears to have some serious shortcomings, calculations based on it have little value.

The empirical work by Maurizi and by Benham and his colleagues is primarily descriptive. They use states as the units of observation and regress the number of dentists, dentists per capita, changes in dentists per capita, net migration, and dentists' mean net income on variables that might possibly be related to them. Their findings are generally difficult to interpret, because they do not attempt to provide structural models of the migration process and they rely on the overall failure rate on the state board examination as a measure of barriers to entry. Benham points out that the failure rate is only one indicator of a variety of ways in which licensing impedes mobility and that the overall failure rate does not distinguish between in-state and out-of-state applicants. In addition, it should be noted that the observed failure rate is an *ex post* measure; that is, the observed failure rate is the actual number of failed candidates divided by the actual number of applicants. We would expect that some dentists will be discouraged from applying for a license if their *ex ante* (or anticipated) probability of failure is high. The ob-

---

[19] Ibid., p. 199.

served failure rate will be lower than the *ex ante* probability of failure—which is the more valid measure of restrictiveness.[20]

Two findings from these studies are of some interest. First, migration between states and changes in the number of dentists per capita indicate that there is some spatial economic adjustment. In-migration rates and changes in the number of dentists per capita show positive associations with levels of, and changes in, state per capita incomes and population.[21] Furthermore, "the number of dentists per capita [has] tended relatively to increase in states where their average income was initially high, and relatively to decline in those where the initial number of dentists per capita was high."[22] Second, failure rates show a positive relationship with the level of dentists' net incomes, suggesting that dentists in high-income states may pursue more restrictive policies toward new entrants than dentists in low-income states and that there is persistent excess demand for entrance into states where dentists' incomes are relatively high.[23] The analyses performed by Maurizi and by Benham and his colleagues provide some support for the hypothesis that licensing has impeded the adjustment process.

Corroborative evidence of a different sort is provided in Holen's study. Holen compares licensing restrictions for three professions—medicine, law, and dentistry—and concludes that licensingregulations for lawyers and dentists are more restrictive than those for physicians, primarily because reciprocity is much more common for physicians.[24] She then employs two tests to see whether licensing inhibits mobility.

The first test compares "the ratios of members who moved to different states (from 1949 to 1950) to members who moved to different counties, both interstate and intrastate."[25] She suggests that when interstate mobility is restricted, as in the case of dentists and lawyers, the fraction of migrants who cross state lines should be smaller. From 1949 to 1950, physicians "had the highest ratio, 68 percent, while dentists and lawyers were both under 40 percent."[26] Table 1 updates the Holen test to the period 1965–1970. The within-state migration rates (column

---

[20] For a similar critique of the use of applications of bank charters to measure the restrictiveness of banking legislation, see Sam Peltzman, "Entry in Commercial Banking," *Journal of Law and Economics*, vol. 8 (October 1965), pp. 11–50.

[21] Benham, Maurizi, and Reder, "Migration, Location and Remuneration," table 2, p. 335; and Maurizi, *Economic Essays*, pp. 43–45.

[22] Benham, Maurizi, and Reder, "Migration, Location and Remuneration," p. 341.

[23] Ibid., table 4; and Maurizi, *Economic Essays*, p. 46.

[24] Holen, "Effects of Professional Licensing Arrangements." Holen notes that lawyers are expected to be less mobile, not only because of licensing restrictions but also because laws about which the lawyer must be knowledgeable vary from state to state.

[25] Ibid., p. 494.

[26] Ibid.

TABLE 1

MIGRATION BY OCCUPATION, 1965–1970
(males, age 25–64)

	(1) Total	(2) Changed Counties	(3) Changed States	(4) Interstate Moves as a Proportion of All Moves (3)/(2)	(5) Instate Migration Rates ([2]−[3])/(1)	Interstate Migration Rates (3)/(1)
Dentists						
25–44	40,949	12,622	6,683	0.529	0.145	0.163
45–64	35,588	1,881	544	0.289	0.038	0.015
Total	76,537	14,503	7,227	0.498	0.095	0.094
Physicians (including osteopaths)						
25–44	129,098	51,210	34,900	0.682	0.126	0.270
45–64	102,151	8,605	3,969	0.461	0.045	0.039
Total	231,249	59,815	38,869	0.650	0.091	0.168
Lawyers						
25–44	134,009	43,906	20,054	0.457	0.178	0.150
45–64	85,662	6,167	2,283	0.371	0.045	0.027
Total	219,671	50,073	22,342	0.446	0.126	0.102

SOURCE: U.S. Bureau of the Census, U.S. Census of Population: 1970 Subject Reports. *Mobility Status of Employed Males 25 to 64 Years Old by Selected Detailed Occupation: 1970.* Final Report PC(2)–2B (Washington, D.C.: U.S. Government Printing Office, 1973), table 7, pp. 39–48.

5) for dentists and physicians are similar, but the interstate migration rates (column 6) for dentists are much lower than those for physicians. The pattern of migration for 1965 to 1970 is similar to the pattern from 1949 to 1950; of those who changed counties, the fraction of dentists who also changed states (column 4) is lower than the fraction of physicians.[27] The difference is particularly marked in the older age group.[28] Lawyers are intermediate between the other two professions.

Holen's second test compares

the internal dispersion of income with state-average professional incomes. Where interstate mobility is restricted we would expect to find higher dispersions of average state incomes than seem warranted by the internal dispersion. This is because adjustment to a change in demand for professional services within a state can be made most easily by either drawing professionals from other states or losing professionals to other states. Where this adjustment can take place only with difficulty, it is likely that at any given time differences in supply relative to demand will be pronounced among states. Such a misallocation of resources would be reflected in differences among average state professional incomes.[29]

As an empirical test of this hypothesis, she calculates for each profession the unweighted standard deviation of average state incomes and compares it to the standard deviation of income among all practitioners in the profession for a year near 1950.[30] The ratio of the standard deviation of average state incomes to the standard deviation of income within the profession is higher for dentists (0.26) and for lawyers and judges (0.18) than for physicians (0.13). While Holen did not have data on the number of respondents by state to test the statistical significance of the between-state dispersions, she concludes from her analysis that dentist and lawyer licensing laws were more restrictive than licensing laws pertaining to physicians.

Table 2 presents the results of an analysis of variance for dentists'

---

[27] Data from the U.S. Bureau of the Census 1/1000 public use tapes for the 1960 Census of Population yield similar results for migration from 1965 to 1970. Of 89 dentists, 20 percent changed counties, and only 3 percent changed states; of 219 physicians (including osteopaths), 22 percent changed counties, and 16 percent changed states; and of 224 lawyers and judges, 17 percent changed counties, and 7 percent changed states. See Jack Ladinsky, "The Geographic Mobility of Professional and Technical Manpower," *Journal of Human Resources*, vol. 2 (Fall 1967), pp. 475–94.

[28] In the younger age group, there is some migration associated with schooling and military service, since the migration measure refers to changes in location from 1965 to 1970 and persons in this age group could have moved at any age from twenty to forty-five.

[29] Holen, "Effects of Professional Licensing Arrangements," pp. 494, 496.

[30] Holen employs income data from the National Income Division survey of lawyers (1946 figures), dentists (1948 figures), and physicians (1949 figures).

TABLE 2

F-Tests of Within- and Between-State Variance in Dentists' Net Incomes for Various Years[a]

	1952	1955	1958	1961	1964	1967	1970
Mean net[b] income	$10,574	$12,278	$14,255	$15,803	$19,269	$24,379	$30,035
U.S. standard deviation[b]	6,547	6,914	7,661	8,964	10,612	12,662	16,658
F	7.348	13.958	5.773	7.752	5.717	5.559	5.530
Degrees of freedom							
Numerator[c]	27	32	49	46	47	48	48
Denominator	3827	5640	4528	6539	5601	6733	7124

[a] The F-statistic is the ratio of the variance between states to the variance within states. In all cases, the calculated F-statistics are significant at the 0.005 level.

[b] The U.S. mean net incomes, U.S. standard deviations, and the standard deviations between states are calculated from the standard deviations and mean incomes reported for states in various ADA surveys. It is not possible to use the means and standard deviations of incomes for the United States reported in the surveys because they include observations from states other than those for which state data are reported. The ADA discards returns from overrepresented states in calculating the means and standard deviations. Data reported separately for each state include all usable returns from the state. The U.S. mean net incomes and standard deviations calculated from the state data reported by the ADA are quite close to the means and standard deviations for the United States as calculated by the ADA.

[c] For 1952, data include all dentists. For other years, they include only nonsalaried dentists. The District of Columbia is included as a state for all years but 1952.

83

incomes using Holen's basic approach. In all years, the between-state variance in incomes is statistically significantly larger than the within-state variance (with significance measured at the 0.005 level—that is, we can be 99.5 percent sure that the difference is significant).

There are several improvements that could be added to the Holen test. First, the hypothesis should be formulated in terms of prices of services, not in terms of practitioner incomes. In other words, we should expect that, the ·more effective licensure, the more will the between-state variation in fees exceed the within-state variation. Net income is an inappropriate measure because the levels and dispersion of net income depend on the distributions of dentists' preferences for income and leisure and their abilities to transform inputs (such as hours worked by the dentist, hours worked by auxiliaries, and capital) into services, as well as variations in the prices of inputs and services. Second, fees should be adjusted for variation among states resulting from differences in the age composition of dentists, costs of living, and input prices. No adjustment for fee variations among states resulting from differentials in the quality of dentists is necessary, because variation in service quality is a possible consequence of effective licensure.

Using 1968 American Dental Association survey data, which provide information on fees for more than 5,000 dentists, I have attempted to incorporate these improvements to Holen's procedure. To see whether the differences in fees among states are significantly different from those that would be expected as a result of variations among states in factors cited in the previous paragraph and as a result of the inherent stochastic (or random) variation in fees within the profession, I have regressed fees on variables expected to influence fees with or without licensing and a set of state dummy variables. A dummy variable for a state is a variable that equals 1 if the dentist practices in that state and 0 if he does not. A test for whether fees differ among states after adjustment for variables expected to influence fees with or without licensure is whether the coefficients of the state dummy variables are significantly different from zero.[31]

Table 3 shows regressions of the comprehensive fee and net income of nonsalaried general practitioners on the age of the dentist (and the square of age), the wage rate of assistants (deflated by a state cost-of-living indicator), a set of variables for the size of community in which the dentist practices, and the state dummy variables. Both dependent

---

[31] This procedure for estimating whether fees differ among states after adjustment for variations in variables expected to influence fees with or without licensing is equivalent to analysis of covariance; see Jack Johnston, *Econometric Methods*, 2d ed. (New York: McGraw-Hill, 1972), pp. 192–207.

TABLE 3

EXPLANATION OF FEE AND NET INCOME VARIATIONS

Variable	Comprehensive Fee		Net Income	
	Coefficient	*t*	Coefficient	*t*
Constant (Washington, city size 100,000 to 1 million)	12.30		−25.65	
Age	0.09	0.46	18.97	20.48
Age^2	−0.03	1.33	−2.13	22.06
Wage	0.04	8.89	0.24	10.87
City size				
Under 2,500	−2.36	19.26	−2.92	5.25
2,500–25,000	−1.46	18.43	−0.96	2.68
25,000–100,000	−0.56	6.65	0.18	0.48
Over 1 million	0.30	1.99	−1.21	1.83
Alabama	−2.85	5.82	3.42	2.44
Arizona	−0.68	2.26	−0.41	0.32
Arkansas	−1.31	4.23	1.82	1.37
California	1.51	5.83	3.11	2.95
Colorado	−0.51	1.81	−0.31	0.26
Connecticut	−1.57	5.51	0.87	0.72
Delaware	−0.51	1.67	−1.84	0.53
Florida	0.20	0.70	4.22	3.45
Georgia	−0.96	3.24	9.66	7.66
Hawaii	−1.95	5.08	−1.61	1.01
Idaho	−0.96	2.67	−1.45	0.96
Illinois	−0.96	3.48	1.84	1.58
Indiana	−1.39	4.52	2.90	2.22
Iowa	−0.96	3.27	2.60	2.07
Kansas	−0.43	1.53	2.99	2.56
Kentucky	−1.72	5.62	2.60	1.95
Louisiana	−0.20	0.67	3.32	2.60
Maine	−3.14	9.10	0.13	0.09
Maryland	−0.56	1.89	3.19	2.58
Massachusetts	−1.51	5.15	−1.27	0.95
Michigan	−0.78	2.80	2.54	2.20
Minnesota	−0.74	2.60	2.42	2.04
Mississippi	−1.24	3.67	0.64	0.45
Missouri	−1.16	3.83	2.83	2.21
Montana	−0.56	1.55	−1.87	1.28
Nebraska	−0.13	0.48	2.01	1.69
Nevada	0.50	1.21	2.34	1.29
New Hampshire	−1.08	2.86	1.06	0.64
New Jersey	0.33	1.12	0.23	0.18

TABLE 3 (continued)

Variable	Comprehensive Fee		Net Income	
	Coefficient	t	Coefficient	t
New Mexico	−0.14	0.36	4.24	2.67
New York	−0.86	3.31	1.61	1.50
North Carolina	−1.14	4.00	6.12	5.16
North Dakota	0.07	0.19	4.57	2.77
Ohio	−1.65	5.97	1.09	0.93
Oklahoma	−0.36	1.27	0.79	0.66
Oregon	−0.50	1.67	−1.22	0.99
Pennsylvania	−1.74	5.98	1.35	1.10
Rhode Island	−2.02	3.52	−3.28	2.06
South Carolina	−1.51	4.66	3.65	2.61
South Dakota	−0.25	0.69	2.83	1.77
Tennessee	−1.87	5.81	2.00	2.14
Texas	0.40	1.35	0.36	0.28
Utah	−2.02	6.91	−3.59	2.79
Vermont	−1.49	0.99	2.39	1.34
Virginia	−0.93	3.27	2.94	2.45
West Virginia	−1.23	3.73	3.18	2.20
Wisconsin	−0.70	2.28	1.39	1.08
Wyoming	0.02	0.05	1.50	0.90

$R^2 = 0.28$
$F = 37.24$
$n = 5115$
Mean value of comprehensive fee $= \$12.00$

$R^2 = 0.41$
$F = 21.63$
$n = 5,877$
Mean value of net income (in $1,000) $= 23.25$

variables are deflated by a state cost-of-living indicator.[32] The comprehensive fee is calculated as a weighted average (the weights in parentheses) of the usual fees for a dental prophylaxis (0.16), amalgam filling for a two-surface cavity (0.48), single extraction (uncomplicated with

[32] The cost-of-living indicator used to deflate nominal variables is based on the annual cost of a moderate living standard for a four-person family in the spring of 1967 given in U.S. Department of Labor, Bureau of Labor Statistics, *Handbook of Labor Statistics, 1969* (Washington, D.C., 1969), p. 339. The index for a state is a weighted average of the cost of living of metropolitan areas included in the Bureau of Labor Statistics sample, the regional cost of living for nonmetropolitan areas, and an estimate of the cost of living for metropolitan areas not included in the Bureau of Labor Statistics sample (obtained by multiplying the regional cost of living for nonmetropolitan areas by the ratio of the national metropolitan index to the national nonmetropolitan index). The weights are the proportions of a state's population living in the respective areas in 1970.

local anesthesia—0.32), acrylic jacket crown (0.02), and complete upper acrylic base denture (0.02). The weights reflect approximately the average composition of dentists' output.

The dentist's age was included in the regressions for several reasons. First, skill may vary systematically with age. Younger dentists, because of more recent training, may be more skillful than older dentists, or older dentists may be more skillful because they have acquired skills with experience—or both, in which case there will be no systematic variation with age. Second, age is likely to be a good proxy for length of practice in a community (assuming lack of mobility). If dentists who have been established for a long time in a community have demand curves for their services that differ from those of recently established practitioners, we would want to take that into account in our analysis. In the net income equation, the age variable may also capture some of the age variations in preferences for income or leisure. Because age-income profiles often resemble an inverted U, the square of the dentist's age is also included in the regressions. In the fee regression, the coefficients of the age terms are not statistically significantly different from zero at conventional levels of significance. In the net income regression, both coefficients are statistically significantly different from zero at the 0.01 level (that is, we can be 99 percent sure that the coefficients do not equal zero). Net income peaks at age forty-five.

The wage rate of full-time dental assistants is included to adjust for differences in factor prices and variations in the ratio of local to state costs of living.[33] The higher the prices of inputs, *ceteris paribus*, the higher will be the equilibrium fee. The higher the cost of living, *ceteris paribus*, the higher will be the fee. As expected, the wage coefficient is positive and is statistically significantly greater than zero at the 0.05 level in both regressions (that is, we can be 95 percent sure that the wage coefficients exceed zero).

The regressions also include a set of dummy variables for the size of community in which the dentist practices. In the regression analysis, a community size variable is set equal to 1 if the dentist practices in a community of that size and 0 if he does not. These variables are included to take into account cost-of-living differences by city size and compensating differences for the amenities or disamenities of various sizes of communities. In the comprehensive fee regressions, the coefficients of the city size variables are all statistically significantly different from zero at the 0.05 level: they show that prices increase with city size. Coeffi-

---

[33] When no assistant was employed by the dentist, the assistant's wage used in the regression was the average for full-time assistants in the state in which the dentist practiced.

cients of the city size in the income equation show increases in net income up to city size of 100,000 and decreases thereafter.

The estimated coefficients on the state dummy variables are not particularly relevant to this analysis. They do provide fee differences between states adjusted for the values of other variables included in the regression, and these are preferable to unadjusted differences, such as those employed by Benham and his colleagues in their descriptive analysis. The difference between the highest and lowest adjusted fees is quite large; the adjusted fee in California exceeds the adjusted fee in Maine by $4.65, where this difference is obtained by subtracting the coefficient of the dummy variable for Maine from the coefficient of the dummy variable for California.

The test for whether fees (or net incomes) differ among states after adjustment for variations among dentists in the values of variables expected to influence fees (or incomes) with or without licensure is whether the set of coefficients on the state dummy variables is significantly different from zero. Statistical tests show that the sets of state dummy variables in both the comprehensive fee and the net income regressions are significantly different from zero at the 0.01 level.[34]

As a test of licensure's effect on mobility, the procedure used here is not without shortcomings. First, other factor prices besides the wage rate of aides may vary among states or regions.[35] Failure to adjust for variations in these prices could explain the significance of the state dummy variables. Second, the test only confirms that there are differences in fees between states not accounted for by the variables held constant.[36] It does not tell whether differences have arisen from reduced

---

[34] The F-statistic for the test of the hypothesis that the set of coefficients of the state dummy variables in the comprehensive fee regression equals zero is 17.36 with 48 degrees of freedom in the numerator and 5,538 degrees of freedom in the denominator; the corresponding F-statistic for the net income regression is 5.71 with 48 degrees of freedom in the numerator and 6,388 degrees of freedom in the denominator. Both F-statistics are statistically significant at the 0.01 level, so that we can be 99 percent sure that fees differ among states even after adjustment for variations among dentists in the other variables included in the regressions. Results similar to that for the comprehensive fee are obtained when the extraction fee and the fee for a two-surface amalgam are used as the dependent variables in the regression analysis.

[35] E. Bruce Fredrikson shows, for example, that there are distinct regional differences in residential mortgage yields and explores imperfections in capital markets that give rise to geographic differences in the cost of capital; see E. Bruce Fredrikson, "The Geographical Structure of Residential Mortgage Yields," in Jack M. Guttentag, ed., *Essays on Interest Rates* (New York: National Bureau of Economic Research, 1971), vol. 2, pp. 187–280.

[36] In their discussion of the paper, George Hay and Donald House suggest alternative explanations for the observed geographical variation in prices. Dr. Hay argues that price and income differences among states may merely reflect compensation for the amenities

mobility due to licensure or from other factors contributing to low mobility. A similar analysis of data on physicians or of data on a profession without licensing would provide a standard against which these results could be compared. Unfortunately, no such data are available to the author at this time. When the results of the regression analysis are combined with the migration data of table 1 and the findings of Benham and his colleagues and Maurizi, however, there is a strong suggestion that licensing has inhibited the mobility of dentists and affected their geographical distribution.

The Effects of Licensure Reform

A consequence of restricted mobility is that dental fees are higher and output lower in some states than would otherwise be the case. On the other hand, fees are lower and output larger in states from which dentists would migrate if there were no restrictions, so that the net impact of unrestricted mobility on the price and quantity of services supplied and consumed is an open—and thus empirical—question. This section of the chapter attempts a rough estimate of the effects of nationwide reciprocity or unrestricted mobility on prices and quantities. The procedure for making this estimate involves estimating demand and supply curves for dental services and then reallocating dentists among states until prices are equal in all locations, where the equilibrium price in a state is determined by equating quantities of services supplied and demanded (given the number of dentists and the values of variables influencing demand).

Table 4 presents estimates of constant elasticity demand and supply

---

or disamenities associated with living in those states. To the extent, however, that dentists and their assistants share similar preferences and to the extent that cost-of-living differences incorporate the higher rents of preferred locations, the regression analysis of table 3 (which adjusts fees for assistants' wages and costs of living) should partially control for location-specific amenities. More persuasive evidence that observed price differences reflect more than simple compensation for amenities or disamenities is that the number of out-of-state applicants to a state in 1970 is positively correlated with the adjusted fee differences among states calculated from the comprehensive fee equation given in table 3 ($r = 0.50$).

Dr. House notes that the full price of a dental service is the sum of its money price and the value of time of the patient spent consuming the service. In locations in which the opportunity costs of patients' time are higher, we would expect dentists to devote resources to reducing waiting and treatment time and to charge higher fees. Thus it would be possible to have equal full prices in all locations but still to have variation in money prices. While it is theoretically possible for differences in the opportunity costs of time of consumers among states to explain the fee differences shown in table 3, it is not a complete explanation, since the hypothesis would imply further that net incomes of dentists would be equal in all locations, holding constant cost of living, factor prices, and age of dentist. The net income regression in table 3 does not support this hypothesis.

TABLE 4

TWO-STAGE LEAST-SQUARES ESTIMATION OF THE DEMAND AND
SUPPLY FOR DENTAL SERVICES, 1967,

(all variables in natural logarithms and standard errors in parentheses)

Quantity demanded
$$= 3.5786 - 1.8687 \; FEE + 2.2262 \; YCAP - 0.2389 \; FLUOR + 1.0000 \; POP$$
$$\quad\quad\quad (0.3573) \quad\quad (0.3021) \quad\quad\quad (0.0697)$$

Quantity Supplied
$$= 8.91227 - 0.2809 \; FEE + 0.9959 \; DENTISTS$$
$$\quad\quad\quad (0.0733) \quad\quad (0.0119)$$

NOTE: Quantity demanded and Quantity supplied are the number of patient visits; *FEE* is average price per patient visit measured in dollars; *YCAP* is per capita income in $1,000; *POP* is population; *DENTISTS* is the number of active nonfederal dentists; and *FLUOR* is the percentage of a state's population served by fluoridated water. Average price per patient visit and income per capita are deflated by state cost-of-living indicators. Observations are weighted by the population of the state. The coefficient of *POP* is constrained to equal 1.0. Alaska, Delaware, and the District of Columbia are excluded from the regressions.

functions for dental services.[37] Quantity supplied is a function of the price of dental services and the number of active dentists; quantity demanded per capita is a function of the price of dental services, per capita income, and the fraction of the state's population served with fluoridated water. (In table 4 both sides of the demand equation are multiplied by population to obtain aggregate quantity demanded.) Price and income per capita are deflated by state cost-of-living indicators. The equations are estimated by two-stage least-squares with states as the units of observation, each observation being weighted by the population of the state.[38] Output in each state is measured as the average number of patient visits to active nonsalaried solo practitioners times the number of active dentists. Since gross income is the sum of price-weighted patient visits (neglecting uncollected charges), the average price per patient visit is calculated by dividing mean gross income of nonsalaried dentists by the average number of patient visits. Visits are heterogeneous units. The price calculated here represents the average price paid by consumers and the average price received by dentist per heterogeneous unit. An advantage of this procedure is that price times quantity yields total expenditure by consumers and gross receipts of dentists, thereby permitting estimation of the effects of the redistribu-

---

[37] A discussion of the estimation of supply and demand functions for the services of independent practitioners can be found in Jack W. Wilson and Bryan L. Boulier, "A Model for Reconciliation of Estimates of the Market Demand and Supply of Services of Dentists and Physicians" (unpublished manuscript, 1978).

[38] Alaska, Delaware, and the District of Columbia are excluded because of lack of data.

tion of dentists on consumer expenditures and on dentists' gross revenue and mean gross income. Other alternatives are (1) using the average price of a standard service (for example, two-sided amalgam filling or the comprehensive fee) with the number of visits as calculated above or (2) using the average price of a standard service and deflating gross income by price to obtain a measure of output. Estimates of the equations with these alternatives are less plausible than those reported in table 4. For example, when the comprehensive fee is used as the price variable and patient visits as the quantity variable, the estimated demand curve is price inelastic, and the coefficient of the fluoridation variable is positive, though not statistically significantly different from zero. The price elasticity of demand and the fluoridation coefficient are inconsistent with previous estimates of these parameters discussed below. The estimated price elasticity of supply is even more negative than the one reported in table 4.

The estimated coefficients of the demand and supply equations in table 4 indicate that demand is price elastic, that the income elasticity of demand is greater than one, that fluoridation reduces the demand for dental services, that the supply curve is backward bending, and that a 1 percent increase in the stock of dentists, holding price constant, increases quantity supplied by approximately 1 percent. These findings are generally consistent with other studies using different data. Feldstein reviews previous research on the influence of income and fluoridation on demand.[39] All studies reviewed by Feldstein conclude that the income elasticity of demand exceeds one and that fluoridation reduces demand. Previous estimates of the price elasticity of demand are ordinarily somewhat smaller (in absolute value) than that reported in table 4; estimates of the price elasticity of supply are usually close to zero and are sometimes negative.[40] In a model similar to the one presented in table 4 but using regional mean values from seven ADA surveys conducted between 1955 and 1967, Feldstein estimates a price elasticity of demand of −1.43

---

[39] Paul J. Feldstein, *Financing Dental Care: An Economic Analysis* (Lexington, Mass.: Lexington Books, 1973).

[40] Although this result is consistent with other studies, it is perhaps surprising that the supply curve is negatively sloped. An explanation is that dentists maximize utility rather than profit and that an increase in the price of output has both substitution and income effects; see Uwe Reinhardt, "A Production Function for Physician Services," *Review of Economics and Statistics*, vol. 54 (February 1972), pp. 55–66; and Bryan L. Boulier, "Supply Decisions of Self-Employed Professionals: The Case of Dentists," *Southern Economic Journal*, vol. 45 (January 1979), pp. 892–902. On the one hand, a higher price raises remuneration per hour worked and induces a dentist to substitute work for leisure and to employ additional inputs resulting in increased output. On the other hand, a higher price raises the dentist's income for any given level of output and leads to an increase in the consumption of leisure if leisure is a normal good. The net effect is indeterminate a priori. Because of licensing restrictions that limit interstate migration of dentists, the estimated supply equation represents the net impact of an increase in price on the supply of output of a fixed stock of dentists.

and a positive price elasticity of supply of 0.29.[41] In a replication of Feldstein's work but including two additional surveys, deflating dental prices and income per capita by the consumer price index, and including dummy variables for the survey years in the supply equations, Jack Wilson and I estimated a price elasticity of demand of −1.40 and a price elasticity of supply of −0.32, although the estimated price elasticity of supply was not statistically significant from zero.[42] Estimates of the price elasticity of supply using individual data also indicate a backward-bending supply curve. If it is assumed that the prices of output and inputs for an individual dentist are exogenous, a regression of output on fee and input prices yields an identified supply curve, which can be estimated by ordinary least-squares. Using data from the 1968 ADA survey, I have estimated a price elasticity of supply of −0.23 when the logarithm of output is regressed on the logarithm of the extraction fee and an elasticity of −0.32 (evaluated at the means) when output is regressed on the extraction fee and its square.[43] The consequences of assuming a zero price elasticity of supply or a lower price elasticity of demand are discussed below.

To simulate the effects of nationwide reciprocity, dentists are distributed among states until the real price of services is equalized in all locations, where the price in each state is determined by the estimated supply and demand equations, by state data on real per capita income and the extent of fluoridation, and by the number of dentists allocated to the state. Before the results of the simulation are summarized, a word of caution is in order: because migration costs are not incorporated in the simulation, the actual redistribution of dentists in the short run would be less than what is estimated.

The aggregate effects of the estimated redistribution are relatively small. The average price per visit increases by about 1 percent, from $13.14 (calculated by weighting the average real price in each state by

---

[41] Feldstein, *Financing Dental Care*, p. 144.

[42] Wilson and Boulier, "A Model for Reconciliation of Estimates."

[43] See Boulier, "Supply Decisions of Self-Employed Professionals." Alex Maurizi, using a combination of state data and individual data from the 1962 American Dental Association Survey of Dental Practices, estimates a supply equation with a price elasticity of supply of 0.20; see Alex Maurizi, *Public Policy and the Dental Care Market* (Washington, D.C.: American Enterprise Institute, 1975). (On p. 25 he reports a price elasticity of supply of 0.79, but this value does not correspond to the estimate of 0.20 implicit in the reported supply equation on p. 62.) His supply equation, which includes price, capital, the number of auxiliary workers, and hours worked by the dentist as independent variables, is incorrectly specified, since all of these variables except price are endogenous variables. That is, these variables are not truly independent, since their values are chosen by the dentist at the same time he chooses the level of output to produce. A consequence of including these endogenous variables in the supply equation is that the estimate of the price coefficient is biased.

the number of visits) to $13.29. The number of visits decreases by 223,000, less than 0.1 percent. The mean gross income of dentists and aggregate receipts of dentists increase by slightly less than 1 percent.[44]

That the effect of redistribution is to raise the average price of services and to reduce output is not altogether surprising. Consider the simple case in which all states are identical (that is, by our definition have the same population, per capita income, and extent of fluoridation). Clearly, the outcome of nationwide reciprocity would be an equal number of dentists (and dentists per capita) in each state. Less obvious is the result that the average price of services would be maximized with an equal distribution of dentists among states. While a mathematical proof is necessary for the case in which the price elasticity of supply does not equal zero, the argument is straightforward if it is assumed that output per dentist is fixed. With a fixed stock of dentists, total output is constant (that is, it does not depend on the geographical distribution of dentists), and maximizing total expenditure is equivalent to maximizing average price per visit. A necessary condition for maximizing total expenditure is that the marginal expenditure generated by an additional dentist be equal in all states. Since in this example demand curves are the same in each state, marginal expenditure is equal in all locations when the number of dentists is the same in each state.

While the aggregate effects of nationwide reciprocity are small, there is considerable redistribution of dentists. Table 5 shows the estimated percentage change in the number of dentists by state. Of the forty-eight states included (excluding Alaska and Delaware), eighteen gain dentists, and thirty lose dentists. The estimated impacts of nation wide reciprocity on states such as California and West Virginia are quite large.[45] In California, the number of dentists increases 34 percent, output increases 41 percent, average price per visit falls 16 percent, and mean gross income of dentists decreases 12 percent. In West Virginia, the number of dentists decreases 35 percent, output falls 39 percent, the average price per visit rises 25 percent, and mean gross income of dentists increases 21 percent.

---

[44] In 1967 mean gross income was $45,284, total expenditure was $4.10 billion, and the number of visits was 311,889,664; in the simulation, mean gross income was $46,129, total expenditure was $4.14 billion, and the number of visits was 311,666,944.

[45] The figures presented for California and West Virginia compare conditions after redistribution with the initial equilibrium values of price, quantity, and gross income estimated from the supply and demand equations, the values of per capita income and fluoridation for each state, and the initial number of dentists. If actual values of price and gross income were used in the comparison, the percentage decreases in price and gross income in California would be somewhat larger than reported in the text, and the percentage increases in these variables in West Virginia would be smaller than reported. It should be remembered that the actual values of these variables are based on rather small samples in some cases and are subject to measurement error.

TABLE 5

PERCENTAGE CHANGE IN THE NUMBER OF DENTISTS BY STATE
ASSUMING NATIONWIDE RECIPROCITY, 1967

Percentage Change	States
Increase	
0–4	Florida, Michigan
5–9	Illinois, Ohio, Wyoming
10–14	Indiana, Massachusetts, North Carolina, South Carolina, Texas
15–19	Georgia, Kansas, Maryland
20–24	
25+	California, Louisiana, Nevada, New Hampshire, New Jersey
Decrease	
0–4	Missouri
5–9	Connecticut, Oklahoma, Pennsylvania, Utah, Vermont, Virginia
10–14	Alabama, Arizona, Iowa, Kentucky, Mississippi, Montana, New Mexico, South Dakota
15–19	Idaho, Maine, Nebraska
20–24	Hawaii, New York, Tennessee
25+	Arkansas, Colorado, Minnesota, North Dakota, Oregon, Rhode Island, Washington, West Virginia, Wisconsin

NOTE: Alaska, Delaware, and the District of Columbia are excluded because of inadequate data.

Given that nationwide reciprocity would lead to considerable redistribution of dentists, an increase in average price per visit, and a decrease in quantity of services produced, an important question is whether welfare increases or decreases. To measure the consequences for consumers, the estimated supply and demand curves were used to calculate the change in consumers' surplus resulting from the redistribution of dentists. The procedure for calculating the change in consumers' surplus is illustrated in figure 1 (for California). Before redistribution, the average price per visit is $15.94, and 34 million visits are consumed; after redistribution, the average price per visit is $13.29, and 47 million visits are consumed. The welfare gain (or increase in consumers' surplus) for Californians consists of the monetary saving of approximately $90 million on the initial 34 million visits consumed (the difference in price times 34 million visits, or the area *ABCD* in the figure) plus approximately 16 million dollars (the area *CED* in the figure), which is the difference between what consumers would have been willing to pay for the additional 13 million visits and the amount they have to pay. Of course, consumers in states from which dentists

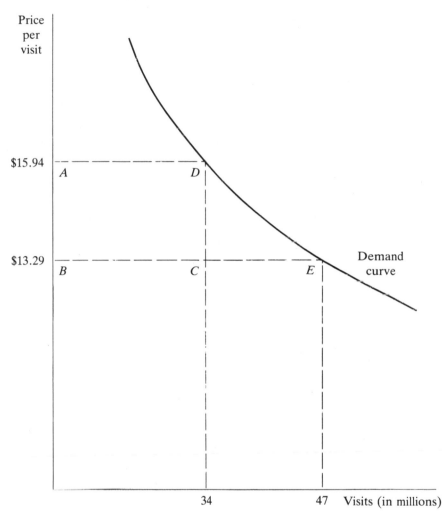

FIGURE 1
WELFARE GAINS TO CALIFORNIANS
FROM NATIONWIDE RECIPROCITY

migrate lose consumers' surplus. The net increase in consumers' surplus for all states combined is slightly less than $28 million in 1967 prices ($52 million in 1978 prices). Hence, consumers would be better off as a result of the reallocation of dentists.

While it is impossible to calculate the change in producers' surplus, because we have only the backward-bending portion of the supply curve,[46] it is reasonable to conclude that dentists are also potentially better off, because aggregate receipts of dentists increase as a result of the redistribution. As total quantity produced diminishes, the aggregate net income of practitioners must increase by an even larger amount than the increase in aggregate receipts.

These results depend, of course, on the estimated parameters of the supply and demand curves. Nearly identical results are obtained if it is assumed that the demand curve is the same as the one used in the preceding simulation but that the supply curve of services is perfectly price inelastic and a 1 percent increase in the number of dentists raises output supplied by 1 percent.[47] If it is assumed that the price elasticity of demand is smaller (in absolute value) than -1.87, both the extent of the redistribution of dentists with reciprocity and the net gain in consumers' surplus would be smaller than estimated above. With a less-elastic demand curve, the number of dentists who would need to leave or to enter a state to bring the state's fee to the national average would be smaller, since a given change in the stock of dentists would induce a larger change in fee.

The net increase in consumers' surplus would also be smaller, since a given decrease in price would increase consumers' surplus by a smaller amount in states that gain dentists and a given increase in price would decrease consumers' surplus by a larger amount in states that lose them.

Conclusion

This paper has demonstrated that the present dental licensing system limits the mobility of dentists and has affected their geographical distribution. A simulation analysis has shown that removing licensing constraints on mobility of dentists through nationwide reciprocity would have little effect on the average price of dental services or the aggregate quantity of services produced and consumed but would result in a significant geographical redistribution of dentists and dental services as

---

[46] For a discussion of the calculation of producers' surplus for backward-bending supply curves, see R. Albert Berry, "A Review of Problems in the Interpretation of Producers' Surplus," *Southern Economic Journal*, vol. 39 (July 1972), pp. 93–106.

[47] When the number of visits per practitioner is held constant at the national average and dentists are redistributed among states until prices are equal in all locations, price per visit increases by approximately 1 percent to $13.29; mean gross income and total expenditure increase by a similar percentage. To the nearest million dollars, the net increase in consumers' surplus is identical with that derived from the equations reported in table 4 ($28 million).

well as increases in consumer surplus and in mean net incomes of dentists. Gains to dentists from reduction in costs of applying for licensure in new locations and nonmonetary gains to dentists from changing locations have not been measured.

Commentary

George A. Hay

Both chapters in part 2 are laudable attempts to quantify the impact of licensing restrictions. On the basis of my experience with the regulatory reform movement, I am certain that such efforts are an essential part of any attempt to reform or eliminate licensing restrictions not in the public interest. Of course such papers are necessarily fairly technical, and my remarks are for the most part technical suggestions about how the papers might be improved and the results strengthened.

White's paper is in two parts. In the first he attempts to explain the rate of conversion by states from voluntary to mandatory licensing. While the ratio of nursing personnel to all hospital personnel at the start of the measurement period (1950) had some impact, the explanatory power of his regression equation is low overall.

In the second part, White uses estimated supply and demand functions for states to gauge the impact of mandatory licensing on wages and employment of RNs. Following Boulier's lead, he might have included in the supply function a measure of the extent to which restrictions on reciprocity or other artificial obstacles to interstate migration affect the supply of licensed nurses in a state.

The results of Professor White's research are tantalizing in that he finds no significant impact of mandatory licensing in 1960 or 1970. This suggests that hospitals in states without mandatory licensing laws[1] appear to use no fewer nurses despite their presumed greater flexibility in substituting practical nurses or other lesser-trained personnel. The obvious question is why this should be so. While anecdotal evidence can rarely prove a point, White might have made some effort to learn from hospital administrators in both sets of states whether, in their view, the mandatory licensing statutes make any difference and, if not, why not.

---

[1] The terminology here is misleading. RNs must be licensed in all states. Mandatory licensing (sometimes called nurse practice legislation) means that certain tasks can be performed only by licensed nurses.

My own limited efforts to address this question (by phone calls to nursing supervisors after reading the paper) produced the response that, even in voluntary states, "tradition" determines the role of nurses. While in a normal business context such an answer would be largely incredible, it occurred to me that a salient characteristic of most hospitals is their nonprofit status and thus insulation from competition. In such an environment it is certainly possible that tradition can be given a prominent role. In this case it would be highly informative to redo the equations, focusing only on proprietary hospitals, for whom substitution of lower-cost personnel may yield a real advantage. I do not know whether the data exist to perform such a study. White's own explanation of his "nonresult" is that accreditation standards may provide the operative constraint. If so, it would be interesting to learn the degree to which nurses have influenced the accrediting agencies.

The main task of Professor Boulier's paper is to estimate the impact of conversion to full nationwide reciprocity on dental service prices. As in White's paper, a supply and demand model for individual states is the vehicle used for reaching his results.

The demand function excludes two variables one would think important. The first is the extent to which the population is covered by dental insurance. Since the equations are estimated for 1968, it might be argued that there was too little dental insurance in existence to matter. While this is probably true, it suggests that the 1968 estimates are of little relevance in 1980, when dental insurance is a significant factor and the extent of coverage varies dramatically across states. The second variable is the degree to which state welfare programs cover dental bills (combined with the percentage of the state population that is covered by welfare). This ought to have been significant even in 1968.

The supply function treats the number of dentists in the state as an exogenous variable. Implicit in this is the view that, without restrictions on mobility, the number of dentists practicing in a state will be whatever is necessary to equalize real prices across states. Indeed, Boulier's measures of the cost of reciprocity restrictions come precisely from the exercise of reallocating dentists until prices equalize—that is, he solves the supply equation for the quantities necessary to equalize prices.

Boulier might have done well to construct a more realistic model to explain the number of dentists in a state. One's impression is that such factors as where one grew up or where one went to dental school (although the latter may be largely endogenous) are major determinants of location and would be major determinants even in the absence of restrictions on reciprocity. This would cast doubt on the assumption that, even in a fairly long run, one would expect sufficient migration to equalize prices.

There are other reasons to question the assumption that a full equilibrium would involve equal prices across states. First, if prices in a state are initially above a competitive level, there are two ways in which they can be forced down. The first is through in-migration, which, as Boulier indicates, is impeded by discriminatory treatment of non-residents on the state's exam and by failure to grant reciprocity. The second, which ought to operate independently of any reciprocity restrictions, is from expansion of the intrastate supply, in the short run through more new graduates remaining in the state and in the longer run through increased enrollment in the state's dental schools. Before I would accept the hypothesis that fees in a given state are above a competitive level I would want to determine (1) that there was less out-migration than would otherwise be expected and (2) that the supply of dental school slots was being held below the demand. While precise tests of these conditions may not be feasible, crude tests probably are.

Second, there is evidence suggesting that differentials may exist even in equilibrium. Specifically, as Boulier points out, many states now subscribe to a regional exam for purposes of licensing. Fourteen states, for example, accept certificates on clinical examinations from the North East Regional Board. This means that a dentist who is licensed, say, in Connecticut by virtue of having passed the North East Regional Board exam is free to migrate, say, to Pennsylvania. Hence persistent differences between oral fees in Connecticut and Pennsylvania cannot be attributed to competitive disequilibrium and must reflect locational preferences. Since such preferences apparently exist, it cannot be true that full equilibrium means equalized prices. I might add that, within regions covered by regional board exams, these preferences appear to be capable of estimation, and one could use the estimates in reaching a closer approximation of the full competitive equilibrium (although, because regional boards did not come into existence until after 1968, Boulier's 1968 data base would not yield such estimates). It would be interesting to see whether the existence and use of regional boards has narrowed the fee differentials across states that participate.

The impact of what I have said so far is to reduce the actual size of the welfare cost of nonreciprocity. In what follows I point to reasons why Boulier's analytical approach *underestimates* the total cost.

First, Boulier's method for estimating the welfare cost assumes that—as a result of the migration that would follow from nationwide reciprocity—prices would come down in states where they are high and go up in states where they are low. There is serious reason to doubt that the latter would occur except in the very short run. For it to happen would mean that prices are currently *below* a competitive level in those states. Since enrollment in dental schools in not compulsory, there is no reason why prices should be below a competitive level. Licensing restrictions may have held prices *above* a competitive level in some states, but there is no reason to believe that prices are at anything other than a long-run competitive level in the "open" states. Hence, while the instantaneous opportunity to migrate to California will draw dentists away from West Virginia, over the long run their place ought to be taken by increased entry into dentistry by persons attracted by the temporary "excess profits" to be made in West Virginia. Only an unmovable ceiling on dental school slots would prevent this result.

However, if prices would not rise in the "open" states and if in the "closed" states they would fall to the competitive level, then Boulier seriously underestimates the welfare gains from nationwide reciprocity. By my reasoning, some states would gain while (at least in the long run) none would lose.

Second, while there are geographic preferences explaining why many dentists would remain in their native states even if they could earn more elsewhere, there are doubtless geographic preferences explaining why some dentists would move even with no direct financial gain from doing so. (One thinks of older dentists who would opt for warmer climates and dentists who move with their spouses in an effort to maximize total family income or utility.) Hence, even where prices are equalized, some migration would occur in a free market, and restrictions on this mobility are a real social cost. Hence, in this respect, also, Boulier (as he states in the paper) has underestimated the benefits of nationwide reciprocity—although I have no suggestions about how one might get a quantitative handle on this issue.

Finally (and this is speculation), I wonder whether restrictions on mobility have had any significant impact on the diffusion of new technology. Dentists from various states doubtless discuss ideas at their frequent conventions in tropical climates, but one wonders if the competition from in-migrants who bring superior technology from their home states might not promote a more rapid adoption of such technology. If others place as much value on freedom from pain as I, any improvement in this area would dwarf any dollar savings in the price of an average visit.

Donald R. House

Professor White's paper offers an appealing approach describing the restrictive effects of mandatory licensing in the market for nursing services. Readers are encouraged to view the ANA as a group of professionals seeking protection from competing services. Through mandatory licensure, purchasers of nursing services are forced to alter their input mix in favor of ANA members. Changes in this input mix must result in higher prices of nursing care, but the final effect on wages and employment of ANA members, as a theoretical proposition, is left indeterminate. The empirical results do not settle the issue.

The reason for the indeterminate effect of mandatory licensing on wage rates among ANA members stems from the existence of the output effect at the firm level. Since licensing promotes higher prices of nursing care, the quantity of nursing care demanded must decrease, which reduces the industry's output. With higher prices of nursing care and the resulting decreased quantity demanded, the final effect on the demand for ANA members is not clear. If the demand for ANA nursing decreases, the market wage received by ANA members decreases in response to mandatory licensing. The likelihood of this result depends on the price elasticity of demand for nursing care. The more inelastic the demand, the less likely it becomes that mandatory licensing will promote decreases in wage rates among ANA members.

White's discussion of the decreasing wage effect of mandatory licensing raises serious questions about the behavior of organized nursing. It is difficult to explain the behavior of groups seeking to decrease their value in the marketplace. Assuming that ANA nurses are informed and seek increases in their wages, White's decreasing wage result is inconsistent with observed ANA behavior. If mandatory licensing does promote decreases in wage rates, the ANA should organize against such restrictions and in favor of less-expensive nurses' aides. The fact that they do not may be sufficient reason to dismiss the decreasing wage result.

The empirical results may be weakened by an inability to observe wage rates among nurses. White's use of only the median income as a dependent variable introduces into his equations the confounding effects of differences in nurses' labor supply decisions. Increases in the wage rate could promote decreases in the median income measure. Although few would expect this to be true, it illustrates the potential measurement error in using income instead of a wage rate in his equations.

The success of the 1950 estimations and the failure of the 1960 and 1970 estimations in identifying significant licensing effects may suggest a structural change during the period examined, or the difference may relate to additional measurement problems. With rapid inflation (and thus automatic tax increases) beginning in the 1960s, employees have demanded more payment in the form of fringe benefits. Since wage measurement excludes fringe benefits, additional measurement error is introduced into the equations. Even if income is sufficiently correlated with the wage rate (reducing the size of the error mentioned) income becomes less correlated with the value of the entire payment package as more and more fringe benefits are added. If the median income variable used in the equations is not strongly correlated with the value of the pay package, White's estimates have little chance of offering support to his theory.

Finally, the analysis should include the state's attempts to enforce mandatory licensing statutes. If a state's attorney general ignores violations, employers have little incentive to employ the more expensive licensed nurse. The existence of the restriction may, in some states, mean little. Enforcement of such regulations often requires the same political pressures needed to enact mandatory legislation. It seems likely that in those states where the ANA's influence is weak (those states that take more time to secure mandatory licensing legislation), the ANA may not promote vigorous enforcement. States with older legislation may enjoy strongly enforced mandatory licensure, whereas states with more recent legislation may not have the necessary enforcement behind the statutes. If this is true, White's poor results reported in the 1960 and 1970 equations are not surprising.

I find Professor Boulier's paper particularly interesting because I have examined the reciprocity issue in my own research. His critical review of the existing literature is quite useful and is recommended to anyone seriously examining state restrictions to entry in dental care markets. However, it is his empirical analysis that I wish to emphasize here.

In my own research, I found that identifying the reciprocity postures of states is exceedingly difficult because of the ambiguities of legislative language. Relying only on the state practice acts for information is occasionally misleading, because some states offer licensure by credentials. Boulier fails to designate any form of reciprocity posture among states, but this is not overly objectionable considering that designation would require extensive effort with questionable success.

Instead, Boulier treats all states as unique. His statistical test does not examine the effects of licensure alone but determines the existence of any state differences. No basis is provided by which differences can be attributed to licensure. While state licensing restrictions may contribute to possible differences, restrictions on expanded functions among auxiliaries, limitations of firm size, or policing efforts enforcing state practice acts could also contribute. Boulier's empirical design is expedient, but it fails to focus on the effects of licensure restrictions alone.

Part
Three

The Federal Trade Commission and Occupational Regulation

Kenneth W. Clarkson and Timothy J. Muris

As the evidence mounts that state regulation of occupations often harms consumers, the question arises whether this evidence is leading to decreased regulation. We discuss one possibility for reducing state control of the occupations, the occupational licensure program of the Federal Trade Commission (FTC). Having asserted that it can preempt state law, the FTC is in a position to reshape the legal environment affecting the occupations.

After briefly stating our understanding of the economic case against occupational regulation and describing the FTC's program, we turn to our major topic, assessing what that program is likely to accomplish. In particular, we ask whether the agency is likely to use its preemption power primarily to deregulate existing state requirements without creating new federal ones or, instead, to impose new federal regulations.[1] To answer this question, we must analyze at least three institutions: the commission itself, Congress, and the courts. In the process of analyzing the commission's use of the power to preempt state law, we will necessarily consider factors outside the narrow scope of the FTC's occupational licensure program. Accordingly, much of what follows is relevant to many other commission activities.

The Economic Consequences of Occupational Regulation

Almost all economists agree that at least some forms of occupational regulation harm consumers. Occupational regulation can reduce the welfare of consumers both through limiting the groups or individuals who engage in a particular business and through controlling the terms of competition (such as advertising and solicitation) for those allowed to compete. The effects of regulation may come in many forms, including

NOTE: We thank John Prather Brown, Jared Lobdell, and Alan C. Swan for helpful comments and Andrew D. Caverly and Randy S. Chartash for valuable research assistance.

[1] To simplify analysis, we define "deregulation" as elimination of existing legal requirements and "regulation" as imposition of new legal requirements. Of course, not all regulation harms consumers, nor does all deregulation benefit them.

higher prices and restricted choice of goods. Unlike private cartels, which often do not have reliable methods of controlling cheating, occupational regulation uses an effective monitor of cheating—the power of the state.

The past decade has seen a considerable amount of evidence supporting the proposition that much occupational regulation harms consumers. George Stigler, for example, found that the median earnings of licensed occupations, including architects, chiropractors, dentists, embalmers, lawyers, professional nurses, optometrists, pharmacists, physicians, and veterinarians, were 50 percent greater than median earnings of unlicensed occupations, including artists, clergymen, college teachers, draftsmen, reporters, editors, musicians, and natural scientists.[2] Further, partially licensed occupations, such as accountants, engineers, and elementary school teachers, had median earnings about 14 percent higher than the unlicensed occupations. The FTC's Bureau of Economics has found that television repair prices are higher in areas (Louisiana) with occupational licensure than in those with mere registration systems (California) or no regulation at all (the District of Columbia).[3] Lee Benham and others have found that laws restricting advertising raise prices to consumers.[4]

Scholars have also directly challenged the claimed justifications for regulation. In particular, it has often been argued that restriction of competition is necessary to guarantee high quality and reduce fraud. By itself, however, increased quality does not justify occupational regulation.

Even where regulation does increase quality, the relevant question is whether consumers are willing to pay the costs. Moreover, regulation does not necessarily improve quality. Over twenty years ago, Walter Gellhorn showed that the relationship between many occupational requirements and quality was tenuous at best.[5] More recently, case studies have indicated that some regulations may actually reduce quality. For example, the FTC study of television repair found that fraud through the replacement of parts that did not need to be changed was higher with licensure (Louisiana) than without licensure (California).

---

[2] George J. Stigler, "The Theory of Economic Regulation," *Bell Journal of Economics and Management Science*, vol. 24, no. 1 (Spring 1971), pp. 3–21.

[3] Jack Phelan, *Regulation of the Television Repair Industry in Louisiana and California: A Case Study* (Washington, D.C.: FTC Bureau of Economics, 1974).

[4] See, for example, Lee Benham, "The Effects of Advertising on the Price of Eyeglasses," *Journal of Law and Economics*, vol. 15 (October 1972), pp. 337–52.

[5] Walter Gellhorn, *Individual Freedom and Governmental Restraints* (Baton Rouge, La.: Louisiana State University Press, 1956).

In addition, a study of a legal firm that advertised heavily found lower prices and, at least by some measures, significantly better quality.[6]

In short, what economists assert is that a relatively unregulated marketplace, because of its advantages in allocating resources and promoting consumer welfare, should be the norm. Of course, the proponents of deregulation of some parts of occupational licensure are not asserting that all government intervention is unjustified. For example, the antitrust rules banning practices such as price fixing (tacit and explicit) and mergers leading to monopoly are beneficial forms of regulation, as are rules against fraud and duress. Further, the FTC television repair study found that random government purchases of repair services to check for parts fraud reduced such fraud. In general, what separates these beneficial forms of regulation from harmful regulation is the degree of government involvement in the provision of goods and services. When the government limits its role to the assignment and enforcement of property rights, regulation is likely to be beneficial. On the other hand, governmental attempts to control the production process usually increase the costs of resource use.

The FTC's Occupational Licensure Program

In early 1974 an intra-agency task force was formed to make recommendations concerning the prescription drug market. Headed by Wesley J. Liebeler, newly appointed director of the FTC's Office of Policy Planning and Evaluation, the task force produced a report a few months later, concluding that the major cause of high retail prices was state prohibition of advertising. The task force proposed a novel solution, formulated by Liebeler and his principal assistant, Mark F. Grady: The commission should preempt the offending state laws. This recommendation led to the FTC's first foray into occupational regulation, the proposal of a preemption rule in June 1975.[7]

In July 1974, after the commission's warm reception of the drug report, Liebeler proposed creation of a more general occupational licensure program. The memorandum in support of this proposal, written by Grady, presented the economic case against occupational regulation that controlled entry or means of competition, such as advertising.[8] In

---

[6] Timothy Muris and Fred McChesney, "Advertising and the Price and Quality of Legal Services: The Case for Legal Clinics," *American Bar Foundation Research Journal*, vol. 1979, no. 1 (Winter 1979), pp. 179–207.

[7] 40 *Federal Register* 24031, 24032 (1975).

[8] This memorandum was reprinted in the *Antitrust and Trade Regulation Reporter*, December 1974.

its deliberations concerning the budget for fiscal year 1976, conducted during the summer of 1974, the commission created an occupational licensure program.

The program lay dormant, however, until January 1975, when FTC Chairman Lewis Engman created a new task force. In a flurry of activity, several industries were selected for detailed investigation. Although many of the investigations have since been closed, industries in which investigations continue include dentistry, eyeglass materials and services, law, accounting, real estate, and veterinary services. Only the investigation involving eyeglasses has produced action overturning occupational regulations, with the mid-1978 promulgation of a rule primarily preempting state laws that forbid advertising of ophthalmic goods and services. (The prescription drug rule was abandoned after a U.S. Supreme Court decision that allowed drug advertising under the First Amendment to the U.S. Constitution.)

Though not formally part of the occupational licensure program, other commission activities involve occupational regulation, the most prominent of which concern health care and the funeral industry. The former has thus far produced proceedings involving the American Medical Association, the American Dental Association, Blue Cross–Blue Shield, and other major entities involved in the regulation of health care, and the latter has produced a rule that the commission will promulgate some time in 1979, limiting the use of certain forms of regulation, such as restrictions on advertising.

The economic foundation of the program—at least of those parts that have reached conclusion—is simple. The case against antiadvertising laws flows directly from the theoretical work of George Stigler and the findings of Lee Benham and others: prohibiting advertising raises prices.[9] In other words, at least this part of the occupational licensure program and the similar efforts in health care and the funeral industry are entirely market (as opposed to regulation) oriented. Remove the anticompetitive laws, the commission argues, and the market will lower prices. Thus this aspect of the program is *deregulatory*, showing considerable confidence in the ability of the market to maximize the welfare of consumers.

The legal foundation of the program, however, is not simple. Indeed, it is unclear whether the FTC will eventually prevail in preempting state law. Because court decisions have limited the ability of the gov-

---

[9] George J. Stigler, "The Economics of Information," in *The Organization of Industry* (Homewood, Ill.: Richard D. Irwin, 1968), pp. 171–90; and Benham, "The Effects of Advertising," n. 4.

ernment and private individuals to attack state law under the Sherman Act, an unresolved question remains. A major problem is whether the "state-action" doctrine of *Parker* v. *Brown* will apply to the commission.[10] *Parker* involved California laws designed to maintain the price of raisins by restricting the supply that could be sold. Although California's scheme was obviously inconsistent with the Sherman Act, the Court refused to apply that statute because of the state's involvement.

There the matter lay until the mid-1970s, when the Court reaffirmed that some state action was exempt from the Sherman Act. For the commission, *Bates* v. *State Bar of Arizona* is the most troubling of the recent cases.[11] In *Bates*, the state bar charged two lawyers with violating the state supreme court's disciplinary rules prohibiting media advertising. Although the lawyers prevailed under a First Amendment theory, the Court found that the *Parker* exemption precluded an antitrust attack. The Court did not engage in a detailed analysis of the state action exemption but did stress that the Sherman Act claim was in effect against the state itself, not against private parties. Further, the state had a substantial and long-standing interest in the regulation, the disciplinary rules reflected clear articulation of state policy, and the appropriate state body, the Arizona supreme court, continually reexamined the rules. Thus a clearly anticompetitive state law of the very kind at which the FTC's occupational licensure program is aimed is exempt from the Sherman Act. If the Sherman Act standard applies to the FTC Act, then the FTC's ability to attack occupational regulation will be reduced substantially.[12]

The FTC, relying heavily on congressional intent in the 1975 Improvements Act, which set standards for the agency's rule makings, has a strong argument that it can preempt. We will not address that issue

---

[10] *Parker* v. *Brown*, 317 U.S. 341 (1942).

[11] Bates v. State Bar of Arizona, 433 U.S. 350 (1977).

[12] As with the Department of Justice's Antitrust Division, the FTC could still attack regulation where the level of state action was not sufficient to invoke Parker. See Phillip Areeda and Donald Turner, *Antitrust Law* (Boston: Little, Brown, 1978), vol. 1, pp. 58–221.

One commentator has recently suggested that the Court's latest Parker decision, City of Lafayette v. Louisiana Power and Light, 98 S. Ct. 1123 (1978), which refused to exempt local governments under Parker, will "open up" occupational licensure to Sherman Act attack. Joe Sims, "Antitrust Comes to City Hall," *Regulation*, vol. 3 (July/August 1979), pp. 35–43. If true, the FTC could strike down occupational regulation, even if Sherman Act standards apply to the agency. Under Lafayette, however, it appears easier to sue a locality than a licensing board, since the latter will be better able to point to a state policy "to displace competition with regulation," the Lafayette test for state action. See 98 S. Ct. at 1138. In any event, the decision has added to the already considerable confusion over the contours of the Parker exemption.

here since it has been fully discussed elsewhere.[13] Despite the legal uncertainty, the FTC has committed considerable funds to the program, nearly $1.5 million in fiscal year 1979 alone. What will come of this effort is uncertain. The remainder of this paper attempts to reduce that uncertainty, not by addressing the legal issues concerning preemption but by assuming that the FTC can preempt and then by considering how the FTC itself, Congress, and the courts (in addressing nonpreemption issues) will act. By so doing, we hope to see whether the agency will use preemption primarily to deregulate state laws without adding new federal ones or instead to create a new level of federal regulation. Although we do not discuss the legality of the FTC's preemption power, we do, as we shall make clear below, question the wisdom of the FTC's having such a potent new power.[14]

The Future within the Agency

Despite large budget allocations,[15] the FTC has shown few results in the five years it has scrutinized occupational regulations, except for the attack on advertising restrictions and some progress in the health care program. A reason frequently given for caution is that the commission is uncertain about preemption. Although this may explain some of the delay, it seems unlikely that it is the sole, or even the dominant, source. Other innovative commission programs have proceeded vigorously under similar legal uncertainty, including the industrywide antitrust program and the program on advertising substantiation.

At least two additional reasons explain the delay in the occupational licensure program. First, there has been no one individual with control over sufficient staff resources and over the program generally. At least

---

[13] See note, "The State Action Exemption and Antitrust Enforcement under the Federal Trade Commission Act," *Harvard Law Review,* vol. 89, no. 4 (February 1976), pp. 715–51; Verkuil, "Preemption of State Law by the Federal Trade Commission," *Duke Law Journal,* vol. 1976, no. 2 (May 1976), pp. 225–47; Federal Trade Commission, *Report of the State Regulation Task Force,* March 14, 1978. All three conclude that the agency can preempt. As they note, though with varying degrees of detail, it is not even clear that state action, which is an *exemption,* will be directly relevant to the question of whether Congress intended *preemption.*

[14] If Congress intended that the FTC have preemptive power, the agency has the legal authority, regardless of the wisdom of Congress's action. If, however, congressional intent is unclear, a showing that the use of preemptive power could cause harm (that is, be unwise) might influence a court in concluding whether Congress must give a clearer indication before the FTC will be allowed to preempt.

[15] U.S. Congress, House, Appropriations Committee, Subcommittee on State, Justice, Commerce, and Judiciary Appropriations, *Hearings on the Budget of the U.S. Government,* appendix, Washington, D.C., 1970–1980 (hereafter House Appropriations Committee Hearings).

occasionally during the history of the program, the individual with ostensible authority over the program (or a part thereof) has had difficulty in making progress because he or she lacked effective control of the resources that the commission had assigned to the program.

Second, and perhaps more important, there is a fundamental inconsistency between the program as originally conceived and many of the other activities the FTC undertakes. Those who favor a curtailment in occupational regulation argue, as we have noted, that the relatively unregulated market will normally produce better results for consumers. In rejecting the necessity of advertising bans to protect consumers, the FTC itself has echoed this argument:

> the public policy of this country favors the existence of free markets to the maximum extent possible. While the complexity of the modern economy often necessitates a departure from free market organization, as a general proposition a market-perfecting solution to a perceived problem is preferable. There should be a heavy burden of proof on those who would opt for a different form of organization.[16]

Nevertheless, the FTC has had a long history of skepticism toward market forces, a skepticism that continues today. Rather than impose a "heavy burden of proof" in favor of the market, the agency has been willing to regulate on the slightest pretext. Before 1970 this was best seen in two areas: enforcement of the Robinson-Patman Act, which penalizes large firms for their efficiency, and advertising regulation, which assumed that many consumers were not capable of making choices in a market without substantial government assistance.

The agency's view of these consumers is particularly important, given that it is at the heart of the defense for much occupational regulation. As one commentator described the FTC's view of certain consumers:

> General stupidity is not the only attribute of the beneficiary of FTC policy. He also has a short attention span; he does not read all that is to be read, but snatches general impressions. He signs things he has not read, has marginal eyesight, and is frightened by dunning letters when he has not paid bills. Most of all, though, he is thoroughly avaricious.[17]

In the 1970s the preference for regulation has, if anything, increased, particularly in the Bureau of Consumer Protection, of which the occupational licensure program is a part. The commission has proposed

---

[16] 43 *Federal Register* 24001–24008 (1978).

[17] George Alexander, *Honesty and Competition* (Syracuse, N.Y.: Syracuse University Press, 1967), p. 8.

rules for many largely unregulated industries that alter substantially their existing methods of doing business. As several scholars have shown, many of these proposals are harmful to consumers as a class.[18] Further, the notion that consumers are often inept remains strong, particularly in proposals to rewrite consumer contracts. Finally, there is open disregard of the cost/benefit trade-offs that occur in the market. For example, in justifying part of a proposed rule that would rewrite credit contracts to eliminate or restrict certain remedies that creditors now use, the FTC staff argued that the proposal should be adopted "regardless of cost considerations."[19]

The FTC's preference for regulation and corresponding distrust of the market have at least two consequences for the occupational licensure program. First, these attitudes may in part explain the delays. To date, most of the program has dealt with advertising bans, now commonly accepted as anticompetitive. The commission approaches other forms of occupational regulation very tenderly—being particularly tender toward restrictions on who can compete. Part of the reason may be that proponents of these provisions often justify them with the same reasons the commission finds so persuasive in other areas. Second, the preference for regulation has a potentially more dangerous consequence. If the commission has the power to preempt state law, it may substitute its own regulatory regime for that of the states. Although the performance of the states is often bad, the performance of the commission could be worse. For example, in preempting numerous state laws, the available empirical and theoretical evidence indicates that the creditors' remedies rule will harm consumers, particularly poor ones.[20]

---

[18] See Dorsey Ellis, "FTC Rulemaking," in Kenneth Clarkson and Timothy Muris, eds., *The Federal Trade Commission since 1970: Economic Regulation and Bureaucratic Behavior* (Cambridge: Cambridge University Press, forthcoming); and FTC Office of Policy Planning and Evaluation, "1975 and 1976 Mid-Year Reviews" (reprinted in *Antitrust and Trade Regulation Reporter,* July 1975 and 1976, respectively). As a further example, see De Alessi, "An Economic Appraisal of Mobile Homes Regulation," in Clarkson and Muris, *Federal Trade Commission since 1970.*

See also the recent proposal of the Administrative Conference of the United States that the FTC use information from disciplines other than law in determining whether to propose rules, discussed in *Antitrust and Trade Regulation Reporter,* no. 903, p. A–15 (1979). This recommendation appears to carry with it a condemnation of the agency for ignoring such disciplines, particularly economics.

These sources, along with the other references to the paragraph in the text that accompanies this footnote, elaborate in great detail on the conclusions given in this paragraph.

[19] For a compilation of this and other similar statements, see Muris, "Evaluation of Proposed Creditors' Remedies Rule," on file as part of rule-making record (November 1974), pp. 15–16, 34, n. 16.

[20] Richard Peterson, "The Federal Trade Commission's Trade Regulation Rule on Creditors' Remedies: Theory and Evidence," in Clarkson and Muris, *Federal Trade Commission since 1970.*

New regulatory requirements are already appearing in the occupational licensure program. Consider the eyeglass rule. Although the major part would preempt state laws prohibiting advertising, another provision is designed to force separation of examination from dispensing by requiring doctors to furnish a copy of the prescription immediately after the examination.[21] The commission argues that without this provision its "efforts to insure maximum useful information in the market will have little effect."[22]

The proposal reflects the commission's willingness to regulate without adequate justification. The Bureau of Consumer Protection report, upon which the commission relies heavily, makes a two-pronged argument to support separating examination from dispensing. First, it argues that consumers would not otherwise be able to gain from any increase in advertising; second, it argues that without separation there would be little or no incentive for dispensers to engage in advertising. Both of these arguments are weak. In states where advertising is currently allowed, the evidence discussed in the commission report suggests that prices are lower. Yet in at least some of these states, the commission found that advertising and dispensing are often not separated. Indeed, the commission concluded that "in virtually every instance in which practicing optometrists were surveyed, it was found that in excess of 50 percent imposed some restriction on the availability of the patient's prescription."[23] If separating dispensing and examination is as indispensable as the commission asserts, it is not clear why Benham and others have found significantly lower prices despite the apparent tying of dispensing to examination.

The second prong appears to be directed particularly at opticians, who cannot survive as independent businessmen without consumer prescriptions because they do not examine eyes. Of course, unless opticians can provide lower-cost or higher-quality service than other dispensers of ophthalmic goods, their extinction would be of no moment to consumers. If opticians cannot so provide, there appears no reason why examiners, given their ability to advertise, could not effectively compete with each other in dispensing as well as in examination. If opticians are in some sense superior to dispensers, then even without separating examination and dispensing, they could easily avoid the problem of not being able to examine through vertical integration. Large chains, using

---

[21] See 43 *Federal Register* 23992, 24007–24008 (1978).

[22] Ibid., p. 24003.

[23] Ibid., p. 2398. See generally Federal Trade Commission, *Staff Report on Advertising of Ophthalmic Goods and Services and Proposed Trade Regulation Rule* (1977), pp. 252–78. The analysis in the text is not meant to be an exhaustive empirical evaluation. It does suggest, however, that the explanation of the commission is, at the least, too facile.

advertising to become increasingly prominent sellers of ophthalmic goods, could combine examination by optometrists with dispensing by the lower-cost (or higher-quality) opticians, producing the best possible package for many consumers.[24]

In addition, a priori economic analysis provides two possible explanations why some practitioners and consumers might want examination and dispensing from one source. First, because a consumer who receives a detectably inferior product will often not know whether to blame the examiner or the dispenser, he could refuse to patronize either in the future, thus giving the "innocent" party the incentive to combine both stages for better quality control. Second, integration of the two functions may reduce costs, including the expense of finding and using a dispenser.

Finally, even if the absence of competition without advertising meant that separation of examination from dispensing would be necessary for advertising to increase price competition, it would presumably be unnecessary once competition became effective. Accordingly, the FTC could have written a sunset provision into the rule, allowing the separation requirement to expire after a period of time. Failure to include such a provision is further indication of the FTC's distrust of market forces.

To summarize this section, the future of a deregulatory occupational licensure program within the commission is in doubt. Since there is no adequate theory to explain why the FTC acts as it does, we cannot predict the agency's future actions with full confidence. To the extent that the past actions of the FTC toward regulation are a trustworthy basis of prediction,[25] however, it appears likely that most future FTC preemption rules will require new regulations, not merely eliminate those of the states.

Having seen how the program might fare within the agency, we turn outside to see what impact first Congress and then the courts are likely to have on FTC deregulation and regulation rules.

The FTC and the Congress

In 1975 members of the 94th Congress introduced a resolution "that the Congress has not delegated to the Federal Trade Commission any

---

[24] If the problem is that ethical or other restrictions prevent opticians from integrating, these restrictions should be attacked directly, not through commission regulations to separate examination from dispensing.

[25] One recent change that may moderate the FTC's preference for regulation is the involvement of the agency's economists in rule making. Although the commission has stated that economic considerations are paramount in its rule-making decisions, the economists became involved on a systematic, continuous, and widespread basis only in 1978. It is too early to assess what impact, if any, this change will have.

authority to preempt the laws of the states in their political subdivisions."[26] Although this resolution did not pass, it reveals that at least some members of Congress wished to curtail the FTC's preemptive authority, an authority that is the heart of the commission's occupational licensure program. This section examines the forces that led to this resolution, which in turn will help answer questions about the future of the occupational licensure program. These questions include why the FTC was able to institute its program with little effective congressional opposition and whether producer groups will succeed in modifying the program.

Answering these questions entails an investigation of congressional ability to direct and monitor the activities of the commission. Congressional authority over the FTC can be divided into four major categories. First, Congress can shape the agency through the annual authorization and appropriation process. Second, Congress can engage in overall oversight or surveillance of the agency through questionnaires, investigations, and hearings. Third, Congress may focus at any time on specific questions, a process we refer to here as "ad hoc monitoring." Finally, Congress may change its legislative authority to govern the commission's programs.

Congressional Authorization and Appropriation. Many scholars contend that the most effective means of constraining agencies lies in control over authorization and appropriations.[27] Congress influences agencies both by adjusting the overall level of funds appropriated to the agency and by allocating expenditures among various agency programs. Congress may encourage particular policies through earmarking funds or discourage other policies through limitations on the use of funds. Specific FTC examples include the earmarking of separate funds for truth-in-lending enforcement in fiscal years 1969 and 1970 and for study of the oil industry following the energy crisis of 1973–1974.

If we focus on the overall congressional constraint on the total budget and allocations between the FTC's two major tasks—maintaining competition and providing consumer protection—we find that Congress has only rarely acted to limit the agency's proposed allocation of budget resources, despite often considerable opposition to many FTC policies. In each year since fiscal year 1970 (except for fiscal year 1979), FTC budget requests have been equal to or below the amount that Congress

---

[26] H.R. Con. Res. 483, 94th Congress, 1st session, 1975.

[27] Richard Fenno, *The Power of the Purse: Appropriations Politics in Congress* (Boston: Little, Brown, 1966). See also Aaron R. Wildavsky, *The Politics of the Budgetary Process*, 2d ed. (Boston: Little, Brown, 1974).

authorized. In many cases supplemental appropriations have been approved, making actual spending higher than the original appropriations.

An investigation of direct program expenditures on occupational licensure and related activities yields similar conclusions, despite the reservations many congressmen have had about the commission's actions in these programs. In recent years, planned occupational licensure program expenditures have been growing both absolutely and relatively (when compared with total consumer protection spending, of which occupational licensure is a part). Thus in fiscal year 1976 the request was $580,000, or 3.5 percent of the consumer protection mission. In fiscal year 1977 the occupational licensure program's planned expenditures had grown to $787,000, or 5.1 percent of the consumer protection mission. By fiscal year 1978 the planned expenditure was $1,197,000, or 6.1 percent of the consumer protection mission, and in fiscal year 1979 it was $1,480,000, or 7.2 percent of the consumer protection mission.[28]

These outcomes, of course, merely reflect a political environment "favorable" to the FTC. Even if congressmen strongly oppose FTC actions, the environment will still be favorable so long as enough members support it (or are at least lukewarm). An unfavorable political environment toward the FTC could lead to massive FTC budget cuts and legislation reducing or eliminating FTC powers (either in general or over particular industries). The environment would have to be so unfavorable, however, that legislation would pass both houses and be signed by the president. Thus the FTC does not need much influence or support in Congress before these controls over the agency become, as a practical matter, ineffective. There is no doubt that Congress is more hostile toward the FTC today than it has been at any time in the 1970s. Yet that hostility is not so strong that it effectively constrains most commission activities. For example, despite numerous congressional hearings and other inquiries, the commission's budget is still growing. Nevertheless, this hostility probably has made the commission more cautious in starting new programs.

In any event, even if it effectively controlled the FTC's overall budget, Congress is not likely to be able to use its control to direct the allocation of resources *within* the FTC. An understanding of the operation of the commission and of the budget process reveals congressional limitations in shaping the direction of the FTC's programs. The commission's budget is roughly divided among the maintenance of competition, consumer protection, and other activities (economic support, compliance, and administration make up most of this last category).

---

[28] House Appropriations Committee Hearings, 1970–1980.

Within the two major categories—the maintenance of competition and consumer protection—there are hundreds of activities. Thus, if Congress wanted to stop or expand a certain activity, it could not do so either by dictating the commission's total budget or by dictating its budget by mission; instead, it would have to address the specific activity. Further, an inability to obtain and digest the vast amount of information necessary to judge the merits of individual activities makes such analysis difficult, thereby further reducing congressional ability to control the commission. Even when knowledge about specific programs is available and understandable, it must be continually updated.[29] These two stumbling blocks—lack of knowledge about particular commission activities and the inability to constrain such activities through overall budget limitations—reduce congressional power to control the FTC through the budget.

The condominium industry presents the exceptional case where Congress actually changed FTC resource allocation. In 1975, when the commission decided to curtail its investigations of this industry, Congress forced continuation by appropriating resources specifically for law enforcement in this industry. What is notable about this effort, however, is that it virtually stands alone, and the resources involved were less than 0.2 percent of the FTC's total budget.[30]

Because Congress does not have complete information, it gives the agency effective power to reallocate resources (or "reprogram") to meet changing economic and social conditions. Reprogramming is clearly within the scope of commission alternatives. The actual appropriation language is extremely loose, permitting great flexibility. In fiscal year 1979, for example, the appropriation to the FTC was "for necessary expenses of the Federal Trade Commission . . . $64,750,000."[31] Fur-

---

[29] Suppose that the first congressional hurdle is overcome, allowing Congress to acquire adequate information about the general nature of the hundreds of individual FTC activities. Given such knowledge, Congress could specify actual resources in both dollars and personnel for each activity. Circumstances change, however, and unless Congress has continued access to information to modify commission activities, misallocation of public resources is likely to result. Most important, note that these powers would effectively turn Congress into an administrative agency, a transformation that is not possible.

[30] U.S. Congress, Senate, *Condominium Consumer Protection Act of 1975, Hearings on S. 2273 before the Senate Committee on Banking, Housing and Urban Affairs*, 94th Congress, 1st session, 1975, p. 244. See also U.S. Congress, House of Representatives, *Federal Trade Commission Condominium Decision and Operations, Hearing before the Subcommittee on Commerce, Consumer and Monetary Affairs of the House Committee on Government Operations*, 94th Congress, 1st sesssion (1975), and *Condominium Development and Sales Practices, Hearings before the Subcommittee on General Oversight and Renegotiation of the House Committee on Banking, Currency and Housing*, 94th Congress, 2d session, 1976.

[31] 92 Statute 1040 (1978).

thermore, the comptroller general of the United States has stated that he was "not aware of any statute or regulation which requires committee approval of reprogramming by the FTC."[32] Although some congressmen have been concerned about the ability of the agency to shift its funds from one activity to another and in fiscal year 1975 the appropriations committee even proposed (but did not pass the proposal) that "except as provided in existing law, funds provided in the act shall be available only for the purpose for which they were appropriated," the FTC's reprogramming power remains intact.[33]

Oversight. Oversight includes legislative proposals and reforms, as well as activities of the General Accounting Office (GAO), the Congressional Budget Office, and the committees of Congress. An examination of the record from 1970 through 1977 reveals that Congress did not use these activities to constrain the FTC. Although there were, for example, a number of GAO inquiries that resulted in reports,[34] there appears to have been little, if any, official action by Congress in response to the reports. For example, in 1974, Congress directed the GAO to work with the FTC to resolve some of the important problems associated with the commission's line-of-business program, which would require business firms to report financial data by each major sales category. The GAO reported a number of problems in a March 1975 communication to the Committee on Appropriations.[35] Information available from congressional hearings reveals that the House Committee apparently ignored the GAO findings. The only questions during the hearings concerning the line-of-business program focused on total expenditures and the confidentiality of the data. There is no reference to GAO's

---

[32] Letter from the comptroller general of the United States to John E. Moss, chairman, Subcommittee on Commerce and Finance (June 24, 1974).

[33] H.R. Rep. No. 93–1120, 93rd Congress, 2d session, 1974, p. 12.

[34] On the effect of the reprogramming power see U.S. Congress, House of Representatives, Subcommittee on Commerce and Finance of the House Committee on Interstate and Foreign Commerce, *Staff Report*, 1975, p. 21. A letter supplied by the GAO identified fifteen accounting office documents issued between 1970 and 1977 that dealt with the FTC. Nine of the fifteen were letters sent by the GAO to the FTC or congressmen, dealing with such topics as the Flammable Fabric Act, government procurement, the line-of-business program, information search and copy fees, and monitoring of the oil industry. The other six documents dealt with fees and charges of regulatory agencies, the advertisement substantiation program, the Webb-Pomerene Act, the energy industry, and the GAO's responsibilities under the Federal Reports Act. A survey of official documents and interviews with previous FTC commissioners and officials suggest that the effects of GAO inquiries were minimal.

[35] Letter from the comptroller general of the United States to the chairman of the Committee on Appropriations of the House of Representatives, March 5, 1975. See fiscal year 1976 House Appropriations Committee Hearings, pp. 386–94.

criticisms in the hearings, and the commission did not alter its line-of-business program.[36]

In fact, there is no evidence indicating any substantial change in FTC line-of-business activities as the result of outside pressures, including pressures from producers' groups seeking to abolish or reduce the scope of the program. The inability of other parties to influence the commission through Congress and of Congress itself to influence the commission is in part a function of differential interests and incentives within Congress. There was, in our present example, a House/Senate difference over support for the line-of-business program. When such differences occur—and on issues affecting the FTC they have been frequent—the commission is able to side with the position closest to its own. Of course, the commission must often expend considerable resources in lobbying. Although its opponents can thus force the commission and particularly its top staff to spend many hours dealing with Congress, they have great difficulty in limiting the activities that the commission can pursue.

Sometimes the commission is subjected to hearings before the oversight committee assigned to the FTC. Generally these hearings have focused only on progress reports of various FTC programs, often trying to answer the question why there has been delay in certain cases or rules. For example, in 1976 oversight hearings were held to examine the effectiveness of the FTC in eliminating unfair and deceptive advertising practices. The data presented and the testimony of FTC officials amounted to a description of what progress the FTC was making and what resources it was expending on the matter.[37]

Finally, the oversight committee faces the same information problems as the appropriations committee. Even if congressmen or staffers are able to acquire some information about a program, the commission can pool several experts on the subject who in sum (and often individually) know more about the topic than the congressmen or their staffs. For this and the other reasons discussed, one should not expect the oversight committee to be an effective constraint on the FTC.

Ad Hoc Monitoring. Another form of monitoring involves hearings or

---

[36] See U.S. Congress, House of Representatives, *Departments of State, Justice, Commerce, and the Judiciary, and Related Agencies Appropriations for 1976, Part 7, Hearings before the Subcommittee on Departments of State, Justice, Commerce, and the Judiciary, and Related Agencies of the House Appropriations Committee,* 94th Congress, 1st session, 1975.

[37] U.S. Congress, House of Representatives, *Federal Trade Commission Oversight, Hearings before the Subcommittee on Commerce, Consumer and Monetary Affairs of the House Committee on Governmental Operations,* 94th Congress, 2d session, 1976.

congressional inquiries focusing on particular issues. During the 1970s there were a number of these inquiries. For example, Chairman Calvin Collier's confirmation hearings focused extensively on his expected enforcement (or lack of enforcement) of the Robinson-Patman Act.[38] The questions were sponsored by a coalition of members of Congress who—pushed by small business groups—strongly favored continuation of Robinson-Patman cases. Despite extensive questioning on this issue and the existence of a special subcommittee (Ad Hoc Subcommittee on Antitrust, the Robinson-Patman Act, and Related Matters of the House Committee on Small Business) to pressure the FTC. enforcement of the Robinson-Patman Act remained minimal after Collier's appointment as chairman of the commission.

An examination of other FTC hearings during the 1970s reveals that they are often used by Congress for ducking issues rather than for monitoring the commission. For example, when the "shortage" of canning lids occurred in 1974, the FTC, apparently at congressional urging, spent a number of man-years investigating the shortage. The FTC investigation, which produced no cases, was finally stopped when a decline in public pressure permitted the commission to redirect its resources to other tasks.

The case of the canning lids does illustrate one frequent influence of Congress. Congress is often able to "persuade" the FTC to investigate. Just because Congress is able to get an investigation started, however, does not mean they can get law enforcement.

There is, however, no doubt that Congress has recently attempted to monitor the commission more closely than previously. FTC appearances before Congress from fiscal year 1970 through fiscal year 1978 increased dramatically. In the first five years of the 1970s, the number of hearings for appropriations, supplementals, and other factors was relatively constant and below thirty per year. Beginning in 1975 there was a substantial increase (more than one-third more) in the number of congressional hearings. These hearings greatly increased the time and effort spent by the commission in responding to congressional inquiries, but they only rarely resulted in the commission's bringing or not bringing a case or rule.

An examination of hearings involving the funeral rule, which involves aspects of occupational regulation, provides an example of the commission's spending more time with Congress but not substantially altering its activities. The industry representatives appearing before Congress were generally funeral directors who were officers in such

---

[38] U.S. Congress, Senate. *Nominations, Hearing before the Senate Commerce Committee,* 94th Congress, 2d session, 1976.

industry organizations as the National Funeral Directors Association.[39] Their main objection was that the rule was not necessary because there were very few complaints. Furthermore, industry spokesmen asserted that the rule would increase the cost of funerals and would reduce the number of funeral homes by 25 percent, driving smaller homes out of business. The spokesmen also raised various legal arguments, such as whether the FTC has the authority to preempt state law, and they alleged that certain practices in the commission's rule-making proceeding were unfair. Furthermore, according to the spokesmen, the FTC action created suspicion that damaged the reputations of reputable funeral homes.

The members of the congressional committee that questioned the FTC were hostile toward the agency. The congressmen focused on the point that the FTC had spent $450,000 and ten man-years from January 1, 1975, until the date of the hearings (September 1976) on a program that was initiated at a time when the commission had received fewer than a dozen complaints about the funeral industry. The committee members were also upset because the commission did little in the way of consulting state officials. They felt that the commission had wasted money, because there were so many Robinson-Patman complaints to which it had not responded.

Like an increasing number of industries under FTC scrutiny, the funeral industry has sought to use Congress to restrain the agency, and the FTC has been forced to expend resources to defend itself. One would be hard pressed, however, to find tangible evidence that such pressure has constrained the FTC in choosing what industries it will sue. Indeed, because Congress has tools that are ineffective in checking the agency and because the agency has successfully found congressional supporters of its activities, the funeral industry, the line-of-business inquiry and (thus far) children's advertising are merely the most prominent of several examples where considerable congressional opposition has not deterred FTC action.[40]

Finally, there may be informal ad hoc contacts between members of Congress and the commission. A politically powerful congressman may have personal and close relationships with one or more commissioners. Such relationships increase the probability that certain matters will come before Congress or the commission. It is doubtful, however,

---

[39] See, for example, U.S. Congress, House of Representatives, *Regulations of Various Federal Regulatory Agencies and Their Effect on Small Business, Hearings before the Subcommittee on Activities of Regulatory Agencies of the House Committee on Small Business*, 94th Congress, 2d session, 1976.

[40] The commission is currently considering a proposal to modify some parts of the funeral rule, although the proposed changes do not deal with the deregulatory aspects of the rule.

that such relationships could significantly modify commission activities and outcomes on their strength alone, because the institutional structure of Congress does not vest power in a single person.

Congressional Incentives and Control of the FTC. Despite the increased FTC time before Congress, there appears to be little congressional influence on the direction of resources within the commission, a result consistent with the incentive structures for both. Although a complete specification of the incentive structures facing individual members of Congress and the FTC is not possible here, our observations, coupled with the earlier findings in this section, suggest certain implications regarding the Congress-FTC relationship.

First, the incentives of individual congressmen to monitor the FTC are less than their incentive to monitor many other agencies. The FTC has a relatively small budget, and it does not hand out subsidies, resource rights, or other direct benefits sought by individual groups. Of course, the FTC regularly engages in policies that have harmful or beneficial effects on producing and consuming groups—some of which provide major political support to members of Congress—but, given that the FTC is not limited to performing a narrow range of actions, Congress will find it harder to regulate all these effects. This is in part because the commission may reprogram its resources or take from one program what it gives in another.

Second, the general inability of Congress to monitor individual FTC programs implies that it will neither seek complete information nor engage in extensive questioning during FTC hearings. Although it is impossible for us to formulate a specific test for rejecting or accepting the proposition that Congress will not seek complete information, an examination of appropriation hearings from fiscal year 1970 through fiscal year 1979 generally confirms our prediction. The official record suggests that congressmen do not make use of complete information on the proposed FTC budget. For example, an examination of hearings from fiscal year 1970 through fiscal year 1979 reveals that information on FTC programs in addition to the brief FTC budget summaries are often not provided to either the Senate or the House, presumably because they are not requested.[41]

Even more revealing are the number and types of questions that the commission is asked during the hearings. Our own reading of the

---

[41] Notable exceptions include a statistical analysis of FTC Robinson-Patman enforcement activities for 1954 through 1970. In the FY 1971 appropriation hearings, one letter charging lack of oversight was included with the budget. The FY 1972 Senate authorization hearings included an FTC response to the appropriations committee report on the FTC.

questions for each of the hearings for fiscal years 1970 through 1979 suggests a definite pattern. First, there are few questions. Second, the questions seek general information, such as how many dollars are allocated for enforcement of the textiles and fur acts or how many cases have been instituted under section 7 of the Clayton Act. Third, the commission is asked to explain certain processes such as rule making and case selection. Finally, questions may focus on status reports for particular programs. Such "monitoring" places few, if any, constraints on the agency.

Modifying Congressional Controls. In recent years, Congress has sought methods of more effective control over the independent and executive agencies, including the FTC. New legislation has frequently been discussed and could be a very powerful tool with which to constrain the commission. Through legislation, industries could be exempted from FTC rules, all new programs could be stopped, or general rule-making power could be removed from the agency. Legislation, however, must be passed by both houses and signed by the president. The more likely the legislation is to constrain the commission, the less likely it is to pass (all else being equal), given the commission's ability to manipulate the political environment. Unless the political environment is very unfavorable to the FTC, the threat of new legislation is largely ineffective.

The most prominent piece of legislative control of the FTC under discussion is the legislative veto, a device by which Congress (or in some cases one house of Congress) may stop proposed regulations or actions of independent or executive agencies. The legislative veto provision for the FTC, like other legislative veto proposals, has been opposed by the president and the commission on the ground that it is unconstitutional. Furthermore, there is a House/Senate split, with the Senate support much weaker than that of the House.[42]

Resort to the legislative veto does indicate that other methods of controlling the FTC have not been effective. The FTC is becoming increasingly unpopular with many congressmen, who apparently realize that their effective control over the agency is minimal. It is not clear, however, that a legislative veto would provide the type of control Congress seeks. First, it would not solve the problem of lack of information discussed earlier in this section. It seems doubtful that Congress, even with its large support staff, has the capacity or interest to master the intricacies of the dozens of rules that the FTC is likely to pass. Second, a legislative veto would place more direct responsibility on Congress since it would not allow Congress to solve ("duck"?) a problem by

---

[42] *Antitrust and Trade Regulation Reporter*, January 18, 1979, p. 879.

referring it to an agency. It is not clear that congressmen desire to have such responsibility. Finally, the congressional necessity for compromise might well dilute the effectiveness of the legislative veto as a constraint.

For these reasons, direct control of the commission's behavior in the form of legislative veto is not likely to be successful. Even when many congressmen actively oppose an FTC rule, the legislative veto would by no means be a sure-fire way of stopping the occupational licensure program. Advocates of deregulation and some consumer groups would surely oppose a legislative veto of deregulatory rules. In short, there may be enough controversy over occupational regulation rules for a legislative veto not to be automatic.

Only if Congress is prepared to modify *all* FTC programs in the same way will it constrain the FTC. Congress could, for example, impose a cost-benefit standard for all commission activities. If all programs are subject to the same rule, the commission will not be able to redirect resources among programs. For the sake of a single small program like occupational licensure, it is highly unlikely that Congress would take this type of general stand to achieve its goals.

Overall, we conclude that, given the current political environment, congressional ability to monitor individual FTC activities, such as those in the occupational licensure program, is limited. In the next section, we consider a constraint potentially tighter than the legislative veto and more likely to occur than a major shift in congressional political forces.

The Commission and the Courts

Assuming that the FTC can preempt state laws, how will the courts influence the agency's occupational licensure program? To answer this question, we must consider to what extent the courts limit the FTC's substantive powers.[43] Specifically, when the commission considers

---

[43] We treat as substantive the question of what evidence the FTC needs to prove before a court will sustain its findings. Though ignoring procedural cases here, we note that these can be important and do constitute a majority of FTC cases in the federal courts. (For example, of the forty-four cases in 1975, only five were substantive.) Besides limiting ourselves to substantive cases, we consider only the commission's enforcement under section 5 of the Federal Trade Commission Act, not the commission proceedings specifically under one of the antitrust statutes or under a theory solely relevant to one of those statutes. In addition, we do not separately consider court review of the scope of FTC orders under which the agency defines impermissible activities and with which the courts have been traditionally somewhat less deferential than when determining substantive legality. Some recent decisions have indicated an increasing judicial willingness to limit FTC orders. See Chrysler Corp., 561 F.2d 357, 564 (D.C. Cir. 1977); Warner-Lambert Co., 562 F.2d 749 (D.C. Cir. 1977); and Standard Oil Co., 577 F.2d 653 (9th Cir. 1978). (Unless otherwise indicated, the FTC is a party in all cases discussed in this section of the paper.)

whether a form of occupational regulation is illegal, will it be the agency or the courts that determine the standard for legality?[44] Moreover, what burdens will the commission be under to demonstrate the ill effects of occupational regulation? Finally, when the commission seeks to promulgate requirements of its own for various occupations, to what extent will the judiciary defer to the agency's judgment as a protector of the public interest?

We begin with a discussion of the traditional relationship between the courts and the FTC. We then consider whether in recent years the relationship between courts and agencies, including the FTC, is changing and how any changes might affect the occupational licensure program. Finally, we discuss the effect that requiring the FTC to employ cost/benefit analysis would have on its rules and on its relationship with the courts.

The Traditional Relationship between the Courts and the Federal Trade Commission. Initially, the courts attempted to limit the commission's freedom to act. During the commission's first sixteen years, three Supreme Court cases indicated that the judiciary would not give the agency wide freedom.[45] In these decisions, court review of FTC actions was not limited to asking if the facts indicated that the practices that the FTC alleged took place; instead, the courts reversed the commission on important policy issues such as whether a practice was illegal or its prohibition in the public interest.

In the mid-1930s, the courts began a shift toward deference to the FTC.[46] A good example is deception cases. In a 1937 decision, the Supreme Court found that a business's representation to consumers violated the Federal Trade Commission Act despite a lower court conclusion that only fools would be deceived.[47] As time passed, no matter how stupid the FTC assumed that some consumers were or how ben-

---

[44] Or, put in a form perhaps more comfortable to lawyers: assuming no dispute over the facts, will the courts routinely allow the FTC to decide whether those facts constitute illegality? In short, the question is whether the courts or the commission will decide what the Federal Trade Commission Act means.

[45] Gratz, 253 U.S. 421 (1920); Klesner, 280 U.S. 19 (1929), affirming 25 F.2d 524 (D.C. Cir. 1928); and Raladam, 283 U.S. 643 (1931).

[46] It is not our primary purpose here to determine the reasons for judicial deference. Whether the courts acted out of agreement with the FTC's substantive positions, a feeling that the problems before the commission were too trivial for judicial concern, a belief that deference was the proper judicial role, a determination that questions such as deception were inherently factual and hence should be left to the agency as the finder of fact, or for some other reason, the result was that the FTC was free of an effective judicial constraint in deciding what practices were illegal.

[47] Standard Education Society, 302 U.S. 112 (1937).

eficial to consumers a challenged claim might be, the courts refused to curtail agency action. For example, in 1965 the Supreme Court upheld a commission finding that the continual offering of paint on a "buy one, get one free" basis was deceptive because the second can was not actually "free," despite the practice's apparent benefits in encouraging price competition.[48] Further, when an advertiser claimed that a hair application could "color permanently," the commission ruled that the claim was illegal because some people might believe it would color hair that had not yet grown out of the scalp. The U.S. Court of Appeals for the Second Circuit, apparently constrained by the Supreme Court's command to defer to the FTC, affirmed the agency.[49]

As to the standard of deception, the courts eased the FTC's burden of proof by conceding that actual deception was unnecessary; the FTC need only show a "tendency or capacity to deceive."[50] Coupled with the standard for judicial review of commission actions—a commission finding would be affirmed if supported by substantial evidence on the record—this test made it extraordinarily difficult, if not impossible, to reverse commission findings of deception.

If this is not enough to show the commission's freedom, it should also be noted that the courts held the meaning of an advertisement to be a matter "committed to the discretion" of the FTC.[51] As one author has stated, "this modest sounding rule is a principal reason that the commission has managed to prevail in the appellate courts in the overwhelming majority of its [deception] decisions that have been appealed."[52] Moreover, the commission can determine how consumers understand an advertisement without even sampling public opinion.[53]

As illustrated in the most recent Supreme Court case dealing with the FTC's substantive powers, the 1972 *S&H* decision, the ability of the FTC to act with confidence that it will receive judicial support is not confined to deception. S&H, the owners of "green stamps," attempted to prevent commercial exchangers and redeemers from, among other things, giving discounts in return for stamps without S&H approval. When the commission argued that S&H's practices restrained trade under the principles of antitrust law, the Fifth Circuit Court of Appeals

---

[48] Mary Carter Paint, 382 U.S. 46 (1965). See Robert Pitofsky, "Beyond Nader: Consumer Protection and the Regulation of Advertising," *Harvard Law Review*, vol. 90, no. 4 (February 1977), pp. 688–89.

[49] Gelb, 144 F.2d 580 (2d Cir. 1944).

[50] See Alexander, *Honesty and Competition*, p. 69, for a detailed discussion.

[51] See Ernest Gellhorn, "Proof of Consumer Deception before the Trade Commission," *Kansas Law Review*, vol. 17 (1969), pp. 559–72, for a leading article on this point.

[52] See Pitofsky, "Beyond Nader," pp. 677–78.

[53] See, for example, Zenith Radio Corp., 143 F.2d 29 (7th Cir. 1944).

reversed, holding that the practices did not violate either the letter or the spirit of the antitrust laws.[54] Only when it came before the Supreme Court, nine years after the proceeding began, did the commission apparently begin in a serious way to move beyond antitrust considerations to focus on a new theory: S&H had committed unfair acts or practices under the Federal Trade Commission Act.

To the Court, whether the FTC could attack the practices as unfair turned on two questions: (1) whether the act empowered the commission to proscribe as "unfair" practices that did not violate either the letter or spirit of the antitrust laws and (2) whether the act empowered the commission to proscribe practices as "unfair" because of their effect on consumers, regardless of their nature or quality as competitive practices or their effect on competition. The Court found that the commission had these powers:

> [L]egislative and judicial authorities alike convince us that the Federal Trade Commission does not arrogate excessive power to itself if, in measuring a practice against the elusive, but congressionally mandated standard of fairness, it, like a court of equity, considers public values beyond simply those enshrined in the letter or encompassed in the spirit of the antitrust laws.[55]

This decision raises at least three points. First, and probably least important, it demonstrates one form of judicial check upon the FTC: the reviewing court will not affirm the agency on a theory that was not raised in the FTC hearings on the matter. S&H is in a very narrow sense a defeat for the FTC, inasmuch as the case was remanded to the commission because it had been tried under an antitrust theory, the circuit court had concluded that the practices did not violate either the letter or spirit of the antitrust laws, and, before the Supreme Court, the commission had not attacked this conclusion of the circuit court. Although this principle limits the FTC, it requires only that the commission be careful in its procedures; it does not in itself limit the substantive areas the agency can regulate. Second, the statement that the commission can consider public values beyond those in the antitrust laws may be particularly relevant for the occupational licensure program. In their most basic sense, if not always in their specific application, the policies underlying the antitrust laws are based on the same presumption in favor of the market that underlies the criticism of occupational regulation. Thus the statement that the commission can go beyond the policies of the antitrust laws may provide a substantive basis

---

[54] 405 U.S. 233 (1972).
[55] Ibid.

TABLE 1

SUBSTANTIVE FTC COURT OF APPEALS CASES, 1970–1974

Year	Won	Partially Won	Lost
1970	4	2	1
1971	3	1	2
1972	3	1	0
1973	5	1	0
1974	3	2	1
Total	18	7	4

SOURCE: Federal Trade Commission, *FTC Statutes and Decisions.*

for rules that substitute FTC regulations for those of the states. Finally, the court may have given the commission near limitless discretion in defining "unfairness." *S&H* may free the commission to find "public values" where it will be subject to minimal court review. Since the commission has only started to test the powers of *S&H*, however, it is too early to tell.

Besides the evidence already discussed on the freedom of the FTC from judicial interference, some additional information can be gleaned from two sources. First is the commission's record in the Supreme Court on substantive cases. Before 1934 the agency won only four of twelve cases; from 1934 until 1958, it won twelve of twenty-one; and since 1958 it has won each of the seventeen cases before the Court.[56] Further, of the nine (at least partial) losses since 1934, four involved the Robinson-Patman Act, a traditional area of judicial hostility. None of the others held that a practice was within the reach of the FTC Act, yet still lawful; rather, the commission lost on such grounds as lack of jurisdiction because the practice was not in interstate commerce or was exempt from FTC scrutiny because of another statute.[57]

Second, we may consider the commission record in the courts of appeals in recent years. Table 1 summarizes the FTC's record on substantive cases in these courts during the first five years of the 1970s.[58] If only part of the order was upheld, the case is listed as a partial victory, even if the part reversed was insignificant.

Although one might suggest that at least a partial defeat in 38

[56] See A. Everette MacIntyre and Joachim Volhard, "The Federal Trade Commission and Incipient Unfairness," *George Washington Law Review*, vol. 41 (1973), pp. 433–35.

[57] Bunte Bros., 312 U.S. 349 (1941) (not in commerce); National Casualty Co., 357 U.S. 560 (1957) (McCarran-Ferguson Act prevented FTC authority over advertising of insurance company).

[58] The list of cases was obtained from *FTC Statutes and Decisions.*

percent of the cases indicates a shift from wide judicial deference to more careful scrutiny, a closer look belies that suggestion. First, the commission did not lose (even part of) one case because the practice it attacked was not an unfair method of competition or an unfair or deceptive act or practice within the meaning of the FTC Act. Further, the courts affirmed an important expansion of commission regulation: advertising substantiation.[59] Finally, prohibition of a merchandising claim that probably few, if any, consumers would misunderstand was upheld in 1974, despite a strong attack by a dissenting judge and a dissenting commissioner that the problem was too trivial for FTC concern and that there was no proof of public injury.[60]

Analysis of three of the four defeats also reveals business as usual. Two involve procedural matters: in one the commission lost when it did not follow its own rules and when a commissioner prejudged the matter;[61] in the other, involving a game of chance, the court held that the commission's action was arbitrary because in some industries the FTC regulated the practice while in this case it banned it.[62] A third commission order was reversed when the commission found a violation upon a theory presented neither in the complaint nor before the hearing examiner.[63] The fourth defeat, in which the court held that the commission lacked the power to order restitution, may reveal a less deferential judicial posture, because the court was unwilling to endorse the FTC's interpretation of the FTC Act.[64] This issue is now of diminished importance, however, because Congress in the 1975 FTC Improvements Act allowed the commission to pursue such a remedy.

Of the seven cases that the commission lost in part, two involved the commission's failure to try the case on the theory apparently underlying the challenged provision of the order.[65] Two concerned various sections of the Clayton Act, an antitrust statute under which the courts do not totally defer to the commission regarding the determination of illegality.[66] Two other cases also appear to typify the deference discussed above. In one an order provision was overturned as too broad when

---

[59] Firestone Tire & Rubber Co., 481 F.2d 246 (6th Cir. 1973), cert. denied, 419 U.S. 886 (1974).

[60] Spiegel, 494 F.2d 59 (7th Cir.), cert. denied, 419 U.S. 896 (1974).

[61] Cinderella Career and Finishing School, Inc., 425 F.2d (D.C. Cir. 1970).

[62] Marco Sales Co., 453 F.2d (2d Cir. 1971).

[63] Bendix Corp., 450 F.2d 534 (6th Cir. 1971).

[64] Heater, 503 F.2d 321 (9th Cir. 1974).

[65] Golden Grain Macaroni Co., 472 F.2d 882 (9th Cir. 1972), cert. denied, 412 U.S. 918 (1973); and Abex Corp., 420 F.2d 928 (6th Cir.), cert. denied, 400 U.S. 865 (1970).

[66] Harbor Banana Distributors, 499 F.2d 395 (5th Cir. 1974); and United States Steel Corp., 426 F.2d 592 (6th Cir. 1970).

the commission gave almost no justification for it; in the other, part of the order was too vague.[67] The remaining case, involving the First Amendment, might restrict FTC regulation (although not deregulation) of advertising, but is not directly relevant to any other aspect of the occupational licensure program.[68]

Given congressional impotence regarding the FTC's substantive programs, the historical deference of the judiciary toward the commission, the FTC's enthusiasm for regulating the marketplace, and the perverse consequences of some of the agency's efforts, it is easy to understand the concern that the FTC's assertion of preemptive power has caused in many quarters. The agency has enormous and, it appears, largely unconstrained power.

As we shall see in the remainder of this section, however, a force may be emerging to check the commission, at least occasionally. The judiciary is shifting away from its traditional deference toward administrative agencies in general. We first consider this shift toward agencies as a group, then discuss some of its specific applications to the FTC.

The New Administrative Law. At least until 1960, what has come to be known as the "traditional" view of administrative law reigned supreme. Still reflected in some opinions today, this view was mainly concerned with limiting an agency to actions authorized by its statutes and with guaranteeing "fairness" in an agency's application of its mandate. Underlying the traditional view was a confidence in the ability of the administrative state to perform its assigned tasks competently without extensive court supervision. The long-standing freedom of the FTC appears at least partially a product of this traditional view. But since this view cannot reconcile the enormous power and discretion of agencies with the idea that intrusions into the rights of private individuals can be taken, if at all, only by the legislature, it is losing some of its force.[69]

---

[67] Papercraft Corp., 472 F.2d 927 (7th Cir. 1973); and National Dynamics Corp., 492 F.2d 1333 (2d Cir. 1974), cert. denied, 419 U.S. 993 (1975).

[68] L. G. Balfour Co., 442 F.2d (7th Cir. 1971). We are not asserting that the commission will always find that the practice it is considering violates the law. For a variety of reasons, respondents do win in the FTC. The staff may be unable to prove the facts as alleged in the complaint, or a majority of the commissioners (often not members when the complaint was issued) believe that the facts as proved should not constitute a violation. Our point is not that all companies charged with violating the Federal Trade Commission Act lose but that the courts have historically had little influence on the substantive grounds determining victory or defeat.

[69] See Richard B. Stewart, "The Reformation of American Administrative Law," *Harvard Law Review*, vol. 88, no. 8 (June 1975), pp. 1667–1814, from which this paragraph draws heavily.

Recently courts have placed more stringent requirements on the agencies, particularly in their rule-making activities. Many cases closely scrutinize agency decisions to see precisely what empirical data and analytical resources the agencies used in making those decisions.[70] While much of traditional administrative law is concerned that the agency be fair, these new cases may be arguing that the agency should also be competent.

Let us consider the application of the recent cases to rule making, the activity that will most affect the occupational licensure program. Traditionally, a court upheld a rule upon finding a plausible hypothesis to support it, with the judges showing extensive deference to agency expertise. A rule would be upheld without a detailed record or a showing of the precise link between the materials in the record and the decision that was made. In contrast, recent cases have required a detailed record, revealing the relevant facts and reasoning that led to the decision. Courts have refused to uphold rules where the facts in the record were inadequate, where the agency failed to respond adequately to important comments from parties before it, and where the agency statement of basis and purpose for the rule was unduly vague and not properly linked to the record.[71]

Those who have followed the evolution of the judiciary/agency relationship might question whether the Supreme Court's 1978 *Vermont Yankee* decision will curtail the thrust of what we are terming the "new administrative law." For this reason and because the lower court's *Vermont Yankee* opinion is an important example of the new judicial attitude (at least in its result if not in all of its reasoning), we will consider that case in some detail. For our purposes, the most important issue concerned rule making involving the environmental problems created by disposal of radioactive waste. Relying on a "vague but glowing"[72] analysis by one of its staff scientists, the Nuclear Regulatory Commission (NRC) assumed that problems would be minimal. The scientist's statement contained a very general and conclusionary description of a novel method of surface warehousing for waste—a method that the NRC has since abandoned. Without benefit of detail, this statement in effect merely offered reassurances that the problem would eventually be resolved.

The U.S. Court of Appeals for the District of Columbia remanded

---

[70] See James DeLong, "Informal Rulemaking and the Integration of Law and Policy," *Virginia Law Review*, vol. 65 (1979), pp. 257–356.

[71] For a discussion of these and other requirements, see Kenneth Culp Davis, *Administrative Law* (St. Paul, Minn.: West Publishing Co., 1972), pp. 139–56.

[72] National Resources Defense Council, Inc. v. United States Nuclear Regulatory Commission, 547 F.2d 633 (D.C. Cir. 1976).

the rule-making proceeding to the NRC. While the majority of the court seemed to stress the inadequacy of the NRC's procedures, Judge Tamm's concurrence expressed concern that the agency might have "uncritically adopted as its own the undocumented conclusion of a single witness that the waste storage issue is a non-problem."[73] Accordingly, he agreed to remand, although he disagreed with what he felt was the majority's requirement of further proceedings more adversarial than those previously held. Neither opinion allowed the agency to use its expertise to dismiss objections to its rules; rather, the NRC was in effect told to demonstrate that its handling of the waste disposal issue made sense.

In an opinion extremely critical of the lower court, a unanimous Supreme Court reversed. Although the circuit court's opinion is susceptible to different readings, the Supreme Court treated the lower court as saying that the administrative procedures were inadequate. The Court concluded that the lower court should not have strayed beyond the procedural format of the Administrative Procedure Act. Superficially, the result is inconsistent with the trend we have described, but on closer analysis, the impact of the decision for our purposes turns on whether Judge Tamm's view will be sustained. If agencies could dispose of crucial issues by accepting conclusionary, undocumented statements of their staff, the judicial constraint upon the agencies would be minimal.

The Supreme Court's *Vermont Yankee* opinion indicates that the Court is not tampering with the Tamm view. The Court remanded the case to determine "whether the challenged rule will find sufficient justification in the administrative proceedings," specifically noting that Tamm found it did not.[74] Further, the Court stated that upon remand the lower court was "entirely free to agree or disagree" with Tamm.[75] The Court thus may have been saying only that the rule could not be set aside because of inadequate procedures. The practical difference between Tamm's opinion and the requiring of additional procedures seems small for our purposes.[76] Whether courts can require more specific procedures or tell the agency that it did not provide an adequate record, the effect will be closer scrutiny than traditional of the agency action. Thus, unless the Supreme Court goes beyond this holding, the new

---

[73] 547 F.2d at 658 (Tamm, J., concurring).

[74] Vermont Yankee Nuclear Power v. Natural Resources Defense Council, Inc., 435 U.S. 519 (1978).

[75] 435 U.S. at 535, 536 n. 14.

[76] For the agency, however, the Tamm approach may be preferable, leaving to the agency the decision of what procedures to adopt to make the record "adequate." Since the agency is presumably in a better position than the court to know what procedures are best suited for it, *Vermont Yankee* will be beneficial if read to support the Tamm view.

administrative law will continue as a constraint upon the substance of agency action.[77]

The FTC and the New Administrative Law. What does all of this mean for the FTC in general and its occupational licensure program in particular? Although the agency has precedent supporting broad discretion, including the recent *S&H* decision, there is no reason it should be immune from changing judicial attitudes toward the administrative state. Indeed, there are two reasons why the commission will be affected. First, the commission is no longer involved in trivial matters, as it was when the courts decided most of the important cases affecting the FTC/judiciary relationship. Many commission activities, including the occupational licensure program, now have enormous potential impact on consumers and producers. Second, although it is much too early to consider this a trend, a few recent FTC cases may indicate a changed judicial attitude toward the commission. We here discuss those cases and then consider application of the "new administrative law" to rulemaking activities such as these in the occupational licensure program.

Recent FTC Decisions. From 1975 through 1978, the commission's record in the courts of appeals included ten victories, ten partial victories, and one defeat. Four of the decisions indicate that courts may be taking a harder look at what the commission does, one even indicating that the courts may overrule the commission on the definition of illegality under the FTC Act.

Ger-Ro-Mar,[78] decided in 1975, was the first of these decisions. The commission attacked a scheme to merchandise lingerie and similar items through what appeared to be a pyramid selling system. Using a mathematical formula, the FTC argued that the number of people attempting to sell the goods would quickly reach a level at which there would not be enough customers available for all sellers. The court found

---

[77] *Vermont Yankee* indicates that the Court rejects that part of the new administrative law requiring procedures beyond the Administrative Procedure Act (APA).

Further, the Court has not faced up to the full implications of *Vermont Yankee* since the Tamm position also strays beyond the APA. See Stephen L. Breyer and Richard Stewart, *Administrative Law and Regulatory Policy* (Boston: Little, Brown, 1979), pp. 521–22. Since the Court not only failed to condemn the Tamm view but seemed to endorse it as a general approach, it is unclear how literally one can take the Court's allegiance to the strict letter of the APA. As indicated in the preceding footnote and the accompanying text, however, judicial imposition of specific procedures is unnecessary and less to be preferred than what we refer to here as the Tamm position.

The impending decision in the Benzene case may indicate whether the Court will cut back further on the new law, although that case could be decided on a narrower point, namely statutory construction.

[78] Ger-Ro-Mar, Inc., 518 F.2d 33 (2d Cir. 1975).

that, although the agency was correct in the abstract, it had not considered the realities of the marketplace. More important for us, the court stated that it was for the courts, not the commission, to decide what unfair competition is—a distinct throwback to the view of the 1920s. Although the commission failed to rely on evidence of harm to consumers other than its formula, the court's deference appears less than traditional. The court simply refused to defer to the commission's judgment unless that judgment had factual support.

In the 1977 *Chrysler Corporation* case,[79] Chrysler claimed that *Popular Science* magazine tests showed that its small cars got better fuel economy than the Chevrolet Nova. Although the court affirmed the commission's finding that this claim was deceptive, it struck out two paragraphs of the order as too broad. One paragraph prohibited representing the results of tests unless the "representation fully and accurately reflects the test results and unless the tests themselves were so devised and conducted as to completely substantiate each representation concerning any characteristic tested." The court said that this was potentially almost limitless and found that another provision, prohibiting petitioners from "misleading in any manner . . . the purpose, context or conclusion of any test" was limitless. Since the FTC conceded that the violations were unintentional, not continuing, and confined to only two of fourteen advertisements, the court said there was no rational justification for the sweeping provisions. The court thus applied a standard of its own, rather than leaving it entirely to the commission to establish criteria by which to justify the order provisions.

In the other two cases, the violation was also unintentional. In both, the court overturned part of an FTC order as too broad, citing the lack of bad faith in striking the order provision.[80] Further, one of the cases, *Standard Oil of California,* decided in 1978, appeared to question the agency's freedom to determine the standard for deception. The commission had found that an advertisement for a gasoline additive, F–310, was deceptive in part because it allegedly implied that the additive would completely reduce pollutants. The court disagreed, stating that it did "not think that any television viewer would have a level of credulity so primitive that he could expect . . . [complete reduction]." Finding that the record did support "the Commission's interpretation of the meaning the commercial would have to the average viewer," the court affirmed the agency as to other alleged deceptions. Nevertheless, an average viewer standard is harder for the FTC to meet than a test designed to protect fools.

---

[79] Chrysler Corp., 561 F.2d 357, 564 (D.C. Cir. 1977).
[80] Warner-Lambert Co., 562 F.2d 749 (D.C. Cir. 1977); and Standard Oil Co., 577 F.2d 653 (9th Cir. 1978).

Rule Making. Thus far, there has been no substantive court review of commission rules. Nevertheless, it appears that what we have termed the new administrative law will have an important effect on the FTC, including the occupational licensure program. Under these decisions, we believe it will often be easier to deregulate than to regulate. This conclusion follows from the economic case against occupational regulation, with its powerful theoretical and empirical arguments that the market is generally a better tool for serving the interests of consumers than government regulation supplanting the market. Thus the commission will be able, if it chooses, to promulgate deregulatory rules with records and reasoning withstanding scrutiny under the recent administrative law decisions.

On the other hand, when the commission decides that the unregulated market produces results that it does not like, its resulting rule may not be as easy to justify. Many such rules will impose costs, and the commission may, under the recent decisions, be forced to rebut evidence that the costs exist or to justify their imposition. Particularly when the issue is the economic welfare of consumers, the FTC will often have to overcome theoretical and empirical evidence that its regulation is not warranted.

As examples of possible court review of FTC rule making, let us consider three FTC rules. First, the agency has preempted state laws that prohibit advertising of ophthalmic goods and services. The resulting rule, deregulatory in nature, has strong theoretical and empirical support, including refutation of the arguments made in favor of the advertising bans. At the other extreme is the commission's creditors' remedies rule, which will rewrite credit contracts. The rule-making proceedings here have included substantial economic testimony, from both FTC and industry witnesses, that the costs of modifying or eliminating creditors' remedies appear to be substantial in relation to any benefits.[81] An FTC justification of this rule as benefiting consumers, particularly poor ones upon whom the costs fall heaviest, will be difficult to sustain under the more stringent judicial review of recent years.[82]

An intermediate case (in that the major problem is with the rule's justification, not necessarily with its impact) is that part of the eyeglasses rule requiring separation of dispensing and examination. The commis-

---

[81] Peterson, "FTC's Trade Regulation Rule."

[82] By applying different evidentiary standards to evidence of costs than to evidence of benefits, the FTC's presiding officer for the creditors' remedy rule making has reached a different conclusion from the one in the text. It remains to be seen whether an appellate court will allow such manipulation of the evidence to support the agency position. If the commission adopts the presiding officer's conclusion *and* reasoning and if a court then affirms the FTC, it would imply that the courts will be a minimal constraint on the agency.

sion's justification for the provision—that the removal of the advertising laws will have little impact without separation of dispensing from examination—is questionable given lower prices in states with advertising but without separation of examination and dispensing. If this point had been developed in the rule-making proceeding, the commission could ignore it only at its peril in future court review.[83]

All of this is not to say that the courts will force the FTC to conform strictly to economic analysis in its rule making. The agency may have considerable discretion. If, as *S&H* implies, the commission can promulgate rules on the basis of vague policies whose appropriate application is left largely to FTC discretion, the agency may often avoid close judicial scrutiny.

Thus, when the commission attempts to justify the rules by economic analysis, the judiciary is likely to be a more effective constraint than when the agency uses a less rigorous standard. For example, let us consider again the provision of the eyeglasses rule separating dispensing from examination. The commission is attempting to justify the provision as necessary to allow advertising to function, a proposition susceptible to close empirical scrutiny. On the other hand, let us suppose that the commission sought to justify the rule on the basis of the "freedom" of consumers to have prescriptions or on the "freedom" of opticians to practice as independent businessmen. If the courts were to allow the commission to pursue such policies, what would be the applicable standards? What evidence would be relevant? What of the examiners' rights? What if the consumer's right to a prescription raises prices? Once the commission moves beyond reliance on only economic analysis,[84] the decision calculus may involve only a nebulous, ad hoc balancing. The less rigorous the justification that the FTC must give for a rule, the less effective judicial review of the decision process will be, reducing the constraining power of the courts.

Given that even the recent judicial decisions may allow the commission to promulgate regulations harmful to consumers, the question

---

[83] From a reading of the commission's statement of basis and purpose and the staff report of the Bureau of Consumer Protection, it does not appear that this point has been analyzed. Furthermore, a theoretical case exists that this proposal will have costs, although the commission statements on the rule do not discuss this possibility. If opponents of the regulation had seriously argued—with well-developed theoretical and empirical analyses—that the rule's impact would be to raise costs, the agency could have ignored this argument only at its peril.

[84] Economic analysis does not ignore the claims discussed in the text. The market would allow individuals to have these "rights" if they desire to pay for them. Underlying our argument for effective judicial scrutiny is the assumption that if the political choice is to be made that costs are to be imposed upon consumers without compensating benefits, Congress, not an administrative agency, should make the choice.

arises whether, assuming that the FTC's rule-making authority continues, a more effective judicial constraint can be devised. We turn next to one such possibility.

Cost/Benefit Analysis. The Fifth Circuit Court of Appeals has recently applied the cost/benefit approach.[85] For example, the Consumer Product Safety Commission (CPSC) promulgated a Safety Standard for Swimming Pool Slides requiring manufacturers to include warning signs on new slides, limiting installation of large slides to water more than four feet deep, and, because of the danger of drowning, requiring a ladder chain device to warn children to stay off slides. The court held that the CPSC must take a hard look not only at the nature and severity of the risk but also at the possibility that the standard would actually reduce the severity or frequency of the injury and at the effect the standard would have on the utility, cost, or availability of the product. Particularly given the infrequency of the risk involved, the commission had to produce evidence that the standard actually promised to reduce the risk. Further, the CPSC did not know whether the required signs would be so explicit and shocking in portraying the risk of paralysis as to constitute an unwarranted deterrent to the marketing of slides.

Judge John Minor Wisdom, in concurrence, aptly summarized the court's opinion on this point:

> The balance the Commission draws between the benefits and the costs must have support. . . . The benefits from these signs have no reasonable relationship to the costs they will impose. With no evidence on the cost side of the ledger, the Commission's cost-benefit analysis is without substantial evidence for support.[86]

This case relied heavily on the applicable agency statute, and it is not at all clear that the FTC Act will be similarly interpreted.[87] Accordingly, legislation may be necessary to guarantee cost/benefit review. The superiority of this approach for the FTC is that it focuses rule making on consumer welfare. The commission acts in the name of protecting the consumer, and cost/benefit analysis is the ideal tool to determine whether a rule will in fact serve that end.

Of course, there will be objections to cost/benefit analysis. Most

---

[85] Aqua Slide 'N' Dive Corp. v. Consumer Prod. Safety Comm'n, 569 F.2d 831 (5th Cir.); and Petroleum Inst. v. OSHA, 581 F.2d 493 (5th Cir. 1978), cert. granted, 47 USLW 3541 (Feb. 20, 1979).

[86] See Aqua Slide 'N' Dive Corp. v. CPSC.

[87] Although it is conceivable that the FTC Act could be interpreted to require something approaching the cost/benefit standard, it could also be interpreted to allow the commission to ignore these considerations. See DeLong, "Informal Rulemaking."

prominent among them is that benefits and costs cannot be appropriately measured. For four reasons, this objection should not bar the proposed reform. First, there is reason to be skeptical about statements that the relevant costs and benefits are not measurable:

> If there is a demand for information, the cry goes out that what the organization does cannot be measured. . . . Often times this is another way of saying, "mind your own business." Sometimes the line taken is that the work is so subtle that it resists any tests. On other occasions the point is made that only those schooled in esoteric arts can properly understand what the organization does and they can barely communicate to the uninitiated. There are men so convinced of the ultimate righteousness of their cause that they cannot imagine why anyone would wish to know how well they are doing in handling our common difficulties. Their activities are literally priceless; vulgar notions of cost and benefits do not apply to them.[88]

Second, under this approach the FTC will not be involved in making judgments based on noneconomic criteria (such as distributional effects) that would complicate cost/benefit analysis. The focus will be on the economic welfare of consumers and on this issue alone. Third, the FTC will rarely be involved in resolving great scientific controversies that complicate cost/benefit analysis in areas such as nuclear power. Fourth, we would not always require the agency to show with certainty that benefits exceed cost. Where it cannot prove that the benefits exceed the cost, the agency should be allowed to act if it has preliminary evidence that sufficient benefits are likely to exist but cannot be demonstrated at the time of the proceeding. In such a case, FTC rules should contain an automatic five-year sunset provision. If the agency cannot show at the end of the five years that benefits exceed cost, the rule will lapse. This will allow the agency to collect before-and-after data to demonstrate the net benefits of its action.

This is not to say that the cost/benefit standard will guarantee an end to anticonsumer regulation. The commission would still have broad discretion in some cases, particularly where there was a serious conflict of evidence. Requiring the FTC to show that its cases produce benefits exceeding costs would at the very least, however, limit FTC discretion to impose costly regulation upon consumers. It would be an important step to changing the agency from one not subject to meaningful court review into one based on the appropriate rule of law: the welfare of consumers.

---

[88] Aaron Wildavsky, "Rescuing Policy Analysis from PPBS," in R. Haveman and J. Margolis, eds., *Public Expenditures and Policy Analysis* (Chicago: Rand McNally, 1970), p. 461.

Conclusion

Upon initial scrutiny, the FTC's occupational licensure program, based on presumed FTC power to preempt state laws, appears to encourage those who favor curtailment of occupational regulation. Closer analysis, however, casts considerable doubt upon such a conclusion. The source of this doubt is within the agency, rather than outside it. Within, the FTC's schizophrenic attitude toward the market is likely to be resolved in many cases in favor of regulation rather than of deregulation. We do not conclude that the agency will never pursue deregulatory cases and rules, but it would not be at all surprising if FTC activities preempting state laws were rarely deregulatory. Even for advertising, where the FTC's position has been consistently deregulatory, the FTC's preemptive power is now of questionable value. Although the prescription drug rule with which the occupational licensure program began promised to be extremely beneficial to consumers, the Supreme Court's protection of commercial speech has greatly decreased the necessity for FTC intervention.[89]

Outside the agency, the picture is somewhat different. Although there is growing congressional opposition to the FTC's foray against occupational regulation, unless it gains considerably more clout than it now possesses, such opposition is unlikely to curtail the program, in either its regulatory or its deregulatory aspects. Congress can force the agency to appear before it, force it to explain its actions, and even force it to investigate certain industries, but Congress's ability to require or stop specific FTC law enforcement is, given all but a political climate extremely hostile to the FTC, limited. As to the courts, if they conclude that the commission can preempt, they are unlikely to oppose a deregulatory occupational licensure program and more likely to constrain new regulation than the other two institutions that we have studied. Unfortunately, without cost/benefit review, even the courts may often constitute only a limited constraint on the commission's tendency to promulgate regulatory rules that reduce consumer well-being.

---

[89] After Bates v. State Bar of Arizona (433 U.S. 350, 1977), the unconstitutionality of laws against advertising for ophthalmic goods and services is clear. Indeed, in a recent case in which a federal district court found such a law to be unconstitutional, those supporting the law did not even bother to appeal that part of the opinion to the Supreme Court, although they did appeal, and win, on other issues. See Rogers v. Friedman, 438 F. Supp. 428, 432–434 (E.D. Tex. 1977), rev'd in part, 47 U.S.L.W. 4151 (1979).

Will the Sun Set on Occupational Licensing?

Donald L. Martin

Within the last three years, over half our state legislatures have passed laws requiring termination of large numbers of government programs, agencies, and laws by specific dates. These laws have been given the name "sunset" because they require that specific legislation be allowed to expire on a given date unless the state's legislature votes to reenact it. In other words, at the end of some evaluation period, the sun will be allowed to set on laws that cannot demonstrate the confidence of the people's representatives.

Prominent among government activities subject to sunset legislation are regulatory agencies and, in particular, occupational licensing boards. The purpose of this paper is to discuss the probable effects of sunset laws on the fate of occupational licensing. To do this we will examine the limited experience states have had, to date, with sunset and licensing and analyze the prospective costs and rewards to occupational licensing boards.

First, we will look, very briefly, at the pros and cons of occupational licensing, using economic analysis. Next we will describe sunset legislation in historical perspective and highlight significant differences in legislation among states. Then, in the major part of the paper, we will examine actual sunset experience with occupational licensing boards and discuss the question of whether sunset will have a significant effect on the pervasiveness of licensing and on the efficacy of licensing practices in the future.

Occupational Licensing

Proponents of occupational licensing have long argued that this form of regulation serves society for any one, or for all, of three reasons: First, the prohibitive cost of information makes it impossible for consumers to distinguish competent from incompetent sellers of certain professional services. Regulation prohibiting the sale of such services by persons either unable or unwilling to satisfy legally specified minimal standards of expertise is thought to protect consumers from incompetence and fraud.

Second, in the absence of licensing, a consumer may knowingly or unknowingly choose a quality of professional service so "low" or "inferior" that it produces harmful effects for third parties. Regulation that establishes minimal professional standards of service is said to preclude such third-party effects. A common example, often cited by the medical profession, is one where consumers' choices of low-quality health care may lead to the spread of communicable disease to third parties.[1] The same type of externality might also arise from the sale of "low-quality" unlicensed plumbing services, electrician services, barbering services, and so on.

Third, there is an interdependence of utility functions among voter-consumers. Voluntary individual consumption choices of quality levels of professional service that are lower than some socially determined standard may generate risk to the individual consumer that fellow voters believe he or she should not take, because that harm will affect *their* sense of well-being. This is the "society knows best" reason for licensing.[2] Interdependent utilities among voter-consumers may be more prevalent in the consumption of professional services in some occupations, such as medicine and law, than in others, such as economics and astrology.

A significant amount of occupational licensing has been adopted in every state in the union (and in the District of Columbia).[3] The social benefits claimed for this form of occupational regulation, however, are held suspect by members of at least one unlicensed occupation, the economics profession. Economists have, for some time, suspected that occupational licensure operates as a legally sanctioned cartelization device, restricting entry of would-be professionals and restraining competition among incumbents. Prohibitions against advertising, price cutting, and other competitive activities are usually enforced by the threat of license revocation. Licensing boards and standards committees are almost invariably populated by members of the occupation being regulated, giving rise to the charge that such agencies have been captured

---

[1] See, for example, Keith B. Leffler, "Physician Licensure, Competition, and Monopoly in American Medicine," *Journal of Law and Economics,* vol. 2 (April 1978), p. 174. See also Thomas G. Moore, "The Purpose of Licensing," *Journal of Law and Economics,* vol. 4 (October 1961), pp. 93–117.

[2] See Moore, "The Purpose of Licensing."

[3] In 1973 the American Bar Association reported 307 different occupations subject to licensure in the states and the District of Columbia. The average number of occupations subject to state licensure was thirty-nine. See Senate Governmental Operation Committee, State of Florida, *Manual of Instruction for the Implementation of the Regulatory Reform Act of 1976,* app. D, March 1977, pp. 84–90.

by the self-interested members of the professions.[4] Excessive limits on entry, together with professional standards that penalize price competition, can result in monopoly rents for members of the profession and higher prices and fewer services for consumers. Thus any social benefits that result from licensing, it is suspected, may be more than offset by the social costs arising from cartelization.

Recently economists have been joined in their suspicion of occupational licensing by lay groups interested in occupational regulation as it relates to consumer protection and in the growth of government regulation in general. These groups, for example, have attacked both the legal and the medical professions for using the threat of license revocation as a means of enforcing antiadvertising rules that sustain higher-than-competitive prices for professional services sold to the public. Moreover, government reform groups, such as Common Cause, and consumer advocates, such as Ralph Nader, have begun to popularize the role the government has played in permitting the licensing functions to be captured by the professionals themselves. Scientific and lay criticism of occupational licensing, as well as of other economic regulation, focuses on the anticonsumer effects of special-interest influence on licensing boards and other regulatory agencies. If board members were to face incentives that made anticompetitive policies more costly to adopt (short of abolishing the licensing process), a major source of criticism might be answered. Likewise, if the public "need" for occupational licensing by government were periodically subject to reevaluation, the political process would be better provided with information relevant to the maintenance or abolition of licensing.

The Rise of Sunset

A cry for *accountability* in the administration of economic regulation (and for that matter in the administration of government in general), rather than for deregulation, has given rise to sunset legislation, the latest innovation in government managerial tools. Demands for economy in government and for limited government are not new. Program evaluation and budget review efforts have been with us at least since

---

[4] See George J. Stigler, "The Theory of Economic Regulation," *Bell Journal of Economics and Management Science*, vol. 2, no. 1 (1971). For a modification of the capture theory, see Sam Peltzman, "Toward a More General Theory of Regulation," *Journal of Law and Economics*, vol. 19, no. 2 (August 1976).

the end of World War II.[5] Between 1969 and 1974, federal expenditures on program evaluation rose from $20 million to more than $130 million.[6] Program evaluation efforts at the state level have also been significant in at least twenty-five state legislatures.[7] Budget review processes, both federal and state, also reflect efforts to evaluate the results of government activities. Program budgeting in the 1960s and zero-based budgeting in the 1970s are attempts to gain control of the budgeting process and meet the rising demand for less expensive and less extensive government.

The relatively sudden popularity of sunset laws, however, is dramatic recognition of the failure of existing legislative evaluation mechanisms in regulating government size and performance.[8] As we noted earlier, the unique feature of the sunset idea is its requirement that laws, programs, or agencies terminate at a specified date unless recreated by the state's legislature. This feature is supposed to force legislatures to evaluate the results of what they have done, with hoped-for effects on the size and efficiency of government. Unless agencies and programs can justify their existence on the basis of criteria contained in sunset legislation, they will cease to exist.[9] To institutionalize the action forcing sunset process, most sunset legislation provides for periodic termination of programs, agencies, or legislation that has survived previous sunset reviews.[10]

Seven states have passed comprehensive sunset legislation covering

---

[5] See Legislative Reorganization Act of 1946, Section 136, ch. 253. This act required each substantive committee of Congress to "exercise continuous watchfulness of the execution of the administrative agencies concerned of any laws, the subject matter of which is within the jurisdiction of such committee." Later acts, such as the Legislative Reorganization Act of 1970, called for the review and analysis of government programs and activities carried on under existing law by the comptroller general and the General Accounting Office (both congressional agencies).

[6] See R. Knezo, *Program Evaluation: Emerging Issues of Possible Legislative Concern Relating to the Conduct and Use of Evaluation in the Congress in the Executive Branch,* 31, Nov. 16, 1975 (Washington, D.C.: Congressional Research Service, Library of Congress), p. 1.

[7] See Council of State Governments, *State Government Program Evaulation Activities,* Summer 1972.

[8] In 1976 Colorado enacted the first sunset law in the United States. Today twenty-nine states have enacted such laws. For brief but informative descriptions of sunset legislation in each of the twenty-nine states, together with a discussion of how sunset "should" work, see *Making Government Work: A Common Cause Report on State Sunset Activity* (Washington, D.C.: Common Cause, December 1978).

[9] Of the twenty-nine sunset states, only Alabama did not enact an automatic termination provision. Alabama's sunset law requires action by both houses of the legislature after a two-hour debate for each program or law (Common Cause, *Making Government Work*).

[10] Arkansas, Indiana, North Carolina, and South Dakota have no provisions for periodic termination in their sunset legislation. Ibid., p. 10.

almost all government agencies and programs.[11] Most states, however, have been more selective. Interestingly, regulatory agencies, and occupational licensing boards in particular, have been a popular target for sunset legislation. This focus may be explained, as Common Cause and many economists have suggested, by the fact that regulatory agencies often produce indirect social costs leading to citizen dissatisfaction with government. Moreover, regulatory agencies are not normally subject to legislative oversight evaluations, since their budgets involve little direct state appropriations.[12]

Sunset and Occupational Licensing

Of the twenty-nine states that have passed sunset legislation, only Louisiana has exempted occupational licensing. The rest have identified between thirty and forty licensed occupations each, to be subjected to the sunset process over a specified period in successive review cycles.

Unfortunately, it is too soon to evaluate the sunset experience of all twenty-nine states. Only fifteen have conducted sunset reviews for at least some licensing boards, and only ten have taken legislative action based on those reviews. Nevertheless, it may be instructive to examine their experience and to evaluate it in the light of incentives for legislators and their staffs in sunset states that have yet to vote on the fate of their occupational licensing boards.

Table 1 presents the disposition of occupational licensing boards under sunset legislation during 1977–1978.

Roughly 35 percent of the licensing boards reviewed by sunset committees were recommended for termination. The committees recommended that 29 percent of the boards reviewed should be consolidated or otherwise modified, in an attempt to improve their performance, and that 11 percent be continued unaltered.

How were these recommendations received by the respective legislatures? Six of the fifteen states shown in table 1 did not vote on recommendations in 1977 or 1978, and, as the table reveals, two states, Georgia and New Mexico, did not authorize recommendations from their committees. This leaves ninety-one occupational licensing boards for which both recommendations *and* legislative action were authorized during the study period. Thirty-seven of these boards (40 percent) were recommended for termination, but only sixteen were actually terminated, which is 43 percent of those recommended for termination. If we include all occupational licensing boards on which legislative action

---

[11] Ibid., p. 8.
[12] Ibid.

TABLE 1
Disposition of Occupational Licensing Boards under Selected Sunset Legislation 1977–1978

State	Licensed Occupations	Sunset Reviews	Termination		Modification		Continuance	
			Recom-mended	Action taken	Recom-mended	Action taken	Recom-mended	Action taken
Alabama	40	40	11	0	0	0	0	40
Colorado	48	10	4	3	4	4	3	3
Florida	51	12	5	4	7	5	0	2
Georgia	53	10	NA[a]	0	NA[a]	0	NA[a]	10
Hawaii	47	6	4	2	2	2	0	2
Montana[b]	50	10	2	—	5	—	3	—
Nebraska	39	8	0	0	0	1	0	7
New Mexico	43	19	NA[a]	5	NA[a]	13	NA[a]	1
North Carolina[b]	30	14	4	—	10	—	0	—
Oklahoma	39	8	7	1	0	0	0	7
Oregon[b]	45	10	4	—	2	—	4	—
South Dakota	33	7	6	6	0	0	1	1
Texas[b]	40	15	3	—	12	—	—	0
Utah[b]	38	8	3	—	2	—	3	—
Washington[b]	33	5	1	—	1	—	3	—

[a] NA means committee recommendations not authorized.
[b] Legislation not due for vote until 1979.

SOURCES: Telephone interviews with state sunset evaluation officers; Common Cause. *Making Government Work*; and Senate Governmental Operations Committee, State of Florida. *Manual of Instruction*.

was taken, including those for which no recommendations were provided, the number of boards actually terminated represents only 17 percent of the total. This should not be taken to suggest, however, that the success or failure of sunset legislation turns on the percentage of licensing boards terminated.

As we noted earlier, many proponents of sunset legislation have not sought deregulation or "delicensing" but rather greater government "accountability" to the "public interest." This purpose is surely consistent with a relatively low termination figure. On the other hand, for those who saw in sunset legislation the opportunity to break the monopoly hold of professional occupations by terminating large numbers of occupational licensing boards, the evidence thus far has not been encouraging.

One of the main reasons that more boards have not been terminated has been the significant amount of special-interest lobbying, from federal and state regulators and from occupational representatives. Before we discuss some of the other reasons for this result, it may be instructive to examine the data in the remaining columns of table 1.

Of the ninety-one boards for which recommendations were supplied, thirteen were recommended for modification by consolidation or by some form of rule change, including switching from licensing to registration.[13] All but one of these boards slated for modification were so modified by their respective legislatures. These twelve, together with the thirteen boards in New Mexico that were modified without benefit of committee recommendation, represent 21 percent of all those boards reviewed and subjected to the legislative process in 1977 and 1978. However, since the Alabama sunset law prohibits agency modification (an agency is either terminated or continued), modifications were actually carried out on 31 percent of eligible licensing boards reviewed and subjected to a sunset vote.

Relatively few licensing boards, four, were recommended for unaltered continuation. However, legislators disregarded recommendations in dramatic fashion, continuing as many as sixty-two boards in those states where recommendations were encouraged, though not necessarily required, and legislative action could be taken in 1977–1978. If we include those states for which recommendations were not sought, continuances rise to seventy-three. That is, about 61 percent of all licensing boards reviewed for action in 1977–1978 were continued unaltered. Taken together, sunset deliberations have re-created roughly

---

[13] This change was specifically considered in Colorado and South Dakota and recommended in Oklahoma.

82 percent of the licensing boards legislated for termination in the period studied.

There are several reasons for the relatively low proportion of terminated and modified licensing boards in this first round of sunset deliberations. First, Alabama dominated the sample with forty boards subject to sunset review. Since its sunset law prohibited modifications in licensing board rules and structure and legislators were severely limited in the time allotted for floor debate (two hours), it is not so surprising that a majority of representatives refused to terminate any of the boards. But even if Alabama's forty boards are excluded from consideration, licensing boards continued *without* alteration still constitute the largest group of outcomes.

A second reason for this phenomenon may be the heavy amount of lobbying by both the regulators and the regulated to prevent board terminations or significant modifications.[14] Cosmetologists, barbers, morticians, harbor pilots, court reporters, podiatrists, massage parlor operators, dental hygienists, physical therapists, landscape architects, and others used lobbying pressures to mitigate sunset staff recommendations.[15] These pressures are not likely to subside when physicians, nurses, psychologists, optometrists, lawyers, and chiropractors are reviewed in later cycles. Thus re-creation of licensing boards without alteration is owed, at least in part, to special-interest pressures—pressures that were, by the way, conspicuous by their absence when watchmakers and polygraphers were scheduled for termination. No doubt the values of rents forsaken by watchmakers and polygraphers were not worth the costs of lobbying against termination. Other terminations involved licensing agencies that had never actually been formed, such as those for escort agencies and photography studios in Hawaii.[16] These groups could hardly generate a constituency sufficiently threatened to fight licensing termination. Likewise, it should not be surprising that these boards are the first to be chosen for termination, offering as they did the least resistance and the lowest political risk to legislators.

Prospects for Occupational Licensing under Sunset

The fate of occupational licensing under sunset legislation depends on two factors: the first is the criteria states adopt for evaluating the efficacy of licensing boards—criteria that, as might be expected, are neither uniform across states nor applied with uniform effort. The second is the

---

[14] See Common Cause, *Making Government Work*, pp. 26–27, 53, 56–57, 59, 73.

[15] Ibid., p. 59.

[16] Ibid.

incentives legislators face in voting whether to terminate, modify, or continue licensing boards and laws unchanged. This factor will be treated after we examine variations in sunset criteria and the quality of sunset reviews.

Although every sunset state has adopted criteria for carrying out sunset reviews, these criteria differ in important ways. For example, one requirement for justifying the continuance of a licensing board in the state of Maine is that "public benefits from the program are sufficient to justify the cost."[17] Each licensing board is required to submit a report to the legislature responding to this point. Unfortunately, no way of evaluating costs and benefits is specified. Moreover, licensing boards and other agencies are not required to divulge the models, analyses, or studies supporting their claims for continuance. By contrast, Oregon requires licensing boards and other agencies to respond to relatively specific questions designed to measure any cost arising from licensing. For example, licensing boards are required to specify whether, and to what extent, their regulations have the effect of directly or indirectly increasing the cost of any goods or services associated with the occupation licensed.[18] They are also asked whether the increase in cost is greater than the value of the harm that could result from the absence of regulation.[19] Oregon law further demands that boards provide a list of models, analyses, or studies supporting their conclusions and recommendations for continuances. Similar detail is required of Tennessee licensing boards under that state's sunset legislation.[20] On the other hand, Alabama sunset legislation specified no quantitative information beyond the amount of service the licensing board has provided to the public, with service measured in terms of licenses issued or consumer complaints processed.[21]

As Common Cause observes, however, most state regulatory agencies and licensing boards have had difficulty collecting quantitative data for evaluating the costs and benefits of licensing to the public. The Utah approach to the estimation of net benefits from veterinary licensing is typical:

> In our opinion, the continued licensing of veterinarians is necessary to protect the health, safety, and welfare of the public. In forming this opinion, we noted that veterinarians work with diseased animals and with controlled substances (drugs). We

---

[17] See State of Maine P.L. 554–1977 and P.L. 683–1978.
[18] Specifically, see House Bill 2323, Oregon Legislature Assembly, 1977, p. 15.
[19] Ibid.
[20] State of Tennessee, Chapter 452 of 1977.
[21] State of Alabama, Act No. 512 of 1976.

also noted that federal regulations of interstate transportation of animals require enforcement by licensed veterinarians.[22]

While the Utah legislative audit staff may, in fact, be right in recommending continuation of veterinary licensing, it has made no quantitative attempt to estimate and compare the expected harm from alternatives to licensing with the costs to the public under existing licensing legislation.

Even if such a comparison were made, however, it is not clear what measures of cost would be employed. The Utah auditor general's report on veterinary licensing and, for that matter, his report on every licensing board reviewed calculates the cost of regulating professions solely in terms of administrative resources forsaken.[23] These, of course, are only the direct costs of regulation. An examination of sunset reviews for Alabama, New Mexico, Florida, North Carolina, and Tennessee revealed similar deficiencies in the application of the opportunity cost concept to estimating the cost of regulation in occupational licensing.[24] Indirect costs (i.e., the welfare losses from cartelization), are systematically ignored. This suggests that, since the great majority of consumer benefits claimed for occupational licensing are often direct and much of the cost of such licensing indirect, most sunset evaluations will be biased toward nontermination. Moreover, the licensing boards that are recommended for termination are more likely to have been regulating occupations associated with smaller welfare losses than other licensing boards. For example, assume that a given state's legislature has chosen licensing boards A and B for sunset evaluation. Assume also that the total social costs of licensing these occupations are $10 million and $20 million respectively and that the social benefits from licensing are $5 million and $10 million respectively. Other things being equal, a cost/benefit test would condemn both boards to termination. The sunset review staff of this state, however, ignores the indirect cost component of regulation; that is, it ignores the welfare losses that arise from limiting competition in professional services. These indirect costs, however, are not uniform across licensed occupations, nor are they a uniform function of the total social costs across occupations. In the present example, assume that the direct cost of regulation is 60 percent of the total social costs in occupation A and only 45 percent of total costs in occupation B. Assume further that there are no indirect benefits of licensing in

[22] "A Performance Audit of Licensing in Utah," Salt Lake City, Office of the Legislative Auditor General, February 1978.

[23] Ibid.

[24] Noteworthy is Oregon's attention to indirect costs. See, for example, *Legislative Staff Sunset Review, State Board of Auctioneers*, prepared pursuant to Chapter 842, Oregon Laws 1977 (Oregon Legislative Assembly, April 1978, pp. 27–28.)

either occupation. In this case, the sunset staff will recommend termination of licensing board A but not of licensing board B. Only in the latter case do the direct benefits exceed the direct costs.

It is likely that differences in the direct costs of licensing different occupations will be smaller than differences in the indirect costs. Therefore, licensed occupations generating relatively larger welfare losses will be the least likely to be affected by sunset legislation, even in the absence of vigorous lobbying on their behalf. This proposition appears to be consistent with the evidence presented earlier. The 1977–1978 experience revealed that boards regulating watchmakers, polygraphers, escort agencies, photography studios, and the like were terminated. Licensing in these occupations, relative to that for barbers, morticians, podiatrists, veterinarians, and harbor pilots, is more likely to be associated with "low" indirect costs. Future sunset reviews will deal with law, medicine, accounting, architecture, optometry, dentistry, and other occupations with relatively large indirect components to their regulatory costs.[25] It is therefore doubtful that sunset legislation will have a significant effect on occupational licensing. Perhaps the most significant modification that may be imposed on licensing boards with any monopoly power will involve the addition of nonprofessional members representing "the public." This recommendation appears in a large number of sunset reviews from the thirteen sunset states for which staff reports were available as of February 1979.

No matter what recommendations are submitted to the respective legislatures, however, the effect of sunset laws will turn on the way legislators vote. As we have seen from table 1, sunset staff recommendations are not uniformly adopted by state legislatures. Invariably, legislators terminated or modified fewer boards than their staffs recommended.

Put another way, legislators chose to continue or re-create licensing boards, unaltered, more often than staff reports found such continuation warranted. This result should not be surprising. To the extent that terminations and modifications have a significant impact on licensees, we should expect the licensees to devote resources to persuading legislators against these actions. If terminations and wealth-reducing modifications are made more costly to legislators, the legislators will tend to vote for

---

[25] These professions have been examined by some economists and found to have significant indirect effects. See, for example, Reuben Kessel, "Price Discrimination in Medicine," *Journal of Law and Economics* (October 1958); Lawrence Shepard, "Licensing Restrictions and the Cost of Dental Care," *Journal of Law and Economics*, vol. 21, no. 1 (April 1978); and Lee Benham, "The Effect of Advertising on the Price of Eyeglasses," *Journal of Law and Economics*, vol. 15, no. 2 (October 1972).

re-creating these licensing boards unaltered.[26] As mentioned earlier, telephone conversations with the audit directors of several sunset states and reports from Common Cause[27] confirm that occupational lobbying has been important in persuading legislators to ignore staff recommendations where they have threatened the survival or prosperity of occupations subject to licensing.

This is not to suggest, however, that legislators are the captives of licensed occupations. Legislators have constituencies that include the consumers of licensed services. Occupational licensing that results in the extraction of *maximum* consumer surplus by licensees may cost some legislators significant numbers of votes or even their jobs.[28] Occupational lobbying is thus not the only source of rewards or opportunity costs faced by legislators. One benefit of sunset legislation may be the information it generates about the voting records of legislators faced with decisions to terminate, modify, or re-create occupational licensing boards. Legislators who support stronger licensing laws or modifications that favor licensees, at the expense of consumer-voters, will be more exposed to the latter under sunset legislation. This should slow the progress of monopolistic occupational licensing.

Periodic termination has been adopted in all but four sunset states. Its intended effect is to force government into an ongoing evaluation effort, thus lowering the probability that licensing boards—and other agencies and programs—will outlive a defensible reason for their existence. To the legislator, however, periodic termination may appear a convenient means for procrastination. If program terminations are politically unpopular with lobbying groups, legislators may vote for continuance under the guise of monitoring board performance until the next termination review (usually six years). So long as termination is possible next time, consumer-voters may accept this as a reasonable response to a weighty question. The legislator will have managed to finesse the difficult situation that would have arisen had his state failed to adopt periodic termination. Of the four states that failed to adopt periodic termination, only one, South Dakota, has provided data on both sunset recommendations and legislative action. Although examination of these data does not constitute a test, it is instructive that only South Dakota of all twenty-nine states has terminated the number of

---

[26] Although consumer lobbies are now active in urging change, the intensity of their effort is not expected to be particularly sensitive to variations in the efforts of occupational lobbying groups.

[27] See Common Cause, *Making Government Work*.

[28] See Peltzman, "Toward a More General Theory," for this modification of the capture theory of regulation.

licensing boards its staff has recommended in the 1977–1978 cycle. The other states have terminated fewer than the number recommended (see table 1).

Conclusions

Although more than two-thirds of state licensing boards have yet to be subjected to sunset review in the twenty-nine sunset states, the outcome has already been determined. Poorly defined and often irrelevant review criteria, together with strong occupational lobbying and periodic sunset evaluations, will all work to maintain the status quo in occupational licensing for most occupations now subject to, and benefiting from, regulation by licensing.

Commentary

Mark F. Grady

The principal papers conclude that neither the Federal Trade Commission nor the states have made very much progress in reforming occupational regulation. The natural question is who has a comparative advantage at reform. It makes sense to distinguish two types of occupational reform, reform of "entry restrictions" and reform of "practice restrictions." Entry restrictions limit who may engage in a particular occupation (for instance by establishing minimum educational or knowledge qualifications). Practice restrictions limit how business may be done in an occupation (for instance by prohibiting competitive bidding and advertising or by limiting where firms can locate—in some states opticians have been forbidden to practice in a building occupied by optometrists). My view is that the states often have a comparative advantage in reforming entry restrictions while the FTC may do well to continue to concentrate on practice restrictions. I have three kinds of reasons for this opinion: institutional, political, and legal.

From an institutional point of view, Martin points out that state legislatures in conducting sunset evaluations frequently do not have enough economic expertise to assess all the indirect costs of occupational regulation. While both entry restrictions and practice restrictions raise significant economic issues, frequently the problems with practice restrictions are more subtle. For example, the commonplace view has sometimes been that advertising increases prices by adding overhead cost. Under this view, it follows that a prohibition of advertising should reduce prices. Of course, economists have generally found the opposite: that advertising actually reduces prices. Building a convincing case that practice restrictions harm consumers often requires a good deal of economic expertise, especially when practitioners have built their case for the restriction on commonplace, but inaccurate, notions of how the market works. Because the FTC can draw upon its well-staffed Bureau of Economics and Office of Policy Planning, it could easily have an advantage over the states in undertaking this kind of reform.

On the other hand, the FTC may have no institutional advantage in reforming entry restrictions. The economic issues raised by these restrictions tend to be fundamental—such as, for example, whether the government should prevent consumers from purchasing inferior goods and services. While it is certainly important for economists to assess costs, most observers are likely to see reform of entry restrictions as an issue extending beyond economics into areas of public health and safety. Because the FTC has no greater expertise than the states in health and safety matters, it does not have the same advantage in dealing with entry restrictions as with practice restrictions.

Reforming entry restrictions can also lead the FTC onto new and uncertain ground. While practice restrictions can be reformed simply by eliminating them, the most persuasive kind of reform of entry restrictions frequently involves imposing different, less anticompetitive regulation—as in substituting state certification of practitioners for state licensing. Implementing this kind of remedy would thrust the commission into new regulatory areas where it has no particular experience. In addition, as Clarkson and Muris argue, the commission's substitute regulation may be no better than the old state regulation that it would replace.

From a political point of view, the commission conserves good will by tackling problems within its own traditional sphere. Because practice restrictions often look like private restraints of trade that the commission has previously prosecuted, the FTC might expect to encounter less political resistance in this area than in reforming entry restrictions— which practically epitomize the state police power.

Both papers indicate that any occupational reform attempt encounters political resistance from practitioners who stand to lose. The issue for reform is where the resistance is likely to be less. On the state level, reformers must make the case many times, but opponents must also oppose it many times. Reformers may gain more than they lose by balkanizing the resistance. In opposing occupational reform, a legislator may trade votes for contributions. Under one view, reformers will try to increase the vote loss by publicizing the undesirable consumer welfare effects of occupational regulation, while opponents will try to increase the contribution loss by offers to legislators. If this rather simple view approaches reality, pursuing reform on the state level may favor reformers who can publicize the issue nationally to voters or use the same studies in each state and may tend to disfavor opponents who must transact with the members of fifty legislatures rather than the smaller number of persons in Congress.

From a legal point of view, Clarkson and Muris say correctly that there is no express impediment to the FTC's striking down state-created entry restrictions. The courts have held that the commission has the power to preempt in other areas, and there are good arguments that the *Parker* v. *Brown* doctrine should not apply as strictly to the FTC as to private actions under the Sherman Act. But *Parker* seems to be based partly on ideas of federalism—that the states should have some power to protect their regulation from attack under federal law. To take an extreme example, if the FTC were ever to determine that state laws licensing physicians are repugnant to the Federal Trade Commission Act, a federal court decision upholding this action would by implication give the FTC the power to second-guess the reasonableness of virtually all state law. This is because Congress has imposed few subject-matter restrictions on the FTC and because the courts have imposed few doctrinal limitations on what the commission can say is unlawful. While the Supreme Court has said that Congress has a comprehensive power to strike down state law in the name of regulating commerce, it could easily recoil from giving a commission majority the same power. Of course, just how the courts might fashion a distinction between FTC action preempting practice restrictions and FTC action preempting entry restrictions is extremely problematic. Again, Clarkson and Muris are correct that no distinction currently exists. If pressed, however, the courts might create such a distinction, if not in exactly these terms.

To conclude, I think that Martin might be unduly pessimistic about the states as reformers of occupational regulation. I found his results more encouraging than he. Clarkson and Muris may underestimate the problems that the FTC would encounter with some reform, particularly the elimination of entry restrictions. I should also say, however, that I agree with Clarkson and Muris that the FTC has a great deal more potential than it is now using and that when entry restrictions merge into practice restrictions (as when a state has forbidden licensed denture manufacturers from dealing directly with consumers), I would favor investigation, as I think they would.

Benjamin Shimberg

Clarkson and Muris have given us some useful insights about the FTC, pointing out in particular the schizophrenia that exists within that agency. I think the authors are on target when they suggest that FTC intervention, even if successful, would probably not lead to deregulation, but instead to more regulation. Regulation of certain aspects of an occupation might be relaxed, but it would almost certainly be replaced by other forms of regulation.

Regulation of trade practices seems to be the FTC's stock in trade, as Mr. Grady indicated. If we look at the rules promulgated in con-

nection with the funeral industry, we see heavy emphasis on trade practices. We also know about the regulation of advertising claims. Certainly
in the case of trade schools, the FTC has clearly indicated that it has
some reservations about a freely operating marketplace. In short, here
is an agency that has always shown a profound distrust of the marketplace. It seems convinced that the man and woman in the street need
protection against predators. It is hard to believe that this same agency
is now going to say, "Get rid of all this licensing of occupations. Let
the free market operate. Give the consumer access to facts, and he will
be able to sort out conflicting claims and make wise choices." It is just
not in character.

The authors' discussion of the role of Congress left me somewhat
perplexed. They emphasized its inability to monitor or control FTC
programs. This observation should surprise no one who has watched
either state or federal administrative agencies. We know that they take
on a life of their own. They defy efforts by their creators to influence
programs or to set priorities. So, while the analysis seemed sound and
persuasive, I was not sure whether the authors were expressing pleasure
or regret that Congress could not step in to put an end to the commission's involvement in occupational regulation. At times I sensed they
felt that Congress ought to stop this nonsense but that it could not.

They mentioned, for example, that despite hostile testimony by
representatives of the National Funeral Directors' Association before
sympathetic congressmen, the agency nevertheless went ahead with
promulgating tough rules for the funeral industry. In other words, the
hearings had relatively little impact on the commission: the commission
did largely as it pleased. Were the authors suggesting that the agency
should have backed off just because the funeral industry did not like
the proposed rules and had managed to get some friendly congressmen
to give them a forum in which to express their objections?

Clarkson and Muris's paper also refer to some congressmen's objections to an investigation of the funeral industry in the first place.
Evidently the agency admitted having received fewer than a dozen complaints from consumers. The congressmen believed that responding to
such a small number of complaints reflected misplaced priorities. My
own view is that the number of complaints received is *not* a dependable
criterion for deciding whether to launch an investigation. The FTC
report on the funeral industry, as well as other reports I have seen,
clearly suggests that there are indeed serious problems in that industry.
The message that I get from the FTC report is that if the states do not
"clean up their own acts," the FTC will use its powers to clean them
up.

This brings us to the role of the courts. The authors suggest that the courts may be taking a tougher stance on rule making by government agencies by requiring agencies to back their determinations of need with supporting evidence and perhaps even by requiring some type of cost/benefit analysis. Such requirements, they suggest, might curb rule making by overzealous bureaucrats so determined to pursue preconceived ideas that they will not be deterred by facts indicating that the proposed remedy might, in some cases, have unintended side effects that could be worse than the original malady.

Perhaps the most important issue raised in the paper is that of preemption. In their legal analysis—especially in their discussion of *Parker* v. *Brown*—the authors suggest that the preemption doctrine is not likely to survive a legal challenge in the courts. That is why I was somewhat surprised to find in their conclusion the following: "if [the courts] conclude that the commission can preempt, they are unlikely to oppose a deregulatory occupational licensure program and more likely to constrain new regulation." So I am not sure what the authors think. Will preemption stand or will it fall? No one really knows what the courts are going to do. Yet clearly the resolution of that issue lies at the heart of the whole FTC program.

I would like to make a few general observations about the paper's conclusions. The authors seem to be saying that they have serious reservations about the FTC foray into occupational licensing. It is not in keeping with the traditions of the agency, they say, which has always had a regulatory rather than a deregulatory thrust. They also seem to believe the program is essentially unproductive. They mention that many hundreds of thousands of dollars have been spent with little to show for the expenditure. There has been very little in the way of actual deregulation—an important matter if one assumes that deregulation was, indeed, the main purpose of the FTC activities.

It is on this point that I would like to disagree most strongly. It is regrettable that the authors limited their analysis to the agency, Congress, and the courts. They seem to have overlooked the fact that licensing is essentially a state matter. They failed to ask, What impact, if any, has the FTC occupational program had on the states? My own view is that the program has had a great deal to do with regulatory reform efforts now under way in many states.

Before the chairmanship of Lewis Engman and the support that he gave to the occupational regulatory program, there was little interest or concern about occupational licensing. Most state legislators viewed it as a form of consumer protection. They saw licensing as a method of screening out unqualified practitioners, ensuring continued competence, and providing redress against incompetent or dishonest practitioners.

If you will forgive a personal reference, I would like to mention that in the early 1970s I conducted a number of studies of occupational licensing under a grant from the Employment and Training Administration of the Department of Labor. I wrote a book calling attention to many of the abuses that have since become fairly widely known.[1] I wish I could say that the book produced controversy and motivated people to initiate needed reforms. But in actuality it had little impact. No one got excited about my findings. No one rushed forth to implement the reforms I suggested were needed.

Then along came Lewis Engman. The fact that he held a high federal office gave him instant visibility. The fact that he spoke about FTC studies, worked on by the Bureau of Economics, gave whatever he said considerable credibility. His statements and allegations about the anticompetitive aspects of licensing made news. And he made people aware that some boards were using their powers to prohibit advertising and competitive bidding and that such restrictions were not in the public interest. He charged that boards were restricting entry and limiting mobility and that the restrictions had implications for the availability, the quality, and the cost of services to consumers. It was Engman more than any other person who stimulated consumer and public interest groups to take an interest in occupational licensure. These groups began to see licensure as a pocketbook issue.

In time, these concerns began to be felt at the state legislative level, as well. In two states, Minnesota and Virginia, legislators have established procedures and criteria that make it much more difficult for new groups to become licensed. These procedures and criteria are working. They are tough, and they are cutting down greatly on new licensure.

Professor Martin points out that twenty-nine states have passed sunset laws, which set specific dates for terminating certain state agencies. If the agency is not given a new lease on life, it goes out of existence. A number of other states have passed laws without automatic termination dates. But the legislature still determines which agencies are to be reviewed and which ones will be terminated.

It is no accident that, in nearly every state, sunset laws have focused on occupational regulation agencies as their initial targets. Frankly, I do not expect sunset to result in the wholesale abolition of regulatory boards. The groups that benefit from regulation have an enormous stake in preserving the status quo. They are willing to spend a lot of time, money, and effort in lobbying. In the face of very poorly organized consumer groups, it is safe to predict that lobbying by regulated groups is likely to be successful in warding off efforts to terminate the laws under which they operate.

---

[1] Benjamin Shimberg et al., *Occupational Licensing: Practices and Policies* (Washington, D.C.: Public Affairs Press, 1972).

In the end, a few boards will be abolished, a few will be consolidated, most will remain in business. But in some states, at least, it may not be "business as usual."

During the past eighteen months, I have had the opportunity to meet with legislators in at least a dozen states. These lawmakers are questioning the need for as much regulation as they have. They realize that the occupational group, rather than the public, is often the primary beneficiary of licensing. They recognize that many of the abuses in licensing are the result of boards' having too much autonomy. They see a lack of adequate accountability and of checks and balances. These regulatory system shortcomings are just beginning to dawn on legislators. Until recently they have not paid much attention to boards. They now realize that some boards have gone off and done pretty much as they pleased with little or no legislative oversight.

Legislators are also hearing more and more about the unresponsiveness of certain boards to complaints from consumers. They are hearing that some boards appear to be unwilling to investigate complaints vigorously and to take real disciplinary action against licensees who are incompetent, negligent, or just plain crooks. These concerns may not bring about deregulation, but they could eventually lead to structural reforms.

I realize that I may be giving Mr. Engman and the FTC too much credit for the movement toward regulatory reform, but I fear that the authors have not given either sufficient credit. Even if the preemption doctrine is struck down, even if no new rules are promulgated, even if the FTC decides to get completely out of occupational regulation, I think the program itself will have had a significant impact. The climate of public opinion toward occupational regulation has changed during the past decade, and it is my contention that the FTC has played a major role in bringing about that change. Whether that is what the FTC had in mind when it started I am not sure. Nor am I sure that it really matters. The fact remains that the program has played an important role in laying the groundwork for regulatory reform.

I sometimes wonder if Mr. Engman was not using both his position as chairman and the doctrine of preemption as a way of educating the public on the need for change. Maybe he felt all along that the threat of federal intervention would stimulate the states to take corrective action on their own. Maybe he had more faith in the marketplace than I have given him credit for having. Maybe he believed that, given the facts, the people would act in their own best interests to bring occupational regulation under greater social control. If that was his purpose, I would say he has succeeded far beyond his own expectations.

Part
Four

The Effect of Occupational Licensure on Black Occupational Attainment

Richard B. Freeman

It is well known that occupational licensing and related requirements for entry into an occupation can reduce the number of workers and raise earnings in a field[1] and reduce the rate of mobility across areas.[2] Licensing laws can also affect the employment opportunities of disadvantaged groups either directly (as a result of discriminatory application of the laws) or indirectly and even inadvertently (as a byproduct of the lower level of education and scores of the group on licensure exams).

This paper examines the impact of licensure laws on the proportion of workers in a given occupation who are black, the examination being carried on in two distinct settings. The first setting is the U.S. South in the period from the 1890s to 1960, during which white-dominated southern states often enacted or applied licensure laws discriminatorily. In this situation one would expect licensure to reduce the proportion of members of occupations who were black. The second setting is the United States in 1960, when discriminatory application of the law was less frequent and licensing exams and procedures likely to be at least "facially" fair. In this situation one would expect licensure to have more complex effects on black representation depending on the nature of the licensing requirements and the education and training of the black population.

Empirical analysis finds, as expected, that in the period of severe discrimination occupational licensure tended to reduce black representation in various craft occupations, though not by enormous magnitudes. While not a major element in economic discrimination in the United States, licensure laws were one of a set of policies by which discriminatory state governments reduced black employment opportunities.

Empirical analysis finds a different picture for licensure and black occupational attainment in recent years. While blacks have lower rates

[1] Simon Rottenberg, "The Economics of Occupational Licensing," in H. G. Lewis, ed., *Aspects of Labor Economics* (New York: National Bureau of Economic Research).

[2] Peter Pashigian, "Occupational Licensing and the Interstate Mobility of Professionals," *Journal of Law and Economics*, vol. 22 (April 1979), pp. 1–25.

of passing some licensure examination than whites and may be adversely affected by licensure in other ways, overall they are as equally represented in occupations that are licensed as in those that are not. The implication is that licensing laws were a barrier to black economic advance during the period when licensure was explicitly for discriminatory purposes but are now a barrier in only a limited set of occupations when licensure is not a tool of discrimination.

Occupational Licensure and Black Employment in the Discriminatory South

From the 1890s through the 1950s, black Americans were effectively disfranchised in most states in the U.S. South. As a result, southern state governments operated to benefit white citizens at the expense of blacks, adopting diverse policies designed to redistribute economic opportunities and income toward whites.[3]

Given white control of licensing boards, occupational licensure laws were a potential tool for reducing black employment in various "desirable" craft jobs. Either by setting licensure standards that required more formal schooling than most blacks attained or by discriminatory application of licensure standards, white-dominated boards could reduce black competition and raise the wages of white craftsmen.

White-dominated craft unions—such as the plumbers, electricians, and railroad firemen—explicitly advocated licensure laws for the purpose of disqualifying black competitors. According to Greene and Woodson, a "favorite method of barring them [for example, blacks] from plumbing and electrical work was to install a system of unfair examinations which were conducted by whites."[4] Spero and Harris report that plumbers' licensure was favored in Virginia so that blacks could be "entirely eliminated" from the craft.[5] In the *Locomotive and Firemen and Engineermen's Magazine*, licensure of locomotive firemen in Georgia was supported on the grounds that "if the act is sound and becomes a law it is expected to have the effect of reducing to a minimum the number of Negro firemen eligible to fill that position on locomotives in the state of Georgia."

Even in the northern states, white-dominated licensing boards were reported to discriminate against blacks: "in a city like Philadelphia, the licensing board will not grant a Negro a license—in Chicago the Negro

---

[3] See Richard B. Freeman, "The U.S. Discriminatory System" (unpublished manuscript).

[4] Lorenzo J. Greene and Carter G. Woodson, *The Negro Wage Force* (New York: Russell & Russell, 1969), p. 192.

[5] Sterling D. Spero and Abram L. Harris, *The Black Worker* (New York: Atheneum, 1968), pp. 59, 478.

plumbers have failed to gain advances after years of effort."[6] While specific cases do not of course "prove" that licensing reduced black representation in crafts, they provide sufficient basis to justify more rigorous analysis of the effect of licensure laws on black employment in the era of severe discrimination in the U.S. South.

Econometric Analysis. To examine the effect of occupational licensure laws on black occupational attainment between 1890 and 1960, information was gathered from decennial censuses of population on employment by race in seventeen crafts in seven southern states.[7] For comparative purposes, similar information was also gathered for four nonsouthern states.[8] Additional data on presence of laws and diverse "control" variables were also obtained (see data appendix). The various sets of data were pooled into time-series/cross-section samples, which provide information on the effect of licensure laws by comparisons over time and across crafts at a specified time.

The dependent variable in the analysis is the relative penetration of blacks in a craft in a state in a given time period—RP_{ijt}—with relative penetration defined as the fraction of workers in the craft who are black divided by the fraction of workers in the state who are black. The subscript i indexes the craft, the subscript j indexes the state, and the subscript t indexes the time period.

The principal independent variable is a licensure dummy variable—L_{ijt}—which takes on the value one when a craft is licensed in a state in a given year and the value zero otherwise.[9] Because of the inadequacies in the basic data, the licensing variable is subject to potential error, which may bias its coefficient downward.[10]

Table 1 shows the pattern of licensing of craft occupations over time in the seven southern states. The data show that licensure was

---

[6] Spero and Harris, *Black Worker*, p. 68.

[7] The workers represented are barbers, bakers, blacksmiths, carpenters, compositors, electricians, foremen and overseers, machinists, masons, mechanics, molders, painters, plasterers and cement finishers, plumbers, shoemakers, tailors, and locomotive engineers and firemen. The states covered are Alabama, Georgia, Louisiana, North Carolina, South Carolina, Tennessee, and Virginia.

[8] The states covered are New York, Ohio, Illinois, and Pennsylvania.

[9] Information on this variable was obtained from Council of State Governments, *Occupational Licensing Legislation in the States* (Chicago, 1952); U.S. Department of Labor, Bureau of Labor Statistics, *Labor Laws of the United States* (Washington, D.C., 1896, 1908, and 1925); and other sources.

[10] There are several problems with the data. First, different sources give different information about licensing. Second, state laws differ in applicability, some requiring licensing in cities above a certain size and others permitting cities to license occupations. Third, it is difficult to determine from available published sources when occupational licensing laws were effectively dropped.

167

TABLE 1

CRAFT AND YEAR LICENSED IN SEVEN SOUTHERN STATES

State	Barbers	Plumbers	Electricians	Locomotive Engineers
Alabama	—	1935	—	1887
Georgia	1914	—	—	—
Louisiana	1928	1902	1925[a]	—
North Carolina	1929	1931	—	—
South Carolina	1937	1914	—	—
Tennessee	1929	1925	1925	—
Virginia	1910	1904	—	—

[a] Approximate because of data limitations.
SOURCE: See data appendix.

concentrated in barbering, where blacks predominated, and in plumbing. North Carolina and Tennessee licensed three of the crafts considered while Georgia licensed only one.

Additional variables used as controls in the calculations are as follows:

1. The proportion of workers in the craft employed by the government. Employment by the government is expected to reduce black representation in an occupation because white-dominated governments are more likely to be discriminatory than private employers. For the years 1940 through 1960, the proportion is based on census data for the specific years. For the years 1890 through 1930, the 1940 census figures are used.

2. The proportion of workers in a craft who are self-employed. Self-employment is expected to increase black representation because self-employed persons can avoid "employer" discrimination. For the years 1940 through 1960, the proportion is based on census data for the specified year; for the years 1890 through 1930, the 1940 census figures are used.

3. The level of education in the craft, with a high level expected to reduce black representation. For the years 1940 through 1960, the level of education is measured by the median years of schooling of all workers in the craft; for the years 1890 through 1930, the 1940 census figures are used.

4. The ratio of the median years of schooling of blacks in the state to median years of schooling of whites. A higher ratio should raise black representation, particularly in crafts with higher median years of schooling. For the years 1940 through 1960, ratios of education are measured

by the median years reported for each state in the census of population; for the years 1890 through 1930, cross-section data on education by age from the 1950 census were used to estimate the median years of the two groups, as described in the data appendix.

5. The proportion of workers in the craft unionized. A higher proportion is expected to reduce black representation in crafts where whites can reasonably be expected to control entry but not in crafts where unions could not organize the market without admitting black workers.[11] This variable is obtained from diverse figures, as described in the data appendix.[12]

To evaluate the effect of licensure laws, variants of the following basic regression were estimated:

$$RP_{ijt} = \alpha X_{ijt} + bL_{ijt} + cS_j + dZ_t + \mu_{ijt} \qquad (1)$$

where X_{ijt} = value of explanatory variable X_{ij} in year t

S_j = dummy variable for state j

Z_t = dummy variable for year t

μ_{ijt} = residual

State and year dummy variables are entered in the regression as controls for otherwise unmeasured state or year effects. With these controls the analysis focuses on the position of blacks in crafts in a given state and year.

The resulting estimates are presented in table 2. Column 1 deals with the seven southern states while column 2 treats the comparison group of four nonsouthern states.

The regressions show that in the discriminatory South licensure laws reduced the relative employment of blacks by a significant and sizable amount but that comparable laws in the nonsouthern states had little or no impact on the relative penetration of blacks into the crafts. Crafts licensed in the South have relative penetration ratios 33 percentage points lower than crafts not licensed. By contrast, in the nonsouthern states, crafts that are licensed have a penetration ratio an insignificant 4 points lower than crafts not licensed.

Let us look briefly at the other variables. The percentage of workers employed by the government reduces black representation in both the southern and nonsouthern samples, while the percentage self-employed

---

[11] The hypothesis is that in crafts that have relatively many blacks before union organization drives, unionization requires nondiscriminatory admission policies because discrimination will hamper successful organization.

[12] Lack of data on unionization by craft within states dictated the use of the craft unionization figures rather than the more desirable figures for crafts within states.

TABLE 2

EFFECT OF LICENSURE LAW ON PROPORTION OF WORKERS WHO ARE BLACK IN SEVENTEEN CRAFTS, 1890–1960: REGRESSION COEFFICIENTS AND STANDARD ERRORS FOR EQUATIONS

Explanatory Variable	Southern States	Nonsouthern States
Licensure law	−0.33(.07)	−0.04(.17)
Percentage employed by government	−0.02(.006)	−0.02(.01)
Percentage self-employed	0.01(.001)	0.01(.003)
Percentage unionized	0.36(.11)	0.01(.26)
Log of median years of education in craft	−1.92(.22)	−0.75(.53)
Log of ratio of nonwhite to white years of schooling in state	−0.33(.26)	−0.17(.46)
Percentage black in state	0.37(.38)	0.15(.43)
State dummies	6	3
Year dummies	7	7
R^2	0.37	0.12
Number of observations	952	544

SOURCE: Calculated from data described in data appendix.

raises representation in both. Surprisingly, the percentage unionized has a positive impact on black employment, largely because, for some crafts (such as masons), where blacks tended to predominate before unionization, successful unionism required admission of blacks and partly because of the inability of some unions to restrict entry. On the other hand, the higher the median years of schooling in a craft, the lower is black representation. Finally, relative amounts of schooling appear to have little relation to black craft employment, though additional experiments (not reported in the table) show relative schooling to affect black employment in crafts with high levels of education.

While by no means definitive, the computations in table 2 suggest that, during the period of black disfranchisement in the South, occupational licensure was a reasonably successful tool for reducing black employment in craft jobs, roughly as intended by many of its proponents. Other factors—such as educational attainment, government employment, and so on—were, however, also important determinants of black representation.

Effects of Licensure in 1970

Is occupational licensure a barrier to black advancement in the 1970s, despite the reduced discrimination and increased antibias activities?

To the extent that the negative effect of licensure on black employment in crafts found in table 2 represents discriminatory application of licensing exams, one would expect the effect to be greatly muted in the 1970s. Indeed, because licenses represent a credential guaranteeing a level of knowledge, it is even possible that groups discriminated against might prefer licensed to nonlicensed fields: discrimination based on unfounded views about competence would be reduced if one had the appropriate credential.

On the other hand, to the extent that the negative effect of licensure on black representation in crafts represents problems in passing "facially fair" licensing examinations (as a result of lower educational attainment and poor quality of schooling), blacks could be expected to be underrepresented in licensed occupations. Which forces predominate will differ among fields depending on the nature of licensing and the occupation.

This section analyzes the relation between licensure and black employment in occupations in the 1970s in three ways: (1) by examining rates of passing certain licensure exams; (2) by regression analyses linking the proportion of workers who are black in various occupations in the United States as a whole to measures of licensure; and (3) by regression analyses linking the proportion of workers who are black to the presence or absence of licensure in the various states.

Passing Rates. Limited evidence on the proportion of persons passing licensing exams for some high-level professions suggests that in these occupations licensure remains a barrier to black occupational attainment. As table 3 shows, blacks appear to have greater problems in passing the exams for the legal profession than whites.

Information on the rate of success of black and white applicants for teaching jobs in the New York City schools shows a similar pattern for those taking the state's exams. In New York the Board of Examiners of the state designs examinations and determines required pass/fail scores for certification. The state law requires that appointment of teachers be based on rank on the examination, with some exceptions for affirmative action purposes. As the data in table 4 show, black applicants have passed the New York exams at a lower rate than white applicants, creating significant racial disparity in the New York City school system.

While persons may retake exams or, in the case of the schoolteachers in New York City, qualify through a different examination (the National Teachers' Exam) or procedure, the net effect of the lower pass rates should be to reduce black representation in the fields considered.

171

TABLE 3

PERCENTAGE OF LAW SCHOOL GRADUATES PASSING BAR EXAM

State and Year of Data for Minority	Black or Minority	White[a]
Alabama, 1968–1973	32	76
California, 1975	28	61
Colorado, 1972–1973	43	76
Washington, D.C., 1973	8	66
Georgia, 1971	0	50
Illinois, 1972–1973	25	81
Indiana, 1972–1973	23	84
Maryland, 1970–1972	25	58
Missouri, 1972	25	71
New Jersey, 1970–1974	61	80
Ohio, 1972	62	86
Pennsylvania, post-1970	60	90
Rhode Island	35	74
Virginia	20	73

[a] 1972–1975 except for Georgia (1971) and Pennsylvania (post-1970).
SOURCE: Symposium on "The Minority Candidate and the Bar Examination," delivered at University of California at Los Angeles School of Law, May 1, 1976, Keynote Introduction by Lennox S. Hinds.
Third World Coalition for Justice in the Legal System, *4 Point Plan for the California Bar Examinations,* pp. 2, 3.

Though "facially" fair, at least some licensure procedures appear to lower black employment in selected fields.[13]

Occupational Employment in the United States. To examine the effect of licensure of occupations on black occupational attainment in the United States as a whole, I obtained from the 1970 census of population data on the proportion of workers who were black, the percentage employed by the government, the percentage self-employed, and median years of education in an occupation. The principal measure of the extent of occupational licensure is the number of states that license each occupation, as reported by the U.S. Department of Labor. If licensing reduces black representation in an occupation, the number of states

---

[13] Courts have upheld the constitutionality of bar examinations despite disproportionate failure rates of minority applicants. See, for example, Aluin, Dwightment Pettit et al. v. Vincent C. Gingerich, Chairman, et al., Civ. No. B-72-964. U.S. District Court D., Maryland, February 22, 1977. For a valuable discussion of the problem of minority candidates and the bar examination, see the symposium "The Minority Candidate and the Bar Examination, University of California at Los Angeles, School of Law, May 1, 1976.

TABLE 4

RACIAL IMPACT OF REGULAR NEW YORK TEACHER LICENSING
EXAMS ON PASS RATES

Name of Exam	Percentage of Blacks Who Passed	Percentage of Whites Who Passed
Early childhood	33	82
Cannon branches	35	65
Social studies, junior high school	14	47
Math, junior high school	75	47
English, junior high school	57	59
Social studies, DHS	4	38
Math, DHS	30	50
English, DHS	46	61

NOTE: Unweighted average of percentages on tests taken on two or three different dates.
SOURCE: U.S. Department of Health, Education and Welfare, Office of the Secretary, letters to New York schools chancellor Irving Anker, November 9, 1976.

TABLE 5

REGRESSION COEFFICIENTS AND STANDARD ERRORS OF THE EFFECT
OF LICENSURE ON BLACK REPRESENTATION IN OCCUPATIONS, 1970

	Male	Female
	(1)	(2)
Constant	15.2	18.0
Number of states licensing occupation	−0.01(.24)	−0.01(.28)
Percentage in government employment in occupation	0.00(.02)	0.03(.03)
Percentage self-employed in occupation	−0.12(.03)	−0.07(.05)
Median years of schooling in occupation	−0.49(.17)	−0.63(.24)
R^2	0.09	0.06
Number of occupations	173	173

SOURCE: Licensure data: U.S. Department of Labor, Manpower Administration, *Occupational Licensing and the Supply of Nonprofessional Manpower*, Manpower Research Monograph no. 11, 1969.
Employment data: U.S. Bureau of the Census, *Census of Population 1970*, Detailed Characteristics.

with such provisions should be negatively related to the proportion of workers who are black.

The regressions in table 5 show essentially no relation between numbers of states with licensing laws and black representation in crafts.

The calculations show that, for both men and women, the licensure variable obtains a negative but insignificant coefficient. From these calculations, licensure does not appear to be a major factor in black occupational attainment. Of the other variables, the percentage of workers government-employed and the percentage self-employed have negligible or oppositely signed coefficients from those obtained in table 2, presumably as a result of equal opportunity and affirmative action policies after the passage of the Civil Rights Act of 1964 and the Voting Rights Act of 1965.

There are three possible reasons for the fact that licensure (as measured in the table) and black occupational attainment do not seem to be related: (1) In some occupations, blacks could be deterred from employment in states where the occupations are licensed and overrepresented in states where they are not (this possibility is examined and rejected below). (2) Blacks could be working in the licensed occupation without the license, either because nonlicensed personnel are legally permitted to work, as in architecture or engineering, or because they are evading the law. (3) Blacks might be managing to obtain licenses as frequently as whites in relation to their education and numerical representation, in contrast to the situation in the fields in tables 3 and 4. While we lack sufficient quantitative data to differentiate between the second and third possibilities, discussion with knowledgeable persons suggests that it is not uncommon for blacks lacking licenses to work in licensed occupations in inner cities.

Cross-State Analyses. An alternative way of analyzing the effect of licensure on black occupational attainment is to take the proportion of black workers to the total workers in that occupation in the state and relate it as to whether that occupation is licensed in that state. Regressions of this type, by controlling for the characteristics of occupations, provide estimates of the effect of licensure on employment within an occupation. The regression equation estimated is:

$$P_{ij} = a + bP_j + c\ Educ_j + dL_{ij} + U_{ij} \tag{2}$$

where

$$
\begin{aligned}
P_{ij} &= \text{proportion of workers who are black in craft } i \text{ in state } j \\
P_j &= \text{proportion of workers who are black in state } j \\
Educ_j &= \text{ratio of proportion of blacks who are high school graduates} \\
&\quad \text{to proportion of whites who are high school graduates in} \\
&\quad \text{state } j \\
L_{ij} &= \text{dummy variable that takes the value one if occupation is} \\
&\quad \text{licensed in state } j \text{ and zero otherwise} \\
U_{ij} &= \text{residual}
\end{aligned}
$$

The education variable is entered into the calculation to control for the possibility that the proportion of workers who are black will be positively affected by the relative schooling obtained by blacks and, more important (for estimating the effect of licensure), for the possibility that the variable is correlated with licensure.

Equation (2) can be estimated only for occupations licensed in some states and not in others. Seven such occupations were selected: clinical laboratory technicians, social workers, photographers, funeral directors, electricians, plumbers and pipe fitters, and drillers. As column 1 of table 6 shows, there was sizable variation in the number of states licensing these fields, with all but six licensing funeral directors and only six licensing social workers.

The calculations in table 6 show essentially no evidence of any of the expected licensure effects on the seven occupations considered. The licensure dummy variable obtains a positive insignificant coefficient in five of the seven cases and a negative insignificant coefficient in the other two. Whether these results reflect blacks working in the fields without licenses or roughly proportionate black/white attainment of the licenses remains to be seen.

State data can be used in another way to examine the effect of licensing on black employment: essentially by duplicating for 1970 the regressions performed in table 2. Such calculations yield a positive coefficient of 0.62 with a standard error of 0.25 on the licensure dummy, compared with the negative coefficient of 0.33 found in table 2. The striking difference between the impact of licensure in 1970 and in earlier years in crafts in the South suggests that most of the negative effect of licensing on black employment in that period may be attributable to discriminatory application of procedures in the earlier period, so that licensure was, but is no longer, a major deterrent to black attainment in southern craft jobs.

Conclusion

We have found that occupational licensure had a noticeable though not large effect on black representation in occupations in the years when licensing was purposely used to reduce black employment in crafts, but not afterward. In 1970 the laws had at most a modest effect on black employment. While passing rates were lower in some fields, on average blacks were as proportionately represented in licensed fields as whites. Since we have not yet determined whether blacks employed in licensed areas are as likely to have licenses as whites, these results do not mean that licensure laws may not still have adverse effects on the black eco-

TABLE 6

ESTIMATES OF THE EFFECT OF LICENSURE ON BLACK EMPLOYMENT IN OCCUPATIONS ACROSS STATES, 1970

Occupation	Number of States with Licensure	Mean Proportion Black in Occupation	*Regression Coefficients and Standard Errors*				
			Constant	Proportion black employed	Licensure law	Ratio of percentage of black high school graduates to percentage of white high school graduates	R^2
Plumbers and pipe fitters	39	0.037	−0.01	0.61 (0.04)	−0.007 (0.005)	0.007 (0.011)	0.90
Funeral directors	44	0.070	−0.03	1.07 (0.12)	0.01 (0.03)	0.01 (0.04)	0.76
Electricians	30	0.018	0.02	0.15 (0.03)	0.001 (0.003)	−0.01 (0.01)	0.67
Social workers	6	0.103	0.08	0.83 (0.11)	0.02 (0.02)	−0.06 (0.04)	0.72
Photographers	19	0.021	−0.00	0.27 (0.04)	−0.00 (0.00)	0.00 (0.01)	0.70
Clinical technologists	19	0.062	0.04	0.44 (0.10)	0.01 (0.01)	0.44 (0.10)	0.50
Drillers	30	0.074	−0.08	0.94 (0.13)	0.032 (0.015)	0.07 (0.05)	0.62

SOURCE: Licensing laws: U. S. Department of Labor, *Occupational Licensing and the Supply of Nonprofessional Manpower*, Manpower Research Monograph no. 11, pp. 51–57.
Occupational representation: U.S. Bureau of the Census, *Detailed Characteristics*, state volumes, table 171.
Percentage high school graduates: U.S. Bureau of the Census, *Statistical Abstract*, 1976, p. 126, table 205.

nomic position. If they do, however, the effects are more subtle than simply reducing the black proportion of employment in occupation.

Data Appendix for Historical Data

Unless otherwise stated, everything is from the U.S. Bureau of the Census.

Government and Self-Employed Data

1970—1940 U.S. summary, U.S. Census of Population
1970—section 2, vol. 1, table 225, part (1)
1960—vol. (1), table 206
1950—"Occupational Characteristics," *Special Reports*, tables 12 and 13
1940—"Occupational Characteristics," *The Labor Force*, table 6

Percent Black in Craft

1890—"Census Statistics of Population," U.S. Census 1890, part 2, table 116
1900—table 41, "Occupations at the 12th Census," Special Report U.S. Bureau of Census
1910—U.S. Census, vol. 4, table 2, table 17, *Negro Population in the U.S. 1790–1915*, table 17
1920—U.S. Census, vol. 4, ch. 7, table 1
1930—U.S. Census, vol. 4, table 2, for *each state*
1940—U.S. Census, vols. 2, 3, 4, 5, *The Labor Force*, reports by state, table 13
1950—U.S. Census, vol. 2, tables 77 and 76, for *each state*
1960—U.S. Census, vol. 1, table 122, *for each state*
1970—U.S. Census, vol. 2, table 171, for *each state*

In some cases where employment was missing in year t, the relative number of blacks in craft unions was estimated using the following formula:

$$\frac{(B/W) \text{ U.S. craft } t}{(B/W) \text{ U.S. craft } t + 10} \times (B/W) \text{ craft } t + 10$$

$$= \text{estimated } (B/W) \text{ state craft } t \text{ where } B$$
$$= \text{black; } W$$
$$= \text{white employment}$$

This was done for several crafts in 1890 and 1900.

Union Membership, by Craft

1930–1940, Leo Troy, "Trade Union Membership 1894–1962," table A–1

1910–1920, Leo Wolman, "Growth of American Trade Unions 1890–1932," tables 6, 7, 8, 9. These numbers have been adjusted to reflect the percentage of total union members that were in AFL unions, i.e., in 1910, 74 percent and in 1920, 81 percent, according to BLS estimates or those of Wolman.

1950–1970, data derived from May 1973–1975 CPS tapes, with the same figures used for all years.

Licensing Laws by State

1. "Occupational Licensing Legislation in the States," by the Council of State Governments, 1952, appendix C, and table 1, appendix B, and appendix A.

2) "Occupations and Professions Licensed by the States, Puerto Rico and the Virgin Islands," table 1, December 1968, Council of State Governments.

3) Juvenal L. Angel, *Directory of Professional Occupational Licensing in the United States*, part 3, pp. 149–55.

4) U.S. Bureau of Labor Statistics, *Labor Laws of the United States*, Bulletin no. 370.

Education

1. "Median Year of School Completed for Employed Persons by Occupation," from U.S. Census, 1940, table 4, "Occupational Characteristics"; 1950, tables 10, 11, *Special Reports*; 1960, U.S. Census of Population, Subject Reports 7a, tables 9, 10; 1970, tables 5, 6, U.S. Census of Population, Subject Reports, "Occupational Characteristics," 7A.

2. Median years of school completed by year and state, 1910–1930, based on estimates desired from 1950 age breakdown. It was figured that the median age of a craftsman (1950) was approximately thirty-eight years. By looking at the median year of schooling of that age bracket, we extrapolated backward so that the education level of those in that bracket was taken to be the same as the overall population in these years. Data from:

1940—16th Census of Population, vol. 4, part 2, by state, table 23

1950—U.S. Census, vol. 2, part 2, table 65, by state

1960—U.S. Census, vol. 1, by state, table 103

1970—U.S. Census, *Detailed Characteristics*, PC (1) Final Report, table 148

Bibliography

Angel, Juvenal. *Directory of Professional Occupational Licensing in the United States*. Part 3, pp. 149–55. New York: Monarch Press, 1969.

Council of State Governments. *Occupational Licensing Legislation in the States*. Chicago: Council of State Governments, June 1952.

———. *Occupations and Professions Licensed by the States, Puerto Rico and the Virgin Islands*. Chicago: Council of State Governments, December 1968.

Freeman, Richard B. "The U.S. Discriminatory System" (unpublished manuscript).

Green, Lorenzo J., and Woodson, Carter G. *The Negro Wage Earner*. New York: Russell & Russell, 1969.

Hinds, Lennox S. Keynote Introduction for symposium on "The Minority Candidates and the Bar Examination," delivered at University of California at Los Angeles School of Law, May 1, 1976.

Pashigian, Peter. "Occupational Licensing and the Interstate Mobility of Professionals." *Journal of Law and Economics* 22 (April 1979); 1–25.

Rottenberg, Simon. "The Economics of Occupational Licensing." In *Aspects of Labor Economics*, edited by H. G. Lewis. New York: National Bureau of Economic Research.

Spero, Sterling D., and Harris, Abram L. *The Black Worker*. New York: Atheneum, 1968.

Third World Coalition for Justice in the Legal System. *4 Point Plan for the California Bar Examinations*. San Francisco: University of San Francisco School of Law, pp. 2, 3.

Troy, Leo. "Trade Union Membership, 1897–1962." National Bureau of Economic Research, Occasional Paper 92. New York: NBER, 1965.

U.S. Bureau of the Census, *Census of the Population*.

———. *Detailed Characteristics*, state volumes, table 171. Washington, D.C.: volumes from 1890–1970.

———. *Statistical Abstract*, p. 126, table 205. Washington, D.C.: 1976.

U.S. Department of Health, Education and Welfare, Office of the Secretary, letters to New York school chancellor Irving Anker, November 9, 1976.

U.S. Department of Labor. *Labor Laws of the U.S.*, 2nd Special Report of the Commissioner of Labor. Washington, D.C.: 1896.

———. *Labor Laws of the United States*, 22nd Annual Report of the Commissioner of Labor, 1907. Washington, D.C.: 1908.

———. Bureau of Labor Statistics. *Labor Laws of the United States*, Bulletin #370. Washington, D.C.: 1925.

———. Manpower Administration. *Occupational Licensing and the Supply of Nonprofessional Manpower*, Manpower Research Monograph No. 11, Washington, D.C., pp. 51–57.

Wolman, Leo. *Ebb and Flow in Trade Unionism*. New York: NBER, 1936.

Regulating the Professions:
A Theoretical Framework

Alan D. Wolfson
Michael J. Trebilcock
Carolyn J. Tuohy

In Canada, as in most other Anglo-American jurisdictions, the last decade has been a period of considerable turbulence for the professions. The growth of the consumer movement, increases in government activity, and jurisdictional disputes between and among professional and paraprofessional groups have led to increasing public scrutiny of the professions and in many cases to legislative change. In Ontario the health professions have undergone a process of review and change beginning with the Committee on the Healing Arts in the late 1960s and culminating in the Health Disciplines Act in 1974 (S.Q. 1974 c. 47).[1] In Quebec sweeping legislative change has occurred in the form of a Professional Code (S.Q. 1973 c. 43), governing all self-regulatory professional bodies in the province, and in the establishment of an overseeing body, the Office of the Professions. In Alberta a legislative committee has published two reports on the professions, and the government has recently released a policy paper.[2] In British Columbia, the government has announced that it is considering a study of the self-governing professions. At the federal level in Canada, amendments to the Combines Investigation Act (S.C. 1974–75–76 c. 76), intended to remove barriers to competition within the professions, have resulted in major changes in the policies of professional bodies in such matters as fee determination and advertising.

In the United States, at the federal level, the Federal Trade Commission and the Department of Justice have pursued a similar procompetition policy toward the professions, and the Supreme Court has ruled

---

[1] Government of Ontario, Committee on the Healing Arts, *Report* (Ontario: Queen's Printer, 1970).

[2] Government of Alberta, Special Committee of the Legislative Assembly of Alberta on Professions and Occupations, *Report I*, April 1973, and *Report II*, December 1973 (Edmonton: Queen's Printer, 1973); and Government of Alberta, *Policy Governing Future Legislation for the Professions and Occupations* (Edmonton: Queen's Printer, 1978).

180

against professional fee schedules and advertising prohibitions.[3] Both houses of Congress have undertaken investigations of the accounting profession in the United States, and several state legislatures (most notably California's) have enacted legislation drastically altering the structure of professional regulatory bodies to include "sunset" review.[4] In the United Kingdom royal commissions have recently investigated the professions of law and engineering. In Australia state enquiries into the professions of law and accounting are in progress.

These developments call for a systematic approach to the problems of policy development for the professions. In particular, the traditional academic approach to the study of the professions (which has been dominated by historical and sociological methods) needs to be complemented by political, economic, and legal analyses if we are to move from descriptive to prescriptive forms of analysis. Regulatory principles must be identified, and structures of professional regulation common to or differentiated among the various professional areas must be elaborated.

This paper presents our approach to professional regulation, developed in the course of recent work for the government of Ontario on the organization and regulation of the professions of accountancy, architecture, engineering, and law in that province.[5] The analysis is grounded in political economy, as will be evident from its language and orientation.

We will begin by addressing the concept of "the public interest" and move then to defining the various interests to be considered and the general principles to be applied. Thereafter, we analyze the particular problems of regulating professional areas in the context of the failure of market mechanisms to achieve social objectives. In particular, we emphasize the agency relationships that arise in response to informational problems in these markets, as well as the difficulties created

---

[3] See, for example, Goldfarb v. Virginia State Bar, 95 S. Ct. 2004 (1975); and Bates v. State Bar of Arizona, 97 S. Ct. 2691 (1977).

[4] U.S. Congress, Senate, Committee on Government Affairs, Subcommittee on Reports, Accounting and Management, *Improving the Accountability of Publicly-Owned Corporations and their Auditors* (95th Congress, 1st session, 1977); and U.S. Congress, House of Representatives, Committee on Interstate and Foreign Commerce, Subcommittee on Oversight and Investigations, *Report on Federal Regulation and Regulatory Reform* (Moss Report) (94th Congress, 2d session, 1976). On California, see the California Business and Professions Code, amended by Senate Bills No. 2116 and 1839, approved by the governor and filed with the secretary of state, September 22, 1976.

[5] For a more complete treatment of the public policy issues in these contexts, see Michael J. Trebilcock, Carolyn J. Tuohy, and Alan D. Wolfson, *Professional Regulation*, staff study prepared for the Professional Organizations Committee (Toronto: Ministry of the Attorney General, Ontario, 1979).

by pervasive third-party effects. Finally, we survey some of the regulatory instruments available to respond to market failure.

The "Public Interest"

One would be hard pressed to find any argument for regulatory intervention in a professional area that is not based on the "public interest"— despite the fact that those who advocate regulation are in most cases the providers of services to be "professionalized" rather than the consumers of such services. One might thus be excused for viewing public interest claims with a jaundiced eye. But if not on *some* notion of the public interest, on what is one to base the development of public policy? However much the concept of the public interest may be abused, it is worth rehabilitating rather than abandoning it.

Such a rehabilitation involves altering the idea of the public interest from something substantive to a linguistic device that indicates that a debate about public policy will be conducted on certain terms. Put another way, we do not treat the public interest as measurable by a kind of social welfare function, but instead as describing the process by which the arguments of such a function, the weights to be attached to these various arguments, and the side constraints (if any) with which the function can be maximized are specified.

Given the difference of opinion about social welfare functions and how they might be used, one would anticipate that the *meaning* of the public interest in any particular context will rarely be a matter of general agreement.[6] In fact, it may be most useful to treat the invocation of the public interest as signaling a certain kind of argument, such that, when we hear that "policy A is in the public interest," we know that a particular kind of case is about to be made, implicitly or explicitly, in favor of policy A.

We know that the case will *not* be made by pointing to the benefits of policy A for a small segment of society, nor will it be grounded on principles that do not enjoy wide public acceptance. The phrase "public interest" can be taken as a signal for a case that (1) the policy achieves a just balance among *all* the relevant interests that should be taken into account and (2) the policy is consistent with generally accepted principles fundamental to our economic, political, legal, and administrative sys-

---

[6] On this see, in general, Glendon Schubert, *The Public Interest* (Glencoe, Ill.: Free Press, 1960); Carl J. Friedrich, ed., *Nomos V: The Public Interest* (New York: American Society of Political and Legal Philosophy, 1962); Douglas Price, "Theories of the Public Interest," in Lynton K. Caldwell, ed., *Politics and Public Affairs* (Bloomington: Indiana University Press, 1962), pp. 141–60; and Richard E. Flatham, *The Public Interest* (New York: Wiley, 1966).

tems—principles such as efficiency, accountability, fairness, and practicality. Seen in this way, public interest has meaning only in the context of a full and open debate among representatives of a wide range of interests. Only in the dynamics of that context will the argument implied in the public interest signal be played out. Let us elaborate on this notion.

In a diverse and interdependent society, actions of individuals, groups, or government can affect a wide variety of particular interests. In the professional arena, for example, the relevant interests include (but are not limited to) practicing professionals and their organizations, clients, third parties, potential entrants into the profession, and taxpayers. No action or policy can fully serve all these interests simultaneously. Anyone who contends that a policy is in the public interest must be prepared to meet the counterargument that the policy *really* serves only a particular set of interests and neglects or penalizes others. The very nature of the debate, then, compels the protagonists to take a broad range of interests into account. They must identify who will benefit from a given policy, who will bear its costs, and how the costs and benefits are to be shared.

Moreover, we must consider not only the policy's impact on various interests but also certain general principles. The more widely accepted are the principles invoked in the defense of a policy, the less open is the policy to the charge that it does not reflect a general social perspective. Obviously, there is in any given society a spectrum of principles evoking greater or lesser public acceptance, and they will accordingly be more or less effective in the public-interest debate. We would argue, however, that in any given society there are certain principles whose significance is more than a matter of their public support at a particular time. There are in any society values that sociologists might call institutionalized and political theorists might call constitutional—values that underlie the organization of economic, political, legal, and administrative systems. In Anglo-American societies, these values include those of efficiency, accountability, procedural fairness, and practicality. Apart from questions of the particular balance of interests to be served in a particular question of public policy, members of societies want their economic entities to minimize waste of society's resources, their governments to be accountable, their systems of justice to be impartial and nonarbitrary, and their administrative systems to be manageable. While even these principles have sometimes been challenged, particularly during the 1960s, they remain in an important sense "built in" to our social systems.

Public-interest arguments, in short, will be made in terms of generally accepted social principles, and the dynamics of the debate will cause at least these few "constitutional" principles to be taken into account. Just as it is impossible to promote all particular interests to the fullest extent simultaneously, so must there be compromises among these principles. But defining these compromises is an essential part of the public interest debate.

In discussion and debate about the public interest, as in any intelligent debate, there are other requirements. The debate must be based on as full and complete information as possible, so that it can focus on genuine differences of opinion. Furthermore, the evidence for and line of reasoning in all the arguments must be laid out for the scrutiny of all the parties to the debate.

This rarely happens. The relevant interests may not be clearly or fully defined. General principles may be invoked with little attention to their implications. The demands of "efficiency" or "accountability" may not be made explicit. Most notably, hard information about the effects of particular policies may be lacking.[7] Such information is costly to obtain, of course, and even here judgments must be made about the payoffs from obtaining it. The effects of a policy in any particular area may be so slight as not to be worth investigating. In general, however, unless explicit discussion and investigation of these issues occur, the public interest remains a hollow slogan.

In short, the public interest is part of our political language—a term we use to express concern for all interests affected by a decision and for a set of fundamental social principles. Invoking the public interest requires all parties to a discussion to make their arguments in terms of these interests and these principles, and it requires that the consequences of all proposals be shown and discussed in a public forum.

More than this we cannot expect. The public interest is not a magic formula to determine how particular interests and general principles ought to be balanced. Individual parties to the debate will attach the term to whatever balance of interests and principles *they* judge to be most appropriate, and the dynamics of the debate will cause them to defend their judgments in the ways noted above. It is ultimately the job of institutions of government to strike a socially acceptable balance of interests and principles once the requirements of the debate have been satisfied.

Let us now briefly identify the various interests and the general principles that should be taken into account in making public policy decisions in professional areas. In other words, let us try to flesh out the public interest debate in these areas.

---

[7] Lee and Alexandra Benham, "Prospects for Increasing Competition in the Professions," in Philip Slayton and Michael J. Trebilcock, eds., *The Professions and Public Policy* (Toronto: University of Toronto Press, 1978).

Interests and Principles. The relevant interests can be broken down into three categories: those of first parties (that is, parties who provide professional services), those of second parties (that is, clients or consumers of professional services), and those of third parties (that is, those who are affected by the interaction of the first and second parties). In the first category we include professional practitioners themselves, professional organizations (with their complex mix of the profession's interests and those of the bureaucratic staff itself), aspiring entrants to professional ranks, allied professionals with a stake in the area, paraprofessionals, educational institutions, and professional educators. In the second category, there are clients with a wide range of demands and degrees of sophistication. In the third category we include third parties who are directly affected by the interaction between providers and clients, for example, users of public buildings and citizens at large.

The interests of providers basically center on the rate of return to their investment in their own "human capital," the returns accruing as either monetary or nonmonetary rewards. The interests of clients are in having available for purchase a full array of professional services of varying qualities and quantities priced at their cost of production. Without a full understanding of the benefits to be obtained from the purchase of professional services, moreover, the promotion of a client's interest is contingent on the smooth functioning of the "agency" relationship he establishes with the professional practitioner. (This is an issue to which we return.) The interests of third parties can be measured by the costs and benefits (monetary and nonmonetary) that spill over onto them from the transactions between practitioners and clients. The citizenry at large, which is a special kind of third party, benefits from the diffuse contributions of professionals to the functioning of the society, and citizens as taxpayers subsidize the production of professionals and professional services.

Identifying the relevant interests is not all we need to do in evaluating policy options; one cannot resolve the matter simply by deciding which interests one wishes to favor over others. Indeed, although it is clear that different regulatory policies have different distributive effects (because professional regulation creates property rights by restricting the ability to practice or use special designations), we do not suggest that a consideration of these distributive effects should be one of the principles governing the policy process. Undoubtedly, much professional regulation in the past has been initiated with the purpose of creating such property rights and vesting them in particular interest groups, but we cannot support the idea of regulating professions so as to redistribute income. Even if it were desirable to shift the distribution of income toward professional practitioners (a proposition we very much doubt), there are more direct transfer mechanisms possible, and the use of professional regulation for such a purpose would generate unnecessary problems. Instead of shifting income distribution, public policy toward the professions should rather be designed in accordance with the four principles noted above: efficiency, fairness, practicability, and accountability.

The Four Principles

Efficiency. By efficiency, we mean not only technical efficiency (no waste of resources in the production of professional services) but also economic efficiency. In other words, an appropriate goal of public policy with respect to the professions is the allocation of factors of production and professional service outputs that achieves a social Pareto optimum in which no individual can be made better off except at someone else's expense. Of course, economic efficiency as defined here takes production technology, consumer preferences, and the distribution of income as given. In addition, there is no single Pareto optimum, even assuming given technology and tastes, but rather a multiplicity of such optima corresponding to the multiple possibilities of distributing income in society. We have already noted the desirability of separating distributive policy from the design of professional regulation. We should emphasize here that, in considering economic efficiency, not only do we take distributive shares as given but we also assume that the prevailing technology and consumer preferences are exogenously determined. That is, we assume that the distribution of income is appropriate, that the appropriate technology has been developed, and that individual tastes and values have been appropriately nurtured and conditioned. But in fact all of these are socially determined, at least in part; none is truly exogenous; and the "efficiency" of any economic system cannot, in fact, be determined independently of social values. Nonetheless, within these constraints, the goal of achieving economic efficiency in any sector of society, including the professions, is widely accepted and an important guiding principle in forming public policy. Policies should be developed to ensure that there is minimal waste in the production, distribution, and consumption of professional services, that the least-cost methods are employed in producing the services, and that the real needs of consumers (as well as their purchasing power) are acknowledged in the provision of the services.

Fairness. Efficiency is an important social goal, but it cannot be pursued blindly at the expense of other legitimate goals. Of particular importance in this context is the problem of fairness. Here we use the term "fairness" in a somewhat restricted sense: we expressly do not include any notion of distributive justice or equity. Rather, our concern is procedural—fairness in this context might be and has been called due process. Although this limits the scope of the principle, even within the limits it is not by any means a principle easy to apply.

Fairness in this sense is most relevant in considering the interests of providers: in this context it has a number of dimensions. First, people in similar circumstances must be treated according to the same standard. Applicants for licensure, for example, ought to be judged on the basis only of qualities relevant to the practice of the profession for which they are seeking to be licensed. The suspension or revocation of licenses through the disciplinary process should be equally impartial.

Second, policy enforcement cannot be arbitrary: decisions in individual cases must be taken in accordance with due process of law. This principle, a central tenet of our judicial tradition, is increasingly being extended to the actions of other tribunals.

Third, policies, like horses, should not usually be changed in midstream. A change in policy may have a profound effect on the interests of those who have entered professional markets under different rules. In the professional arena, such disruptive effects are often handled by "grandfathering" into the new regime those who entered the professions under the earlier rules. Whether or not such a provision is appropriate in any given case, the question of some sort of compensation to those whose careers are disrupted because of a change in policy cannot be ignored.

Practicability. Policies must be assessed according to their ease of implementation. One must be able to put the policy into effect, and one must be able to change it if its results are not what was intended. First, the administrative component of a policy must be designed with due regard to information flows and incentive structures. That is to say, those who are charged with administering a policy must know what to do to achieve its goals and must be motivated to do it. To the extent that flows of information are blocked, or that the rewards and punishments for administrators are at cross-purposes with the policy, policy implementation will be thwarted.

The implementation of a policy must also enhance the ability to learn from experience. The real world includes uncertainty and time constraints. A good research and consultation program can help inform policy makers at a given time, but the policy makers must usually act before they are absolutely sure either of their facts or of their judgments. Intelligent policy making should not, therefore, "lock in" a particular course of action, but rather provide for the effects of the policy to be monitored and the policy to be adjusted if its results are not as anticipated.

One must also remember that policy makers are rarely if ever presented with a blank slate, and the field of professional regulation is no exception. In every professional area, regulatory systems are currently in place, and these complicate matters in at least two ways. First, relationships have been established within these systems, and change may be made more difficult by the fact that participants need not only to learn new rules but to "unlearn" old ones. Second, organized interests (notably but not exclusively professional interests) have arisen within existing regulatory systems. Any new policy that fails to take account of these interests may well founder because of organized resistance.

Accountability. Finally, where a policy is to be carried out directly through self-governing institutions or through an agency of government, the principle of accountability must be respected. Those who make public policy decisions ought to be held accountable to those who are affected by their decisions. Those who disagree with the decisions must have apparent and available avenues to seek redress.

Accountability is not simply an abstract concept. It has shaped our political institutions of representative and responsible government. Where governmental powers are delegated to professional or other regulatory bodies, the same principle ultimately obtains. No governmental powers ought to be exercised simply on the basis of a pro forma accountability. Public accountability will be effective only to the extent that all those affected are informed about the actions of political decision makers and can give or withhold their support for those decision makers accordingly. Thus, in designing professional regulatory systems, one must keep in mind that they must function within the context of constitutional government and that accountability requires effective representation of interests and effective dissemination of information.

Rationales for Professional Regulation

This discussion of the public interest provides some guidelines for selecting among the various regulatory options available to policy makers. But before a choice of regulatory instruments is considered, it must be determined that *some* intervention is required in a particular area. The first choice must be whether to intervene at all in the structure and conduct of any occupational group. Aside from issues of creating and distributing "professional" property (dismissed above), the rationales for regulatory intervention must lie in the perception that unregulated activities fail to achieve social objectives—that is, that there exists a market failure.

The failure of markets to achieve the social objective of economic efficiency in the allocation of factors and products (services) forms a prima facie rationale for regulatory intervention. It should be noted, however, that market failure does not of itself always *justify* intervention. Regulation itself is costly and it can, moreover, introduce inefficiencies of its own making. We must consider *net* impact rather than simply the achievement of primary objectives. Nevertheless, the perceived failure of an unregulated service market to operate competitively and achieve socially optimal allocative distributions is a primary rationale for governmental intervention.

In professional sectors, as in others, there are five main reasons why markets might "fail." There may be concentrations of economic power on the supply side or the demand side; there may be barriers to free entry and exit from the market; the services sold in the market may not be homogeneous; complete information about the nature and value of the services sold may not be available to all consumers and producers; and there may be externalities in the production or consumption of services.

It is difficult to speculate on what unregulated markets in many professional areas would look like, because there have rarely, if ever, been any. On the other hand, it does seem possible to identify the main sources of market failure in professional areas.

Although there may be instances where economies of scale lead to concentration among producers of professional services (as, for example, with auditors), in general there are a large number of buyers and sellers in most professional markets. But even apart from institutionalized barriers to entry, the ability of firms to move in and out of the market is encumbered by the high level of human capital required to compete once there. But this characteristic does not differentiate "professional" markets from others requiring large investments of human capital and would scarcely on its own justify significant regulatory intervention in professional areas when it was not justified in other areas. A similar case can be made on the question of product homogeneity. Such homogeneity does not, in general, exist in professional markets, and this is some cause for concern about their ability to operate competitively, but here again professional markets would not appear to be particularly plagued by this source of market failure. A special case for regulatory intervention in professional areas on this ground does not seem to be warranted.

There are, however, two major sources of market failure in professional areas that differentiate them from many other markets and may call for special regulatory intervention: serious information problems and pervasive externalities.

The Informational Problem. The informational problem in professional markets has received considerable attention from academic economists, but despite this (or perhaps because of it) confusion continues to surround the topic.[8] What is at issue here is whether consumers have enough information to assess the *benefits* of professional services with accuracy. It is not important for the market's operation that consumers be knowledgeable about the nature of the professional production process itself and the technicalities involved therein, any more than it is necessary for the efficient operation of the market for transistor radios or pocket calculators that consumers learn how they are made. What is necessary is that consumers be able to judge the *value* to them of the services offered on the market. If this ability is not present, then competitive market outcomes are no longer optimal. To compensate for their inability to assess the value of the services offered, consumers of professional services establish agency relationships with practitioners so that the latter can act on their behalf in making informed decisions about the purchase of services.[9] If these agency relationships function perfectly, the consumer acts as if he were completely informed, and the interaction between independent supply and demand produces an optimum market equilibrium. Unfortunately, the professional agency relationship involves inherently competing interests, because the "demand agent" is often the supplier of services as well.

Professionalism involves the application of a general system of knowledge to the circumstances of a particular case. In treating a client's

---

[8] On the informational problem see, for example, George A. Akerlof, "The Market for Lemons: Qualitative Uncertainty and the Market Mechanism," *Quarterly Journal of Economics*, vol. 57 (1970), pp. 488–500; Kenneth J. Arrow, "Uncertainty and the Welfare Economics of Medical Care," *American Economic Review*, vol. 53 (December 1963), pp. 941–73; Lee Benham and Alexandra Benham, "Regulating through Professions: A Perspective on Information Control," *Journal of Law and Economics*, vol. 18 (October 1975), pp. 421–27; Robert G. Evans, "Models, Markets and Medical Care," in L. Officer and L. B. Smith, eds., *Canadian Economic Problems and Policies*, 2d ed. (Toronto: McGraw-Hill, 1974); M. S. Feldstein, "Econometric Studies in Health Economics," in M. D. Intriligator and D. A. Kendrick, eds., *Frontiers of Quantitative Economics* (Amsterdam: North Holland Press, 1974), vol. 2, pp. 377–434; Alex Maurizi, "Occupational Licensing and the Public Interest," *Journal of Political Economy*, vol. 82 (1974), p. 399; T. G. Moore, "The Purpose of Licensing," *Journal of Law and Economics*, vol. 4 (1961), p. 93; Michael Spence, "Consumer Misperceptions, Product Failure and Product Liability," *Review of Economic Studies,* in press; and Alan D. Wolfson, "The Supply of Physicians' Services in Ontario" (Ph.D. diss., Harvard University, 1975).

[9] For a fuller discussion of this point, see Carolyn J. Tuohy and Alan D. Wolfson, "The Political Economy of Professionalism: A Perspective," in *Four Aspects of Professionalism* (Ottawa: Consumer Research Council, Canada, 1977), pp. 45–86.

problem, this knowledge is necessary (1) to identify the precise nature of the problem (diagnosis), (2) to determine the best way of dealing with it (prescription), and (3) to provide specialized services so as to solve the problem (therapy).

The uniqueness of a professional's role lies in the "agency" functions of diagnosis and prescription. Professionals are charged by their clients with making important decisions on their behalf, and they are compensated for assuming this decision-making responsibility and bringing their knowledge to bear on the decision.

Often, however, this is not the end of the professional practitioner's involvement with the client. After assisting in the decision making, the professional also stands ready to provide the "technical" services necessary to effect therapy. He is compensated as a supplier of these "technical" services as well as for his diagnosis and prescription.

It is here then that the potential conflict of interest arises. Professionals often have a pecuniary interest in advising their clients in their agency role to buy from them (or members of their firm) in their role as suppliers of services. In fact, wherever the agency relationship exists, this potential for demand-generation exists. To the extent that practitioners exploit their agency to generate a demand for their own services greater than that which fully informed consumers would demand in their own right, the resulting level and mix of professional services provided deviates from competitive market solutions, and social welfare is reduced.

The proper functioning of this agency relationship between practitioner and client obviously requires trust between them. The client, in authorizing the professional to act on his behalf, must *trust* his agent to take the client's interest *fully* into account and not let the practitioner's *own* interests enter into the process. Trust of this sort is difficult to establish, especially when it touches upon some of the most fundamental of human affairs, partly because the nature of these agency relationships is at direct variance with the culture of competitive markets (the culture predicated on the belief that the common good can best be achieved by each individual's pursuing his own self-interest). Thus trust relationships preclude the full operation of market forces, and market forces undercut trust relationships. In the latter event, practitioners might abuse the discretion granted them by virtue of their agency function and overprescribe their own services for the client. The medical practitioner who runs a revolving-door practice, generating excessive demand by frequently recalling patients, would show this failure of the agency function.

We do not suggest that there is widespread abuse of the discretion inherent in the professional agency role; there is little *empirical* evidence of such a problem.[10] No doubt in many cases clients are sufficiently sophisticated for there to be no necessity for complete agency. In other cases, undoubtedly, the restraints imposed by professional codes of ethics are important. But it is worth noting that professional codes focus on the practitioner's obligation to consider and promote his clients' interest as determined by the benefits to be derived from recommended courses of action; they are generally less eloquent (and often less than explicit) on the necessity of protecting the clients' *financial* interests by minimizing the cost of services purchased. The tendency for overservicing may thus be inadequately inhibited by the operation of these codes.

The most important restraint on the abuse of professional agency is undoubtedly the self-restraint exercised by the practitioner (agent) himself. Client sophistication is useful, of course, but if clients were fully knowledgeable, there would be no need to establish the professional agency relationship in the first place. Moreover, the enforcement even of restricted ethical codes is inhibited by the sheer number of practitioner-client relationships to be policed and by the fact that the discipline process must generally be initiated by the unsophisticated victim. Clearly, the agency relationship between professionals and clients cannot work satisfactorily if practitioners are not self-disciplined. In this context, it is hard to overemphasize the importance of the "socialization" process inherent in professional education and reinforced by professional norms. The collectivization of appropriate norms and their transmission to individual practitioners are the cornerstones of professional-client relationships. In the absence of self-discipline, the agency relationship must be unsatisfactory.

To the extent, then, that a service market is characterized by the informational problem discussed above and to the extent that agency relationships are established between practitioners and clients in response to this problem, the potential and the incentives for the imperfect functioning of these agency relationships call for a regulatory response. It may be all well and good to emphasize the importance of individual self-restraint by practitioners. But in the absence of regulation, it may be unrealistic to expect much more of these practitioners than of entrepreneurs in general. The imposition of a regulatory structure may be required, and in some cases the "professionalization" of these markets through a self-regulatory regime is indicated.[11]

---

[10] The medical profession has provided the most fertile ground for investigation of this phenomenon. For a review of Canadian studies on the topic, see R. G. Evans and Alan D. Wolfson, "Moving the Target to Hit the Bullet: Generation of Utilization by Physicians in Canada" (paper prepared for the National Bureau of Economic Research Conference on the Economics of Physician and Patient Behavior, Stanford, California, January 1978).

[11] See Carolyn J. Tuohy and Alan D. Wolfson, "Self-Regulation: Who Qualifies?" in Slayton and Trebilcock, *Professions and Public Policy*.

Externalities. Most analyses of professional markets have focused on the informational problems, perhaps because medicine and law have been taken as archetypes. In these two "senior" professions, the primary problem *is* informational, and regulatory responses are principally addressed to market failure through lack of information. On the other hand, it would be a mistake to assume that informational problems are the main point of concern in all professional markets. In accounting, architecture, and engineering, to name but three, there do not appear to be serious informational problems. Consumers of services in these markets are relatively sophisticated and do not, in general, need to establish "agency" relationships with practitioners to compensate for their own ignorance.

There are, however, pervasive externalities in these markets. The purpose of auditing is to lend credibility to the client corporation's financial statements (which are used by third parties in making investment decisions). In building design, the "neighborhood" effects are evident. In almost every branch of engineering—chemical, mining, aeronautical, nuclear, whatever—the potential effects of bad design on public health and safety are dramatic. It is, in fact, externalities of this kind that necessitate a regulatory response.

Externalities or third-party effects occur, as we know, when some of the costs of producing services are not borne by the producers (here, the professionals) or when some of the benefits of what is consumed do not accrue to the consumers (here, the clients). In these cases the production decisions made by firms and the consumption decisions made by individuals will not be socially optimal. The firm has no incentive to consider external costs of production that are not internalized and is thus likely to produce more of whatever it produces than it would if it had to bear all the costs itself. An example would be afforded by physician overuse of hospital laboratory services. In other words, the availability of seemingly free resources encourages excess production— "excess" in the sense that if societal costs were acknowledged in the production decision, fewer total resources would be devoted to that economic activity.

For consumers, there is an analogous situation where benefits accrue to others than the direct purchaser of services. Thus, if an individual obtains an innoculation against polio, not only does he receive the benefits of immunization, but third parties with whom he comes in contact are protected against contracting polio *from him*. If these third-party interests are not introduced into the decision-making process and individual consumption decisions are made as though only those who made purchases were affected, the societal consumption of these goods and services would be less than optimal. Thus, on both the supply and demand sides of the equation, the existence of externalities leads to a market failure to achieve optimality and *may* call for governmental intervention.

In fact, in many professional markets, market failure of this sort provides the most important argument for regulation. One suspects that references to the need for regulation to protect the public interest are often based on concerns for third-party effects rather than the protection of clients themselves. Certainly such concerns have some validity. Our discussion of professionalism above focused on the agency role of the professional in the decision-making process, but this agency role does not exhaust the professional's responsibilities. In general, a responsible professional must take into account not only the interests of his client but the legitimate interests of third parties who may be affected by the decisions he makes on his client's behalf. The only interests he should *not* take into account in this decision-making process are his own. In this context, then, the professional assumes a second "agency" function acting on behalf of affected third parties.

Just as regulation is required to ensure that the practitioner fulfills his agency responsibilities to his client in markets plagued with informational problems, it is required to ensure that the services provided take into account the interest of third parties where externalities represent the important source of market failure.

Quantity, Quality, and Price. Where markets perform imperfectly, we have reason to be concerned that the goods and services produced and consumed will be inappropriate in number, quality, price, or any combination of these—inappropriate meaning either too little or too much.

Quantity. Where there are monopolistic practices, either by individual firms or by cartels, supply is kept below the optimal quantity forthcoming in a perfectly functioning market. On the other hand, in professional markets there can be demand-generation through exploitation of the agency relationship between practitioner and client. In many professional areas, there may be an inappropriate level of services in an unregulated market as the result of third-party effects. Here we could reasonably assume that ignoring the interests of third parties would yield a level of services lower than what would be socially optimal if all interests were taken into account—because the clients (second parties) who purchase professional services would demand only enough to satisfy their own needs and protect their own interests. The concerns of affected third parties might plausibly require additional professional services that clients are unlikely to purchase at their own expense unless required to do so by the state. Thus, for example, a steel mill may desire engineering services to design better processes for burning fuel in order to increase the efficiency of its production, but the profit-oriented company is unlikely, on its own account, to purchase the additional engineering services necessary to purify the combustion process further to avoid polluting the air.

To summarize, in the absence of regulation, markets characterized by informational problems may exhibit unnecessary demand-generation by suppliers, while markets in which third-party effects are important are likely to exhibit deficient service levels.

Where externalities are significant, regulatory policy must thus ensure that *sufficient* services are purchased to protect third-party interests. Where informational problems are significant, regulatory policy must address the potential for demand-generation yielding *excessive* use of services. The former can be achieved through regulating the "demand" for professional services; the latter can be effected only by regulating the *suppliers* of these services to ensure that practitioners do not take advantage of unsophisticated clients by exploiting the professional agency relationship.

Intervention on the demand side can take a number of forms. The purchase of professional services might be subsidized through programs such as Medicare and legal aid. Typically, however, "demand" for professional services can be created by *requiring* (through statute or regulation) that in particular circumstances services be purchased. Examples of this kind of demand-side regulation abound. In accounting there are "statutory" audits; in building design, building codes often require an architect or engineer for the construction of certain kinds of buildings; in engineering, there is a variety of statutes concerning public health and safety.

Quality. In general, the protection of third-party interests requires that a sufficient quantity of services be purchased *and* that these services be of an appropriate quality. Quality regulation alone would not suffice, because professional agency on behalf of third parties could not be ensured without requiring the purchase of some "professional" services in specified circumstances. On the other hand, quantity regulation alone is also clearly inadequate, because one must ensure not only that services are purchased but that the services purchased are of the appropriate quality so that third-party interests are adequately protected. Thus, where the primary rationale for regulatory intervention is the protection of third parties, we perceive the need for parallel regulation to ensure that *enough* of the *right* kind of services are purchased.

The purchase of inappropriately large quantities of professional services stemming from the imperfect functioning of the agency relationship between professional and client cannot be addressed by "demand-side" regulation. Rather, the identification of unnecessary service blends into scrutiny of the quality of services in general and can be pursued only by policies designed to regulate the supply of professional services.

For the quality of services, as for the quantity, it is possible for market imperfections to yield either too low or too high a level. Unscrupulous or negligent practitioners may deliver services of poor quality without being detected. Moreover, the needs of third parties may dictate modifications in the nature of services provided, as well as in their number. If the legitimate interests of clients and third parties are not taken into account, the resulting quality of services provided could be too low. On the other hand, it is possible to find quality standards too high to be justified from a cost perspective. In the absence of competitive pressure, it may be possible for providers to offer only Cadillac services even when a Chevrolet variety would suffice. Practitioners may make more money by providing only high-priced, high-quality services. Or, economic motives aside, they may obtain personal satisfaction from providing only the "very best," even if it means that some consumers will not receive any service at all because of the resulting (real or perceived) economic barriers to access. Thus, while the primary problem in quality regulation is that of ensuring high standards, excessive quality levels may sometimes also constitute a problem.

It should be emphasized that regulation of the *supply* of professional services—professional regulation, in other words—is primarily concerned with the *quality* of services provided. Concern about an inappropriately large *quantity* of such services (demand for which is generated by a practitioner acting imperfectly as an agent for his client) can be addressed only by regulating the practitioner himself. One cannot intercede directly on the demand side to correct these distortions, because without the professional agency relationship the *need* for services cannot be specified. Thus, although regulation of the *suppliers* of service cannot totally ignore questions of quantity, it is fair to say that the primary concern with appropriate quantity relates to third-party interests, and this concern is by and large properly addressed by requiring certain purchases of professional services. This we have called demand-side regulation. The emphasis of supply-side regulation of professionals themselves is on the quality of the services they provide.

Price. There is one final dimension of interest in professional services that needs to be considered, and that is price. It is a commonplace that market imperfections that undermine the effectiveness of competition result in unnecessarily high prices.

Whereas inappropriate levels of the quantity and quality of professional services delivered call for regulation of both demand and supply, the problem of inappropriately high prices can be addressed in a manner largely independent of the determination of the regulatory frameworks for these markets. In other words, the questions of minimum or maximum fee schedules or price advertising can be addressed outside the context of demand and supply regulation. This is not to suggest that price determination itself is independent of the regulatory framework in each market. On the contrary, as we have suggested, prices are affected by the strength of competitive forces in the market, and these in turn can be influenced by regulatory intervention. But the resolution of pricing issues is not contingent on the other regulatory decisions: one can, in essence, graft pricing policy onto any regulatory framework.

Options for Professional Regulation

In the previous section, we sought to identify factors that might justify some form of regulatory intervention in professional markets. Here we attempt to review and assess the strengths and weaknesses of the principal regulatory strategies available to policy makers. As we noted, the quantity of professional services can be regulated primarily through demand-side legislation, and price regulation can be treated within the context of any regulatory framework. Professional regulation—that is, regulation of the *supply* of professional services—centers on quality assurance. And before we examine the principal instruments available for regulating service quality in professional markets, some clarification of what is meant by "quality" may be useful.

Problems of quality in professional markets center on the relationship between the nature of services provided and the outcomes of those services. There are other aspects to quality, such as the empathy with which the practitioner deals with his client, his attentiveness and promptness in execution, his patience in communicating, and so on, but quality in professional services essentially relates to effecting satisfactory outcomes. The quality problem exists in professional markets for two reasons. First, clients may not be sufficiently sophisticated to determine what quality of service they need. For one price one can get tax advice or criminal advocacy from one's family lawyer; for another price one can get tax advice or criminal advocacy from the top experts in the country in their fields. Quality involves matching the level of services used to the need for such services, given that higher-level services are also more expensive. The problem of matching services to needs is solved only by the activities of an ethical professional who takes all the relevant second- and third-party interests into account in making his service decisions, while ignoring his own interests.

197

Even if consumers know what service they need, however, they may not be able to evaluate the services received. Services of proper quality are those that are appropriate as measured by client and third-party needs and that are well performed. These two dimensions of quality can be regulated either by regulating the services produced or the producers of services, the output of professional markets or the inputs.[12]

Two forms of output regulation are available. Civil liability for the performance of professional services addresses the quality of services produced and, more important, addresses it in terms of the outcomes resulting from such services. Standard setting and enforcement focus directly on outputs, but not necessarily on outcomes. On the other hand, one can attempt to ensure that high-quality services are produced by regulating the *producers* of services rather than the services themselves, and here again two forms of regulation are available. One can certify providers—that is, ensure that certain qualifications are met before a provider can identify himself by a restricted designation. Or one can license providers, prohibiting unqualified practitioners from offering services altogether rather than prohibiting them from calling themselves qualified. In all cases, what one would eventually want to influence through regulation is the *outcome* of professional services.

Output Regulation: Civil Liability.[13] Probably the least interventionist and longest established response to quality breakdowns in professional markets is the civil liability suit for professional negligence. Here the injured client (or in some cases the injured third party) is given a private right of action against a provider guilty of negligence in the provision of professional services. Typically, the standard to which the provider will be held is the standard of competence and care that generally prevails throughout the profession in question. If the plaintiff has suffered damage as a result of a provider's failure to adhere to this standard, the plaintiff will receive compensation in the form of a damages award against the negligent provider.

---

[12] See D. Wittman, "Prior Regulation versus Post Liability: The Choice between Input and Output Monitoring," *Journal of Legal Studies*, vol. 6 (1977), p. 193.

[13] See, on this, Edward P. Belobaba, *Civil Liability as a Professional Competence Incentive*, Working Paper no. 9 prepared for the Professional Organizations Committee, 1978; Robert S. Prichard, "Professional Civil Liability and Continuing Competence," in Slayton and Trebilcock, *Professions and Public Policy*; G. Calabresi, "The Problem of Malpractice: Trying to Round Out the Circle," *University of Toronto Law Journal*, vol. 27 (1977), pp. 131ff.; R. Epstein, "Medical Malpractice: The Case for Contract," *American Bar Foundation Research Journal*, vol. 1 (1976), p. 87; Spence, "Consumer Misperceptions, Product Failure and Product Liability."

At first glance, the civil liability suit appears to have many attractions as a response to the quality control problem:

1. It keys on outcomes, in the sense that liability ensues if a service fails to achieve the purpose that it was reasonably intended to serve as a result of negligence in its provision. Obviously the interest of a client in professional services that he has purchased is, ultimately, in the outcome of such services, and civil liability systems address that question directly and explicitly.

2. It constitutes an external constraint on professional behavior inasmuch as suits for its enforcement are initiated by parties external to the profession (clients or third parties), and it is adjudicated by an agency external to the profession (the courts).

3. It simultaneously achieves both compensation and deterrence. To the extent that civil liability *fully* compensates victims for damage sustained as a result of professional negligence, the victims become indifferent to poor quality service. To the extent that the negligent provider is required to face the full social costs he has inflicted on other parties, he will have incentives to provide a quality of service that will avoid those social costs.

4. It is dynamic in the sense that the standard of quality demanded shifts over time to reflect changes in norms and procedures in a profession.

5. Because it is a decentralized and private form of law enforcement, it does not lead to a public monopoly over the law enforcement function.

These strengths are not trivial. But in many professional markets, the system is afflicted by a number of disabilities that are also not trivial:

1. The system is victim initiated. In many contexts, this implies that a victim can obtain and digest the kind of information needed to know that he has been victimized. Often the mere fact that the client thinks the outcome of a professional service is negative implies nothing about the quality of the service. For example, in most lawsuits involving two parties, one party must lose. Treatment for many medical problems, no matter how good, may have only an outside chance of ameliorating them. Negative outcomes in both these examples may be attributable to poor quality service, but they may not. The client will be able to resolve this question only either by mustering sufficient personal expertise to make a judgment on the matter (in which case he should consider switching sides in the marketplace) or by purchasing the advice of another expert. In this latter case, the

client may find himself in the invidious position of trying to decide which of two conflicting experts is right, at least in the preliminary fashion involved in deciding (probably with the help of a third expert) whether to sue. These information costs may be even more acute in the case of third parties at least one stage removed from any direct interaction with the service provider.

2. The injured party may have difficulty obtaining the services of a second expert. Here the collectivization of professional values may tend to manifest itself in a conspiracy of silence.

3. The problems associated with uninformed enforcers (clients) may be compounded by the dependence of the system on inexpert adjudicators (courts). In short, the probability of error in determinations of competence may be quite high.

4. The system is costly to administer because of the difficult technical determinations required case by case.

5. In many contexts, the system will not compensate or deter. While some forms of loss sustained by clients as a result of incompetent professional services may be fully compensable by damages (misappropriation of trust funds, for example, where a sum of money can be substituted for a like sum), other forms of injury are not perfectly compensable through monetary awards (death, for instance). As a matter of equity, there is a serious defect in a system that permits sudden, drastic losses that are not fully compensable to fall unevenly on relatively few people. Moreover, the system will not achieve an optimal level of deterrence if victims, through ignorance, do not sue for incompetence or, because of the costs of bringing suit, are deterred from doing so.

More important, to the extent that a market for professional services is less than perfectly competitive, a provider may not be required to weigh the social costs of incompetence against the social costs of avoiding that incompetence. If both sets of costs are not fully internalized, he is likely to end up providing "too much" or "too little" competence. He may provide too much competence to the extent that the client can be induced to accept unnecessary precautionary procedures that the client is persuaded he needs or that, through the existence of a third-party payer (Medicare, for example), he has little incentive to refuse. A professional may provide too little competence to the extent that victims, because of information or transaction costs, fail to initiate suit against him in situations where negligence has in fact occurred.

How one weighs these various strengths and weaknesses of the civil liability system obviously depends on the nature of the professional market. If one is dealing with a market where clients and third parties are relatively well informed and sophisticated and the cost of error by the provider is fully compensable by a damages award, civil liability can and should play a central role in ensuring an appropriate quality of professional services in that market. If one is not dealing with such a market or if third parties at jeopardy are numerous and the transaction costs entailed in multiple lawsuits are high and not reducible (through improved class action rules, for example), civil liability can be assigned no more than a secondary role in the search for assurances of professional competence.

Output Regulation: Standard Setting and Enforcement. The second form of regulating professional output is by establishing standards of performance and monitoring or reviewing professional activities to ensure that they conform to those standards. The setting and enforcement of standards could each be done either directly by a branch of government or, through delegated authority, by a professional group. The regulatory process itself could include client complaints, inspection, peer review, and practice audits.

There is a fundamental difficulty entailed in this kind of regulation of professional market outputs. The ability of a regulator to prescribe desired product or service outcomes is circumscribed by the unique nature of professional services. The application of general systems of knowledge to individual circumstances produces widely diverse service outcomes, incapable of being fully regulated by general, predetermined standards. Despite this, attempts are commonly made to monitor and regulate outputs. For example, in building design and construction, building code and planning acts often confer extensive municipal powers to prescribe structural, aesthetic, and other standards for new buildings.[14] More generally, most professions maintain a disciplinary apparatus to monitor and sanction delinquent members.

Obviously, standard setting and enforcement constitutes a more substantial or more specific form of intervention in professional markets than civil liability. A specialized agency is vested with authority to develop and enforce detailed norms of behavior specific to a given profession. In theory, one could regulate quality in a professional market solely through standard setting and enforcement, thus entailing free entry into a professional market but, where justified, enforced exit from it.

There are certain advantages to this form of intervention in professional markets:

---

[14] See Donald N. Dewees, Stanley M. Makuch, and Alan Waterhouse, *An Analysis of the Practice of Architecture and Engineering in Ontario*, Working Paper no. 1 prepared for the Professional Organizations Committee, 1978, pp. 299ff.

1. Standard setting and enforcement key directly on outputs, which are closer than inputs to the ultimate interest—the outcome.
2. Like any other specialized tribunal, a disciplinary body can bring a great deal of highly specialized expertise to bear on developing and enforcing appropriate standards of conduct and performance.
3. To the extent that the standards are specified and enforced through a collegial agency within a profession, the credibility of the process may be heightened and self-adherence to the norms promoted, thus reducing enforcement costs.
4. An expert agency is not afflicted with the lack of information and expertise besetting the individual client-victim contemplating a civil liability suit. Thus the system may generate fewer errors (both in enforcement and in adjudication) than the civil liability system.
5. Because an expert agency can be given power to enforce exit from the market, the system may take care of recidivists more effectively than they are taken care of under civil liability regimes.

On the other hand, standard setting and enforcement suffer from some very substantial disabilities:

1. Like the civil liability system, the process of monitoring and review is highly individualized and involves costly determinations of difficult factual and technical issues case by case.
2. To the extent that administrative regulation of outputs involves standard setting, there is a danger that excessive rigidities may constrain innovation.
3. In enforcement an agency faces an invidious choice between relying on victim-initiated complaints (with all the problems noted) and engaging in extensive independent practice reviews and quality audits that are both costly and likely to be damaging to trust between professionals and clients.
4. To the extent that the administrative process is triggered by victim-initiated complaints, there may be a disabling absence of economic incentives for the victims to pursue complaints (an absence in contrast to the compensatory attractions of a civil liability suit).
5. Where the enforcement agency is a profession's disciplinary body, the sanctions available to it are generally crude, and it is not easy to make the provider weigh the social costs of incompetence and the social costs of avoiding it and select the smaller. The disciplinary process is unlikely to confront a provider with both sets of costs with any degree of accuracy.

6. If the regulatory process is administered by the profession being regulated, there is a danger that its priorities will be distorted by professional self-interest. Competitive behavior such as advertising, for example, may be heavily penalized, while complaints about excessive delays or fees may be downplayed.

Input Regulation: Certification (Reserved Title). If, for the reasons noted, judicial regulation and administrative regulation of outputs are thought to be inadequate guarantors of service quality, the broad alternative is input regulation. In professional markets, the two basic forms of input regulation available are certification and licensing.[15] By certification we mean that some authority or agency is empowered by statute to certify individuals to the public as having satisfied particular educational and training requirements judged (by the certifying body) to indicate competence in a particular range of professional services. (We do not here consider groups awarding designations on a purely private basis as "certifying" bodies within the meaning of the word.) Certification typically involves exclusive legal appropriation of a generic occupational description, usually in conjunction with such a term as "registered" or "certified" (for example, "certified public accountant"). With certification, uncertified individuals are not legally prevented from offering services in competition with certified individuals. In contrast, with licensing, only individuals licensed after attaining prescribed educational and training standards are legally permitted to offer the relevant services.

The strengths of a certification system are these:

1. It responds directly to the problem faced by an uninformed public trying to determine competence. It does this by "grading" service providers into at least two categories, certified and uncertified (although in theory a certification system could attempt to differentiate the quality of service providers more finely by creating a variety of grading categories along the quality continuum).
2. It is relatively flexible. While it attempts to segregate providers in the market by informing consumers about relative degrees of competence, it nevertheless preserves free entry into the market. (In this respect it contrasts sharply with licensure.)
3. Certification systems permit competing and parallel certif-

---

[15] See Milton Friedman, "Occupational Licensure," in *Capitalism and Freedom* (Chicago: University of Chicago Press, 1962); T. Moore, "The Purpose of Licensing," *Journal of Law and Economics,* vol. 4, no. 93 (1961); A. Maurizi, "Occupational Licensing and the Public Interest," *Journal of Political Economy,* vol. 82, no. 399 (1976).

icates to be offered by a number of rival organizations, which would create strong economic incentives for each organization to police the competence and conduct of its members to enhance the credibility of its own certificates.

4. Certification systems may serve to counterbalance concentration tendencies in a professional market. For example, a market entirely unregulated as to inputs but subject to major information deficiencies on the demand side may of its own motion generate certain adjustment processes (such as heavy advertising of "brand-name" firms as a proxy for more specific service information desired by consumers). If a certification system provides consumers with information about the relative competence of alternative providers, smaller firms may be able to compete in quality with larger firms, and the competitive vigor of the market may be enhanced.

5. In markets characterized by quality uncertainty, high-quality providers may be driven out unless there is a means (such as certification) of enabling them to differentiate their product and obtain appropriate rewards for superiority. Certification may prevent the degeneration of such a market.[16]

Despite their strengths, certification systems also exhibit a number of significant weaknesses:

1. Like licensing systems, they make large (often heroic) assumptions about quality correlation between inputs and outputs. More specifically, both systems assume that simply by prescribing a given set of educational and other inputs as a condition for certification or licensing, we can be assured of the provider's ability to furnish us with the desired quality of service forever after. While this assumption may hold reasonably well in some cases, it is unlikely to hold for all practitioners for all services undertaken by them at all times. The more narrowly defined the prescribed inputs and the more widely differentiated the desired outputs, the weaker will be the correlation between them. Some who have attained the required certification standard will not provide competent services; some who have attained the required standard and do provide competent services could have reached the standard more efficiently by means other than fulfilling the prescribed training requirements.

---

[16] See Michael Spence, *Entry, Conduct and Regulation in Professional Markets*, Working Paper no. 2 prepared for the Professional Organizations Committee, 1978; George A. Akerlof, "The Market for Lemons," p. 488; and W. K. Wiscusi, "A Note on Lemons' Markets with Quality Certification," *Bell Journal of Economics*, vol. 9 (1978), p. 277.

2. Prescribing and enforcing a uniform quality of inputs is likely to be difficult. Ensuring a uniformly satisfactory quality of formal education or on-the-job experience, for example, may entail extraordinary monitoring costs.
3. If a particular market is afflicted with a high measure of uncertainty about quality or high risks from poor quality, the public's reliance on a certificate in choosing a practitioner may become so strong that a certification system functions de facto as a licensing system, with whatever rigidities this form of entry control might in particular cases imply.[17]
4. In attempting to redress informational deficiencies, certification systems have their own potential for introducing misinformation if inappropriate criteria are chosen for differentiating the quality of the various providers in a market. If consumers are misinformed, some providers will be given unfair advantages, and others will be unfairly penalized. The problem is that, to some extent, all certification schemes are inherently misleading: they can never tell a consumer what, precisely, a provider is certified as competent to do, or how well. Inevitably, no provider will be equally competent at all tasks in the field covered by certification. Moreover, certification schemes tell a consumer nothing about the quality of service to be expected from (or risks entailed in dealing with) an uncertified provider. To the extent that certification is generally taken to imply a marked quality differential between certified and unqualified providers, at the margin it is likely to be misleading.
5. In markets where the costs of error in the provision of a professional service are high, certification may not be a sufficient guarantee of service quality. For example, if the cost to a patient of choosing an incompetent medical practitioner is death, the information conveyed to the public through a simple listing of practitioners as certified or uncertified may be of limited value.
6. In the absence of regulation requiring the purchase of services (and from certified providers), certification systems do not address third-party effects. Essentially they leave it open to consumers to retain uncertified providers, assuming whatever risks are inherent in this, both to themselves and to third parties. If demand-side regulation is instituted to protect third parties, the certification regime becomes, in effect, licensure.

---

[17] See Walter Gellhorn, "The Abuse of Occupational Licensing," *University of Chicago Law Review*, vol. 44 (1976), pp. 21ff.

7. Conferring on professional associations the legal ability to certify the competence of their members may tend to convert certification schemes, however desirable, into licensing schemes, however undesirable. Exclusive licensing schemes create monopolies for licensees and thus may be more attractive than certification schemes. Licensing schemes may involve coerced membership in a professional association, where that association is the licensing body. This would drastically reduce the transaction costs entailed in organizing a large group of people by providing a large captive membership and dues-paying base and accordingly would enhance the prestige and power of the staff bureaucracy and elected leaders of the association. Thus certification regimes may involve an inherently unstable political dynamic.

Input Regulation: Licensure (Exclusive Right to Practice). Licensure may arise in several ways. The state may license service providers directly; it may delegate this function to another agency (as, for example, a self-governing profession); or demand-side legislation or institutions may require that certain functions be performed only by persons with a prescribed designation. An occupational licensing system, under which only licensed providers are legally permitted to provide services to consumers, offers several advantages over other forms of regulation:

1. Licensure is anticipatory. That is, it attempts to exclude all incompetent practitioners from the market and thus keep the costs of incompetence from materializing. This contrasts with all the previous strategies and takes into account the fact that some costs of incompetence can never be fully compensated for through civil liability damage awards.
2. Licensure, by setting standards for providers rather than for transactions, economizes on enforcement costs.
3. Licensure (much more than certification) creates valuable property rights for practitioners in their legal ability to practice. In principle, the possibility of extinguishing those property rights by disciplinary action for incompetence should be a significant and general incentive to competence throughout a profession.
4. A licensing system may, in theory, substantially reduce the information costs faced by consumers by providing a central agency, able to exploit economies of scale, to obtain information about the competence of aspiring practitioners, licensing being based on that central pool of information.
5. A licensing system directly addresses the problem of third-party costs and externalities by removing from the provider

and client the unfettered right to make any quality choice or assume any risks they please.

6. A licensing system (more effectively than certification) may reduce economic concentration in professional markets by reducing the public uncertainty in dealing with small, non-"brand-name" firms.

7. Again, licensure may (more effectively than certification) prevent the degeneration of a market through the exodus of high-quality providers unable to differentiate their product from that of incompetent practitioners.[18]

The weaknesses of an occupational licensing system are potentially serious, however:

1. Like certification, licensure dubiously assumes a high correlation between required training inputs and desired service outcomes.

2. Of all the regulatory strategies surveyed, licensure introduces the greatest numbers of rigidities and elements of arbitrariness into a market. It acts as though the market were static, isolating at a given time certain functions as requiring licensing and prescribing certain educational and training requirements to be met as a condition for licensure. In a technologically changing market, this static model may exact serious social costs in creating impediments to innovation. On the demand side, changing consumer demands and, on the supply side, technological changes will over time call for different configurations of skills and manpower resources. A licensing regime is unlikely—and may be unable to keep pace with these forces.

3. All standard-setting mechanisms, including licensing, necessarily proceed on the assumption that quality is a discontinuous attribute.[19] A licensing regime assumes that either one satisfies the required licensing conditions and provides a corresponding quality of service or one does not meet the standards and is not permitted to provide any lesser quality

---

[18] See Hayne E. Leland, "Minimum-Quality Standards and Licensing in Markets with Asymmetric Information," in part 5 of this volume.

[19] For discussions of problems raised generally by public standard setting, see, for example, W. Oi, "The Economics of Product Safety," *Bell Journal of Economics*, vol. 4 (1973), pp. 3ff.; P. Sands, "How Effective is Safety Legislation?" *Journal of Law and Economics*, vol. 11 (1968), pp. 165ff.; Nina Cornell, Roger Noll, and Barry Weingast, "Safety Regulation," United States National Science Foundation, mimeo., 1976; Spence, "Consumer Misperceptions, Product Failure and Product Liability"; V. Goldberg, "The Economics of Product Safety and Imperfect Information," *Bell Journal of Economics*, vol. 5 (1974), pp. 683ff.; Sam Peltzman, "An Evaluation of Consumers Protection Legislation: The 1962 Drug Amendments," *Journal of Political Economy*, vol. 81 (1973), pp. 1049ff.; and "The Effects of Automobile Safety Regulations," *Journal of Political Economy*, vol. 83 (1975), pp. 761ff.

of service on any terms. But consumers may still use unlicensed services. The consumer's choices are to buy the quality of service that conforms to or exceeds the prescribed standard, to dispense with the service entirely, or to use some substitute service of indeterminate quality that falls outside the licensed domain. For example, if lawyers are licensed, a consumer who wishes to purchase legal services may buy services of a quality that satisfies the prescribed standards, or he can dispense with the service altogether (perhaps substituting his own services by reading "how to be your own lawyer" handbooks), or he can rely on legal advice from nonlawyer friends or businessmen or other counsellors (such as social workers). It is not clear that the result produced by a licensed regime, net of these substitution effects, is higher in average quality than it would be in a market not subject to licensure. The failure to regulate all substitutes for licensed services, no matter how remote, creates the possibility of consumers' drawing misleading inferences about the quality of those substitutes.[20] In this case licensure in one market may induce imperfections in related markets. Where supply and demand forces generate a strong market for substitutes, there will be persistent tension between suppliers in the licensed and unlicensed markets over the demarcation of the licensed territory. This may result in the licensed profession's attempting to extend the scope of its license progressively.

4. Even assuming the absence of such substitution effects, consumers who would have preferred to purchase inferior-quality services at a lower price and now must purchase higher-quality service at a higher price are thus forced to reallocate resources away from some other area of preferred consumption, with an unclear but probably negative impact on their general welfare.

5. For consumers who choose to purchase services from providers satisfying the required entry standards, licensing is only a crude quality signal. Inevitably, some tasks within the licensed domain are likely to call for a relatively modest degree of skill, others for highly sophisticated skills. A one-level licensing regime, like a one-level certification scheme, sends fuzzy quality signals to consumers of professional services. If, on the other hand, one attempts to reflect the continuous nature of the quality attribute through multiple or hierarchical licensing tracks, the problems of rigidity in-

---

[20] A problem raised by the economic theory of second best; see R. Lipsey and K. Lancaster, "The General Theory of Second Best," *Review of Economic Studies*, vol. 24, no. 1 (1956–1957).

herent in any licensing scheme are correspondingly multiplied.

6. On the assumption that a single licensing standard for a given professional market is necessary and feasible, the question of where on the quality continuum that standard should be set raises formidable policy issues. How "safe" should a doctor (engineer, lawyer) be before he is let loose on the public? How much of society's resources is it worth investing in further training an aspiring doctor to increase by 10 percent the probability of his "saving" one additional human life over the course of his professional career? Unfortunately, in answering such questions, there is no way of avoiding an access-quality trade-off, access being contingent on both the quantity and the price of services offered. Broadly speaking, the lower the quality threshold demanded of practitioners, the greater the access to the market by aspiring entrants and the greater the access to services on the part of potential consumers. The higher the quality threshold demanded of potential providers, the less the access to the market by aspiring entrants and the less the access to services on the part of potential consumers. There is no available policy that is capable of making all those affected better off.

The choice of a preferred policy, reflecting as it does the choice of a preferred pattern of distribution of social costs and benefits, while assisted by a technical analysis of social costs and benefits, is not ultimately a technical question on which any body of experts has a special claim to wisdom. This is not to say that the problem is peculiar to occupational licensure. An unregulated professional market may hold advantages for the informed and sophisticated while imposing costs on the uninformed and unsophisticated. The task of carrying out the requisite social calculus is not made easier by the fact that different interests win or lose in different ways under different options.

7. To expect that the legal system can frame rules precisely differentiating complex occupational functions either horizontally (lawyers' functions from accountants' functions, engineers' functions from architects' functions), or vertically (engineers' functions from engineering technologists' functions) may be to expect an unattainable degree of regulatory refinement.

8. To the extent that professional interests influence both the setting and the enforcing of licensing standards, there is a risk that standards will be set too high in order to restrict entry and drive up the incomes of existing practitioners. The emphasis placed by most professions on technical ex-

cellence over other dimensions of service quality and over issues of cost and access is likely to increase this risk.

9. A licensing scheme once in place is difficult to remove. Forms of regulation conferring windfall gains on parties (exclusive licenses, for example) typically induce early capitalization of those gains, so that investments by subsequent parties in the regulated sector will reflect a relatively normal rate of return.[21] Thus revoking regulation will inflict real welfare losses, a prospect likely to be vigorously resisted by those whose interests are in jeopardy. The ideological primacy accorded to private property rights in our society is likely to reinforce hostility to expunging or interfering with those rights, however created.[22] Exclusive licensing laws, once enacted, thus tend to be politically irreversible.

These weaknesses of an occupational licensing system are formidable and suggest that licensure should be reserved for professional markets characterized by high costs of provider error, high consumer information costs, or substantial and widespread negative third-party effects not fully compensable by damages.

Direct or "Professional" Regulation. Even if one were satisfied that quality assurance in a professional market required input regulation (whether certification or licensure), one would be faced with the further question how the input regulation should be administered. In particular, a case for input regulation in any market does not constitute a case for self-regulation by the practitioners. Since regulatory powers are state powers, one might expect that, whatever the appropriate regulatory response, the regulation would be undertaken by the public authority. One does not observe the state delegating self-regulatory powers to taxi drivers and airline pilots, for example. Those occupations are "regulated" to some degree directly by the state, either through a branch of government or through a regulatory board. Indeed, this is the norm of "occupational licensure" rather than the exception. Self-regulatory powers are accorded to only a relatively small number of occupational groups, and it can be argued that this is a central feature of their "professional" status. The appropriateness of self-regulation is thus contingent on more than a demonstration of market failure in the absence of regulatory intervention. The delegation of regulatory authority by govern-

---

[21] See Gordon Tullock, "The Transitional Gains Trap," *Bell Journal of Economics*, vol. 6 (1975), pp. 671ff.

[22] See Carolyn J. Tuohy, "Private Government, Property and Professionalism," *Canadian Journal of Political Science*, vol. 9 (1976), p. 668; and G. Tullock, "On Dismantling Regulation: A Public Choice Perspective," *Regulation*, November/December 1978, p. 50.

ment to a self-governing professional body requires a demonstration that self-regulation is more effective than direct regulation. Once a need for *some* regulation has been established, the case for professional self-regulation turns on four kinds of considerations: the costs of information, the costs of error, the costs of enforcement, and the establishment of trust.[23]

Although there is great diversity in the activities of the different professions, there are common elements. In each case, we find the application of a body of knowledge that is systematic and sometimes arcane, which, by its nature, can be acquired only by long and arduous training. Second, the activities of the professions touch on some of the most fundamental of human affairs. Third, professional practitioners are numerous while their clients are even more numerous. Professional services intrinsically involve the application of general knowledge to particular cases and are therefore essentially individual in scope. Finally, the essence of the professional relationship involves the assumption of an agency role by the practitioner, acting on behalf of all the relevant interests involved in decision making (the client's interests and those of third parties) and suppressing his own interests altogether. This agency function cannot be established or maintained in the absence of trust. Professionals must be trusted to act for their clients rather than for themselves, and they must be trusted to be sensitive to the interests of third parties. Without trust, professional relationships would founder.

The choice between direct regulation and self-regulation of quality in these professional markets is affected by these four characteristics. The determination that a service is of high quality or that a practitioner is adequately qualified can be made only by the application of the systematic knowledge required of the profession's members. If the state chooses to regulate the quality of professional services directly, it may, of course, hire "experts" to assist it in its task. Clearly, however, the acquisition of this information is costly, no matter how it is acquired. The delegation of regulatory powers to the profession itself would place the responsibility for quality assurance in the hands of people with sufficient knowledge to do the job.

High costs of error, like high costs of information, may argue for professional self-regulation. Where the activities of professionals involve vital practical affairs, the performance of poor-quality services (or, more generally, the certification or licensure of unqualified practitioners) generates social costs. In extreme cases, public health and safety may be imperiled. Even in less dramatic circumstances, the state cannot easily countenance "errors" made in assuring quality in such

---

[23] See Tuohy and Wolfson, "Self-Regulation: Who Qualifies?"

markets. Such errors will, of course, be more numerous when the regulator lacks the information necessary to assess quality. The combination of high costs of acquiring such information with high costs of doing without it argue in favor of delegating the regulatory function to a profession itself.

There are further arguments supporting such delegation. The fact that professional practitioners are so numerous and that their services are so myriad implies that enforcement of quality standards will be formidable. Strong allegiances to the profession and its norms, developed by members as part of their education and training, serve to enhance compliance with quality standards. The enforcement costs of monitoring and policing legions of practitioners can thus be substantially reduced by delegating this responsibility to a profession as a whole.

Finally, in our impersonal society, trust relationships are extremely fragile. But trust is fundamental to the professional's role; the professional agent cannot perform his function without it. We would argue that individual clients and the public at large are more likely to have confidence in the activities of practitioners when the state has indicated its confidence in the profession as a whole. The delegation of regulatory authority to a self-governing body of the profession signals such trust and thereby reinforces individual trust relationships.

It is important to note that the delegation of regulatory authority is not itself without costs. There are risks that a self-regulating profession will not adequately discharge its responsibilities, particularly when conflicts of interest arise. These are likely to be particularly pronounced when the profession's economic interests are at stake, such as in the protection of a professional monopoly over rights to practice and in the discouragement of competitive practices among its members. Such dangers exist, and the state must be alert to them.

In light of these potential costs of delegating regulatory authority, self-governing status ought not to be easily granted. In fact, unless there is evidence that all four conditions are met—that there are high costs of error, information, and enforcement and a need to reinforce trust between practitioners and clients—we would not, in general, suggest such delegation.

General Points of Emphasis

By way of summary, let us note the general points of emphasis in our approach to regulatory policy for the professions. First, however, let us note two major regulatory issues that, for reasons of length, we have not addressed in this paper. One relates to policies regarding the structures and processes of the regulatory system. In general, we advocate that powers of licensure and certification be used only in compelling circumstances. It follows that where they *are* necessary, they must be treated as serious governing instruments. Powers to certify, as well as to license, ought to be based on statutes that specify the structures and processes through which they are to be exercised. And these structures and processes must promote a politics of the public interest—that is, they must provide the conditions under which the public interest debate can be carried on. Accordingly, they must ensure that all relevant interests have access to information on the decisions of professional regulatory bodies and have the opportunity to challenge or support those policies. More specifically, the structures and processes of professional regulation must provide for the representation of relevant interests on professional governing bodies, for the maintenance of a publicly available information base on the professions, for a requirement that the policy decisions of regulatory bodies be approved by the political executive, and for periodic legislative review of the statutory base of professional regulatory power.

In addition, whereas in this paper we have focused primarily on the broad issues relating to the need for regulation per se and the options for regulating professional practice in general, we ought to point up the importance of regulating post-entry conduct. Public policy toward the professions cannot be viewed solely in terms of controlling entry to professional markets. Equally important are issues relating to the conduct of practitioners after entry. Indeed, rules of professional conduct that are either too lax or too restrictive may be at least as detrimental to consumer or third-party interests (to say nothing of the interests of the profession) as standards of entry that are either too low or too high. Careful attention must therefore be paid to questions of continuing competence mechanisms, disciplinary processes, fee determination, advertising, and the structure of firms. In this context, it is worth emphasizing the importance of innovation in professional markets and the correlative importance of eliminating unjustified regulatory constraints on the ability of individual professionals and professional firms to innovate. To review our central points:

The public interest is not in itself a substantive concept that can guide policy determination; it is a signal for a particular kind of political debate in which all the relevant interests are taken into account and in which certain general principles dominate. These principles are efficiency, fairness, accountability, and practicality. The interests to be taken into account include those of providers, consumers, and third parties.

We have analyzed the rationales for regulatory intervention in professional areas and found market failure to be a precondition for intervention of any kind. Two kinds of market failure are particularly troublesome in professional markets. The classic informational problem of uninformed consumers unable to assess their needs for professional services (or to evaluate the services they receive) leads to the formation of agency relationships with providers. The establishment, maintenance, and monitoring of these agency relationships call for regulation, lest practitioners take advantage of vulnerable clients. In some professions—accounting, architecture, and engineering, for example—the principal regulatory problem revolves around the protection of third-party interests, not second-party (client) interests as in the archetypical professions of medicine and law. This poses special challenges in designing regulatory strategies to ensure not only that any professional services purchased are of appropriate quality but that an appropriate quantity of services is purchased to protect these third-party interests. In other words, parallel regulation of the demand for and supply of professional services is required. This issue has been little addressed in previous analyses of the professions.

We have reviewed a number of regulatory options. A case for regulation per se does not constitute a case for a self-governing licensure regime. In the first instance, the regulation of professional market outputs by civil liability rules or standard setting and enforcement must be considered. In input regulation, restrictions on the use of title (certification) may constitute an alternative to restrictions on the right to practice (licensure). Indeed, licensure is justified only by the most compelling circumstances. In general, one should limit the scope of licenses as much as possible, insofar as this is consistent with the need to protect vulnerable clients and third parties.

Once a case has been made for regulation of any professional market, appropriately tempered forms of self-regulation are sometimes to be preferred to direct state regulation. Professionals could not perform their unique functions without their clients' trust. The confidence in a profession shown by the state in its delegation of regulatory authority to a self-governing body reinforces this trust. Thus we see self-regulation endorsed by the state as a vital element in the protection and promotion of the trust that must characterize the relationships between professionals and their clients.

Commentary

Jack A. Meyer

Wolfson, Trebilcock, and Tuohy's assessment of what constitutes good federal regulation is useful, and their four criteria (of efficiency, fairness, accountability, and practicality) are helpful. Some of their discussion shed new light on the notion that regulating, like politics, is often the art of the possible and needs to involve people in ways that the people consider fair. I believe, however, that their conceptual framework gives inadequate—and, in some cases, inappropriate—attention to the question whether, or under what conditions, regulation should be pursued at all.

This reflects a general problem: the tendency to jump to *regulation* without adequately considering alternative public or private responses to a problem. This tendency, regrettably, lingers even when the authors properly acknowledge that market failure, per se, is not a sufficient rationale for rgulation. Rarely does the cost of regulation initially appear to be greater than the cost of the market failure to which it is addressed. Later, we frequently find that the cure is worse than the disease. How does this criticism apply to the authors' analysis of the criteria for regulation and of the appropriate types of regulation?

The authors specify two basic rationales for government regulation: inadequate information and externalities. They argue that professionals in certain fields are imperfect agents for their clients or patients, but imperfect agency or imperfect information, per se, does not constitute a rationale for federal regulation. There may be preferable ways to increase the flow of information. Let me illustrate this point with the physician-patient relationship.

It is often said that consumers' ignorance leads them to rely on doctors for decisions about treatment, rendering notions of consumer choice useless in an analysis of health care costs. Physicians are said to control demand and dictate for themselves a "target" level of income. Stories are recounted to show that when one is admitted to an emergency room, he is not about to question the doctor's judgment about treatment. But it can be quite misleading to jump from these emergency treatment cases, in which the patient has no real input in the selection of a treatment, to a presumption that the patient is ignorant. It is an even greater jump to presume that, where he *is* poorly informed, this can be cured through additional government regulation.

Patients frequently have enough information to generate outcomes as close to a competitive norm as would occur with most other services. There are numerous constraints on physician abuse of the kind of agency relationship described by the authors. These include consumer information acquired from friends and relatives, limited competition from alternative delivery mechanisms, peer pressure, and the fear of malpractice suits. The fact that patients have little influence over emergency care does not mean they are without influence over routine care. Furthermore, cost considerations should not be immaterial at the point when consumers purchase insurance, particularly where they can reap the savings from selecting a low-cost health plan.

One of the problems of excessive regulation is that it frequently glosses over—and diverts our attention from—the fundamental forces driving the consumption of services and inflation. For instance, in health care costs, such factors as open-ended federal tax subsidies for health insurance, the job-centered nature of insurance (with typically little or no incentive for employees to pick low-cost plans), and physician and hospital reimbursement mechanisms that encourage excessive purchases of equipment and treatment are at the heart of cost escalation—but they are not really addressed by proposed regulation. Indeed, the growing body of federal and state regulation of the health care industry is as much a *part* of the health care cost problem as it is a cure for it.

The hospital cost-containment legislation now under consideration in Congress demonstrates the folly of trying to regulate away the problem—to paper it over by placing caps on hospital expenses and revenues. These caps, which accept base costs and limit the growth of costs, reward and entrench inefficiency.

A similar problem attaches to the authors' discussion of externalities. Again, they jumped too quickly from the presence of a problem (externalities) to the need for regulation. There is a tendency to equate a rationale for government intervention with a rationale for regulation. The externality may justify a government role, but why must that role be a regulatory one? The authors fail to make Charles Schultze's important distinction between the "command-and-control" and the "tax-and-subsidy" approaches to correcting a market imperfection.

Let me comment briefly on the authors' discussion of the various types of solutions, such as civil liability standards and licensing. They presented a very good analysis of the advantages and disadvantages of the alternative remedies, but there was too little attention devoted to the larger issue: whether or when any of these interventions is needed. When this issue is posed, the matter is too often depicted as a choice between state regulation and self-regulation, begging the question of the need for regulation at all.

Again, this is reminiscent of the hospital cost debate, in which the industry and the government fight over whether there should be voluntary controls or mandatory controls, whether the industry should be allowed to regulate itself or be regulated by the Department of Health, Education and Welfare. Rarely does anyone consider whether this approach to health care inflation is appropriate at all.

In fact, the regulatory approach is now frequently crowding out more systemic solutions—those that would permit self-corrective mechanisms to work in ways involving the parties directly. Other vehicles for problem solving, such as collective bargaining, are often replaced by regulation, even though they can meet such criteria as accountability and fairness, which were highlighted in this paper.

The authors assume that regulation is needed to protect third parties from the providers of services. Too frequently, however, when government intervention takes the form of regulation, rather than the provision of incentives or penalties, what starts as an attempt to protect the public becomes a mechanism for shoring up the providers. The inclination to shelter regulated interests from outside competition and the tendency of the regulated interests to gain the ear of the regulators, deflecting policies that appear harmful, are inherent in the regulatory process. This is true of occupational licensure, but it is also true of Interstate Commerce Commission regulation of the trucking industry, and "captive" regulatory relationships characterize other sectors of our economy.

It is not that I believe the analysis in the paper is wrong; rather, I would prefer to have seen this additional basic dimension added.

Robert B. Reich

There was once a kingdom that boasted impressive monuments, historic buildings, rich memorials to its heritage, museums, curiosities, and artifacts of all kinds. The opening of a royal highway to the kingdom brought thousands of tourists to marvel at the splendor of it all. The tourists naturally wanted to be guided to the most spectacular sights and to hear the most colorful and interesting historical anecdotes. So a few residents of the kingdom, who knew every nook and cranny of it and had thoroughly studied its history, decided to offer themselves as guides. The tourists willingly paid $50 a day for their valuable services.

Soon the guide business proved so profitable that other residents offered themselves as guides. These other residents knew far less about the city's attractions than the first guides and knew almost no history. Instead of showing tourists the most impressive monuments, they showed tourists the kingdom's sewage disposal treatment center and its morgue. They concocted historical anecdotes from their dull imaginations. Obviously tourists were less impressed with the kingdom when guided by these less experienced guides. As a result, tourists were willing to pay only $30 when they sought a guide for the remainder of their stay, and they decided to leave the kingdom earlier than they had planned.

The best guides, who knew most about the kingdom and its history, now had difficulty attracting tourists for $50 a day. At $30 it was hardly worth their while to offer their services as guides. They could earn more by using their knowledge of culture and history as curators in the king's museums.

Now the king owned all the hotels in the kingdom. As a result of the deteriorating condition of guide services, fewer tourists came to stay in the king's hotels, and those who came soon left. Eventually the king was visited by a delegation of his hotel managers. "Something must be done!" they cried. "Soon no one will come to marvel at this kingdom, your hotels will be empty, and we'll be out of jobs."

The king was worried. He understood the problem. Tour guides had no need to offer good quality because (1) tourists were not repeat purchasers of tour guide services and (2) in any event, tourists had no way of evaluating the services they were getting. The king had heard the royal economists talk in hushed tones about such things, which they called "market failures."

The king summoned three scholars from the University of Toronto, who offered several possible remedies. First, the king could pass an ordinance imposing civil liability on guides who failed to offer "reasonable" services. For this to work, however, tourists would need to be able to evaluate the quality of guidance they received. This option would also clog the courts with difficult case-by-case determinations about the reasonableness of guide services. The king rejected this option.

A second option was for the king to establish minimum performance standards for tour guides. But these standards would be costly to monitor and enforce, particularly because tourists who cannot evaluate what they receive cannot be relied on to complain about substandard services. The king did not care much for this alternative either.

A third option was to certify guides who met certain minimum criteria as "official royal guides." Because different tourists were apt to be interested in seeing and hearing different things, however, the criteria for certification would not match the wants of many tourists.

Certification might also discourage guides from offering new and innovative ways of showing the kingdom. No good, thought the king.

Finally, the scholars suggested that the king license guides who passed an examination about the kingdom's culture, history, and special attractions and prohibit all others from offering their services. This option, however, shared many of the disadvantages of the others and also would prevent tourists from being able to choose cheaper, less expert guides; tourists who did not want to pay for an expert would have to do without any guide at all. This option would also facilitate collusion among tour guides, who would probably end up running the Royal Board of Tour Guide Examiners and thereby deciding on how much competition they would tolerate. The king did not like this alternative either.

The king was in a quandary. All of these options had severe disadvantages. Each seemed a clumsy way of remedying the problem. Was there nothing else he could do?

The king thought and thought. "Perhaps," he mused, "I can give tour guides the means of differentiating themselves from one another, without getting the kingdom into the business of setting standards, certifying, licensing, or adjudicating civil liability. I'll allow each guide to establish a trademark that no other guide can use. I'll also allow the guides to advertise and solicit tourists. And I'll allow guides from various kingdoms to combine into partnerships and franchises and to enforce minimum quality standards for themselves across kingdoms, so that tourists can rely on the trademark wherever they travel." The king smiled. "By these means I'll establish property rights in reputation, and the market will take care of itself."

The king tried out his plan. Soon the royal highways were dotted with brightly colored neon and plastic signs announcing McDonald's Tour Guides and Hertz's Tour Guides. Tourists started flocking back to the kingdom.

Before long, however, there were only two giant tour guide companies left. All the rest had either merged or gone out of business because they could not afford the advertising and promotion—even though some of them had offered unique services better suited to the particular needs and tastes of some of the tourists than the two giant companies. The price of tours went up to seventy-five dollars. Once again fewer tourists came to the kingdom, this time because they could not afford the high tour guide prices. The king's hotel managers again complained to him.

The king was perplexed. "How can I keep tour guide services competitive, while ensuring that tourists don't get poorer quality than they want?"

The king sent his emissaries to other lands to look for a remedy. The emissaries returned with exciting news: "There is a solution, Highness," they said. "Give property rights to 'information brokers' who can profit by locating for tourists just the guide services they want. Because the brokers will deal with many tourists and many guides, they can aggregate consumers' experiences over the long term and learn a great deal about each guide."

The emissaries told of brokers who act as private certifiers, such as *Good Housekeeping* and *Consumers' Union*; other brokers who refer particular consumers to particular sellers, such as real estate agents, consulting physicians, stockbrokers, and independent insurance agents; and brokers who directly control quality on behalf of consumers, such as department stores and automobile clubs.

In each of these markets the brokers are competitive with one another. Each broker has a strong stake in consumer satisfaction because each hopes that the consumer will depend on it in the future for various other transactions. While the consumer may have difficulty in evaluating the quality of a particular service to which he is referred by the broker or may not need that particular service again, the broker will want the consumer to use his *brokerage* service again and therefore will want to provide the consumer with the means of evaluating what he has received.

The king was intrigued. Who, he wondered, was best situated to act as broker for tour guide services in the kingdom? Why, of course—the hotels! Surely they could aggregate consumers' experiences with tour guides over the long term and efficiently learn about price and quality. If the hotels were competitive with one another, they would have a strong stake in consumer satisfaction. Each would want tourists to stay on its premises and to return in the future. Each would want its guests to know that it had aided them in obtaining the best guide services for the money.

The king summoned his hotel managers. "From now on," he declared, "each of you is on his own. I'll collect a tax, of course, but I hereby give you property rights to your individual reputations. It is up to you whether tourists come to your hotels. You will bear the costs of finding tour guides that meet the wants of your guests and passing on these costs in your rates. And I will make sure that you do not collude in any way."

The plan worked like a charm. Many tour guides were established, with varying prices and quality. Tourists who came to the kingdom found just the quality of tour guide they wanted, at the price they wanted to pay. The kingdom prospered. So did the king, who had his royal engraver inscribe these words on the royal coat-of-arms:

GLORIA CONTENTIOQUE SUPER OMNIA

which, roughly translated, provides a moral for our tale: develop property rights in reputation and ensure vigorous competition before you try anything else.

Part
Five

Professionals and the Production Function: Can Competition Policy Improve Efficiency in the Licensed Professions?

Robert G. Evans

Professions as Source of and Response to Market Failure

The economic analysis of the professions is the study of market failure. The professions are associated with a particular subset of productive activities, all of which are to a greater or lesser degree hedged about with legal restrictions impeding or preventing the normal operation of market forces. The production of professional services and associated goods is, of course, an economic activity in the ordinary sense, using up scarce resources of human time and embodied skills, capital, and so on, to produce outputs valued by consumers, patients, or clients. Thus one can think of the professional industries as one of the many possible subdivisions of the set of resource-using and value-generating productive activities that make up the overall economy. The optimum allocation of social resources to these industries is part of the general economic problem.[1] What appears distinctive about the professional industries, however, is that they all function within a special framework of public regulation over both entry and conduct. Moreover, this framework is administered, and to a large extent created, by private associations of professionals, exercising delegated state authority.

Authority delegated for self-regulation with the force of law thus appears to be the characteristic of the professional industries that distinguishes them from, say, professional sports or from occupations, such as public relations, that attempt to appropriate the "professional" title for its presumed status connotations. Legally sanctioned self-regulatory power may not be a sufficient condition for professional status—agricultural marketing boards come to mind as counterexamples—but it seems to be a necessary condition.

Such generalization may be helpful for taxonomic purposes, but it

---

[1] It may be noted that I am focusing on professional *industries* as a type of production activity rather than the more usual discussion of professional *occupations*. The choice of focus is deliberate, and (as I hope to show) the distinction is of considerable importance.

begs the more interesting analytic question *why* certain industries have become professionalized. It is clear that the process of resource allocation through market forces that economists often think of as normal cannot be assumed to function in an industry where associations of providers have legal authority to set conditions of entry and to specify and enforce both economic and professional conduct.[2] In this sense, the very existence of "professional" institutions implies market failure.

Underlying these institutions, however, there may be presumed to exist special characteristics of professional goods and services that (as perceived by the public or by the legislators who delegate legal authority to private associations) lead to inferior resource allocation outcomes if constraints are not placed on market forces. Analysts of health care, in particular, have attempted to isolate the special aspects of that commodity that violate the assumptions necessary to derive a restricted form of optimal allocation from market institutions.[3] All emphasize the lack of full information that exists between the buyer and the seller of professional services. This asymmetry leads to the creation of a professional role as agent on the buyer's behalf as well as economic principal acting on his own behalf—an inherent conflict of interest that seems to be the essence of the professional role. Carolyn Tuohy and Alan Wolfson in a more extended analysis have suggested that the self-governing professions possessing private governmental authority emerge from a dual agency relation, the individual professional as agent of the consumer/patient/client and the collective profession as agent of the state for quality monitoring and disciplinary processes. Survival of a profession, they suggest, depends on informational asymmetry at both levels; and if the information differential is eroded at one level, it cannot be indefinitely sustained at the other.[4] Pharmacy may be in the process of "deprofessionalization," since the pharmacist has virtually ceased to be an agent and become only an arms-length principal; thus in pharmacy collective self-government is threatened. Indeed, the pharmacist is increasingly not even a principal but merely a salaried manager employed by a strictly for-profit corporation with no agency role whatever. In

---

[2] If such a distinction is possible. "Professional" activity is clearly resource using and output producing and therefore economic. The usual distinction is one of motive.

[3] See Kenneth J. Arrow, "Uncertainty and the Welfare Economics of Medical Care," *American Economic Review*, vol. 53, no. 5 (December 1963); H. Klarman, *The Economics of Health* (New York: Columbia University Press, 1965); A. J. Culyer, "The Nature of the Commodity 'Health Care' and its Efficient Allocation," *Oxford Economic Papers*, vol. 23, no. 2 (July 1971).

[4] Carolyn J. Tuohy and Alan D. Wolfson, "The Political Economy of Professionalism: A Perspective," in Michael J. Trebilcock, ed., *Four Aspects of Professionalism* (Ottawa: Consumer Research Council of Canada, 1977); see also their paper in this volume.

response, organized pharmacy struggles to rediscover an agency role at the individual level to protect its collective position.

Studies currently under way by the Professional Organizations Committee in Ontario indicate that informational asymmetry at the individual provider/client level may also be a relatively insignificant feature of the market for engineering, architecture, and accounting services, again calling into question their collective possession of delegated state power.[5]

While the crucial role of informational asymmetry and agency behavior in the creation of the professional relationship is now generally understood and accepted, there is not such wide agreement on the implications of professionalization for resource allocation and efficiency. What, if any, is the economic problem of the professions? Presumably, public policy toward regulation or deregulation should be rooted in some clear picture of the present pattern of resource misallocation and what should be done about it. Unfortunately, there appear to be several different and inconsistent perceptions of the underlying problem, which give rise to radically different policy recommendations. In what follows I try to trace the evolution of perceptions of the "professional problem," with particular reference to health care because analysis has been pushed furthest in that area. In the process it should become clear how different policies relate to different perceptions and also that all professions are not the same—far from it. The degree of information failure, agency, and professionalism varies both from one profession to another and across types of services supplied by the same professional group, and appropriate regulatory policy must be formulated accordingly.

Professions as Monopolies: Restricted Entry and Elevated Price

The earliest and simplest analyses of the "professional problem" seem to have focused on the implications of licensure and restricted entry for resource allocation. The straightforward application of an elementary price-theory model gives the obvious result that restricted entry into an industry protects the above-normal profits in that industry that have

---

[5] Like the pharmacists, these professions respond by trying to rediscover an agency relationship of some sort. Professionals may perhaps be agents of unrepresented third parties—unsafe buildings may fall on innocent bystanders, ugly buildings are an eyesore, unreliable financial statements may mislead the investing public. These third-party interests cannot be dismissed a priori, but the classical self-governing profession with its intimate professional/client relationship does not appear optimally adapted to meet them. Unrepresented third parties do not pay the bills or enter into follow-on contracts. Their interests may be in conflict not only with those of the professional as economic principal but also with those of the second-party client who retains the professional, thus adding an additional dimension to the conflict of interest inherent in the professional/client relation.

been achieved by curtailing output (and thus moving up the demand curve).[6] There are several variants to the restricted entry story.

One can have price competition among those in the industry with rising long-run firm supply curves and restricted entry. In this case, price would equal short-run marginal costs for each firm but exceed what long-run industry marginal costs would be if new firms entered. Individual firms would be selling at prices above short-run average costs and—if the long-run cost curve is U-shaped—would be operating at levels of output above those at which they would be most efficient. Short- and long-run average costs will be above their lowest possible levels.[7] Professionals will "work too hard," drawn by high prices for services; production will be unnecessarily costly in terms of resources used; but the real resource-allocation problem for society as a whole is the restricted output of services. In this model, professional services are underproduced while prices and professional firm profits are above market levels. The policy solution is more entry; if those in the industry are already behaving competitively, all else follows.

Alternatively, one can assume local monopolies or other forms of differentiated product combined with blocked entry; in this case price may vary from firm to firm but will be set to exceed short-run marginal cost in each firm. The collective behavior of the profession will now seek to maximize professional incomes by reducing the extent to which the demand for one firm's services is sensitive to another's price or output behavior—for example, by restrictions on advertising and other forms of competition. In this way the demand curve faced by any in-

---

[6] Probably the most widely disseminated version of this model is in Milton Friedman, *Capitalism and Freedom* (Chicago: University of Chicago Press, 1962), but the model frequently lies behind discussions of medical care in the business press (see "Keeping Up," *Fortune,* December 18, 1978, advocating increases in physician supply to drive down price). The historical role of the American Medical Association in constraining the supply of physicians to protect physicians' incomes has been widely discussed, as by Reuben A. Kessel, "The A.M.A. and the Supply of Physicians," *Law and Contemporary Problems* (Symposium on Health Care, part 1), vol. 35, no. 2 (Spring 1970). In the elementary price-theory model, supply restriction drives up incomes through its effects on market-clearing prices, but the income result can easily be achieved without the price effect (or with perverse effects) in alternative models.

[7] If the long-run average cost curve of the firm is L-shaped, both prices and average costs will fall to the technological miniumum as firms in the industry expand their capacity and output. (Operation on the left-hand or falling section of the average cost curve is ruled out by the assumption of perfect competition in the industry.) In this case, barriers to entry are ineffective in constraining industry output. In the case of professional services firms, however, such expansion can only come about by raising the output from existing professionals with clearly rising costs or by hiring more professionals. The supply of professionals is restricted by entry barriers. Any technology permitting the expansion of output by existing firms at more or less constant long-run costs (through use of capital or non-restricted-entry labor substitutes for professionals) would, of course, destroy the value of entry barriers to existing suppliers.

dividual firm at any price and market share combination is made steeper, and the probability that price cutting will appear profitable to the individual firm is reduced. In the limit, when each firm can be entirely isolated from effects of others' price variations, the firm demand curves become independent of one another, and market shares depend on relative prices only insofar as the pricing decisions of each firm influence its own sales levels. For such a policy to be profitable for all professional firms taken together, there must be a relatively inelastic market demand curve for professional services.[8]

In this environment a policy of stimulating free entry up to its competitive limit would lead to the standard monopolistic competition result: tangency of demand and average cost curves, but firms too small and unit costs too high. Total industry output would still be too small relative to the competitive optimum, and the resource allocation problem remains underprovision of professional services. Public policy in this case would have to be focused on increasing the sensitivity of each firm's sales to the price behavior of others by, for example, removing regulatory prohibitions on advertising as well as liberalizing entry. If it turns out that the cross-elasticity is still relatively low when regulatory restrictions are removed—that is, that local monopoly or "brand preference" continues to inhibit interfirm price competition—then presumably the best that deregulation can produce is the monopolistic competition equilibrium of constrained output and small, high-cost firms.[9]

---

[8] If the market demand curve does not have an elasticity less than unity (absolute value), there may not be monopoly gains to be made by pushing up individual prices. Of course, the isolated, individual firm demand curves need not each have the same elasticity as the market curve; some could be greater and others less. Complete equality of elasticity could be achieved by means of a perfect cartel with collusive pricing and organized market sharing. Reuben A. Kessel, "Price Discrimination in Medicine," *Journal of Law and Economics*, vol. 1, no. 2 (October 1958), describes in considerable detail the mechanisms whereby cartel discipline is maintained in medical care markets; many of the same formal and informal sanctions appear possible of application in other professional groups. Collusive behavior seems to focus both on discouraging price or quantity competition and on creating an institutional environment (low cross-elasticities) where such competition is unlikely to be profitable. Collusion does not extend to formal output allocation, however, except perhaps in group practices.

[9] One should, however, note the distinction between this discussion and the usual monopolistic competition case. In the conventional model, consumers are presumed to have full knowledge of all market prices. Advertising of product characteristics is perceived as generating or promoting real or illusory differences between the products of different firms so as to lower cross-price elasticities. The objective is the same—market segmentation—but in the professional services case, cross-elasticities are held down by prohibiting *price* advertising and so restricting the availability of such information. The usual defense of monopolistic competition—that its "excess costs" reflect merely consumers' purchase of diversity—obviously does not apply in this case.

As K. J. Lancaster has shown, however ("Socially Optimal Product Differentiation," *American Economic Review*, vol. 65, no. 4 [September 1975]), monopolistic competition with increasing returns to scale will lead to too much product differentiation and too many

Finally, there is the interesting variant on the restricted-entry, imperfect-competition model analyzed by Kessel.[10] If professional firms not only face independent downward-sloping demand curves but also have the power to set different prices for different customers, then, of course, professional profits are higher still. Individual firms would then expand output to the point where the price charged the marginal buyer equaled the marginal cost for each firm. *If* (a qualification that turns out to be critical) the cost curve is not affected by a shift from uniform to discriminatory pricing (and if income effects on buyers are small), the problem of service underprovision resulting from imperfect competition disappears, and the only remaining difficulty is blocked entry.[11] On the other hand, perfectly free entry and perfect price discrimination would appear to lead to excessive entry and the dissipation of all producers' and consumers' surplus in the industry: all consumer surplus would be converted into profit, and all supranormal profit would be eliminated by entry. Marginal cost would equal marginal revenue (price of last unit sold) for each individual firm and would be less than average price, but average cost would lie above price on the marginal unit sold and average firm size would be even smaller than in the standard monopolistic competition case. As Oliver Williamson has pointed out, the resource-allocation advantages of price discrimination in imperfect competition (as against uniform pricing by each firm) depend on costless extraction of the necessary information and costless prohibition of intercustomer trades.[12] If resources are used in locating and protecting

---

products. This conclusion is based on the assumption that goods are bundles of characteristics and different products in a monopolistically competitive market represent different bundles of the same characteristics. If diversity per se is valued, of course, the "too many products" argument may fail, but the utility functions of the consumer begin to look rather peculiar, having as arguments not only commodities or characteristics but the number of different (measured how?) commodities, bought or unbought, in the market.

[10] Kessel, "Price Discrimination in Medicine."

[11] If these qualifications are not met, there may still be Pareto optimality—resources will still be allocated so that price equals marginal cost. But price and marginal cost of professional services will be higher and output lower than in the alternative Pareto optimum that would have obtained if suppliers could not charge different prices to different customers and had raised output to the point where price equaled marginal cost. Price discrimination is thus akin to a lump-sum transfer to professional service suppliers that raises the opportunity cost (forgone leisure) of such services and lowers the incomes of service consumers.

[12] O. E. Williamson, *Markets and Hierarchies: Analysis and Anti-Trust Implications* (New York: Free Press, 1975). The point, of course, generalizes; from the social point of view, all resources invested by the industry in maintenance of cartel discipline and in generating the information needed for its optimum exploitation are dead-weight losses. These costs are likely to be higher than costs of transacting in normal competitive markets because in the normal case transaction prices are themselves readily accessible "sufficient statistics," encapsulating necessary trading information. In cartelized and discriminatory markets, this is no longer true.

markets in which customers are willing to pay very high prices (the upper branch of the demand curve), each firm will invest in such information and protection up to the usual maximum profit point, but this is a dead-weight social loss. For professionals, ability to exploit the upper reaches of the demand curve increases the payoff for policies that restrict cross-elasticity, and Kessel has provided considerable detail on the process of maintenance of "cartel discipline" by formal and informal means.

The extension of anticombines policy and legislation to the service industries in Canada appears to be explicable if it is assumed that the "professional problem" is merely another case of imperfect competition. Like the shift in the U.S. legislative interpretations and antitrust policy, the new deregulatory approach appears to restrict the powers of professional regulatory bodies to regulate their members' conduct. Assuming that such an extension of Canadian federal competition policy to provincially regulated professions is not beyond the implied powers (*ultra vires*) of the federal government, such policy would be expected to increase the cross-elasticity of demand among professional firms for any given shape of the market demand curve.[13] This, in turn, should flatten the demand curve faced by each firm and lead to increases in output per firm, lower prices, and a reduction in above-normal profits. Whether total costs of professional services rise or fall depends on the elasticity of the market demand curve; but if it is inelastic, they should fall. The resource misallocation to be remedied, however, is the restriction of output by existing suppliers. The problem of restricted entry is not addressed; but in most professions in Canada, entry is now in the hands of universities and behind them the hands of provincial governments; so in very few professions is there still any significant power by the profession to control access to qualification. Entry is far from unrestricted, but the incentives facing those who control entry differ significantly from those facing the self-regulating professions.[14] There does

---

[13] The issue is currently before the courts in British Columbia and will presumably go to the Supreme Court. The constitutional question is whether a federal statute, the Combines Investigation Act, can be applied to a professional body (in this case the B.C. Law Society) whose powers are derived from a provincial act. If it cannot, then of course the powers of the provincially established professional regulatory and licensure bodies are beyond the reach of federal competition policy.

[14] Articling requirements for lawyers (service for a specified time with a law practice after graduation as a condition of licensure) give the profession some control, but not collectively. A systematic failure to provide sufficient articling opportunities for provincial university graduates *somewhere* would invite intervention. Hospital residency positions depend on the budgetary decisions of provincial hospital reimbursing agencies, not on the professions. Access to existing firms may be restricted—law, accountancy, engineering—but new entrants can certainly set up new firms. A new solo practitioner may not compete on equal terms with Price, Waterhouse; but that is another problem.

231

appear to be a connection, though ponderous and clumsy in some cases, between demand for entry by would-be students and supply of training places. One might then expect that an aggressive anticombines policy aimed at removing regulatory restrictions on the competitive conduct of professional firms, together with public educational policies adjusting training capacity to demand for access to the professions, could solve the "professional problem"—if that is principally the conventional monopoly problem of undersupply and excessive price. Of course, if market or industry demand is inelastic, increased competition will lead to lower profits and higher outputs per firm or lower incomes/higher workloads per professional, and demand for entry may fall off. But any new lower-price equilibrium on the industry demand curve will, of course, have to be at a higher overall level of output of professional services.

Inadequacy of the "Monopoly" Perspective

So much for the deregulatory anticombines (or antitrust) policy solution. Unfortunately, for several professions it may be the "solution" to the wrong problem. By taking the nature of the professional firm as given and equivalent to an ordinary for-profit firm in received microeconomic theory, it focuses attention on the relations between firms. Problems internal to the firm are ignored. Technical inefficiency is ignored except insofar as firms may be led to operate at an inefficient scale, and, of course, supranormal profits may generate distributional problems in the form of excessive professional incomes; but the central resource allocation problem is undersupply of professional services.

One obvious difficulty is that this analysis focuses only on the characteristics professional firms have in common with all other industries—there is no allowance for whatever special characteristics have led to the emergence of professional institutions in the first place. In its simplest terms, the competition-inducing policy amounts to assuming that, for regulatory purposes, the professions should be regarded as no different from the rest of the world. In discussions of health care policy, for example, the question "Is health care different?" has been debated for years among economists. Yet, as we have noted, the answer must be that professional services *are* different; otherwise it is hard to explain why self-regulatory professions exist at all. Why not repeal all provincial medical practice acts? A more relevant set of questions takes off from what we already know about the "differentness" of professional services, and explores how (if at all) we might wish to modify the analysis based on the simple monopoly view and the policy conclusions that flow from it.

These questions can be grouped under three headings, according to their implications for regulatory policy. These are (1) the sources of market power at the firm level, (2) the central role of the professional individual as labor supplier in the management of the professional firm, and (3) the instability of the demand function and its limited relevance as a policy guide in the presence of asymmetric information.

The first heading accepts the allocation problem as that of restricted output and elevated price but questions the capacity of conventional anticombines (or antitrust) policy to promote significant increases in interfirm price competition in all professions. "Conscious parallelism" (implicitly coordinated behavior recognizing mutual interdependence without overt collision) in a very general form may require a redefinition of the nature of the professional firm, in some professions, to induce the desired behavior. Changing the formal regulatory relationships among existing firms may make very little difference.

The second set of issues also focuses on the nature of the professional firm. As J. E. Meade has pointed out, most professional firms are labor managed in the sense that the chief supplier(s) of labor to the firm are also its managers and residual claimants to its profit stream.[15] Even if the professional firm is a large one, containing many non-professionals or paraprofessionals, management is usually vested by law in the professional group whose members alone are permitted to be employers, issuers of bills, and residual claimants to earnings. Under these circumstances, the firm may well choose input mixes that are far from cost minimizing in the usual sense, because what is maximized is a combination of profit and quasi rents (earnings above those in the next best possible occupation) to a particular class of labor. Hence, whatever the overall output of professional services may be, there is no reason to assume least-cost production. In several professions, there is extensive evidence of very substantial departures from least-cost production, through choice of "wrong" input mixes, as a result of the fact that professional firms are labor managed. The more important problem of the professions may thus be not restricted output but technically inefficient production and excessive cost. A regulatory or deregulatory policy to deal with this technical inefficiency must be more subtle and more extensive than one that merely encourages professional advertising.

Finally, the concept of imperfect buyer information and seller agency throws into question the stability and significance of the demand curve. A long debate continues among economists in health care about

---

[15] J. E. Meade, "The Theory of Labour-Managed Firms and of Profit-Sharing," *Economic Journal,* vol. 82, no. 325S (March 1972 supplement), and "Labour-Managed Firms in Conditions of Imperfect Competition," *Economic Journal,* vol. 84, no. 336 (December 1974).

the extent and significance of the direct influence of professionals—particularly physicians and dentists—on the utilization of their services independent of price. The debate is fueled by extensive medical evidence of overutilization of services—that is, their use beyond the point of contribution to health. Unnecessary, inefficacious, or excessive servicing is not only a waste of resources but a positive threat to health. In this context the normal assumption of consumer sovereignty is abandoned by those who define overutilization by health criteria, that is, efficacy, not preferences. The fact that patients willingly accept and pay for useless or harmful services or drugs is interpreted as resource misallocation by waste, not as revealed preference. Furthermore, it appears that "supply creates its own demand" in the sense that further entry of new professionals/firms increases service levels not by bidding down prices along a fixed market demand curve but by shifting the whole curve outward: prices may even rise. Seen from this perspective, the resource allocation problem in the professions may be one of oversupply rather than undersupply, and high prices may indicate too much, rather than too little, entry. The standard anticombines model is not merely incomplete, or beside the point, but backwards.

A problem of oversupply or excessive allocation of resources to professional services cannot be addressed by attempting to increase competition among firms supplying professional services. Quite the contrary: a failure of consumer information assumptions and consumer sovereignty criteria for resource allocation requires rather a regulatory solution or solutions. There may, however, be scope for restructuring some markets for professional services in such a way as to permit competitive rather than regulatory solutions, and this precisely in those areas where the imperfections of information are most severe.

Problems in Promoting Competitive Behavior

The first set of issues or problems in the application of procompetitive policy to the professions arises if we accept the traditional "monopolistically restricted output" conception of the resource misallocation problem. Procompetitive policy is then aimed in the right direction, but there are several reasons why it may be ineffectual. These include (1) aspects of the professional product itself, (2) special characteristics of the relationships among professional firms, (3) the training, socialization, and value systems of professionals, and (4) the probable overall quantitative significance of such monopoly-induced distortions.

Defining the Product or Service. There is frequently a problem in defining just what is the professional service product to be priced. A set of eyeglasses, a will, an uncomplicated land conveyance, or a dispensed prescription (the dispensing act, not the drug itself) are well defined, relatively standardized, and capable of being advertised at various prices by different suppliers. Problems of heterogeneity wash out on average, and competitive price shopping is, in principle, easy. More uncertain is the preparation of a tax return or a tooth restoration; standard prices may be quoted for different types of complexity, but the professional's judgment will determine whether the tooth is a one-, two-, or three-surface restoration. One supplier may quote a lower price schedule but bill a higher proportion of his work as multiple surface. Corporate or criminal legal service or incompletely defined medical problems constitute undefined packages or services whose extent and costs cannot be determined in advance. A lawyer's hourly rate means very little until one knows his average productivity and thus the total costs of handling different problems. Moreover, a professional price quotation in the middle of a sequence of services may or may not help. As Oliver Williamson points out, the professional first consulted has a "first mover" advantage over other potential competitors in that he or she has specialized knowledge of the customer's problem, which it would be costly for other suppliers to acquire.[16] Yet without that knowledge, they cannot submit competitive bids. Of course, this problem is not always insurmountable; one may have a dentist recommend a course of orthodontia or a complex form of fixed restoration in terms sufficiently specific that competing price quotations on the same service are costless or almost so. (Hence the importance of arguments over such things as who owns the patient's radiographs.) But seeking a set of additional price quotations and possibly shifting suppliers on that basis in the middle of a course of medical treatment—or a criminal action—are clearly costly in psychic and economic terms. Moreover, in such areas as corporate law or accountancy, the possibility that one's former professional adviser might go to work for a competitor must give pause.

Hence the development of the professional/client or doctor/patient relationship, not merely an agency relationship in an individual instance but a long-term agreement, often implicit, to deal with each other in a set of future unspecified or incompletely specified circumstances according to certain rules.[17] The relationship is not a series of spot con-

---

[16] Williamson, *Markets and Hierarchies.*

[17] V. Goldberg, "Regulation and Administered Contracts," *Bell Journal of Economics,* vol. 7, no. 2 (Autumn 1976), provides an interesting discussion of the situations in which uncertainties and irreversibilities make the prospect of a sequence of spot contracts undesirable for both parties to the relation. As he points out, in such environments longer-term, incompletely specified relationships are developed that create a set of rules (implicit or explicit) governing the adjustment of the interests of both parties as the future unfolds. Long-run optimization thus requires restrictions on spot optimization.

tracts. The professional implicitly agrees not to charge all that the traffic will bear in each instance and to be available to his/her patients/clients even at some personal cost when there is a need, although new or unaffiliated customers (with whom there is no implicit contract) may be turned away. On the other hand, the customer/patient implicitly agrees not to shop around or to shift suppliers frequently in searching for the lowest spot price. The resulting series of spot prices in the continuing relationship are thus neither as low as energetic shopping could make them nor as high as could be charged for a life-threatening or liberty-threatening midnight emergency (or as the result of a strategic threat to go on holiday before a critical trial or emergency).

Such implicit contracts may indeed be an efficient way of dealing with situations of uncertainty, high fixed costs for the supplier (acquisition of information about the client/patient's problem), and shifts in demand elasticity. It is not clear how or if these can be reconciled with the promotion of effective price competition in individual spot markets for particular services. As we will note, these may simply be the wrong markets. An alternative solution may be to make the implicit contracts explicit and price those explicit contracts competitively. For groups of customers this may be possible—it often is in health care—but for many professions adverse selection (the tendency of bad risks who cannot be identified in advance to seek out explicit contracts) may rule out such individual contracts. The implicit contract protects the professional by charging the bad risks more (on average) than the good risks, while the explicit contract has a fixed price. Still, there seems to be a good deal of scope for creating more flexible price structures between the poles of fee for service and fixed price per time period.

Implicit Coordination of Professional Behavior: Conscious Parallelism. Apart from the difficulties of defining professional products for pricing purposes, there are further problems caused by the relations among firms. The combination of common training, geographic proximity in local markets, and continuing association in professional activity (the hospital, the courtroom, the professional association, the continuing education functions) and often social relations as well creates ideal conditions for conscious parallelism. Most of the dentists in even a moderate-sized city seem to know each other, for example, so that adoption of an aggressive competitive strategy would succeed by taking business away from known colleagues and (perhaps) friends, not from faceless competition. An impersonal market may appear to include a large number of suppliers, but each individual firm is for geographic reasons in competition with a much smaller number. On the other hand, accounting firms with national or international markets or chain-managed pharmacies function in a much wider arena.

For professionals with geographically localized markets, the inherent awareness of interdependence encourages parallelism because retaliation is likely if not inevitable if the impact of an aggressive competitive policy falls most heavily on a few nearby suppliers—a point reinforced by the peculiarly steep cost curves of the firm. Thus each individual professional will realize that a "successful" market share expansion policy is likely to succeed only until others discover that it is working. Then all prices will fall, and if market demand curves are relatively inelastic, everyone is worse off. Moreover, collusion is easy: although formal fee schedules may be illegal, informal discussions are not. Price advertising may be permissible but not mandatory. Even fairly complex fee guides could (if necessary) be developed by having an article written for a professional journal describing relative time requirements for different services. It has been suggested that a unit-value fee schedule may actually be a stimulus to competition, where services can be clearly defined, because firms need only advertise their different conversion rates of units into dollars. Although such values are easiest for consumers to compare in price shopping, they are also easiest for professionals to set collusively in informal discussion.

The importance of conscious parallelism in subverting the aims of competitive policy should not be underestimated. William Stanbury and Gilbert Reschenthaler have described its development in the Ontario steel culvert industry, noting its sociological and unidirectional nature. An energetic "educational" campaign was carried on (by a particular individual) to create awareness of interdependence. At first the mixture refused to "jell"—the message did not get across—but, once the learning process was complete, collusive behavior in pricing developed without any further overt illegal acts.[18] In several of the professional industries, such mutual interdependence is already well recognized. Even if the cartel discipline breaks and a maverick professional adopts a price-competitive strategy, the damage can be limited so long as professional control over acceptable production processes limits firm size.

---

[18] William T. Stanbury and Gilbert Reschenthaler, "Oligopoly and Conscious Parallelism: Theory, Policy, and the Canadian Cases," mimeo. (Vancouver: B.C. Faculty of Commerce and Business Administration, University of British Columbia, 1976). What is interesting about this case is the irreversibility aspect. Once mutual consciousness of interdependence occurred, it created a change in each firm's behavior and its expectations of its rivals' behavior that required no further overt coordination. The relation, then, between explicit activities and collusive behavior is sharply discontinuous; when the activities cease, behavior does not revert to its former pattern. Moreover, if a collective identity is already in existence and reinforced by a strong ideology and value system, then the behavior of colleagues/competitors is sufficiently predictable that parallel behavior never requires explicit coordination.

Finally, there are the barriers to competition implicit in the value systems of professionals themselves. George Akerlof, for example, has analyzed the behavior of markets in which participants value reputation as well as economic benefits, in which reputation depends on conformity with social custom or a code of behavior, and in which social custom shifts over time depending on what most participants do. Depending on the parameters involved, one can get equilibria in which almost everyone continues to obey custom despite apparent economic advantages that would accrue to its violation.[19]

Such a process can easily subvert competition in professional markets. Professional training and value formation are intended to—and do—influence professionals so that they place a high value on their reputation with their peers. Economic success does not in itself damage this reputation—quite the contrary—but competitive practices clearly do. On one level the loss of reputation may be rationalized by saying the price cutter is not "good enough" to draw business any other way; on another level the price competitor loses reputation because he is a direct economic threat to other suppliers. Various forms of social sanction are to be expected. Thus a more general formulation of the objectives of the professional as entrepreneur will include noneconomic variables (because the entrepreneurs are in this case specific people), and in the professional industries these variables will probably be negatively dependent on the kinds of competitive practices an aggressive competitive policy is intended to promote.

These difficulties should not necessarily be viewed as arguments against such policy. There are clearly professions (pharmaco-ophthalmic dispensing, parts of law, or professions with large markets and sophisticated clients) where these restrictions do not apply. Moreover, even if the policies are inefficacious—say, price advertising is legalized, and either no one does it or market shares do not respond—no harm has been done. To say this, of course, assumes that the definition of the

---

[19] George A. Akerlof, "A Theory of Social Custom, of Which Unemployment May Be One Consequence," mimeo., Special Studies Paper no. 118 (Washington, D.C.: Division of Research and Statistics, Federal Reserve Board, June 13, 1978). There is significant emphasis in professional training on the inculcation of sensitivity to professional norms, values, or customs and the insertion of peer or professional standards into the individual professional's personal utility function.

Since this paper was written, the British Columbia Supreme Court has ruled that price advertising by lawyers is legal. The law society is responding by trying to establish a form of "ethical" advertising, in keeping with the dignity of the profession, which appears to be an attempt to restrain by collective parallelism or the creation of custom what can no longer be restrained by threat of delicensure. By specifying what forms of advertising are appropriate, the professional organizations may be able to educate their members in their common interest in not behaving competitively and so to maintain the cartel.

basic resource allocation problem as restricted supply is correct. What does appear to follow, though, is that removal of the most overt self-regulatory restrictions on competitive behavior will not necessarily constitute an adequate policy. Other forms of restriction and collusion exist that will require more subtle forms of intervention to promote competition. In extreme cases competition policy may simply fail, leaving options to regulate or do nothing. It would be the height of folly and circular reasoning to assume that when overt anticompetitive practices or regulations were removed, professional resource allocation processes would necessarily follow market-determined—much less socially optimal—channels.

Even the potential usefulness of conventional procompetitive policies is severely limited by the specificity of the particular resource misallocation problem they address and by the relatively small welfare impact of such misallocations. Since the impact of monopoly-induced price increases is primarily distributional (from consumer to monopolist), the actual welfare costs can easily be shown (given assumptions on market-demand-curve elasticity) to be very small indeed relative to total expenditure. A unit-elastic demand curve with prices 20 percent above competitive levels as a result of monopolistic restriction (and constant long-run marginal cost) generates a net welfare burden somewhat less than 2 percent of total industry revenues. On the other hand, a 20 percent price differential resulting from failure to minimize costs or a 20 percent overproduction of excessive or unnecessary professional services corresponds (subject to some qualifications) to a proportionate real resource cost and welfare burden.[20] Thus the issues surrounding these kinds of distortions in professional service markets are quantitatively much more important than those resulting from simple monopoly, while the remedial potential of conventional competition policy is limited (in the cost minimization case) and may be nonexistent (in the overproduction case).

Technical Inefficiency in Professional Firms. Without answering the

---

[20] The systematic choice of high-priced (professional own-time) over lower-cost (auxiliary or capital equipment substitutes) inputs may not all represent excess resource use if part of the price of the high-cost input is itself monopoly rent. Furthermore, the provision of inefficacious services need not represent waste if consumers derive utility from the services themselves, not from their contribution to the resolution of a health, legal, or accounting problem. One cannot, of course, know with certainty whether hypothetical fully informed consumers would choose to undergo inefficacious surgical procedures or whether professional time (adjusted for productivity) would cost more than paraprofessional time in some ideally competitive long-run equilibrium world. But then, of course, recognition of the inherently second- (or nth-) best nature of the real world leads, if pushed to its logical extremes, to complete policy agnosticism and quietism. While perhaps philosophically respectable, such a stance has few other attractions.

239

question whether professional firms will engage in more aggressive price competition among themselves if self-regulatory restraints on such competition are removed, this discussion has followed most conventional economic theory in assuming that they will adopt a least-cost technology in producing whatever level and mix of output they make available. This least-cost assumption includes both efficient management (that is, operation on the production function with a given set of inputs) and, most important, choice of the least-cost input mix. This rules out preferences for "organizational slack" and also preferences defined over the mix of inputs used. The exclusion of organizational slack may be justified on the argument that, if market power can be removed by enhanced price competition, tastes for organizational slack will be competed off the market or will be indulged at the expense of normal profit levels. The problem of input mix, however, is much more serious and demands further exploration.

The market analysis of professional firms tends to confuse professionals themselves (as particular types of workers with special skills and legal rights) with the firms in which they work, which by law (in most jurisdictions) only they may control. In principle there is no obvious reason why nonprofessionals should not hire professionals and enter markets for professional services; in practice this does not happen because of legal prohibition.[21] Whether it would happen in the absence of such prohibition depends on the strength of the social and reputational sanctions that the professional community can bring to bear; potential profits to such a nonprofessional entrant would have to be large enough to enable him to compensate professional employees for the (capitalized) value of such loss of reputation, which could be very large indeed.[22]

For the professional-controlled professional firm, however, it is obvious that the time input of professionals as workers, that is coordinated by professionals-as-entrepreneurs (often the same), is only one of several inputs. Even the traditional solo practitioner—doctor, dentist, or lawyer—used a variety of forms of capital equipment (black bag, chair and drill, law books) and almost always some secretarial or other nonprofessional assistance. The services were not, after all, produced on the front lawn. The modern professional firm, whether solo or group, draws heavily on nonprofessional or paraprofessional labor as well as on various forms of capital. Thus the supply of professional *services* is

---

[21] Again, pharmacy forms an exception in some jurisdictions, but its professional status is correspondingly tenuous.

[22] The formal structure of Akerlof's model ("A Theory of Social Custom") enables one to show the balance between the costs and payoffs of breach of custom. If the payoff is large enough, violators of custom become numerous, and custom changes. A smaller payoff, however, will not shift the equilibrium.

not necessarily controlled by restricting the supply of professionals. Each individual professional will have a rising supply curve of own-time (or an income-leisure trade-off) that will serve to restrict the available input of professional time if the number of professionals is restrained. Furthermore, if, as is usually assumed, professionals value additional leisure more highly in relation to additional income as their income rises, then the supply-price of professional time will rise (at any work-load level) in response to an exogenous income increase—as from, say, a general increase in the price of professional services. Since the cost of professional time is a major component of the cost of professional services, this means that the marginal cost of professional services (and hence the supply curve) cannot be defined independently of the demand.

Although this introduces an extra complexity into the analysis and, in the absence of perfectly free entry *and exit*, reduces the supply response to demand shifts (because of the leisure adjustment), it is not a fundamental analytic problem. It does, however, reinforce the concern about conscious parallelism (or mutually perceived interdependence) previously raised. If the time input supply curve of each professional, and hence the effective supply of professional services, is steep for each firm, each firm will be aware that others are unlikely to cut output or leave the market in response to price competition. This will obviously lower the payoff to be expected from a strategy of aggressive price cutting unless some firm believes the whole market demand is much more price sensitive than its rivals think. But the probability of price response to a "successful" (that is, market-share-increasing) price-cutting policy and thus (if total market demand is inelastic) losses all round is surely increased if the steeply rising opportunity cost of the professional's own time dominates the firm's marginal cost curve. Firms with steep marginal cost curves cut price, not output, when they start to lose market share. The huge write-off of human capital (to say nothing of personal identity) implied in exit from the industry by the professional himself makes this option unattractive. What will seem most plausible to a professional price cutter is that, if his strategy really does start to cut into the market share of his rivals/colleagues, they *must* follow him down.

The more interesting analytic point about the confounding of the entrepreneurial and labor supply roles, however, is its impact on the choice of inputs and the bias it creates in favor of excessive use of professional own-time (and thus failure to use less costly auxiliary or paraprofessional personnel). This issue has been explored in some detail by Robert Evans and Malcolm Williamson who—in the course of an investigation of the economics of universal dental and pharmaceutical insurance in Ontario—noted the very large opportunities for substituting less highly trained and costly paraprofessionals for relatively expensive dentists and pharmacists.[23] The peculiar features of pharmaceutical retailing and the overtraining of pharmacists for the relatively straightforward dispensing function (on a part-time basis) are, of course, widely known. Less well known is the information, derived from Canadian government surveys of dental practice and supported by experimental evidence, that a very high proportion—80 to 90 percent—of the work of a general dentist (time, procedures, or billings) can be performed by a high school graduate with twenty months' postsecondary training. Quality standards for these procedures match or exceed those of general dentists.[24] These facts are no longer challenged by organized dentistry.[25]

There is also an extensive literature on the untapped or partially tapped potential for paraprofessional use in medicine—nurse practitioners (pediatric or otherwise), midwives, physician assistants, medexes, nurse anesthetists, operating-room technicians, and so on. In this field, however, the very wide range of different functions and activities makes generalization more difficult. The use of paraprofessionals is also a topic of lively interest outside the health professions; but documentation, measurement, and analysis do not appear to have progressed very far.

The quantitative implications of suboptimal paraprofessional use may be very large indeed. Evans and Williamson estimate, on what they believe to be fairly conservative assumptions, that a dental care system making optimal use of paraprofessionals (and somehow eliminating the excess dentists) could reduce costs of care in Ontario by 30 to 40 percent. This estimate reflects the dramatic differences in annual income between

---

[23] Robert G. Evans and Malcolm F. Williamson, *Extending Canadian Health Insurance: Policy Options for Pharmacare and Denticare,* Ontario Economic Council Research Study no. 13 (Toronto: University of Toronto Press, 1978), chap. 6.

[24] Province of Saskatchewan, *Saskatchewan Dental Plan Report, September 1, 1976 to August 31, 1977* (Regina, 1978), or any recent year, describing the functioning of a program that will—when fully phased in—provide dental services to all children up to age thirteen in a population of over a million with a staff of about twenty dentists. Blind trials of quality of care provided are described in Saskatchewan Dental Plan, *A Quality Evaluation of Specific Dental Services Provided by the Saskatchewan Dental Plan: Final Report* (Regina, February 1976).

[25] See, for example, the editorial in *Operative Dentistry,* "Expanded Duties: An Economic Fallacy," no. 2, 1977, conceding that the capabilities of auxiliaries have been conclusively demonstrated, although individual dentists may remain ignorant. The profession nevertheless recommends against use of such auxiliaries and supports their legal prohibition, on the grounds that economic benefits from their use will be illusory and that patients demand not merely technically competent care but also more comprehensive "professional" services. The analysis is fuzzy to nonexistent; but if the argument that auxiliaries would be uneconomic and unacceptable were true, a legal prohibition would obviously be unnecessary. If it is false, the prohibition is clearly counterproductive—though necessary to protect dentists!

dentists and the projected two-year auxiliaries and overestimates the true savings of resources insofar as the current incomes of dentists include a significant monopoly rent. It is difficult to know what the social opportunity cost or competitive market wage of a dentist might be, but it is clear that the large amount of embodied human capital must be paid a return even in a hypothetical rentless world. Estimated reductions in drug costs by similar rationalization of pharmacy are smaller—11 to 17 percent—but this is because the dispensing process is only about half of drug costs.[26] Thus dispensing costs appear to be capable of reduction by 22 to 33 percent, again on fairly conservative assumptions about productivity. For medical care, Uwe Reinhardt in the United States has developed estimates of the physician office services production function using cross-sectional data and has similarly shown that auxiliary use could be pushed much further than it presently is.[27] The resulting reduction in unit costs of services could be passed either forward in lower prices or backward in higher net receipts of physicians. Assumptions vary, but the potential cost reductions in shifting to optimal use of aides are in the 15 to 40 percent range. Moreover, the regression methodology is conservatively biased, since it can use data only from practices employing existing types of auxiliaries. The further gains from use of paraprofessionals of a technically feasible but legally prohibited type cannot be discovered by such a technique. This explains the finding (from regression studies of dental practice) that increasing numbers of aides contribute to output per dentist but that the specific type of aide training does not matter. This may well be true of current practice patterns but is obviously not true of dental auxiliaries trained to handle the entire task of diagnosing carious cavities, preparing them, and placing fillings. Regression analysis cannot measure the productivity of impermissible technologies.[28]

---

[26] Economic analysis of the market for prescription ingredients raises an entirely different set of issues, but they do not relate to the professions.

[27] Uwe E. Reinhardt, *Physician Productivity and the Demand for Health Manpower* (Cambridge: Ballinger, 1975).

[28] Uwe E. Reinhardt, "Manpower Substitution and Productivity in Medical Practice: Review of Research," *Health Services Research,* vol. 8, no. 3 (Fall 1973), provides a discussion of alternative methodologies. K. E. Kilpatrick et al., "Expanded Function Auxiliaries in General Dentistry: A Computer Simulation," *Health Services Research,* vol. 7, no. 4 (Winter 1972), provides a powerful technique for going well beyond regression studies to explore the productivity implications of radically new types of auxiliaries in various practice settings. The value of this computer model for areawide and provincewide program planning was shown in the *Report* of the British Columbia Children's Dental Health Research Project (Victoria: The Queen's Printer for B.C., 1974, released 1975), which modeled a range of alternative delivery systems for children's dental care in the province. The same model was later used by Evans and Williamson (*Extending Canadian Health Insurance*) to cost out different plans in Ontario.

The evidence of very large quantitative effects from underuse of paraprofessionals and overuse of costly professional time seems to be confined to health care. The role of legal secretaries, engineering technicians, and architectural draftsmen is far from trivial, of course, and anecdotally one gets the impression that most of the services involved in, for example, a routine will or land conveyancing can be and often are provided by paraprofessionals. Experimental and cross-sectional productivity studies do not appear to be available in the nonhealth professions, but the extensive and consistent evidence in health care suggests that overuse of professional time inputs in the production of professional services should be looked for outside health as well. If this sort of resource misallocation is a serious problem in professional services generally (and even if it is not, health care is a large enough professional subsector to make misallocation there significant), the obvious questions are Why? and What can public policy toward self-regulation do about it?

Inefficient Input Mix: Collective Constraint or Individual Choice? The high-cost input bias can arise at one (or both) of two levels. It may be that collective self-regulation is used deliberately to exclude lower-cost technologies because of their threat to the earnings of professionals as labor suppliers. This is the easier case for policy to deal with (professionals collectively acting like a labor union to ensure the demand for their own services), since presumably specific limitations on this regulatory power can solve or at least mitigate the misallocation. Less tractable is the situation that arises if the high-cost bias is inherent in the structure of the individual professional firm as a result of its being labor managed. In this case, a broader public policy aimed at restructuring the nature of the firms in the industry may be necessary.

In the first case, professional associations obviously place restrictions on the tasks auxiliaries are allowed to perform. This may be accomplished explicitly by legislation or authoritative bylaws enumerating permitted or excluded tasks or, alternatively, and more difficult to influence from outside, by applying standards of "ethical" or "unethical" practice that will be employed in internal disciplinary proceedings or when defending or not defending a member on malpractice or negligence charges. Such restrictions, by imposing restraints on the use of nonprofessional inputs, force a professional firm to expand output by using professional time with its steeply rising marginal cost. The sole practitioner trying to expand output cannot hire auxiliaries but must give up sleep instead. Of course, firms may expand by hiring more professionals, but that, given limits on the supply of professionals themselves, simultaneously removes or shrinks another firm; it does not increase the supply of professional services. Thus the constraint on use of auxiliaries, the supply of whom may be assumed (given short training periods) to be relatively elastic, is a way of constraining the growth of individual firms. It reinforces professional disapproval of and sanctions against aggressive price-cutting, market-share-expanding strategies by ensuring that the professional as entrepreneur who adopts such a strategy will rapidly run up against increasing costs.

The "need" for such a constraint from the profession's viewpoint can easily be appreciated if one contemplates the impact (on a group of professional firms in long-run equilibrium in a market with an inelastic aggregate demand curve) of a new technology that shifts long-run cost curves downward and increases significantly the output per firm at which costs per unit of output are minimized. At sufficiently large outputs, of course, unit costs must still rise, since not all professional functions can be performed by auxiliaries. ("Output" is assumed to be a vector of different services in constant proportions.) If the industry is at all competitive, even if each firm has some or considerable market power, the drop in marginal cost would induce an upward shift in output, which, at the aggregate market level, would induce a drop in price. Given inelastic aggregate demand, total market revenues would fall, and costs (net of professional own-time) would clearly rise as more (and more highly trained) auxiliaries were employed. Since professionals/firms will not leave the industry until all their monopoly rents disappear, the result must be losses all around. No one gains but the consumer—not even the firm initiating a move. Hence it is unlikely that individual professional firms would initiate such competitive moves, even if they were not restrained by collective self-regulation. A first mover would have to believe that it can drive some of its competitors out of the industry entirely. For pharmacies, this may be plausible; but for physicians and dentists, it is highly unlikely.

The implication of this discussion is that anticombines policy must go beyond preventing price fixing, restrictions on advertising, and overt collusion. It must also try to eliminate regulations that make competition unprofitable by restricting low-cost, high-volume technology. Seen in this light, section 32, clause 6, of the new federal Combines Investigation Act of 1976 takes on strategic importance.[29]

---

[29] Canada, Parliament, *Combines Investigation Act* (Office Consolidation) (Ottawa: The Queen's Printer, 1976), R.S., c. 314, s. 1. The strategic role of this clause as a device for limiting entry to the professional services market has been pointed out by W. T. Stanbury, *Business Interests and the Reform of Canadian Competition Policy, 1971–1975* (Toronto: Carswell/Methuen, 1977), p. 183. As Stanbury noted, the use of a proxy, such as formal education, for ethical standards and professional competence will permit the maintenance of significant entry barriers. Stanbury emphasizes the tendency of professions to "overprotect" by establishing quality standards too high relative to what the general population would wish, but in fact there are two separate issues here, not one. Professions may surely

The Combines Investigation Act extends federal anticombines legislation from goods to services, including professional services; but 32 (6) creates a defense against criminal conspiracy and similar charges if the otherwise criminal activity "related only to a service and to standards of competence and integrity that are reasonably necessary for the protection of the public." Thus "quality" regulation, including control of the use of auxiliaries and the nature of the production process generally, appears to be untouched. But use of such power to prohibit low-cost, high-volume technology may be as effective as bans on advertising or price fixing in preventing the outbreak of unhealthy competition. Price cutting and advertising are unlikely to be popular if the result is that one gets more customers/patients but works eighteen-hour days. Unless new entry and underemployment of professionals are serious problems, the market is unlikely to change much. As we will note below, even new entry at present relatively rapid rates appears capable of being absorbed without creating a "hungry fringe" in health care. Law may be another story, however, since it appears there that entry is so rapid and access to the lucrative corporate and tax markets so difficult that a competitive consumer law market (that is, a market in wills, divorce, conveyancing) might well develop without any need to address the technology issue. (The foregoing, of course, assumes that the courts will not determine professional regulation to be outside federal jurisdiction—the issue is still sub judice.)

The argument over technology is not merely a plea for yet further deregulation, however. Dismantling of collective self-regulation of market practices among firms may in itself be ineffective, and the generation of true competition may require deregulation of technological practices as well. It must still not be forgotten that professions exist because there *is* a quality problem in these industries, a problem rooted in consumer ignorance, that the market does not solve. In some professions—engineering or architecture, for example—asymmetry of information may be small or nonexistent, and the client may be perfectly capable of protecting against faulty performance. But in health care particularly,

---

establish the "wrong" quality/cost trade-off (wrong from society's perspective), either in honest error or to protect themselves against entry of low-priced competition. But they may also adopt erroneous proxies for "quality." As has been shown for dentistry, a high school graduate with twenty months' training can perform most of the work of a general dentist to equivalent or higher-quality standards. The successful legislative suppression of such auxiliaries over (almost) all North America reflects a barrier *not* to a lower-price/lower-quality supplier but to a lower-price supplier of at least equivalent quality. Formal education turns out to be a bad proxy for quality. Thus professional associations not only may establish faulty trade-offs but, more important, may and do establish faulty quality measures that are structural characteristics (training) instead of outcome (effect of services on the user). Their own services are *defined* as higher quality, in the absence of supporting evidence or even in defiance of contradictory evidence.

professionals' collective power to regulate the process of production is rooted, not without some justification, in the social *desideratum* of protecting the ill-informed patient. If that power is curtailed or removed, alternative forms of quality regulation must be developed. These may require more, not less, direct state intervention, and they should be focused where possible on outcome, not on process measures of professional service quality or adequacy.[30] But if *some* alternative to self-regulation of process as a quality-assurance mechanism cannot be offered, reduction of that self-regulation is likely to be politically difficult. Process self-regulation, in the health field at least, is the most important source of resource misallocation. Evidence shows that the excessive use of high-cost professional inputs is quantitatively far more significant than any monopoly-power-restricted output costs (even discounting the considerations of possible oversupply to be addressed below).

The Need for Entry of New Types of Firms. Suppose, however, that the collective professional restrictions on technology can be swept away and alternative outcome-based quality review techniques (patient sampling, chart or insurance record review, sending "rigged" customers to professional practices, advertising of success rates) take their place. Will professional firms rush to adopt new lower-cost auxiliaries and attempt to bid market share away from each other? Perhaps, but the answer is neither obvious nor automatic, precisely because professional firms are neither profit (only) maximizers nor generally myopic. Much depends on their belief about what volume of their own services their markets can absorb and on their preferences for particular styles of practice.

Most of the literature showing that professional firms overuse professional own-time and underuse auxiliaries has defined underuse by a finding that additional auxiliaries could produce additional output that (valued at current prices or fees) would more than compensate for their wage and other costs. In other words, the value of auxiliary marginal product (*VMP*) exceeds the wage (inclusive of fringe and other costs). Such a finding, of course, does indicate underuse from a social perspective. From the individual firm's point of view, however, the

---

[30] A good example of this concept is the recommendation by the recent report of the Restrictive Trade Practices Commission on ophthalmic products, which, while recommending measures to increase price competition in the Canadian market, simultaneously recommends the establishment of national minimum standards of quality for eyeglasses and contact lenses. Canada, Restrictive Trade Practices Commission, *The Ophthalmic Products Industry in Canada* (Ottawa: Department of Consumer and Corporate Affairs, 1979). Similarly the federal QUAD (Quality Assessment of Drugs) program forms an essential underpinning to efforts to promote competition in drug ingredient markets through compulsory licensure, competitive public bids on contracts to supply bulk ingredients, generic prescribing, or permissive substitution rules.

relevant test is whether the marginal revenue product (*MRP*) of auxiliaries equals or exceeds their wage. This *MRP* will be equivalent to the *VMP* only if the firm can expand its output freely at a constant price, which is obviously a rather special case. For this to hold, either there must be perfect competition among professional firms within the restricted entry industry (such that each must take price as given and beyond its control), or the generation of new demand at present prices must be costless (which would make the failure to generate such demand and raise prices difficult to explain). If, more plausibly, there are downward-sloping demand curves for individual professional firms as a result of locational or reputational differences, the *MRP* of new auxiliaries may very well lie below their wage rate, so that the firms would not hire them even if unrestricted by collective self-regulation.

The interconnection of this with the labor management of the professional firm can be seen if we consider the opportunity cost of professional own-time. The reason auxiliaries appear less costly than professionals is that their wage cost for producing a given increment of output is much lower than the average rate of reimbursement of professional time for the same product. A nonprofessional cost-minimizing and profit-maximizing entrepreneur running a professional firm would (if unrestrained) substitute the less for the more costly input. The implicit wage (average per unit of time input) earned by a professional in his or her own firm is not, however, the opportunity cost of own-time.[31]

---

[31] Exactly how the implicit wage should be calculated is not obvious. In principle, one would presumably want to use an opportunity cost measure, the rate of reimbursement of professional own-time in its next best occupation. But what is that? Using average net revenue per hour worked for each self-employed professional will yield a different "wage rate" for each and will define profits as zero—all monopoly rents or quasi rents to fixed costs will be included in "wages." Taking the same average for the profession as a whole enables individuals to earn positive or negative "profits"; but these must average zero, and again all rents on average enter the wage.

T. Scitovsky, "A Note on Profit Maximization and Its Implications," *Review of Economic Studies,* vol. 11, no. 1 (February 1943), defines the implicit wage as the amount of the self-employed entrepreneur's net earnings, at current levels of time and effort input, that would just compensate for the utility cost of that input—that is, return the entrepreneur to the income-leisure indifference curve running through the zero work, zero income point. The average implicit wage would then equal this amount divided by total time input; but given the usual indifference curve shape, the true shadow price of own-time would be the (larger) marginal income-leisure trade-off. E. O. Olsen, "Utility and Profit Maximization by an Owner-Manager," *Southern Economic Journal,* vol. 39, no. 3 (January 1973), introduces the possibility of a market for hired managerial labor, showing that, given long-run free entry and perfect competition, the wage rate of hired management will be equal to the marginal revenue product of management (profit maximization) and to the managers' marginal rate of substitution of labor for leisure (utility maximization). Earlier G. W. Ladd, "Utility Maximization Sufficient for Competition Survival," *Journal of Political Economy,* vol. 77, no. 4, part 1 (July/August 1969), demonstrated the same point—that if entry and competition drive supranormal profits to zero, then profit and utility maximization are equivalent. In this special case, the shadow price

It contains a large monopoly rent component, as well as a quasi rent earned by the embodied human capital. The professional as entrepreneur may thus be charging himself for own-time at a price much below what society has to pay for it. In such a case, the socially suboptimal use of auxiliaries will be individually optimal for each firm.

Deregulation of process alone (expansion of the possibility of auxiliary use) will thus be insufficient in itself to change production processes; there will also have to be a shift in the identity of the entrepreneur. Whether this be the creation of dental clinics run by a private corporation, such as Sears Roebuck, for example, or of HMOs run by local cooperatives or of neighborhood legal clinics, the critical point is that the management of at least some professional firms will have to be exercised by cost minimizers who are not simultaneously selling their own services to the firm. If deregulation is to result in the major potential benefits of improved technical efficiency in professional service production, it will have to go beyond modifying the relations among existing firms to promoting changes in the nature and objectives of the firms themselves. As noted, however, the caveat must be added that if one deliberately adopts a policy of shifting the structure and objectives of

---

of own-time equals its market price and its social opportunity cost. It may be such a special case that was in the mind of one of the commentators on this paper, who asserted in discussion that professional time shadow prices must, in fact, reflect social resource costs. (Thus, presumably, there would be no resource allocation problem, despite the evidence?)

But if there are market imperfections of various types, then, as Olsen shows, the equivalence of utility and profit maximization collapses. In moving from this analysis to real-world observation, however, it must be recalled that, given the nature of wage contracts observed, wages are an *average* return on hours worked. Thus employed and salaried managers or professionals receive a wage that, if the industry is largely self-employed, will be primarily determined by the available earnings in self-employment (adjusted where relevant for risk, responsibility, etc.). If there is not free entry to the profession, this observed market wage will embody all the rents available to successful entrants averaged over standard hours of work—employment contracts are not, in general, written in wage-per-hour terms with open-ended hours. But there is no particular reason why this restricted-entry average wage should bear any relation to the marginal income-leisure trade-off of the professional, self-employed or salaried. Thus any observed market wage rate for professional time does not permit one to identify the opportunity cost of own-time, relative either to leisure or to the next best occupation. In practice, then, the exact partitioning of professional revenues into implicit wage and rental or profit components does not seem possible.

What one can say, however, is that the utility-maximizing owner-manager will equate his own marginal rate of substitution of income for leisure to his perceived marginal revenue product of own-time input. If this MRP is below the average return to own-time, as it will be because of fixed costs, monopoly rents, or costs (utility or otherwise) or demand generation, then the average price paid by the rest of society for professional own-time will be above the marginal value the professional places on it. Correspondingly, the professional will substitute auxiliary time for own-time only up to the point where the marginal rate of technical substitution is equated to the ratio of auxiliary wage to marginal valuation of own-time, not to the ratio of wage to average social cost of professional time.

professional firms toward the for-profit end of the spectrum, there is a significant possibility that quality control will be eroded. The dental clinics run for profit by a private corporation such as Sears cannot be expected to be self-regulating; external quality monitoring and control will be necessary. The idea that "brand name" and reputation will perform this function is just so much fluff: the whole essence of the professional relationship is that the consumer does not know what he needs before service, nor does he know afterward whether he was adequately served. Furthermore, the services in question are generally considered too important to the consumer to permit a certain amount of routine quality shading in the interests of profit. We really have very little experience, at least in this century, of what an unregulated professional market would look like—there is no a priori reason for optimism. As a political matter it is likely that restriction of self-regulatory powers (in the professional process dimension) and promotion of nonprofessionally controlled firms will require some regulatory substitute. This difficulty is likely to be most acute in the professional fields serving individual and relatively uninformed customers—health care and the individual service part of the legal market. For large engineering, architectural, accounting, or corporate law firms these informational and quality control issues obviously do not arise. This of course raises the obvious question why, in markets with economically large and sophisticated clients, professional self-regulation exists at all.

Professional Control over "Demand": the Ultimate Market Failure

The discussion thus far has assumed the existence of a stable market or aggregate demand curve for professional services of whatever type, restricting individual firms to choose price or quantity of output produced but not both. The two aspects of performance of the professional industries thus far explored have been (1) the way relationships among firms might lead to a nonoptimal level of total output and price (too small and too high) and (2) the way (given any such output/price point) production costs might be upwardly biased by a socially inappropriate choice of input mix. The presupposition that there is a stable aggregate demand curve, however, neglects one of the crucial aspects of the professional relationship. The social institution of the profession, or at least its delegated legal authority, develops because of market failure arising from consumer ignorance and costly information. Accordingly, the professional acts as agent of the consumer, recommending consumption levels and patterns of professional services as well as standing ready to supply those services.

The professional as agent can thus directly affect the level of service use, not merely selecting from points on an exogenously given and negatively sloped demand curve but (by his or her advice) directly shifting the level of use at any given price. The power to do so, of course, varies among different professions and services within a profession. But it appears that such power is the essence of professionalism. Where there is no agency role, there is no profession, and one might as well dismantle the self-governing structure. Hence the pharmacist's problem.

The agency relation is not perfect, however. If it were, one could imagine the professional combining his or her information with the consumer's preferences and making an optimizing decision as if the professional *were* the consumer. The resulting utilization patterns would display the price sensitivity of the hypothetical fully informed consumer. Of course, the professional would have to be perfectly schizophrenic as well, running around the desk after acting as perfect agent to become arms-length economic principal supplying the recommended services.[32]

One could, on the other hand, imagine the professional not as agent but as perfect technocrat, recommending services as a "best-practice" response to consumer "needs" independently of price, preferences of consumer, or the professional's own economic objectives.[33]

Neither of these approximations appears to fit the data or experience well, at least in the health care professions (where study of utilization patterns has been most intensive). There is abundant evidence of the direct influence of professionals on utilization patterns independent of price. Evans and Wolfson have recently surveyed Canadian studies in the medical care field, while Evans and Williamson discuss

---

[32] This schizophrenic aspect of the hypothetical perfect agency relationship raises the interesting question why professional industries have not evolved two types of firms. Specialists in information, brokers or agents, could have arisen to advise patients/clients/customers while service providers operated at arm's length. Whether this has failed to occur because of the inherent informational and technical properties of professional services or because the organized professions have prevented such developments would be an interesting question but beyond the scope of this paper.

[33] The professional or Hippocratic myth is that the professional in the second role applies knowledge and skills to the relief of the patient/client's problem independently of economic considerations. Economists have generally had little difficulty dispensing with such a model, and the fluidity of supposedly objective and scientific standards of best practice across time and regions undercuts its appeal. What is perhaps more surprising is the attraction to economists of the complete agency model, the notion of a "physician-patient pair" as a conventional fully informed consumer. The analytic convenience of this assumption and its politically conservative policy implications seem inadequate compensation for its total inability to generate a sensible model of the provider-as-principal and its empirical difficulties. These are generally sidestepped by circular reasoning of the "if people are informed, then they must will the consequences of their actions; hence their actions are right; hence they must be informed" sort.

some of the dental care literature.[34] This discretionary power is bounded, apparently, by an incomplete agency relation in which the professional seeks to optimize some complex function of his perception of the consumer's best interests. The function defines both the benefits and the costs of direct generation of additional use of professional services. Moreover, the costs of such generation are far from uniform. The dentist encouraging his patient to accept marginally (if at all) efficacious counseling or preventive services suffers little or no professional "cost"; the one who places fillings in healthy teeth clearly does.

Since demand generation is costly to the professional, in the sense of reducing his satisfaction from work, and presumably becomes more costly as it is pushed further on a given base, each professional faces a utility-adjusted downward-sloping demand curve—that is, each additional increment of generated output yields lower net welfare even if price is held constant and cost of production (due to use of auxiliary labor in perfectly elastic supply) is constant. Further details are in Evans and Williamson.[35]

In an environment characterized by direct professional influence over utilization there is no stable negative relation between aggregate utilization and price that is independent of professional behavior. An increase in the supply of professionals, for example, may raise total service output—not by bidding down price and moving along the market curve but by shifting the curve sideways and raising output at all prices. In such a case, as Culyer points out, one can no longer make the positive consumer sovereignty assumption that utilization patterns reflect the price-dependent choices of consumers or the normative assumption that such choices are the appropriate social values to use in guiding and evaluating resource allocation patterns.

This being so, we cannot assume that the resource allocation problem is one of undersupply even when monopoly rents are being earned. Monopoly rents may depend ultimately on restricted supply of inputs, since (by definition) unrestricted entry and persistent supranormal profits will in the long run draw the whole labor force into the professions. Restricted entry is, however, perfectly consistent with oversupply of services (that is, with there being current utilization patterns beyond what fully informed consumers would take off the market at either current prices or true marginal resource cost prices).

Unfortunately, we do not see any of these hypothetical fully in-

---

[34] Robert G. Evans and Alan D. Wolfson, "Moving the Target to Hit the Bullet: Generation of Utilization by Physicians in Canada," mimeo. (Toronto: University of Toronto Department of Health Administration, January 1978); and Evans and Williamson, *Extending Canadian Health Insurance.*

[35] Evans and Williamson, *Extending Canadian Health Insurance,* chap. 6.

formed consumers in action, but in the health care field there is a proxy, or an intermediate step. It is possible in many cases for technically expert third parties to judge the impact of professional health care services on health. If we assume that all or most consumers use most professional services because of an expected health benefit and that, in general, the direct utility effects of health care are negative—that is, its use is painful and unpleasant (dentistry seems an obvious example)— then we can assume that a rational fully informed consumer would not use care beyond the point where the utility value of its expected marginal impact on health status equaled its price to him or her. Even given complete insurance coverage, no one would knowingly use inefficacious or harmful care. If such use is observed, we may call this oversupply.

Such oversupply is a commonplace among students of hospital care and surgical services: almost every third-party observer of hospitals or surgery in North America has pointed to excessive use in a technical sense.[36] Ambulatory care is harder to evaluate, but there are very serious concerns about diagnostic interventions. "Galloping consumption" of drugs known to be inefficacious or harmful in present uses is a wide-

---

[36] On surgery, one should look at J. Bunker, B. Barnes, and F. Mosteller, eds., *Costs, Risks, and Benefits of Surgery* (New York: Oxford University Press, 1977); and for a discussion of the economic issues, E. Blackstone, "Misallocation of Medical Resources: The Problem of Excessive Surgery," *Public Policy*, vol. 22, no. 3 (Summer 1974). The excess hospital use issue is now so widely discussed and documented as to be hard to provide a single reference for, but a recent Ph.D. thesis by M. L. Barer surveys a number of the U.S. and Canadian studies showing how changing the organization and payment of physicians changes patterns of hospital use ("A Methodology for Derivation of Marginal Costs of Hospital Cases and Its Application to Estimation of Cost Savings from Community Health Centres," Vancouver, Department of Economics, University of British Columbia, 1977). New studies continue to appear (for example, an unpublished paper by J. B. Christianson and W. McClure, "Competition in the Delivery of Medical Care," Interstudy, Excelsior, Minnesota, September 1978, showing how HMO plans are increasing their market share in Minnesota and holding hospital use well below state averages), and no one now seems to question overuse. S. Schroeder et al., "Use of Laboratory Tests and Pharmaceuticals: Variations among Physicians and Effect of Cost Audit on Subsequent Use," *Journal of the American Medical Association*, vol. 225, no. 8 (August 23, 1973); and M. Daniels and S. Schroeder, "Variation among Physicians in Use of Laboratory Test: II. Relation to Clinical Productivity and Outcomes of Care," *Medical Care*, vol. 15, no. 6 (June 1977), are among those who have documented wide variations in use of diagnostic services among different physicians, in the absence of any evidence of difference in therapeutic outcome. Articles describing inappropriate drug prescribing are numerous; see, for example (though only as a representative), D. L. Miles, "Multiple Prescriptions and Drug Appropriateness," *Health Services Research*, vol. 12, no. 1 (Spring 1977), and references therein. Most recently a study funded by the U.S. National Center for Health Services Research has concluded that electronic fetal monitoring does more damage than good and imposes significant unnecessary costs on patients and on society as a whole (David Banta and Steven Thacker, *Costs and Benefits of Electronic Fetal Monitoring: A Review of the Literature* [Washington, D.C.: National Center for Health Services Research, April 1979], DHEW publication no. (PHS) 79–3245). And so it goes. A complete literature survey on the problem of incompletely evaluated or inefficacious treatment in health care would be a mammoth study in itself and instantly out of date.

spread fear. The rapid extension, with little apparent justification, of preventive activity in dentistry on very flimsy evidence similarly raises suspicion of overuse. Moreover, there is increasing evidence that overuse is driven by oversupply of professional capacity: more surgeons lead to more surgery, more hospital bed space leads to more bed use, more dentists lead to more preventive care. Nor need this be malfeasance. After all, the assumption that the professional is fully informed is an imperfect one at best. There is, however, widespread and widely quoted evidence that changing the patterns of organization and payment of professionals, as in the HMO phenomenon, drastically changes the mix, volume, and cost of services supplied to a given population. This is hard to reconcile with an exogenous demand curve; it is equally hard to square with interpretations of "the professional problem" as monopoly-induced undersupply.

How serious this problem is in the nonhealth professions is difficult to say. The architect who overdesigns at the client's expense to produce a professional triumph or the overlitigious lawyer may well exist, but their quantitative significance is unknown. More important may be collective professional impact on needs (defined by the professionals). In law, for example, the powerful professional representation in legislatures may well influence the legal framework so as to raise "demand" for legal services. The complexity and cost of land conveyancing in the more progressive provinces of Canada, which have adopted the Torrens system of land registry, are much lower than in Ontario. The problems of title security in the United States strike a western Canadian as absurd. Yet introduction of this more efficient technology, economizing on expensive lawyer time, is not seen as a high priority by the Law Society of Upper Canada or the Ontario legislature. Legislative struggles over no-fault insurance, apart from their other issues, may well have been related to their explicit objective of reducing professional time input and billings. The brief popularity of the tort system in the United States as a device for ensuring quality control in health care (medical malpractice suits) may well have been related to its lucrative potential for lawyers; it is hard to think of other explanations.

Policy Responses to Professionally Induced Oversupply of Services

The difficulty with this third view of the "professional problem"—of agency-induced oversupply—is that it seems largely beyond the scope of competition policy. New entry, price pressure, and aggressive competition among professional firms will make the problem worse, not better, as professionals adjust to new trade-offs between "ethical" and economic objectives. The ethical costs of "demand generation" will fall.

It should be recalled that the original document, the Flexner report, that triggered a revolution in North American medical education (raising quality but cutting throughput) explicitly asserted that too many physicians in a region led to low quality and excessive servicing as a result of economic competition.[37] The fact that supply control also served the economic interest of physicians does not dismiss the substantive point; most recently we have the study of surgical specialties in the United States (SOSSUS) report, arguing that oversupply of surgeons lowers average workloads below the point at which frequency is adequate to maintain competence, while raising overall output beyond the technically efficacious level, and that as a balancing item (to adjust for individual workload drops) prices seem to rise, not fall, with excess supply.[38] It is hard to see how bans on price fixing or open advertising can help here—if, indeed, advertising could lower prices (does one search for the lowest-priced surgeon?), utilization might well go up even more.

In fact, as long as most people have full or extensive insurance coverage, the whole competition policy issue is irrelevant. The point is rather that even if one did move to the high-deductible coverage being advocated in the United States as a panacea for health care costs (reviving the old ideas of the 1950s, evaluated and discarded by the Hall Commission),[39] there is, in an "incomplete agency" world, no reason to believe that competitive pressure on prices, even if it could be

[37] A. Flexner, *Medical Education in the United States and Canada* (New York: Carnegie Foundation, 1910). The significance of this report in providing "quality-control" justification for closing medical schools and restricting the supply of physicians is discussed in Kessel, "The A.M.A. and the Supply of Physicians."

[38] American College of Surgeons and American Surgical Association, *Surgery in the United States* (Chicago: American College of Surgeons, 1975). A useful economic analysis of the report is provided by E. Blackstone, "The Condition of Surgery: An Analysis of the American College of Surgeons and the American Surgical Association's Report on the Status of Surgery," *Health and Society*, vol. 56, no. 3 (Fall 1977).

[39] The Hall Commission (Canada, *Report of the Royal Commission on Health Services* [Ottawa, The Queen's Printer, 1964]) was established to carry out a thorough investigation of alternative ways of establishing universal medical insurance in Canada. Hospital care had already been covered by a series of universal and public provincial plans (under federal guidelines and funding assistance) by the end of the 1950s. The establishment of such a commission had been advocated by representatives of the private insurance industry and the Canadian Medical Association (for example, Vancouver Province, "Study of New Health Scheme Proposed by Insurance Man," February 7, 1956, p. 14) in the expectation that it would lead to adoption of a plan with numerous insurers, significant private participation, and a large role for direct patient payment in the form of coinsurance or deductibles. In fact, many of the features being advocated as "new" ideas in the U.S. debates over health insurance (M. Feldstein, "The High Cost of Hospitals—and What to Do about It," *The Public Interest*, no. 48 (Summer 1977), were advocated in much the same terms by W. M. Anderson in 1952 ("Voluntary Health and Pension Plans—Can They Meet the Major Needs?" *Proceedings, Institute of Public Administration of Canada*, 1952), and their key weaknesses pointed out by J. Willard and M. Taylor in subsequent discussion. In the end the Hall Commission rejected the limited and partial plans that still fascinate U.S. analysts—a decision that looks better and better with hindsight.

achieved, would mitigate the resource allocation problem. If the problem is oversupply resulting from inadequate information, it will get worse.

To this third problem there seem only two basic lines of response. (Of course, "do nothing" is always a default possibility.) For those markets that display significant degrees of professionally induced oversupply, one could expand, not contract, the regulatory process. Alternatively, one could try to encourage a redevelopment of the structure of the professional market and the definition of the product transacted so as to move provider incentives away from oversupply. The first approach could be represented by an extended version of the Canadian hospital and medical insurance system, the second, with multiple competitive HMOs in the medical care market—a vision most recently expressed by Enthoven and Havighurst.[40]

Sole-source public funding of professional services permits regulation of the oversupply problem in several ways. First, direct constraints on service capacity can be imposed by refusal to supply capital funds or, if capital funds are elsewhere raised, refusal to cover operating costs of nonapproved hospital projects. This limits oversupply of services in such facilities but is hard to extend to other professions. Second, direct responsibility for reimbursement gives provincial governments a strong incentive to restrict the supply of physicians and to negotiate aggressively over fees. The former has led to a virtual cutoff of immigration and (with one provincial exception—the minister of education in British Columbia is also a professor in a local medical school) standstills or cutbacks in medical school capacity. The latter (tight fee schedules) has clearly contributed to cost control but has probably pushed utilization up as physicians seek to keep their incomes rising. More sophisticated regulation of specific procedures and monitoring of rates of performance have barely begun—although universal provincial insurance plans create a data base that would support a great deal more epidemiological and economic analysis of what drives performance rates of different services. So far, however, successful cost control in the medical care sector has been predominantly price control with limits on supply. No direct influence has been brought to bear on either the internal efficiency of medical practice or the overall efficacy of the service mix. This type of

---

[40] The most recent exponent of the "world of competing HMOs" concept is A. Enthoven, "Consumer Choice Health Plan—Parts I and II," *New England Journal of Medicine*, vol. 298, nos. 12 and 13 (March 23 and 30, 1978). The same basic idea, of restructuring the health care market to create new "products" so that private for-profit incentives could be used positively to serve a less ill-informed and vulnerable consumer, is expressed in Clark Havighurst, "Speculations on the Market's Future in Health Care," in Clark Havighurst, ed., *Regulating Health Facilities Construction* (Washington, D.C.: American Enterprise Institute, 1974).

regulation to control the mix and volume of professional services supplied could probably also be applied in dental care (selective reimbursement of particular procedures) or pharmacy (a public formulary with refusal to reimburse nonapproved drugs and the monitoring of individual rates of use and mix) if universal insurance plans were set up for these services. Partial plans or fragmented coverage on the U.S. model do not provide this regulatory capacity, of course, because insurers lack leverage in negotiating with providers and data bases are inadequate for monitoring purposes—hence the U.S. failure in cost control.

Such direct regulation has, as noted, a proven record of success. It is not perfect, however, and leaves several areas of potential improvement in efficiency untouched. Moreover, it raises regulatory issues far outside the purview of anticombines or antitrust policy, and its extension beyond the health care field is dubious. Discussion of "Judicare" surfaces from time to time, however, and if some public scheme for paying the legal fees of individuals were established, the same fee and service regulation issues would no doubt arise.

An alternative mechanism for dealing with the oversupply problem—also developed in health care—is the combined professional service and insurance contract. In this device, associated in the United States with the HMO idea, a group of professionals contract to supply all "necessary" services to a particular population for a specific payment per person per time period. This clearly places the onus of controlling excess use on the professionals, and it is indeed a commonplace observation that costs and utilization fall in such organizations, with no apparent indication of deterioration in quality or adequacy of care. The concept could clearly be extended beyond medical care; the corporate for-profit dental clinic has an incentive to overservice even though each service is produced at minimum cost, but the for-profit corporation selling annual dental contracts at X per head (excluding preexisting conditions) obviously does not. Capitation plans have been suggested for pharmacy and could probably be developed for personal legal services as well. Deregulation aimed at removal of legal barriers to development of such professional service-plus-insurance firms, already under way in the U.S. medical industry, could clearly contribute to improved efficiency. The growth of market share for such organizations would then follow from their ability to offer lower annual package costs of professional services, by controlling overservicing as well as choosing more efficient input mixes (assuming input mixes were deregulated as well). Translating this into the Canadian setting, we could say that persons signing up with an Ontario health service organization, a Saskatchewan community clinic, or whatever, would be offered premium rebates or tax reductions equal to their expected savings in service costs. In return, of course, all unauthorized out-of-clinic service use would have to be paid for out of pocket.

As always, though, there is a catch. If entry, expansion, and vigorous price competition over market share are anticipated, some of the firms will have to be profit motivated. How then does one control underservicing, quality shading, and selection only of good risks? Clearly these problems are mitigated by group contracting, since groups can more easily monitor contractor performance. A group purchasing services from a dental contractor might make a side contract with an independent quality review team and build penalties into the main contract for unsatisfactory quality performance. Patient satisfaction depends on dual- or multiple-choice options for group members.

The details of such an approach in health care services have been spelled out by Enthoven; and Christianson and McClure report very encouraging results from five years' experience in Minneapolis with a growing number of HMOs, rapid increases in market share, and falling utilization and cost.[41] The market shares of such organizations are still very small, however, and many large questions have yet to be addressed. It needs to be recalled that market share is not indicated just by proportion of population insured; the 12 percent enrollment achieved by Minneapolis HMOs is concentrated among the young and middle-aged employed. The heavy users of care, however, are the elderly and chronically ill. Market share, from the point of view of the delivery system (though not necessarily of an insurer), means share of health care *sales* (or costs). Insuring the low users—groups of employees and their families—always has a much less than proportionate impact on the delivery system. How are the elderly and chronically ill to be attached to such a system? They are, after all, the main users of health services, and no system can be successful unless it deals with them. What happens when such firms hold a large enough share of the market as to put serious pressure on conventionally organized fee-for-service practitioners? As the hospitals empty out, who folds? How do they fight back—will the HMOs be taken over? The strategy is full of promise, but it is far from proved.

From a regulatory perspective, however, encouraging this sort of organizational change involves a mix of deregulation and further regulation. Regulations, whether collectively self-imposed on and by professionals or built into the terms of public approval and reimbursement, will have to be eliminated if they restrict competition over market

---

[41] Enthoven, "Consumer Choice Health Plan"; and Christianson and McClure, "Competition in Delivery of Medical Care."

share, over nature of contract sold, or over production process. A further regulatory structure will be needed to help detect and discourage professional underservicing or quality dilution of a kind harmful to (and undetected by) customers. Regulation of the assigned-risk type will also be necessary to ensure that the ungrouped poor risks are not excluded from or discriminated against by this type of competitive service system. This problem is a serious one because the poor risks are so many, they are such important users of care, and they are so easily identified; the difficulty has been recognized by proponents of the competitive approach, but their suggested solutions are only sketched in.

The conclusion, however, appears to be that the problem of oversupply of professional services, in those professions where it occurs, must be met by further regulation. If one relies on direct service, price, and capacity regulation of the uniform national health insurance or service type, then anticombines policies become irrelevant. There is no price competition over market share. If one relies instead on enhanced competition among redesigned professional firms selling insurance-plus-service contracts, anticombines policy would have an important role to play in removing regulatory or collusive barriers to the entry and growth of such firms.

Public regulation of a more sophisticated type would still be needed to substitute for the quality control provided by self-regulation, as well as to protect individuals against either undetected underservicing or overt refusal to contract. Of course, self-regulation is not necessarily a guarantee of quality, but there seems reason to believe that quality control and restraints on overservicing in professional markets are better than in, say, used car or auto repair markets. To say that pure profit seeking is likely (if unrestrained) to lead to more serious problems is not to suggest that present systems are either perfect or beyond improvement. The difficulties posed by imperfect information in a market setting can be moderated and shifted, but they never disappear. Fortunately, it appears that overservicing may not be especially serious outside the health care field. Moreover, where it does appear, as in the legal examples cited, the remedies are political, not organizational.

Summary and Conclusions

To recapitulate, then, the problems of resource misallocation posed by professional organization and self-regulation are of three distinct types. Each may relate to the others and in some respects reinforce them as problems, but they have quite distinct policy implications.

The conventional economic view of the professions confounds professional individuals as inputs and professional firms as producing units. It identifies the resource allocation problem as restricted supply of services and elevated price, resulting from restrictions on entry to the industry and collusive behavior (or at least restrictions on competitive behavior) among industry members. The anticombines implications are clear: reduce self-regulatory or other barriers to entry, remove obstacles to competitive behavior (especially in pricing), and seek to prevent collusive behavior. Professional industries are not seen as being intrinsically different from any other industries in any way that is relevant to policy.

As noted, however, the characteristics of the professional service product and of professionals themselves may make the promotion of price competition difficult. The nature of the professional service, which may make price comparison of nonhomogeneous services impossible, the value systems of professionals with their emphasis on reputation and peer esteem, the geographic localization of professional markets, the consciousness of interdependence, continuing occupational education, and social contacts may all combine to thwart traditional competition policy addressing traditional problems of monopolistic supply restriction. Competition policy is an appropriate response, but it may not be effective.

The second view of the "professional problem" suggested in this paper is that confusion of entrepreneurial and labor-supply roles in the professional firm leads to choice of an excessively costly input mix— overuse of expensive professional time and underuse of less costly substitutes. In some professions, at least, the implication of this failure to minimize costs for quantitative resource misallocation appears to be far greater than any possible welfare burdens from monopolistic restraints on supply. In health care—medicine, dentistry, pharmacy—such excess costs are variously estimated at 20, 30, or more than 40 percent of the unit cost of professional services; and, of course, the welfare burden of price increases resulting from lack of cost-minimization is much greater than the burden of equivalent increases resulting from monopolistic restraint.

Dealing with such distortions also involves more complex problems of regulation and deregulation. If increased competition is to be a lever to encourage less costly production, then collective self-regulation of processes of service production, as well as of the economic behavior of professional firms, must be weakened or removed. Moreover, the exclusive link between supply of professional labor or skills and management of professional firms may have to be broken. Entrepreneurs who have no direct economic interest in the sale of professional labor itself may have to be admitted into the industry. Such more extensive deregulation of the professions, however, may be even more difficult to achieve politically than the first stage of deregulation (of economic behavior), and it will leave an obvious gap in quality regulation in those professions where the market cannot seriously be expected to perform that function. If the professions themselves cannot be permitted to regulate production processes, someone else must regulate outcomes.

Finally, a third view of resource misallocation in the professions is based on an extensive literature in health care and draws out the implications of the incomplete agency role of the professional provider: this view holds that in some professions at least, particularly in health care, the problem is not undersupply but oversupply of services. (This is, of course, in no way inconsistent with the second view, which can be combined with oversupply or undersupply.) Many services appear to be provided well beyond a point of positive impact on health, and (even under fairly weak assumptions) we may conclude that a fully informed consumer would not use them at any price. The resources used in their production are obviously wasted, and the problem appears to be of significant magnitude.

This aspect of the "professional problem" is clearly beyond the scope of competition policy, which (given present firm structures) will simply exacerbate the problem. It has been argued here that two radically different strategies are available—either very detailed public regulation of service delivery on the Canadian health system model, only more so, or a competitive market among very different types of professional firms selling not services but maintenance contracts. Either would require close regulation, although the latter strategy would also require anticombines or antitrust policy to maintain competition among these new types of professional firms. The public services model, at least in health care, can show limited but substantial success in practice; the competitive approach on a systemwide basis offers even more promise but also more problems and must still be regarded as unproven. The general intractability of the resource misallocation problems resulting from professional oversupply of services in either system may explain why a number of U.S. health economists insist so energetically that oversupply generated by providers cannot happen. But a good theory is supposed to "save the phenomena," and it is bad methodology (and worse policy) to "save the theory" by jettisoning the phenomena.[42]

This most serious and difficult of the "professional problems" is

---

[42] Certain specific procedures have been investigated in considerable detail—cervical screening, annual health exams—and guidelines for appropriate and inappropriate servicing are being developed in a limited range of areas. But this is only a beginning.

not, however, common to all professions. It is most severe in medicine, is somewhat less so in dentistry, and falls away rapidly thereafter. Similarly, the overuse of professional time in producing services is most acute in dentistry, pharmacy, and medicine. It may be significant also in law, but that is not documented. If we think of the professions not as a uniform group of industries but as distributed across a spectrum according to the degree of informational asymmetry between provider and consumer and the strength of the resulting agency relationship, it is clear that the most serious allocation problems develop at the end where the asymmetry is greatest—that is, at the most "professional" end.

With professions whose customers are informed and sophisticated buyers, there may be no agency relation at all, merely a continuing business association, and professional self-regulation might be dispensed with entirely. Certainly, such professional service markets would appear to benefit from aggressive interfirm competition. Pharmacy has small and unsophisticated buyers; but the agency relation is absent, and the dispensing act is relatively standard. Here there seems a good case for an openly competitive dispensing industry, though with considerable regulation of the manufacturing and wholesaling function and perhaps with public insurance of ingredient costs on the Saskatchewan model. The details and advantages of this system are analyzed in Evans and Williamson[43]—the basic notion being that consumers have no information with which to respond to price signals in selecting among drugs, but quite a lot in selecting among pharmacies.[44]

Eyeglasses, likewise, appear to have been demonstrated to be an area where enhanced competition can have considerable benefits, although there is, of course, a significant difference between the dispensing function of making up a pair of eyeglasses to a prescription and the optometric or ophthalmological function of determining the prescription

---

[43] Evans and Williamson, *Extending Canadian Health Insurance.*

[44] The Saskatchewan drug reimbursement plan, moreover, seems to be working out very much as theory would predict. Centralized public purchase by competitive bid is significantly reducing drug ingredient acquisition costs, and ingredients are supplied free to patients. Pharmacists are permitted to set dispensing fees independently, up to a maximum, and patients pay these fees directly (less a small flat payment by the public program). Formal and informal efforts by organized pharmacy to discourage open price competition over dispensing fees have had only limited success. As a result, Saskatchewan prescription costs (ingredient plus dispensing costs) seem to be lowered significantly by a constructive blend of private market forces (where suppliers are numerous and patients informed—dispensing) and public competitive contracting with no private patient participation (where suppliers are concentrated and patients totally uninformed—ingredients). Province of Saskatchewan, Department of Health, Prescription Drug Plan, *Annual Report 1977–78* (Regina, 1978).

needed.[45] Competition policy may be more help in the former than in the latter market.

Finally, the strongholds of professionalism, dentistry and medicine, pose the most complex problems both for regulatory and for competition policy. Here it appears that a major shift in regulatory policy could lead, in dentistry, to a market for competitively priced annual dental contracts, supplied by a firm (not necessarily owned by dentists) using the optimal input mix and constrained by independent quality-monitoring contracts. The shift from present patterns of practice and regulation would be massive, however, and would go well beyond open advertising and barring of (formal) price fixing. The rewards could be very large, but the rapid spread of private dental insurance in Canada and the United States may be foreclosing this option by destroying the constituency for any such massive deregulation. The providers are quite clear about the benefits of regulation and are well organized to fight for them.

As for medicine, the most professional of professions, there is no "magic bullet" solution to this multiplicity of different resource-allocation problems. Although there may be more scope for competitive or market-type mechanisms to play a useful role than is now used (either in Canada because we regulate or in the United States because they pretend they *have* a market), this component of the professional industry is unlikely—for many reasons—ever to move away from the making of collective choices about resource allocation through extensive regulation of the private sector or through direct public provision. In such an area anticombines or procompetitive policies may, from time to time, play a useful subsidiary role (as, for example, in restraining the enthusiasm of local groups of Ontario physicians for collusively opting out of the provincial insurance system and billing patients at standard fees; in theory, at least, they could go to jail). Even if the United States successfully develops an extensive network of private and competitive HMOs or similar organizations to organize medical care—using competition policy to encourage and protect this development—and even if Canada should move in that direction, an extensive regulatory web will still be necessary to constrain the industry. The types of choices, particularly those dealing with life or death, that must be made in this

---

[45] Lee Benham, "The Effect of Advertising on the Price of Eyeglasses," *Journal of Law and Economics,* vol. 15, no. 2 (October 1972); and Lee Benham and Alexandra Benham, "Regulating through the Professions: A Perspective on Information Control," *Journal of Law and Economics,* vol. 18, no. 2 (October 1975). The Canadian Restrictive Trade Practices Commission (*Report*) appears to have accepted this argument and to have recommended a combination of freedom of price-competitive advertising, divestiture to create a more competitive industry structure, and national quality standards so that consumers can price-shop with confidence

area are ultimately collective choices, and no market, competitive or otherwise, handles those well.[46]

---

[46] The social problems surrounding "pulling the plug" or the use of extremely expensive life-prolonging technologies seem particularly unsuited to a private market. The economic incentives faced by a private, for-profit firm supplying services plus insurance on a capitation basis are obviously to pull the plug but not to tell; those facing a service-reimbursed firm are to keep the machine running and the payments coming in (vegetable gardening or market gardening). The problem is a desperately difficult one, but there is no reason to suppose that private market institutions have any advantages in its solution. Quite the contrary.

Minimum-Quality Standards and Licensing in Markets with Asymmetric Information

Hayne E. Leland

The hand of the government in economic affairs is rarely more visible than in regulating quality. Safety standards have been imposed on drugs, automobiles, microwave ovens, and a host of other products. Bank and insurance portfolios must satisfy certain criteria for soundness. Restaurants are required to meet cleanliness standards, commercial aircraft must conform to maintenance standards, and so on.

Nor are minimum-quality standards limited to products alone. To enter a number of professions, one must pass state-administered tests believed to ensure at least a minimum level of competence. Doctors, lawyers, and contractors, to name but a few, must pass such tests. Moreover, in many professions where the state does not impose requirements, professional groups themselves set standards supposed to improve quality. There is also continual agitation to extend standards to other professions, from automobile repair to investment counseling.

Traditional economic literature gives little guidance on the desirability of such standards. A number of economists have held that they are misguided paternalism at best or an outright grab for monopoly profits at worst. It also seems clear that licensing standards are often written more to protect current practitioners from competition than to protect the public from incompetence.[1] As several papers in this volume bear witness, the current attitude of economists seems to be moving toward eliminating many, if not all, licensing requirements.

In the analysis developed here, and in my recent article in the *Journal of Political Economy,* I reach somewhat different conclusions, showing that certain types of markets may benefit from minimum-quality standards.[2] Even random licensing or entry restriction, which arbi-

NOTE: The author expresses his thanks to the Institute of Business and Economic Research, University of California, Berkeley, for clerical assistance in preparing this manuscript and to the National Science Foundation grant no. SOC 78–08280.

[1] See Milton Friedman, *Capitalism and Freedom* (Chicago: University of Chicago Press, 1962), for example.

[2] Hayne E. Leland, "Quacks, Lemons, and Licensing: A Theory of Minimum Quality Standards," *Journal of Political Economy,* vol. 87, no. 6 (December 1979), pp. 1328–46.

trarily exclude a certain fraction of potential sellers from the market, may be socially beneficial. This paper defines the nature of markets for which standards are desirable. It also examines the standard that might prevail if a profession or industry were empowered to regulate itself. In most cases, my results confirm a popular suspicion: self-regulation results in standards that are too high. Nevertheless, while quality regulation may be misused, this does not alter my contention that it can have beneficial effects.

To reach these conclusions, it is clear that my model of markets must diverge from the model suggested by traditional theory. The key difference is one characteristic of many quality-regulated markets: asymmetric information. By this I mean that the seller has a more accurate perception of true product quality than the buyer. Automobile purchasers have difficulty in assessing the safety merits of alternative gas tank locations. A depositor finds it difficult to assess the risk of his bank's portfolio of assets. And the user of medicines or of a doctor's services may not be in a position to judge their efficacy at the time of purchase.[3]

Of course, buyers usually have some information about the quality of their purchases. The quality of some products can be observed before any transaction is made. Even if direct observation of quality is not possible in advance, experience from prior purchases or friends' suggestions may reduce uncertainty. Consumer information services scrutinize a few major products. And "signals" (such as guarantees offered or diplomas displayed) may provide further insights into product quality. In a number of markets, nonetheless, substantial asymmetries tend to remain. These are the markets on which this study is focused.

In a seminal article, George Akerlof pointed out that problems can arise in markets characterized by asymmetric information.[4] He considered a market for used cars, where quality was assumed to vary from high to low ("lemons"). Akerlof assumed that potential sellers know the quality of their own cars and that higher-quality cars have more value to their owners if they are not sold. Buyers, on the other hand, have difficulty distinguishing good cars from bad. Since no one will pay more for a car that appears to be identical with all others, all cars of

---

[3] An alternative suggestion is that quality regulation occurs in markets whose products are potentially hazardous. But this seems less satisfactory: knives, for example, are potentially hazardous but are not regulated. Bank portfolios are regulated but are not life threatening. While potentially hazardous products do *tend* to be regulated, it is because of difficulties in assessing the hazard (information asymmetry) rather than the hazard itself.

[4] George A. Akerlof, "The Market for 'Lemons': Qualitative Uncertainty and the Market Mechanisms," *Quarterly Journal of Economics,* vol. 84, no. 3 (August 1970), pp. 488–500.

the same model and year have the same price. Akerlof assumed this price reflected the average quality of cars offered for sale—a form of rational expectation on the part of buyers, who know the general quality offered by the market but not the quality of any specific unit.

Problems begin to occur in the used-car market because owners of the highest-quality cars do not find it advantageous to sell at the market price, which reflects the lower average quality. When these sellers withdraw, average quality and price fall further, inducing owners of the next best quality cars to withdraw from the market. Price and quality spiral downward; in equilibrium, Akerlof suggests, only "lemons" will be offered for sale. The steep discount of slightly used car prices from new car prices would seem to add casual empirical support to Akerlof's point.

Akerlof's model is formalized in my recent article in the *Journal of Political Economy*.[5] It is shown there that, although markets with asymmetric information do not always degenerate to the lowest-quality level, there will always be an inefficiency in competitive equilibrium: quality *will* be too low.

The market failure can be explained as follows. In equilibrium, the marginal seller will find market price just equal to his opportunity cost. When opportunity costs rise with quality, the marginal seller will always be of the highest-quality level actually selling. The social value of a unit of the highest quality exceeds the social value of a unit of average quality. Yet the price received by the seller of the highest-quality level is the same as the price received by all other sellers and equals the average value in equilibrium. Thus the market failure can be cast in terms of a simple externality. When a high-quality seller offers his good or service to the market, the average quality rises, and buyers are willing to pay more. But the high-quality seller must split the benefits with all other sellers, who share in the higher price. Because the marginal seller cannot be recognized as the "best," he cannot receive his full contribution to social welfare. This wedge between social and private benefits results in too low quality and economic inefficiency.

Free Market Responses to Market Failure

A number of possible institutional frameworks could be set up to respond to this market failure. Let us first consider voluntary actions on the part of market participants. Here we will examine three possibilities: seller guarantees, private firms that specialize in providing information, and retailers that provide quality screening services.

---

[5] Leland, "Quacks, Lemons, and Licensing."

A number of authors have suggested that sellers could eliminate market failure by offering product guarantees. By voluntarily assuming liability for the failure of a product to attain a certain quality, sellers of the highest-quality product could "signal" their superiority. Sellers of lower quality would find it too expensive to offer as complete a guarantee; they would then face a lower price reflecting the lower average quality after the departure of the best-quality products. Then the next-best sellers might offer a slightly less complete guarantee to separate themselves from the remaining masses. The market would "ravel down" until all but sellers of the worst quality offered some form of guarantee. Products of different quality would then be recognized by buyers and paid for accordingly; while there might be some excess costs of signaling, there would be some promise of welfare benefits.[6]

Guarantees are not voluntarily offered in many markets exhibiting asymmetric information. The lack of guarantees is closely related to the nonexistence of insurance against certain kinds of risks. For many goods and services, the ultimate benefit or quality depends not only on the intrinsic quality of the product but also on how it is used by the purchaser. Separating these two may be difficult or impossible, and there may be incentives for misuse by the purchaser. This "moral hazard" problem, well known in the insurance literature, is an important rationale for the policy of caveat emptor. It explains both the lack of certain forms of insurance and the lack of voluntarily offered guarantees. Guarantees can, of course, be provided *involuntarily* by laws making sellers liable for the (observed) quality of their product.[7] I will return to this question in the concluding section.

An alternative market response might be the emergence of information-providing services. Indeed, there are some examples of these: *Consumer Reports,* restaurant guides, and so on. These services are sold directly to buyers. But therein lies a problem. As is well known, information on quality has many of the aspects of a public good: a consumer can give it away and still have it. Under such circumstances, inadequate resources will be channeled to providing information. If the cost of information provision is not borne entirely by consumers, an equally vexing problem can arise. Consider, for example, magazines that rate

---

[6] See, for example, W. Kip Viscusi, "A Note on 'Lemons' Markets with Quality Certification," *Bell Journal of Economics,* vol. 9, no. 1 (Spring), pp. 277–79. The stability of such a signaling equilibrium is not always assured; see M. Rothschild and J. Stiglitz, "Equilibrium in Competitive Insurance Markets: An Essay on the Economics of Imperfect Information," *Quarterly Journal of Economics,* vol. 90 (1976), pp. 629–50.

[7] See, for example, W. Oi, "The Economics of Public Safety," *Bell Journal of Economics,* vol. 4, no. 1 (Spring 1973), pp. 3–28; and Dennis Epple and Arthur Raviv, "Product Safety: Liability Rules, Market Structure, and Imperfect Information," *American Economic Review,* vol. 68 (1978), pp. 80–96.

restaurants and also receive a substantial portion of their revenues from advertising. It will be in the interest of restaurants to receive a favorable rating. Part of the benefits of a favorable rating could be kicked back to the magazine in the form of additional advertising. The vehement assertions that "we do not accept advertising" or "we are a nonprofit organization" on the part of some of the most respected consumer-testing agencies testify to this problem. A few private information-providing firms that derive their revenues from sellers do exist (bond-rating services, for example), but there is casual evidence suggesting that they make excessive profits, thereby diminishing the advantage of offering inflated ratings, with their subsequent short-term gains but longer-term losses. Indeed, some degree of monopoly power might be regarded as socially desirable if it diminishes the problems of quality deterioration.

Yet another market response is the development of informed intermediaries who sell multiple goods or services. Retailers, for example, typically carry many products. While their customers may purchase a particular item only on rare occasions, they will make frequent purchases from among the *set* of products offered. The retailer will be motivated to monitor and maintain the quality of the products he sells, since a dissatisfied customer will take his business elsewhere. In short, multiproduct retailers internalize the basic information externality. Such an argument can also explain the success of product conglomerates, restaurant chains, and so on. (It is interesting to note that income tax services are now being offered in certain large retail stores.)

While the existence of informed multiproduct intermediaries lessens the problem of asymmetric information, it does not eliminate it. Information to assess the quality of sophisticated products—such as doctors' services, drugs, or microwave ovens—may be difficult or impossible even for a middleman to obtain. And there are many services that do not lend themselves to being offered by multiproduct middlemen.

We conclude that private market responses will not always ameliorate the market failure resulting from asymmetric information. Given that private markets cannot eliminate the problem, the economist trained by the southwestern shores of Lake Michigan might be tempted to conclude that no institutional framework can be devised to improve matters. The following sections show, I believe, that this is not a correct conclusion.

Regulatory Responses to Market Failure

An alternative possible solution to market failure is the use of institutions further restricting the freedom of individual choice. Restrictions may be imposed by a government, by a professional or industrial organization, or by both.

In what follows, we shall look at three institutional arrangements, both separately and in combination. The three possibilities considered are the payment of subsidies to suppliers, the random restriction of entry to a fraction of suppliers (licensing on a random basis), and the imposition of minimum-quality standards (licensing on a quality basis). All involve some extramarket restrictions on individual behavior: the first because it involves the transfer of income through taxation and subsidies, the second and third because restrictions are placed on market entry. Two further possible solutions—certification and (involuntary) seller liability—are noted later.

Let us first examine the desirability of such institutions when welfare-maximizing policies are followed. Welfare is presumed to be the sum of producers' and consumers' surplus. Welfare-optimal policies may be contrasted with those that maximize sellers' profits (producers' surplus), to examine the implications of allowing industry or professional groups to dictate licensing or other criteria for sellers.

A Model of Markets with Asymmetric Information

To present my analysis in a simple but rigorous manner, I am using a model I developed previously, specialized to a linear-quadratic form that permits explicit solutions to be derived and alternative policies to be analyzed.

It is assumed here that sellers offer a specific number of units of goods or services of a given quality level. Without loss of generality, quality and quantity units can be rescaled so that the supply of goods is uniformly distributed over a quality interval from zero to one, where zero is the index assigned to a good of the lowest possible quality and one is the index assigned to the highest quality good. That is:

$$f(q) = 1, \; q\varepsilon[0,1]$$

where $f(q)$ is the number (density) of potential sellers of quality level q.[8]

Sellers of higher quality are assumed to have higher opportunity

---

[8] If $\bar{q}$ is an initial quality index with distribution of sellers given by $F(q)$, then we simply redefine the quality index by $q = F(\bar{q})$, with q now uniformly distributed. Note that the quality of each individual seller is fixed. Extensions of this analysis to include quality choice are discussed in Leland, "Quacks, Lemons, and Licensing." Such an extension does not alter the nature of our conclusions here.

costs. For simplicity, it is assumed here that such costs take a simple quadratic form:

$$R(q) = dq^2 + eq + f \tag{1}$$

with marginal opportunity cost $R'(q) = 2dq + e > 0$. As price rises, higher-quality sellers will be induced to offer their goods. Thus the average quality of goods offered tends to increase with price.

Buyers are presumed to have a marginal willingness to pay (inverse demand) such that:

$$p = a + b\bar{q} - cy \tag{2}$$

where p is the price offered to all units, $\bar{q}$ is the average quality of goods offered for sale, and y is the amount consumed. Thus consumers recognize average quality but cannot distinguish the quality of any particular seller.

Let $\hat{q}$ represent the *maximal* quality level of goods actually offered for sale and L represent the *minimal* quality permitted. Let $M\varepsilon[0,1]$ denote the proportion of sellers with quality between $\hat{q}$ and L who are actually allowed to sell. (If there are many sellers at each quality level, a random entry restriction would eliminate the same proportion at each quality level.) L and M are variables that regulatory authorities may be able to control. In the absence of control, $L = 0$ and $M = 1$.

Given our scaling of q to produce a uniform distribution of potential supply, actual supply will be given by

$$y = M(\hat{q} - L) \tag{3}$$

Average quality can also be related to $\hat{q}$ and L. It will be the average of the highest and lowest quality:

$$\bar{q} = (\hat{q} + L)/2 \tag{4}$$

Note that, given $\hat{q}$ and L, $\bar{q}$ is invariant to M.

Let us consider two alternative environments: (1) where the use of subsidies (or taxes) permit the choice of $\hat{q}$ and (2) where such subsidies are not possible and $\hat{q}$ is determined by the market forces of supply and demand.

If the market determines $\hat{q}$, it will set a level where the opportunity cost of the marginal seller, $R(\hat{q})$, just equals the price he receives. Thus, the market equilibrium $\hat{q}_e$ is determined by this relationship:

$$p = a + b(\hat{q}_e + L)/2 - cM(\hat{q}_e - L) = d\hat{q}_e^2 + e\hat{q}_e + f = R(\hat{q}_e) \tag{5}$$

using equations (1) through (4). This can be solved explicitly for $\hat{q}_e$ as a function of M and L:

$$\hat{q}_e = \frac{\dfrac{b}{2} - e - cM + \left[\left(\dfrac{b}{2} - e - cM\right)^2 + 4d\left(a - f + \left(\dfrac{b}{2} + cM\right)L\right)\right]^{1/2}}{2d} \tag{6}$$

When $d = 0$,

$$\hat{q}_e = \frac{a - f + \left(\dfrac{b}{2} + cM\right)L}{cM + e - b/2} \tag{7}$$

Equations (6) and (7) relate the maximal quality actually sold on the market to demand and cost parameters as well as to the policy parameters L and M. Recall that L is the minimum quality permitted (the "licensing standard") and M is the fraction of potentially willing sellers who are allowed to sell (the "random entry restriction"). Welfare is given by consumers' surplus plus producers' surplus. It is measured by the area under the demand curve (given average quality), less the opportunity costs incurred:

$$\begin{aligned}
W(\hat{q}, L, M) &= \int_0^{M(q-L)} (a + b(\hat{q}+L)/2 - cz)dz \\
&\quad - M \int_L^q (dz^2 + ez + f)dz \\
&= (a-f)M(\hat{q}-L) + \frac{(b-e)}{2} M(\hat{q}^2 - L^2) \\
&\quad - \frac{c}{2} M^2 (\hat{q}-L)^2 - \frac{d}{3} M(\hat{q}^3 - L^3)
\end{aligned} \tag{8}$$

If the market is allowed to determine the maximal quality, $\hat{q}$, (7) can be used to yield an expression for welfare, W, as a function of the policy parameters L and M. However, $\hat{q}$ itself can be chosen independently if subsidies or entry restrictions are used to induce a $\hat{q}$ different from the market equilibrium.

Profits to sellers depend on the price they receive, multiplied by supply, minus opportunity costs. When the market determines $\hat{q}$, profits will be

$$\begin{aligned}
\Pi = py - M \int_L^{\hat{q}} R(q)dq &= [a + b(\hat{q}+L)/2 - cM(\hat{q}) - L]M(\hat{q}-L) \\
&\quad - \int_L^{\hat{q}} (dq^2 + eq + f)\, dq
\end{aligned} \tag{9}$$

272

If, through subsidies, sellers are paid a higher price, equation (9) can be suitably modified.

To examine the impact of alternative policies on welfare and on profit, we set the cost and demand parameters at a fixed or reference level. The effects of changing the parameters from their reference levels will be examined later. Our reference case has:

$$a = b = d = 1$$
$$c = 2$$
$$e = f = 0$$

These numbers were chosen because they yield interior solutions for all problems considered.

Figure 1 shows market equilibrium when no policy instruments are used: $L = 0$, $M = 1$, and $\hat{q}$ is determined by the market. In this case:

$$\text{Maximal quality sold } \hat{q} = 0.5$$
$$\text{Total welfare } W = 0.3333$$
$$\text{Profits } \Pi = 0.08333$$
$$\text{Price } p = 0.25$$
$$\text{Supply } y = 0.5$$
$$\text{Average quality } \bar{q} = 0.25$$

The market failure associated with competitive equilibrium can be shown by differentiating (8) with respect to $\hat{q}$ and using (5), yielding:

$$\left. \frac{dW}{d\hat{q}} \right|_{\substack{L=0 \\ M=1 \\ \hat{q}=\hat{q}_e}} = \int_0^{\hat{q}_e} \left(\frac{1}{2} b \right) dz = \frac{1}{2} b \hat{q}_e > 0 \qquad (10)$$

That is, at competitive equilibrium, a further increase in the maximum quality level $\hat{q}$ would increase welfare.

Welfare-Optimizing Policies

Let us assume now that the regulatory authority can adjust maximal quality sold, $\hat{q}$, the level of random entry restriction, M, the minimum quality level, L, or combinations of the three. The nature of such adjustments and the information requirements to determine optimal policies are briefly discussed below.

Adjustment in $\hat{q}$ to a level above the market equilibrium, $\hat{q}_e$, can be achieved by offering subsidies to sellers. Subsidies bring into the market those who (because of high opportunity costs) were previously

FIGURE 1
COMPETITIVE EQUILIBRIUM

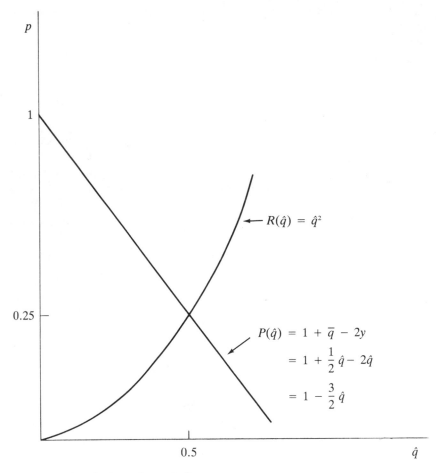

$$R(\hat{q}) = \hat{q}^2$$

$$P(\hat{q}) = 1 + \overline{q} - 2y$$
$$= 1 + \frac{1}{2}\hat{q} - 2\hat{q}$$
$$= 1 - \frac{3}{2}\hat{q}$$

NOTE: $a = b = d = 1$; $c = 2$; $e = f = 0$.

unwilling to sell. The cost of subsidies depends on whether the regulatory authority can identify high-quality sellers. If it can, only these need to be offered subsidies, at a level just sufficient to induce them to enter the market. For example, scholarships might be offered to talented applicants. If the authority offering the subsidies cannot identify the more talented potential sellers, the subsidy would be paid to all. Computation of the optimal subsidy in this case does not require the agency to know the quality of individual sellers but does require knowledge of market demand and opportunity-cost schedules. Even without such knowledge, equation (10) indicates that at least small welfare improvements can be made through small subsidies, because higher-quality sellers will be drawn into the market.

Adjustment of M, the fraction of willing sellers who are actually permitted to sell, requires that the authority be able to restrict entry. The number of licenses might be fixed or places in required educational programs limited. The important feature of M as a policy variable is that knowledge of individual quality levels is not required. It can be viewed as random-entry restriction or licensing—a fraction of potential sellers at all quality levels are refused entry. With entry restricted, price will tend to rise, thereby attracting more applicants and resulting in higher average quality. This higher quality *may* merit the initial restriction on entry.

Adjustment of L, the minimal quality permitted, requires that the authority be able both to restrict entry *and* to ascertain whether the quality offered by any seller lies above or below L.

Table 1 shows the welfare-maximizing levels of the policy variables depending upon which variables the regulatory authority can control. Tables 1 also details the resulting prices, supply, average quality, profit, and welfare for each case.

Use of Subsidies. Because of the nature of market failure, we know that increasing $\hat{q}$ beyond the competitive level of 0.5 will increase welfare. From line B of table 1, we see that the optimal $\hat{q}$ is 0.62, which is achieved by offering a subsidy of 0.31 per unit sold to sellers. Because of the increased supply, the price to consumers falls to 0.07 per unit. Supply and average quality rise markedly; total welfare increases by about 5 percent over the competitive level.

If all sellers are paid the subsidy (rather than only those who require it to offer their services), profit to sellers rises to 0.157. Subsidies improve the welfare of sellers markedly; if consumers of the goods or services are required to pay the subsidies through taxes, their consumer surplus will in fact fall.

Subsidies can also be useful in conjunction with minimum-quality standards. As we see from table 1 (line E), subsidies and minimum-quality standards jointly increase welfare. Both the extent and the total expense of subsidies are less when minimum-quality standards are also enforced (compare line E and line B).

Table 1 lists numerical results for the reference example only. We have also examined the response of numbers in the table to changes in the parameters a through f of our model. The percentage welfare gains from subsidies become larger as (1) the value of low-quality units (pa-

275

TABLE 1

WELFARE-MAXIMIZING REGULATORY POLICIES

Authority Can Set:	Minimum Quality L	Entry Fraction M	Price Subsidy to Sellers	Maximum Quality $\hat{q}$	Price to Consumers	Supply	Average Quality $\bar{q}$	Profit	Welfare
A. Nothing (competitive equilibrium)	0	1	0	0.5	0.25	0.50	0.25	0.083	0.333
B. Subsidy only (determining $\hat{q}$)	0	1	0.31	0.62	0.07	0.62	0.31	0.157[a]	0.348
C. Entry fraction M only	0	0.88	0	0.55	0.30	0.48	0.28	0.099	0.335
D. Minimum quality L only	0.22	1	0	0.70	0.49	0.48	0.46	0.127	0.360
E. Subsidy and L	0.20	1	0.28	0.78	0.49	0.58	0.49	0.199[a]	0.372
F. Subsidy and M	(same as B above: use subsidy only)								
G. M and L	(same as D above: use minimum quality only)								
H. Subsidy M and L	(same as E above: use subsidy and minimum quality only)								

[a] This assumes all sellers are offered the subsidy.

rameter a) is relatively low, (2) the fixed costs of quality provision (parameter f) are relatively high, (3) the sensitivity to quality (parameter b) is relatively high, (4) the marginal cost of providing higher quality (parameters d and e) is relatively small, and (5) the elasticity of demand (at the competitive equilibrium price and quantity) is relatively high. (The last of these involves a simultaneous shift in parameters a and c, which rotates the demand curve through the original price/quantity equilibrium to a steeper slope.)

Use of Random-Entry Restrictions. When no other policy options are available, welfare can nonetheless be improved in some cases by randomly restricting entry. For our reference case, line C of table 1 indicates it is welfare-optimal to exclude 12 percent (include 88 percent) of all applicants. This raises price, thereby inducing higher-quality sellers to apply for entry. Even though some of these higher-quality applicants are (randomly) rejected, average quality and welfare rise. But random restrictions are not always beneficial. The benefits from random-entry restriction increase as (1) the value of low-quality units (a) is relatively low, (2) the fixed costs of quality provision (f) are relatively high, (3) demand is relatively sensitive to average quality (b), (4) demand is relatively inelastic, and (5) the marginal cost of providing higher quality is relatively small (d and e). These situations are similar to those that yield gains to subsidies, except that the effect of demand elasticity differs.

It should again be stressed that random licensing is not *always* beneficial. Welfare may be decreased by such restrictions when markets are not described by these characteristics. Furthermore, the results in table 1 indicate that random licensing is less desirable than other instruments, regardless of parameter values.

Use of Minimum-Quality Standards. Welfare can often be increased by using minimum-quality standards, even when other policy instruments are available. Line D of table 1 indicates that a welfare rise of about 9 percent can be effected by a minimum-quality standard that eliminates the lowest 22 percent of potential sellers. Note that the *net* effect on supply is a reduction of only 4 percent. The elimination of low-quality sellers raises average quality and price, which, in turn, attracts entry of high-quality sellers. Both price and average quality soar from previous equilibria.

Like random licensing, minimum-quality standards are not always socially beneficial. The benefits from minimum-quality standards increase as (1) the value of low-quality units (a) is relatively low, (2) the fixed costs of quality provision (f) are relatively high, (3) demand is

277

relatively sensitive to average quality (*b*), (4) demand is relatively insensitive to price, and (5) the marginal cost of providing higher quality is relatively small (*d* and *e*). Therefore, minimum-quality standards will increase welfare in the same situations where random restrictions will be beneficial.

We found no combination of parameters where random restrictions were preferred to minimum-quality standards. Line G of table 1 indicates that random restrictions will not be useful in conjunction with minimum-quality standards. Thus, from a welfare viewpoint, minimum-quality standards dominate random-entry restrictions, but their implementation requires more knowledge on the part of the regulatory authority. Where knowledge of seller quality is difficult or impossible to obtain, random restrictions may be the only feasible option.

It may be noted from line E of table 1 that minimum-quality standards are useful in conjunction with subsidies. In all cases examined, the optimal minimum-quality standards were less restrictive when subsidies could also be used. A fortiori, markets in which minimum-quality standards alone are not beneficial will not gain from minimum standards when subsidies are possible.

Profit-Maximizing Policies

Let us now consider policies that maximize profits (seller revenues less opportunity costs) rather than welfare. This criterion is adopted as a proxy for a professional group or industry operating in its own interest. This is not to claim that all professional groups should or would operate to maximize producers' surplus—indeed, detailed examination of group decision making would be necessary to specify any particular profession's objectives.

The policy variables are the same as before: $\hat{q}$, the maximal quality seller; M, the fraction of willing sellers who are permitted to sell; and L, the minimum quality permitted for sale. While adjustment of M and L requires the same information and is implemented in the same manner as before (but with a different objective), the choice of $\hat{q}$ is made somewhat differently. It may be recalled that the welfare-optimizing authority was permitted to induce higher-quality sellers into the market by offering subsidies. But to do this the welfare optimizer must have the ability to tax, since subsidies imply revenues paid to sellers beyond those received from the sale of goods or services. (It might be suggested that sellers tax themselves ["union dues"] to subsidize high-quality entrants. If the quality of entrants could not be determined, all entrants would have to be subsidized, with the tax equal to the subsidy—thus rendering no change in the total opportunity cost of entrants. If the quality of entrants could be detected, such a plan might be in the group's interest but only if willingness to pay p were an increasing function of $\hat{q}$.) Let us presume, however, that the profit-maximizing authority does not have the ability to tax and therefore cannot raise $\hat{q}$ above the market equilibrium level, given L and M. Nonetheless, the profit-maximizing authority can reduce $\hat{q}$ below the market equilibrium if it can identify high-quality sellers and prohibit their entry. In certain circumstances, this may increase profits.

Table 2 gives the optimal profit-maximizing policies for the reference example. The rows A-F distinguish alternative combinations of policy variables. The columns show the corresponding profit-maximizing policies and their impact on prices, supply, average quality, profits, and welfare. We offer the following observations.

Restricting Maximal-Quality Level. In the absence of other policy variables, it will be profit maximizing to restrict entry of high-quality applicants. By this restriction price will be driven up while average quality falls. As the price-elasticity of demand rises or as sensitivity to quality increases, this policy becomes less attractive. It should be noted that, for the reference example, *some* restriction of maximal quality was optimal, even when other restrictions could be used. From a welfare point of view, such restrictions are, however, unambiguously bad because they exacerbate the fundamental market failure.

Random Restrictions. Prohibition of entry on a random basis can also increase profits. For the reference example, maximum profits resulted when only 33 percent of applicants were allowed to enter. Both price and average quality were high. In contrast with the welfare-optimizing policies, it was optimal to use random restrictions in addition to minimum-quality standards when both were available. However, both the minimum standard and the fraction refused entry fell from levels that were optimal when only one or the other could be used.

In all cases, profit-maximizing restrictions on entry were stricter than optimal welfare restrictions.

Minimum-Quality Standards. Minimum-quality standards improved profits, whether used alone or in combination with other policies. As demand becomes more elastic and more sensitive to quality, minimum-quality standards become more profitable relative to other policies and will increase welfare above the competitive equilibrium level by larger amounts.

TABLE 2
PROFIT-MAXIMIZING REGULATORY POLICIES

Authority Can Set:	Minimum Quality L	Entry Fraction M	Maximum Quality $\hat{q}$	Maximum q Willing to Enter	Price to Consumers	Supply	Average Quality $\bar{q}$	Profit	Welfare
A. Nothing (competitive equilibrium)	0	1	0.5	0.5	0.25	0.5	0.25	0.083	0.333
B. Maximal quality $\hat{q}$ only	0	1	0.30	0.74	0.55	0.30	0.15	0.156	0.247
C. Permitted entry fraction M only	0	0.33	0.92	0.92	0.85	0.30	0.46	0.173	0.266
D. Minimum quality L only	0.46	1	0.90	0.90	0.80	0.44	0.68	0.144	0.334
E. M and L	0.17	0.41	0.96	0.96	0.92	0.32	0.57	0.177	0.281
F. M and L and $\hat{q}$	0.30	0.65	0.76	0.97	0.93	0.30	0.53	0.189	0.279

For all parametric variations, minimum-quality standards were higher when profit was maximized than when welfare was maximized. Thus the contention that professional groups set standards that are too high seems warranted in markets described by our model.

Some Policy Implications

It is always dangerous to generalize from a theoretical example to real-world markets. A conservative approach would be to interpret our results as a counterexample, disproving the hypothesis that minimum-quality standards (or other policies) can *never* improve welfare. For a market described by a given set of parameters, it has been shown that welfare can be increased by a number of policies, including subsidies, minimum-quality standards, and even random-entry restriction. For subsidies or random-entry restriction, no additional ability to discern individual sellers' quality is required.

To draw positive implications from our model requires review of its key elements: (1) the market must be characterized by informational asymmetries; (2) higher prices must tend to attract higher-quality sellers; and (3) the opportunity costs of higher-quality supply must be convex (that is, opportunity costs increase with q at an increasing rate). Clearly, not all markets fit these requirements, and our results here are not applicable when they do not. When markets *do* fit, (1) there will be market failure in competitive equilibrium; (2) welfare may be increased by subsidies or random-entry restrictions, even if the regulatory authority cannot identify the quality of individual sellers; (3) subsidies can always increase welfare (computation of optimal subsidies requires that the regulatory authority know aggregate demand functions and opportunity-cost functions but not the quality of individual sellers); (4) random-entry restrictions will not always increase welfare but will tend to in markets with relatively inelastic demand, high sensitivity of demand to average quality and low marginal cost of increasing quality; (5) minimum-quality standards will not always increase welfare but will tend to in markets described in (4) (here implementation *does* require knowledge of individual seller quality); (6) minimum-quality standards will always be preferred to random-entry restrictions for welfare optimization, but combination of subsidies and minimum-quality standards will generally yield even greater welfare; (7) optimal policies tend to increase producers' surplus more than consumers' surplus (indeed, in many cases, the latter actually falls); (8) profit-maximizing policies yield higher prices, higher average quality, and lower supply than welfare-maximizing policies (relative to competitive equilibrium, welfare may be higher

281

or lower); and (9) profit-maximizing minimum-quality standards are too high (welfare may be higher or lower than in competitive equilibrium; welfare will tend to be higher as demand is more elastic and more sensitive to average quality).

These conclusions lend some support to both camps on the question whether minimum-quality standards are desirable. On the one hand, standards can be socially desirable. On the other hand, when left to the profession or industry, standards will be set too high, perhaps resulting in lower welfare than when no standards are imposed. And in markets that are *not* characterized by asymmetric information, minimum standards can only serve to lower welfare.

Note that I have not discussed the costs of implementing minimum standards—clearly one would have to weigh benefits against costs to make a correct decision. The burden of the analysis here has been to show that there *may* be positive benefits. The prevalence of minimum-quality standards might be viewed as positive evidence that benefits outweigh costs, although alternative explanations are possible.

Some Extensions

My analysis has been limited to the case where the quality levels offered by individual sellers are fixed and opportunity costs increase with quality and are convex. My recent article indicates that minimum-quality standards may be even more desirable where firms (or individuals) can choose the quality of their goods or services, if informational asymmetries persist.[9] Moreover, decreasing opportunity costs also strengthen the case for minimum-quality standards, since the sellers eliminated by those standards have the highest (rather than lowest) opportunity costs. But random-entry restriction or subsidies would not be desirable for these markets.

(The analysis is greatly complicated when costs are concave. Corner solutions become the rule rather than the exception. Disjoint supply intervals might be preferred to a single quality interval. Except to retain the conclusion that there is market failure in competitive equilibrium, our analysis, as developed here, cannot adequately cover this case. Whether costs are convex or concave is, of course, an empirical question.)

While we have looked at a number of alternative policies, we have ignored two that have been suggested by a number of authors: these

---

[9] Leland, "Quacks, Lemons, and Licensing."

two are seller liability and certification.[10]

Seller liability can be viewed as a compulsory insurance policy issued by the seller to the buyer. It can be beneficial by serving to internalize the basic informational externality. But the fact that seller liability has not come about voluntarily through product guarantees suggests that problems may exist with such an institutional arrangement. In an earlier section, I discussed the problem of moral hazard in limiting voluntary liability agreements. Moral hazard remains a problem with compulsory seller liability; its presence is a fundamental justification for the doctrine of caveat emptor. When it is difficult to separate product misuse from poor product quality, buyers may be led to initiate unwarranted claims, with resulting resource misallocations. For example, it has been claimed that fear of malpractice suits has led doctors to overtreatment of patients. Perhaps more important, the costs of monitoring product quality after use may be greater than the costs of monitoring product quality at the time of sale. This is clearly an empirical question, to which no definitive answer can be offered here.

Certification involves identification of seller quality but not prohibition of sales by low-quality sellers. The information requirements of certification are therefore similar to those for minimum-quality standards. Buyers have a wider range of choice, however, because they can buy low-quality goods or services if they wish. In an earlier section, I argued that private enterprise could not be relied on to provide complete certification, because of the anomalies of information as an economic good. It would still seem that government might perform this service, with higher welfare than would be produced by the enforcement of minimum-quality standards. It would seem that, when possible, certification would be preferred to minimum-quality standards.

There is another crucial difference between minimum-quality standards and certification. Certification involves not only identifying quality offered by individual sellers, but also communicating this information to buyers. In many cases, the latter step may be costly or impossible. Consider, for example, the rating of drugs. This would involve the results of many tests, most of which would require chemical and statistical expertise to interpret. Without such interpretation, the information would be worthless. Correct interpretation by consumers would involve

---

[10] J. P. Brown, "Product Liability: The Case of an Asset with Random Life," *American Economic Review,* vol. 64 (March 1974), pp. 149–61; Epple and Raviv, " Product Safety"; Roland McKean, "Products Liability: Implications of Some Changing Property Rights," *Quarterly Journal of Economics,* vol. 84 (November 1970), pp. 611–26; and Oi, "The Economics of Product Safety" consider seller liability in markets with symmetric information. For a discussion of certification, see Friedman, *Capitalism and Freedom.*

costly education. Rather than incur this expense, consumers might be better off appointing experts as their agents. *But the only action such an agent could undertake that would not require information transfer but would affect consumers' choices would be deciding whether to allow the product to be sold.* In short, because of the cost of information transferral, we wind up with a principal-agent relationship.[11] The relevant policy decision would be whether the principals (buyers) should be able to buy or not—and this is nothing other than the enforcement of a minimum-quality standard.

---

[11] S. Ross, "The Economic Theory of Agency: The Principal's Problem," *American Economic Review*, vol. 63 (May 1973), considers a formal model of principal-agent relationships. V. Goldberg, "The Economics of Product Safety and Imperfect Information," *Bell Journal of Economics,* vol. 5 (Autumn 1974), pp. 683–88, also alludes to the principal-agent relationship in the setting of product standards in his perceptive comments on Oi, "The Economics of Product Safety."

Commentary

William S. Comanor

From the vantage point of public policy makers, it must be frustrating to listen to the advice of economists, to take it seriously, and to try to fashion economic policies from their advice. Economists seem unable to make up their collective minds. Just when a consensus appears to be developing, opposing viewpoints arise, based either on new theory or on new empirical findings. And it is no longer clear what policies should be adopted.

This scenario, I believe, applies to the policy issues discussed here. I had perceived a consensus developing in this area, but the two papers presented at this session point in just the opposite direction.

For many years, economists have emphasized the restrictive and undesirable effects of existing policies toward licensing and the setting of minimum-quality standards. They have emphasized the anticompetitive effects of these regulations, which in turn have led to higher prices to consumers and higher incomes for the protected producers. The classic example has been the medical profession and the ability and effectiveness of organized medicine to employ licensing practices that limit the number of physicians.

The ostensible purpose of these regulations—that of protecting quality levels—has traditionally led to two responses from economists. First, economists have argued that the restrictions have probably not had much impact on quality. They have pointed to cases where the link between the restrictions imposed and quality was tenuous at best. Even where quality differences were present, moreover, the economists have argued that consumers should be free to choose between low-priced, low-quality goods or services and their high-priced, high-quality counterparts. There are, they have said, no good reasons that consumer choice should be limited or restricted in this area: on the contrary, such choices should be free for consumers to make as they will.

This analysis and discussion has largely complemented the growing interest in deregulation, both in Washington and elsewhere. The elimination of licensing and quality standards, in at least some areas, were seen to be an important part of deregulation.

There seemed to be a consensus on these issues among economists and, probably more important, the acceptance of the validity of this position by some policy makers. As fate would have it, however, just at this time, a new line of thought seems to be developing that points in the opposite direction.

The two papers in this session are among this new line of approach which seeks to contradict any consensus that may have been developing. The basic element in this discordant approach, and that which joins these two papers together, is the assumption of asymmetric information: that sellers are fully informed about the quality and the need for the good or service to be exchanged but that buyers are largely uninformed.

Professor Leland's analysis is founded on this premise. In this paper and his article in the *Journal of Political Economy,* he extends the analysis developed originally by George Akerlof. This analysis is based on the premise that sellers have a good perception of quality and indeed face an increasing opportunity cost of improved quality. Buyers, on the other hand, according to Leland, cannot distinguish high-quality from low-quality goods, so that their demand schedules depend on the *average* quality of all similar products in the marketplace.

Leland shows that market failure results directly from this type of asymmetrical information. Maximum-quality levels are too low, which means that higher levels would lead to a welfare gain. His discussion, however, largely ignores another facet of the problem of information, in that he deals in only a minor way with private and public attempts to correct for this imbalance. The problem he poses is not what should be done about asymmetrical information—how can this asymmetry be corrected?—but rather, *given the presence of asymmetrical information,* what is appropriate policy? His concern is not why and whether appropriate information or signals can be provided, but rather the regulatory implications of the information asymmetry that remain after all corrective measures are taken. His conclusion is that there is some beneficial role for appropriate regulatory standards setting—a conclusion that represents a break in what had seemed to be a developing consensus.

Professor Evans's paper also rests on information asymmetries. In his lengthy discussion, he pursues themes he has developed in various writings over a number of years. Implicit in his discussion is the possibility that an informational asymmetry between buyers and sellers can never be corrected, especially in the medical profession, which has long been his primary concern.

Even more than Leland, Evans is directly opposed to what I have characterized as the developing consensus on competition and regulation. First, he argues that quality regulation is required to protect ill-informed consumers, but his position in support of a regulatory structure to protect quality rests more on assertion than on detailed analysis. Even more important is his second theme, which is that "supply creates its own demand." This fulfillment of Say's Law occurs through manipulating the information that suppliers provide with the product. But here Evans departs from Leland. Demand depends, according to Evans, on the information that sellers provide on specific products, rather than on average quality levels.

Of course, this proposition stands conventional economic models on their heads. High prices and incomes call forth the entry of new suppliers, but this leads to still higher prices; and the process repeats itself. Only detailed government regulatory intervention can break the cycle. Evans's call for a substantial regulatory presence is thus strong indeed.

What conclusions can be drawn from this? Clearly, we have conflicting economic models, and the empirical evidence is not sufficiently strong to choose among them. Certainly we need to pay more attention to the way markets function in the presence of asymmetrical information between buyers and sellers than we have in the past, but to what extent is asymmetry a rationale for regulation?

One question presents itself. What is the nature of any trade-off between the price-enhancing effects of regulation, which have lately been emphasized, and the quality-enhancing effects suggested here? And what does this trade-off indicate about the proper scope of quality regulation?

It may have been—and I think it probably was—premature of me and others to talk about the development of a consensus regarding the economic effects of regulation. There are still too many open questions before us, with the inevitable and appropriate controversies that accompany them. Unfortunately, this must reduce the sharpness and clarity of any advice given by economists as to the proper scope of government regulation. We still have some way to go.

Keith B. Leffler

The self-regulation of professional occupations has been of interest to economists since Adam Smith's day. The dominant view categorizes such professional control as one of the many political techniques for gaining and employing monopoly power. A burgeoning literature analyzing the market effects of uncertainty about consumer product quality leads quite naturally to an examination of the social welfare effects of minimum-quality entry restrictions that explicitly recognizes uncertainty.[1]

Professional licensure has a long history as a social institution existing in widely variant political and economic systems. Licensure is not an anomaly. The simple notion that this institution represents successful efforts by occupational groups to transfer rents from consumers is difficult to reconcile with the basic economic assumption of self-interested rational agents. An economic explanation of a stable institution that relies on consumer ignorance or naiveté (this is the simple monopoly theory of licensure) is itself naive. An understanding of occupational licensure and regulation must be based on an understanding of a unique occupational character that buttresses the survival of the institution of licensure.

The overwhelming support for entry restrictions into some occupations (as, for example, medicine) by potential consumers suggests that consumers are not merely the willing victims but rather the beneficiaries of these entry barriers. Nonetheless, an explicit model of Pareto optimal licensing constraints is useful. Such a model at least enables us to identify the quantitative factors increasing the likelihood (or the level) of efficient entry constraints. Professor Leland's paper represents an attempt to establish such a model. Unfortunately, taken together, Leland's host of simplifying assumptions yield an elegant model with trivial and unrealistic results.

Leland's analysis makes use of a generally discarded description of public intervention assuming the existence of an omniscient social planner able to engage in the costless pursuit of Pareto optimality. Naturally, such a knowing planner must have little difficulty improving a society that privately knows naught—he must simply spread the good word. Leland's analysis, however, limits the state's alternatives to costless enforcement of entry restrictions. He then finds that the self-interested behavior of potential suppliers of a service may produce a more desirable result when low-quality suppliers are not allowed into the market. This "possibility theorem" is Leland's fundamental result, although variants of the entry-control technique and of the ownership of the entry-limiting property right are considered.

When the state can obtain information about quality costlessly, as in Leland's analysis, the possibility of efficient minimum-quality standards is unimportant. For illustration, let us consider a slight amendment to Leland's model. He assumes that the potential supply of any partic-

---

[1] Thomas G. Moore, "The Purpose of Licensing," *Journal of Law and Economics,* vol. 4 (1961), pp. 93–117, first examined alternative or complementary rationales for consumers demanding licensure restrictions.

ular level of quality is less than the demand for the occupational service. It strikes me as far more realistic that the *long-run potential* supply of a particular occupational service at any quality level is essentially perfectly elastic (at least relative to the market demand for the service.)[2] Leland's analysis also assumes that consumers face infinitely costly information about suppliers' qualities. When the supply of any quality is elastic and high-quality suppliers provide services, a free-entry market will produce goods or services of only the minimum possible quality. This occurs because consumers are by assumption unable to identify and therefore unwilling to reward any higher quality. The availability of a costless method of changing the minimum quality provided simply allows society to choose what single quality will be supplied. If there is no reason for the lowest possible quality to be identical with the most desirable single quality, Leland's possibility theorem becomes more tenable. When the supplies of services of different qualities are not perfectly elastic, as they are in his model, things are somewhat more complicated.

The specification of the supply of quality used in Leland's analysis also completely explains his "random licensing" suggestion. The supply conditions ensure that in the free-entry market equilibrium *all possible* low-quality suppliers are in the market. If some suppliers are now randomly eliminated (before any specific training), they can be replaced only by higher-quality suppliers. Again, since the random process is costless and licensure application (in Leland's model) also costless, random licensing can improve consumers' well-being. Of course, if low-quality suppliers stand ready to replace those eliminated or if the application for licensure is costly, this theoretical result has no policy relevance.[3]

Leland's analysis of markets with consumer uncertainty about supplier quality makes the same assumptions about consumer uncertainty that are made in Akerlof's model of used cars.[4] Consumers are assumed to be entirely ignorant of a supplier's quality though (implicitly) completely knowledgeable about all market supply and demand curves (in order that they know *exactly* the equilibrium distribution of quality

---

[2] For example, physician services to the entire population are provided by less than 0.5 percent of the labor force. Low-quality suppliers are clearly able to "flood" the market if allowed.

[3] The random licensing procedure must be implemented by a *deus ex machina*. Low-quality suppliers with (by assumption) low opportunity costs would otherwise spend the greatest amount to influence the "random" selection through grade competition, course selection, multiple applications, and "bribes" (say, donations to endowment funds).

[4] George A. Akerlof, "The Market for 'Lemons': Qualitative Uncertainty and the Market Mechanisms," *Quarterly Journal of Economics,* vol. 84, no. 3 (August 1970).

under alternative entry restrictions). Akerlof's uncertainty characterization may be reasonable for purchases of durable goods such as used cars, but it seems completely irrelevant for the consumption of occupational services. Quality is in part a characteristic of the supplier himself (as is implicit in Leland's analysis). Services of about the same quality are supplied continually over time by a particular supplier. Hence consumers will not face infinitely costly information; rather, they have some quality information from past experience and from friends, relatives, or information suppliers. This slight alteration in the model causes fundamental changes in the nature of free market equilibrium. As shown in Klein and Leffler, if consumers are able to check suppliers in *any manner* for veracity, the laissez-faire market equilibrium can support high-quality supply.[5]

Any model intended to demonstrate the possibility of efficient minimum-quality standards should incorporate consumers' search for both price and quality in response to consumers' learning about quality as they try different suppliers. Such a model must describe both sellers' and buyers' search procedures and ensure that the equilibrium supply and demand distributions are consistent with one another and with the assumptions underlying each. The difficulties of a model of this sort are manifest, and the existence of efficient minimum-quality standards is no longer obvious.

Professor Leland concludes his paper by recognizing the long-extant objection to an information cost-efficiency justification for licensure—namely, that certification "dominates" licensure by providing equivalent information and wider consumer choice. Leland argues, however, that certification provides poorer or more costly information than licensure, because consumers require "costly education" to interpret the criteria and evidence leading to certification. This argument is a non sequitur. Consider the certification carried out by the Underwriters' Laboratory. Does the average consumer have the slightest idea of the evidence and testing procedure used? The same is true for the Good Housekeeping Seal and for Moody's bond ratings. The knowledge that experts would not "use" (that is, certify) certain goods provides useful information regardless of consumers' knowledge of the exact standards. If a consumer does not trust his ability to understand the ways in which a noncertified product is inferior, he simply treats a certificate as a license. If all consumers so acted, certification would become de facto licensure. Yet *ex ante* prevention of consumer choice of uncertified quality can be

---

[5] Benjamin Klein and Keith B. Leffler, "Non-Governmental Enforcement of Contracts: The Role of Market Forces in Assuring Quality," UCLA discussion paper 158, July 1979, in press in the *Journal of Political Economy*.

justified only under a paternalistic "society knows best" argument, not by the costliness of information.[6]

Professor Evans's paper ranges far and wide, the central theme being the potential for competition in the supply of professionals' services. Evans emphasizes the special characteristics of professions that must explain the extensive regulation of these industries, and he properly stresses that economic analysis of procompetitive policies must explicitly recognize and evaluate the unique agency relationship between the "expert" professional and the informationally disadvantaged customer. While legal rulings in the United States allow for special treatment of the professions, economic discussions all too often ignore the quantitative differences between professions and other industries.[7]

Evans distinguishes three aspects of the professions as important to an understanding of the role and effects of traditional anticompetitive policies toward these industries: (1) the "natural" power of professions, (2) the labor-managed character of professional firms, and (3) the interdependence of the demand and supply of professional services.

The complexity of the services offered and personal characteristics of professionals' services make price competition intrinsically difficult. Price information is difficult to collect and to evaluate. Information about new technologies and practice techniques is valuable to the professional, and this makes for extensive social and business relationships that are not conducive to price competition. Besides noting these impediments to economic rivalry, Evans presents a creative and instructive analysis of the close relationship of professional regulatory restraints to "consciously parallel" noncompetitive pricing behavior. For example, ethical restrictions on the use of auxiliary personnel are shown to be a rational trade-off between the loss from increased output cost and the gains from stabilization of a cooperative price. This stabilization results from the decreased supply elasticity when physicians' time must substitute for auxiliary personnel.

Notwithstanding Evans's understanding of such practices, he re-

---

[6] See Moore, "The Purpose of Licensing," or Keith B. Leffler, "Physician Licensure," *Journal of Law and Economics,* vol. 21 (April 1978), pp. 175–76, for a discussion of efficient paternalist licensure.

[7] See, on special treatment, Goldfarb v. Virginia State Bar, 421 U.S. 773, where the Supreme Court noted that "it would be unrealistic to view the practice of professions as interchangeable with other business activities and automatically to apply to the professions antitrust concepts which originated in other areas. The public service aspect and other features of the profession may require that a particular practice which could properly be viewed as a violation of the Sherman Act in another context be treated differently" (pp. 788–89). But the special characteristics of professional services are not qualitatively unique. In particular, asymmetric information accompanies nearly all buyer-seller relationships. However, the extent of information costs, risk aversion, interdependent utilities, option demand, and so on makes the professions (particularly health care) quantitatively unique.

mains skeptical that competitive policies can solve the institutionally related pricing problems. His skepticism transcends the social custom, that is, the consumer demand, that restricts price competition in the professions. He argues that the requirement for external quality control is inconsistent with price competition. Evans's analysis dismisses consumers' ability ever to evaluate the quality of professional services. Thus he simply asserts that "the idea that 'brand name' and reputation will perform this [quality monitoring] function is just so much fluff: the whole essence of the professional relationship is that the consumer does not know what he needs before service, nor does he know afterward whether he was adequately served."

If Evans's view of consumers' uncertainty in professional markets is correct, the entire notion of consumer sovereignty, underlying the evaluative standard based on Pareto optimality, is undermined. Between the lines, Evans appears to substitute paternalistic, technological, social welfare criteria ("experts' opinions") for evaluation of the welfare effects of professional service consumption. This approach is not only elitist and unscientific but also unrealistic and unnecessary. We need only some limited long-run ability of consumers to identify and reward high-quality service for markets to monitor and guarantee product quality. Since the notion of repeat sales underlies the market's ability to guarantee quality, it is important to note that, in essence, an economic "repeat sale" need not be an individual consumer's repurchase of a good. Repeat sales incorporate all situations in which a favorable consumption experience by one consumer influences a supplier's future demand. This results from the exchange of information among consumers or between information agencies and the consumer. Hence the notion of repeat sales is applicable even to one-time purchases (such as appendectomies).

Markets can and will impose penalties for the supply of low-quality professional services; however, this does not imply that procompetitive policies necessarily increase efficiency. Self-interested professionals are motivated to control their own and their colleagues' levels of quality because of the future quasi-rent returns from currently satisfied customers. While procompetitive policies will serve to lower price, such policies also simultaneously lower the value of future business and thereby lower the incentive to produce high quality. Indeed, ethical restrictions designed to limit price competition may, as a joint output, increase product quality and consumer welfare.[8]

Evans concludes his discussion of professional market power by

---

[8] See Klein and Leffler, "Non-Governmental Enforcement of Contracts," for a more extended discussion of product quality, product price, and market equilibrium.

recognizing the relatively small welfare impact of price-searcher monopoly distortions. He goes on to suggest that a more important social loss may result from a "bias . . . in favor of excessive use of professional own-time (and thus failure to use less costly auxiliary or paraprofessional personnel)." Evans argues that the input bias is not solely a result of direct regulatory restrictions but also a consequence of the labor-managed nature of (medical or dental) professional firms. Licensure restrictions do limit the organizational structure of many professional firms by retaining to those who supply the professional labor the exclusive property right to the profits from production of professional services. Nonetheless, Evans's analysis of this issue is confused, and the input bias allegation is simply incorrect.

Meade has shown that labor-managed firms will add labor until the value of labor's marginal product equals the average earnings per worker.[9] Because additional labor dilutes the profit share of previous workers, under imperfect competition the labor-managed professional firms will be smaller than entrepreneurial firms (for example, there will be fewer physicians per practice). An individual laborer-partner will supply his own labor up to the point where the marginal value of his time just equals the marginal increment in his share of the profit. In a sole-proprietor professional firm, the reward and cost of own-time will reflect the entire social value and cost; inputs will be efficiently combined. In labor-managed firms with multiple partners, however, each partner will receive a reward from increased time input that is less than the social value (because the increased profits are shares); hence each partner works less than is socially desirable. The resulting input bias is exactly *opposite* to what Evans conjectures. Thus any empirical bias in favor of intensive professional time input rests completely on auxiliary input-use restrictions.[10]

The most troubling aspect of Evans's paper is his emphasis on the conclusion that classic economic principles are impotent in explaining equilibrium prices and quantities in professional services markets. The informational disadvantages of consumers (particularly when purchasing

---

[9] James Meade, "Labour-Managed Firms in Conditions of Imperfect Competition," *Economic Journal,* vol. 84, no. 336 (December 1974).

[10] Evans notes that "the professional as entrepreneur may thus be charging himself for own-time at a price much below what society has to pay for it." This is opposed to his earlier recognition that labor-managed firms will internalize any monopoly rents that might be present if the professionals supplied labor on an hourly wage basis. Indeed, this internalization may explain the empirical claims of excessive professional time input. Use of an implied average wage to the professional can overestimate the true social value of professional time. The correct welfare implication is then that entrepreneurial firms would underutilize professional labor while the professional firms efficiently internalize a pecuniary externality.

medical care) will cause them to rely on the advice of professionals about the value of their services. Thus, the plausible story goes, an increase in supply (as caused perhaps by procompetitive policy) unmatched by an increase in the aggregate "true" market valuation of professional services will result in suppliers' increasing their demands by "exaggerating" the implied valuation advice. Only thereby can the suppliers' desired or expected income be maintained. The resulting interdependence of demand and supply are duly noted as being inconsistent with classic economic descriptions of markets.

While the "supply creates its own demand" scenario can be criticized on many grounds, here I wish to emphasize an aspect of the scenario that is usually underplayed.[11] Consumers clearly recognize doctors as their agents for selecting desired levels of health care expenditures. We should, however, question why patients willingly trust the advice of agents whose short-run interests may frequently be inimical to their own. The answer is obvious only because experience has rewarded the reliance on such advice with satisfactory health and wealth. Certainly, if we visit our trusted family doctor tomorrow and are advised to undergo tests, inoculations, or even "life-saving" surgery, we may accept the physician's implicit estimate of the value of such procedures. If these procedures in fact result from biased advice in response to supply changes, however, patients will eventually recognize a change in the nature of the market. While one individual's health may stochastically decline and this may explain his physician's advice about an increased "value" of medical services, if all friends and relatives simultaneously receive the same advice about increased value of health care services, they should doubt that the change in advice is simply caused by a simultaneous change in all their states of health. Over time, through direct experience and the experience of others, through publicity given to research on the value of health care, and through reports of "unnecessary" surgery, patients will learn to reduce their reliance on the advice of self-interested professionals.

While there are a myriad of studies showing that surgical proclivities rise and prices do not fall when the supply of surgeons increases—and that follow-up visits, diagnostic procedures, and preventive care increase while prices do not fall as the number of primary-care physicians increases—there is absolutely no evidence that, in the long run, consumers do not penalize the "excess" provision of professional services. The

---

[11] I have discussed the inability of the "supply creates demand" model to explain the endogeneity of "desired" income and the cross-specialty, cross-section, and across-time variations in physician incomes in "Explanations in Search of Facts: A Critique of a Study of Physicians' Fees," Law and Economics Center Occasional Paper, 4–9/878, University of Miami School of Law, 1978.

available evidence cannot address the effects of biased advice on consumers' trust. The empirical support for the supplier-induced demand model is either cross-sectional or short run. The fact that suppliers can influence short-run demand does not imply long-run control. It would be folly to alter public policy as a response to a fashionable but unsubstantiated theory that flies in the face of all economic experience. Like most of Evans's analysis, the "supply creates demand" theory ultimately is based on consumers' inability to decide what is best for themselves; it is therefore inconsistent with the entire notion of freedom of choice.

To summarize, Evans bases his paper on the concept of market failure. The failure of the professional services market is alleged to result from asymmetric information and is defined by the incongruence of the equilibrium price-quality-quantity variables in actual markets and those that would occur if only information were free. Yet the costliness of information is a fact of life, and all social organizations fail to achieve hypothetical optima.

Alfred J. Lotka, the eminent mathematical biologist, has stressed the creative role that definitions can have in developing theories and understanding the world.[12] As an example, Lotka noted that "the enunciation of the principle of the survival of the fittest is essentially of the nature of a definition, since the fit is that which survives."[13] Economists, however, seem adept at selecting definitions that confuse and obscure economic theories. The concepts of moral hazard and imperfect capital markets are widely noted examples of misleading definitions. Just as obscuring is the definition of market failure. Markets fail because of asymmetric information just as markets fail because oil is found on the north slope rather than at the gate of extant oil refineries. All real market equilibria could be better, if only . . . if only. . . . The idea of "market failure" holds an implicit false promise—the promise of an achievable superior, nonmarket alternative—and leads therefore to a Sisyphean search for an economic panacea.

---

[12] A. J. Lotka, *Elements of Mathematical Biology* (New York: Dover, 1956), chap. 1.
[13] Ibid., p. 3.

Part
Six

Has Occupational Licensing Reduced Geographical Mobility and Raised Earnings?

B. Peter Pashigian

In principle, there are several ways to determine the effects of occupational licensing on earnings and mobility. It is seldom possible to compare licensed with unlicensed states (since licensed occupations tend to be licensed in all or most states), but one can compare states that apply stringent standards in licensing an occupation with states that enforce less stringent standards. This popular method of measuring the effects of licensing has distinct limitations when state differences in licensing stringency are difficult to measure. An alternative approach would be to compare an occupation before and after the advent of licensing. Unfortunately, many occupations were licensed before the second decade of the twentieth century, and the dearth of information often precludes a before-and-after study.[1] Given these obstacles, one is forced to consider a third alternative. Licensed occupations may be compared with unlicensed occupations to determine how earnings and mobility are affected by occupational licensing. While this approach also suffers from several drawbacks (one of which is the comparability of occupations), it does have the merit of comparing extremes, licensing and no licensing, rather than some licensing versus more licensing. The objective of this kind of study would be to determine if a "representative" licensed occupation differs in important ways from a "representative" unlicensed occupation.

This is the approach adopted here. One hundred and fifty-seven occupations, some licensed and many unlicensed, are analyzed to determine if members of licensed occupations (1) are less likely to move across state boundaries, (2) are less likely to move from one market to another within the state, (3) are less likely to change occupations, and (4) report higher earnings.

NOTE: The author acknowledges the helpful comments by the discussants at the conference, Stuart Dorsey and Janice Madden, and by participants in the Labor Workshop and the Workshop in Applications of Economics at the University of Chicago.

[1] Thomas G. Moore, "The Purpose of Licensing," *Journal of Law and Economics* (April 1961), pp. 93–117.

The first section reviews the existing theory of mobility and considers the different ways licensing may affect earnings. The next defines the mobility variables and proposes a simultaneous equations system to explain the joint determination of intra- and interstate mobility and earnings. The third section introduces the exogenous variables and the fourth discusses the selection of licensed occupations. The fifth section presents the empirical results, and the last section reviews the major findings.

A Review of the Theory

Mobility of Workers. Schwartz has proposed a theory of employee mobility in which age and education are important determinants of the geographical area of search by workers for new jobs and by firms for new employees. The firm minimizes total search costs by selecting the area of search and the share of the working population eligible for the new positions in the firm. Workers learn through formal training and through job experience. The amount and form of on-the-job training varies with the educational requirements of the position. Part of the on-the-job training is general and is useful in other jobs (and in jobs with other firms), and the other part is specific and valuable only for the current job (and with the current firm). Schwartz assumes that the share of specific training increases as the educational requirements of the position increase. This implies that the higher the educational requirements of the job, the more costly it is for employees to switch jobs (because the share of specific investment rises with the educational requirements of the position). When the firm tries to fill positions with higher educational requirements, it will have a greater incentive to expand the area of search or hire younger workers who have not yet made large specific investments. To attract existing nearby workers would require firms to pay excessive wage premiums to offset the reduction in the value of the specific investment made in the past by these workers. Schwartz's analysis suggests that the migration rate (the proportion of employees that move a given distance) should decrease with age and decrease at a faster rate the higher the education level of the employee.

Schwartz also sketches a theory of worker search activity. The worker sets a minimum wage level, called a reservation wage, that he must receive before he will leave his current position. In a given market, Schwartz assumes that the mean length of time before a wage offer exceeds this reservation wage increases with the educational requirements of the position. This would mean that more highly educated workers have greater incentives to reduce the waiting time before a wage offer exceeds the reservation wage. This they can do by searching over a wider area and thereby canvassing more markets. This type of analysis could be extended by assuming that mean waiting time rises with earnings (given age). Workers with higher earnings would also have a greater incentive to search over wider areas. Schwartz's analysis of worker and firm behavior suggests that geographical mobility will rise with education and earnings and decline with age.

Because Schwartz wished to explain the relationship of mobility, education, and age for the work force as a whole, he did not consider the special characteristics of occupations that might affect mobility. To understand differences in geographical mobility among occupations, it is imperative to consider such characteristics. In some occupations members make major location-specific investments. Independent practitioners, businessmen, and craftsmen learn about local markets through experience. Much of their investment in this learning becomes obsolete if a geographical move is made. Investment in local reputation and market is a deterrent to mobility: certainly the empirical evidence supports the notion that local good will deters mobility. I found that interstate mobility was lower in those professional occupations with greater investments in local reputation.[2] The form of the wage and employment contract will also affect mobility. In some unions seniority is not automatically transferred with a job change. Employees of local and state governments face this problem when a job change involves a move across state boundaries. They will be more reluctant than employees of the federal government to move across state boundaries because their pension and seniority rights are likely to be lost or reduced, which is not the case for federal employees.

These comments suggest that geographical mobility would differ among occupations even in the absence of licensing because of differences in age, education, earnings, place-specific capital, and types of employment contracts. Licensing adds to the cost of movement even when some form of reciprocity is practiced. Recent studies indicate that the costs of mobility are even higher when restrictions are placed on reciprocity.[3]

Earnings. The earnings of members of an occupation can change if licensing is imposed. The magnitude of the change will depend on the

[2] B. Peter Pashigian, "Occupational Licensing and the Interstate Mobility of Professionals," *Journal of Law and Economics*, vol. 22 (April 1979), pp. 1–25.
[3] See A. Holen, "Effects of Professional Licensing Arrangements on Interstate Labor Mobility and Resource Allocation," *Journal of Political Economy*, vol. 73 (October 1965), pp. 492–98; and Pashigian, "Occupational Licensing," pp. 11–12.

underlying reason for licensing. Licensing might benefit certain groups of consumers by reducing the numberof lower-quality practitioners and lowering search costs. If so, prices would be higher and the range of qualities more limited, but the rate of return earned on the human capital of the practitioners in licensed occupations would not rise in the long run, so long as there was free entry into those occupations.[4] On the other hand, existing practitioners might use the licensing mechanism to raise the rate of return. They might require new entrants to satisfy progressively higher educational or experience requirements. As these requirements were raised, the current members would achieve short-run benefits when prices and earnings rose as older members of the occupation retired and were not immediately replaced by new entrants because of the higher requirements. After what could be a long time, prices and earnings would rise by enough to justify the greater investment required of new entrants to satisfy the higher requirements. There is no way of telling whether this has in fact happened since no comprehensive study has been made of the comparative growth of educational requirements over time in licensed and unlicensed occupations.

Methods of measuring the effects of licensing on earnings should be discussed at this point. The easiest way to do this is take the simplest though unrealistic case and assume that differences in average earnings between occupations depend only on differences between occupations in the amount of schooling required. This is often called the *pure* schooling model.[5] Annual earnings per member will be determined by the equation $\log E_i = a + bS_i + u_i$, where E_i is the annual earnings per member in the ith occupation, S_i is the years of formal schooling of members in the ith occupation (all members in an occupation are assumed to be alike), and u_i is a disturbance term encompassing all other factors affecting earnings. This equation says that annual earnings must be higher in equilibrium in occupations that require more years of formal schooling. In the absence of licensing, there will be differences between occupations in the amount of formal schooling and corresponding differences in annual earnings. Suppose now that one occupation becomes licensed and formal schooling requirements are raised. After a long time, practitioners in the newly licensed occupation have spent a longer period in school and, once a new equilibrium is reached, the earnings of members in this occupation will have to rise by enough to justify the larger investment by members (in the form of the forgone earnings due

---

[4] Keith B. Leffler, "Physician Licensure: Competition and Monopoly in American Medicine," *Journal of Law and Economics*, vol. 21 (April 1978), pp. 165–86.

[5] Jacob Mincer, *Schooling, Experience and Earnings* (New York: Columbia University Press, 1974), pp. 7–11.

to the longer schooling period). Higher earnings per member come about because licensing will reduce the number of practitioners and cause prices and earnings to rise. Suppose one proposed to measure the effect of licensing on earnings by simply comparing average earnings in many occupations, some licensed and others not. The equation says the log of earnings will be linearly related to years of schooling. Suppose an econometrician wants to measure the effect of licensing and regresses the log of earnings on years of schooling and on a dummy variable set at one if an occupation is licensed and at zero if it is not. The statistical analysis would fail to reveal any effect due to licensing because differences in schooling would explain all the differences in earnings. Licensing has raised earnings by raising schooling requirements, but all the increased earnings in licensed occupations would be explained by the increased schooling requirements. There would be nothing left for the dummy variable representing licensing to explain. To estimate the effect of licensing on earnings would require a considerable extension of the model to explain why schooling levels differ among occupations. This extension is not easily made and is not attempted here but is necessary if the effects of licensing are to be estimated.[6]

The effect of licensing on earnings will be captured through the use of a dummy variable if the current members of a licensed occupation can determine the number of entrants into the occupation. By determining the number and size of training schools and the educational prerequisites for entry into the schools, the members of an occupation can limit the number of entrants into the occupation and thereby raise earnings. Given the required years of schooling, earnings will be abnormally high in the licensed occupation because there is no longer free entry into it.[7] Because earnings are abnormally high relative to years of schooling required, there will be an excess demand for entry into training schools and an incentive for the training schools to raise tuition

---

[6] We might set up an equation that would make schooling a function of licensing and other variables:

$$S_i = S(L_i, V_i) + s_i$$

where L denotes the presence of a licensed occupation, V denotes other determinants of schooling, and s_i is the disturbance term. The net effect of licensing on earnings would then be determined by

$$\log E_i = a + bS(L, V_i) + \varepsilon_i.$$

Hence, if the exogenous determinants of schooling could be well specified, this equation could be used to measure the effects of licensing on earnings.

[7] The current members may find that the lowest-cost method of restricting entry is to control requirements and places. By prohibiting the entry of low-quality training schools, the members of the occupations will secure the support of some educators. This method will yield greater political support than a policy of allowing anyone to complete the schooling requirements but limiting entrants by lowering the pass rate on the entrance exam.

or fees. Present and future members of the occupation wish to limit these increases. Because nonprofit institutions pursue wealth-maximizing activities less actively and employ financial incentives less extensively, members of the occupation will favor nonprofit rather than for-profit training schools. To the extent that tuition increases are controlled, the earnings of members will remain high relative to schooling requirements, and a persistent excess demand for entry into training schools will exist. Because earnings are abnormally high in the licensed industry, the effect of licensing on earnings will be captured in part by the use of a dummy variable representing licensing in an empirical analysis.

This discussion suggests that a regression of earnings on schooling and a dummy variable for licensing will identify only cases where (1) licensing has been combined with other effective entry restrictions or (2) licensed occupations have not yet reached long-run equilibrium because of rising educational requirements. If the regression analysis fails to show a direct effect of licensing on earnings, it may nevertheless be true that licensing has raised earnings through its effect on schooling or experience.

We do not know whether requirements for entry into licensed occupations have been increasing more rapidly in licensed than in unlicensed occupations. If there have been no systematic differences over time, the average earnings in licensed occupations in 1970 are not likely to exceed the average earnings in unlicensed occupations in 1970 (after adjusting for schooling and experience) even though requirements might have been raised around the turn of the century when licensing was first imposed. Most of the members in licensed occupations at the time when licensing was imposed would have been retired by 1970.

If licensing reduces interstate mobility (by raising its cost) it need not simultaneously raise average earnings. Licensing may raise the cost of importing members into the state without restricting within-state production of members. In effect, licensing would encourage a dispersal of training facilities. If the opportunities for interstate mobility are lower in licensed than in unlicensed occupations, members in the licensed occupations would be expected to receive an earnings premium, its size depending on the importance of the restriction of choice. If there are many other local markets within the state, the restriction on interstate mobility would be a modest one, and the premium would be correspondingly small.

Occupational Mobility. There is another way of determining whether earnings in licensed occupations are high relative to the formal educational requirements and on-the-job training of members. The effect of licensing on the probability of licensed practitioners' leaving an occupation will provide indirect information on the effect of licensing on earnings. If licensing does raise earnings relative to schooling, then licensed occupations will be attractive to enter and unattractive to leave. If earnings in licensed occupations are relatively high, the proportion of members leaving them should be lower than the proportion of numbers leaving unlicensed occupations, all other things being equal. The effects of licensing on earnings would be consistent with the effects of licensing on occupational mobility.

Measures of Interstate and Intrastate Mobility

The 1970 census of population identifies the number of individuals in each occupation in 1970 whose *residence* in 1965 was in a different state, a different county of the same state, or a different residence in the same county as in 1970. These data may be used to construct several measures of intrastate and interstate mobility. The three measures used in my earlier study are employed in this study:

1. The interstate migration rate (IMR), that is, the number of members of an occupation in 1970 whose 1965 residence was outside the state of residence in 1970 divided by the number of all members of the occupation in 1970.

2. The probability of an interstate move given an out-of-county move (PIM)—the number of members of an occupation in 1970 whose 1965 residence was outside the state of residence in 1970 divided by the number of those members who lived in 1965 outside the current county of residence (the probability of an interstate move is the conditional probability of moving out of state given an out-of-county change of residence).

3. The probability of remaining in county given no interstate move (PIC)—the number of members of an occupation in 1970 whose county of residence was the same in 1965 and 1970 divided by the number of those members whose *state* of residence was the same in 1965 and 1970 (PIC may be considered a proxy for investments in local good will and will be higher in occupations where members make larger investments in good will, other things being equal).

The three measures are related to each other. Let T denote all members of an occupation in 1970, S denote members in the same residence between 1965 and 1970, INC denote movers who remained in the same county, INS denote movers to a different county in the same state, and $OUTS$ denote movers to a different state. Thus $T =$

$S + INC + INS + OUTS$, and the three measures are defined as follows:

$$IMR \equiv \frac{OUTS}{T}$$

$$PIM \equiv \frac{OUTS}{INS + OUTS}$$

$$PIC \equiv \frac{S + INC}{S + INC + INS}$$

The three measures are related to each other, so that knowledge of PIC and IMR uniquely determines the value of PIM.[8] For subsequent discussion, define POC ($\equiv 1 - PIC$) as the conditional probability of moving *out*-of-county given no interstate move.

The average earnings in an occupation and interstate and intrastate mobility of members may not be determined independently. For example, interstate mobility will be lower in occupations where local good will (with PIC serving as a proxy for local good will) is important. So it is necessary to formulate a system of equations that jointly determines the interstate migration rate, the intrastate migration rate, and the mean earnings of full-time workers. The proposed system of equations is shown here:

$$\ln\left(\frac{IMR}{1 - IMR}\right) = \alpha_0 + \alpha_1 \ln(POC) + \alpha_2 LIC$$
$$+ \alpha_3 \ln(MEF) + \sum_{i=4}^{L} \alpha_i X_i + u_1 \quad (1)$$

$$\ln(POC) = \beta_0 + \beta_1 \ln LIC + \beta_2 \ln(MEF) + \sum_{i=3}^{M} \beta_i Y_i + u_2 \quad (2)$$

$$\ln(MEF) = \gamma_0 + \gamma_1 LIC + \gamma_2 \ln(POC) + \sum_{i=3}^{N} \gamma_i Z_i + u_3 \quad (3)$$

where LIC denotes a dummy variable for licensing (discussed below) and X_i, Y_i, and Z_i stand for other exogenous variables (discussed below). In the first equation, the interstate migration rate is assumed to be

---

[8] The relationship is

$$\left[\ln\left(\frac{PIM}{1 - PIM}\right) = \ln\left(\frac{1}{1 - PIC}\right) + \ln\left(\frac{IMR}{1 - IMR}\right)\right]$$

where ln denotes the natural log.

directly related to the within-state migration rate($\alpha_1 > 0$), inversely related to licensing ($\alpha_2 < 0$) and directly related to earnings ($\alpha_3 > 0$). The variables X_i would include educational attainment and other occupational characteristics. In the second equation, the within-state migration rate is related to licensing, earnings, and other exogenous variables. The licensing variable is introduced in this equation for the following reason. First, β_1 should be zero if licensing only raises the cost of *interstate* mobility (because licensing should therefore not affect the within-state migration rate). In some occupations, however, licensing is also associated with other restrictions that raise the cost of entering any new market—such as the restriction on forms of advertising. If this is the case, licensing will be inversely related to within-state migration. The third equation identifies the determinants of average earnings in occupations. The variables in this equation include educational attainment, experience, licensing, and the within-state migration rate. The within-state migration rate is considered a proxy for non-locality-specific capital. The hypothesis tested is whether earnings are lower in occupations with larger within-state migration rates. This is to determine whether total human capital is larger (given age and education) the smaller the geographical mobility of members in an occupation. Members of these occupations may invest more in knowledge of the job and local market conditions because they anticipate less job and market turnover.

There are 157 occupations in the sample, for the most part corresponding to the detailed census occupations. (A list of the occupations is presented in appendix A.) An occupation was included in the sample if the census of population reported mobility data of males (since we are studying males), if the title of the occupation was not a residual (as, for example, "not elsewhere classified"), and if the relevant economic or demographic data were available.[9]

Definition of Dependent Variables

The definition of and symbol for each dependent variable are given first:

1. Earnings: The mean earnings of male workers employed fifty to fifty-two weeks in 1969 is the measure of occupational earnings. (The use of earnings of full-time workers standardizes for differences among

---

[9] The effects of family structure on mobility are not studied here. See Jacob Mincer, "Family Migration Decisions," *Journal of Political Economy,* vol. 86 (October 1978), pp. 49–74.

occupations in weeks worked.) The letters *LMEF* stand for log of mean earnings of male full-time workers (sixteen years and older) in 1969.

2. Local good will: A proxy for local good will is the probability of remaining in a county given no interstate move. The variable employed in the regression analysis is one minus this probability and is given as *LPOC*, equal to the log of one minus *PIC*.

3. Interstate mobility: The variable used in the regression analysis is the log of the interstate migration rate, divided by one minus this rate, abbreviated *LOIMR*.

4. Occupational mobility: A measure of occupation stability is the probability of remaining in an occupation over a period of time. A special tabulation of census data shows the percentage of workers in an occupation in 1965 still remaining in the occupation in 1970 after adjustments for departures due to deaths.[10] The symbol used for this probability is *PIS*. The variable used in the regression analysis is the Log $(PIS)/(1 - PIS)$, abbreviated *LOPIS*.

5. Interstate migration rate of older versus younger workers: The ratio of the interstate migration rate of older workers to that of younger workers reflects the relative importance of locale-specific investment in the occupation. Occupations with greater locale-specific capital will have smaller ratios. The variable (*IMROY*) is the interstate migration rate of workers between forty-five and sixty-four years old divided by the interstate migration rate of workers between twenty-five and forty-four years old.

Definition of Independent Variables

The independent variables are these:

1. Age of worker: Two variables are used to measure age effects, these being the median age of worker in experienced civilian labor force in 1970 (*AGE*) and the percentage of workers in the experienced civilian labor force less than thirty years old, 1970 (*YOUTH*).

2. Educational attainment: Census estimates of years of formal schooling are deficient inasmuch as the highest measured attainment was the open-ended class of seventeen or more years of formal schooling (and in many professional occupations the median years of schooling would exceed seventeen years). Two substitute measures have been employed, these being percentage of experienced civilian labor force (sixteen years or older) with five or more years of college, 1970 (*PC05*)

---

[10] Dixie Somers and Alan Eck, "Occupational Mobility in the American Labor Force," *Monthly Labor Review*, vol. 100 (January 1977), pp. 3–19.

and percentage of experienced civilian labor force with four years of college, 1970 (*PC*04).

3. Local good will: Two proxies are used to measure the importance of local good will: *POC* (the conditional probability of an out-of-county move) has already been discussed. The other measure is percentage of workers in an occupation in private practice (*PRI*).[11]

4. Growth in market demand: If the growth in market demand for the services of an occupation did not differ among states, the national growth rate would not have a pronounced effect on the interstate migration rate. But the variability among state growth rates can be expected to increase with the growth rate in the occupation overall: faster growing occupations will typically have greater variability among the state growth rates. Variability among state growth rates should raise the interstate migration rate, so that the overall growth rate in members may be directly related to interstate mobility. The variable here is the log of the occupational growth rate in the total number of employed workers (civilian labor force fourteen years and over) between 1960 and 1970 (*LGROW*).

5. Urbanization: Earnings will usually be higher if members of an occupation live in urbanized rather than rural areas. Residence in urbanized areas is also likely to be associated with a higher probability of moving out of one county into another county (in the same urbanized area). The variable here is proportion of employed male workers (sixteen years and over) living in urban areas, 1970 (*URB*).

6. Mean hours worked: Earnings of full-time workers (working fifty to fifty-two weeks) are adjusted for hours worked per week by including the mean hours worked by all *employed* males in 1970 (mean hours worked by full-time workers being a figure not publicly available). The variable is log of mean hours worked per week of employed males (sixteen years or over), abbreviated *LMHW*.

7. Employment by federal, state, and local government: Workers employed by state and local government will have less incentive to move across state boundaries than workers employed by federal government if the job change involves a reduction in seniority or pension benefits. Hence occupations with a larger proportion of workers employed by state and local governments should display less interstate mobility than occupations with a larger proportion of workers employed by the federal government. Within-state mobility of state and local employees may or may not be lower than the within-state mobility of federal employees. Government employment may also affect average earnings. A recent study by Smith shows that earnings of federal, state, and local employees

---

[11] Private practice includes all nonwage, nonsalaried and nongovernment workers.

are higher than in the private sector.[12] If so, average earnings should be higher in occupations with a larger share of employment accounted for by government. The two variables used here are percentage of workers employed by federal government (*PFED*) and percentage of workers employed by state and local government (*PSL*).

8. Unionization: Richard Freeman kindly provided estimates of the percentage of workers in unions by occupation over the 1973–1975 period. The variable is percentage of unionized workers in occupation (*U*).

9. University employment: The number of colleges and universities per state is smaller than the number of firms per state. A location change by a professor has a higher probability of involving an interstate move than a location change by someone in industry. A dummy variable is assigned a value of one if the occupation is composed of college and university teachers, zero if it is not. The variable is employed by college or university (*UN*).

10. Full-time workers: The fraction of workers employed fifty to fifty-two weeks in the year was used to determine if geographical mobility and occupational mobility are lower in occupations where workers make larger investments in the job. The variable is proportion of male experienced civilian labor force (sixteen years and over) working fifty to fifty-two weeks, 1970 (*PWFT*).

11. Interaction effects of age and education: The interaction of age and education on mobility and earnings is captured by the product of median age and the percentage of workers with five or more years of education. The variable is the product of *AGE* and *PC*05 (*PC5AG*).

12. Percentage of occupation members who are male: Some occupations have a small proportion of workers who are males. Males in these occupations could be temporarily employed in the occupation or are of lower quality than other male workers. If females invest less in the job because of a shorter work horizon, then occupations populated mostly by females will attract those males that similarly will invest less in market activities. These arguments imply that average earnings of males will be lower in occupations with a smaller proportion of males. The variable is percentage employed males of all employed workers (fourteen years and over), 1970, abbreviated *PMALE*.

13. Licensing variables: Two standards for licensing are established (see below). For each standard, two licensing variables are defined, one for occupations with few restrictions on reciprocity and the other for more restrictions on reciprocity. A dummy variable is assigned a value

---

[12] Sharon Smith, "Government Wage Differentials," *Journal of Urban Economics*, vol. 4 (July 1977), pp. 248–71.

of one if the occupation satisfies the necessary conditions, zero if it does not. The variables here are licensed occupations under standard I with few restrictions on reciprocity ($AL1$), licensed occupations under standard I with more restrictions on reciprocity ($NREC1$), licensed occupations under standard II with few restrictions on reciprocity ($AL2$), and licensed occupations under standard II with more restrictions on reciprocity ($NREC2$).

14. Dummy variable for the clergy and judiciary: Members of the clergy report very low earnings because part of the total compensation (other than spiritual) is in kind. A dummy variable is assigned a value of one if the occupation is the clergy, zero if it is not. Members of the judiciary are less likely to migrate across state boundaries. Hence a dummy variable is assigned a value of one if the occupation is the judiciary, zero if it is not. The two dummy variables are judiciary occupation (JUD) and clerical occupation (CLE).

A list of the variables and the assigned symbols is reproduced in table 1 for the convenience of the reader.

Selection of Licensed Occupations

Licensed occupations are not easily identified. Information is scarce about the extent of licensing, the forms of licensing, and conditions for reciprocity among states. The limited information must temper the objectives of a cross-occupational study, and the best that can be hoped for is a reasonably accurate classification of occupations into three groups: unlicensed occupations, licensed occupations with few restrictions on reciprocity, and licensed occupations with more restrictions on reciprocity. If this grouping can be made with reasonable accuracy, then the empirical results will allow a comparison of the average (or representative) licensed occupation with the average (or representative) unlicensed occupation. Of course, the effects of licensing on mobility and earnings may differ among the licensed occupations within each of the two groups (few or more reciprocity restrictions). This paper presents some scattered results on these differences, but the primary results should identify the average effect of licensing on mobility and earnings.

Errors in assigning occupations to one of the three groups are bound to creep in because of the lack of information. Some way of determining whether the results are not due to the particular assignment of occupations to the three groups would be helpful. This is done by establishing two definitions for a licensed occupation. A stringent definition (standard I) of a licensed occupation was established, and those occupations satisfying the definition were classified as licensed occupations. A less

311

TABLE 1

DEFINITION OF VARIABLES

Variable	Definition
IMR	Interstate migration rate
LOIMR	Log($IMR/(1 - IMR)$)
PIC	Probability of remaining in county given no interstate move
LPOC	Log($1 - PIC$)
LMEF	Log of mean earnings of male full-time workers
PIS	Probability of remaining in same occupation between 1965 and 1970 given no death
LOPIS	Log($PIS/(1 - PIS)$)
IMROY	Ratio of IMR for workers between forty-five and sixty-four years to IMR for workers between twenty-five and forty-four years old
AGE	Median age of worker, 1970
AGE2	Age squared
PC05	Percentage of experienced/civilian labor force with five or more years of college
PC04	Percentage of experienced civilian labor force with four years of college
PCC4	Percentage of experienced civilian labor force with four or more years of college
PRI	Percentage of workers in private practice
LGROW	Log of the ratio of number of workers in 1970 to number in 1960
URB	Proportion of employed male workers living in urbanized areas
LMHW	Log of mean hours worked per week of all employed males
PFED	Percentage of workers employed by federal government
PSL	Percentage of workers employed by state and local government
U	Percentage of workers unionized
UN	Occupations composed of college and university teachers
PWFT	Proportion of male workers employed for fifty to fifty-two weeks
PC5AG	$PC05 \times AGE$
PMALE	Employed males as a percentage of total employed workers
AL1	Licensed occupations under standard I with few restrictions on reciprocity

312

TABLE 1 (continued)

Variable	Definition
NREC1	Licensed occupations under standard I with more restrictions on reciprocity
AL2	Licensed occupations under standard II with few restrictions on reciprocity
NREC2	Licensed occupations under standard II with more restrictions on reciprocity
JUD	Dummy variable for judiciary
CLE	Dummy variable for clergy
YOUTH	Proportion of workers in experienced labor force less than thirty years old, 1970

stringent definition (standard II) was established, and additional occupations satisfying this less-demanding definition were identified. Licensed occupations under standard II include all licensed occupations under standard I plus additions. Once the definitions of licensed occupations were established, several previous studies of occupational licensing were consulted to determine which occupations met the conditions for inclusion as licensed occupations. Licensed nonprofessional occupations were taken from a list compiled by the U.S. Department of Labor in 1969.[13] Licensed professional occupations were taken from the list in two older publications of the Council of State Governments.[14]

Under standard I the detailed census occupation had to be identical with the occupation listed in these publications, and the occupation had to be licensed in forty or more states in 1969. Under standard II the detailed census occupation was classified as licensed even though it might include several suboccupations, not all of which were licensed—but it was so classified only if the suboccupation was licensed in thirty or more states in 1969. Standard II is less demanding because not all suboccupations in the detailed census occupation are necessarily licensed and because the licensed suboccupation had to be licensed in no less than thirty states. Licensed occupations were then classified into those with more and fewer restrictions on reciprocity. Needless to say,

---

[13] U.S. Department of Labor, *Occupational Licensing and the Supply of Nonprofessional Manpower*, Manpower Research Monograph 11 (Washington, D.C.: Government Printing Office, 1969).

[14] Council of State Governments, *Occupational Licensing Legislation in the United States* (Chicago: Council of State Governments, 1952); and Council of State Governments, Western Office, *Professional and Occupational Licensing in the West* (San Francisco: Council of State Governments, 1964).

313

this division required the use of judgment, because reciprocity requirements are not uniform across states.

The list of licensed occupations under each standard is shown in table 2.

Statistical Results

Table 3 presents mean values of selected variables for licensed and unlicensed occupations. A standardization for the effects of age and

TABLE 2

LIST OF LICENSED OCCUPATIONS

Type of Occupation	Standard I	Standard II
Licensed census occupations with few restrictions on reciprocity		
Architect	X	X
Optometrist	X	X
Pharmacist	X	X
Physician (including osteopath)	X	X
Veterinarian	X	X
Elementary, prekindergarten, and kindergarten teacher	X	X
Secondary teacher	X	X
Insurance agent, broker, and underwriter	X	X
Real estate agent and broker	X	X
Accountant		X
Civil engineer		X
Registered nurse, dietician, and therapist		X
Health technologist and technician		X
Psychologist		X
Stock and bond salesman		X
Optician, lens grinder, and polisher		X
Pilot		X
Licensed census occupations with restrictions on reciprocity		
Lawyer	X	X
Dentist	X	X
Barber	X	X
Hairdresser and cosmetologist	X	X
Funeral director	X	X
Electrician		X
Plumber		X

NOTE: An X denotes that the occupation qualifies as a licensed occupation under the standard.

TABLE 3
Mean Values of Selected Variables for Licensed and Nonlicensed Occupations

Type of Occupation	IMR	PIC	PIS	MEF	PCC4	AGE	MHW	PWFT	Sample Size
Licensed occupations									
Licensed occupations, standard I, with reciprocity	0.108	0.860	0.726	$15,492	70%	42	45.3	71%	8
Licensed occupations, standard II, with reciprocity	0.143	0.850	0.720	14,519	68	40	43.2	75	16
Licensed occupations, standard II, with restrictions on reciprocity	0.066	0.898	0.792	13,423	30	43	44.6	75	7
Nonlicensed occupations									
Professional, technical	0.225	0.834	0.689	13,163	63	38	41.1	79	30
Managers and administrators	0.110	0.879	0.650	12,199	31	46	45.2	86	14
Clerical	0.081	0.903	0.521	8,226	11	37	40.2	77	18
Craftsmen	0.059	0.920	0.645	8,809	1	42	41.3	72	31
Operatives (excluding transportation)	0.054	0.929	0.512	7,059	1	38	40.7	68	16
Laborers (except farm)	0.053	0.928	0.409	6,299	1	33	36.3	51	7
Service	0.058	0.918	0.576	6,961	3	42	40.2	66	7

NOTE: *IMR*—interstate migration rate; *PIC*—probability of remaining in same county given no interstate move; *PIS*—probability of remaining in the same occupation given no death; *PCC4*—percentage of members with four or more years of college; *AGE*—median age of male members; *MHW*—mean hours worked by all male members; *PWFT*—percentage of male members working 50–52 weeks in year; *MEF*—mean earning of members employed 50–52 weeks in year; Sample size—number of occupations in class.

education is desirable before licensed and unlicensed occupations are compared. By comparing licensed occupations with few restrictions on reciprocity with unlicensed professional occupations, a rough control for education, percentage of members with four or more years of college (*PCC*4), and age is achieved. The comparisons show that licensed occupations have lower interstate migration rates (*IMR*), higher mean earnings (*MEF*), a higher mean probability of remaining in the same occupation (*PIS*), higher mean hours worked (*MHW*), and a lower proportion of full-time workers (*PWFT*) than comparable unlicensed occupations. (The higher earnings in licensed occupations may be due to more schooling and experience.) A comparison of licensed occupations having restrictions on reciprocity with unlicensed managerial and administrative occupations also achieves a rough control for schooling and age. These licensed occupations also have lower interstate migration rates, a higher mean probability of remaining in the same occupation, higher mean earnings, and a smaller proportion of full-time workers. This initial look at the data suggests that licensed occupations generally have lower interstate migration rates, higher earnings, a higher mean probability of remaining in the same occupation, and a lower proportion of full-time workers. The mean interstate migration rate in occupations with more restrictions on reciprocity is smaller than the mean interstate migration rate in occupations with fewer restrictions on reciprocity. This is a comforting result and suggests that the information on reciprocity upon which the groupings were made has a rational basis.

These preliminary assessments are tentative and must pass a more stringent test before they can be accepted. What follows will present, first, the regression results for several reduced-form equations showing the net effect of licensing on mobility and earnings and then estimates for several structural equations.

Table 4 shows the estimated coefficients of the reduced-form equations: where each of the jointly dependent variables *LPOC* (the log of the intrastate migration rate), *LOIMR* (the log of the interstate migration rate divided by 1 minus this rate), and *LMEF* (the log of mean earnings of full-time workers) is regressed on the exogenous variables. Because the occupation is the unit of observation, there is more variation in years of schooling across occupation, *PC*05, than in age; hence the variation in the interaction term *PC5AG* is more closely related to the variation in *PC*05 across occupation than in the variation in age. The interaction variable is probably capturing some of the effects of schooling on mobility and earnings. This is reflected in the negative coefficient for *PC*05 and the positive coefficient for *PC5AG* in the earnings equation. If the average age of members in an occupation is forty, the equation indicates that a small increase in the proportion of workers

TABLE 4

Reduced-Form Equations

	Dependent Variable		
	Intrastate mobility (LPOC)	Interstate mobility (LOIMR)	Earnings (LMEF)
Constant	−6.11[c]	−1.41	7.78[c]
AGE	0.0156	0.0342	0.0214
Age squared (AGE2)	−0.0004	−0.007	−0.0002
Five years of college or more (PC05)	0.0300[c]	0.0591[c]	−0.0052
Four years of college (PC04)	0.0082[c]	0.0120[b]	0.0076[c]
Licensed with few reciprocity restrictions (AL1)	−0.0664	−0.4080[b]	0.0862
Licensed with more reciprocity restrictions (NREC1)	0.0381	−0.5567[b]	0.0941
Log of mean hours worked (LMHW)	0.5476	−0.4578	−0.0632
Urbanized (URB)	0.5698[c]	1.287[c]	0.4540[c]
Log of growth (LGROW)	0.217[c]	0.237[c]	0.085[c]
State and local (PSL)	0.0008	−0.0049[c]	−0.0018[b]
Federal (PFED)	−0.0019	0.0013	−0.0003
Clergy (CLE)	1.269[c]	1.051[b]	−0.853[c]
Males (PMALE)	0.177[a]	0.420[b]	0.150[b]
Union (U)	−0.0042[c]	0.0083[c]	0.0020[b]
University (UN)	−0.309[a]	0.143	0.115
Working full time (PWFT)	−0.2347	0.2816	0.6277[c]
Interaction term (PC5AG)	−0.0006[c]	−0.0012[c]	0.0003[c]
R^2	0.749	0.799	0.858
σ_μ	0.237	0.381	0.140

[a] t-statistic between 1.60 and 1.99.
[b] t-statistic between 2.00 and 2.99.
[c] t-statistic greater than 2.99.

with five or more years of college would raise the log of mean earnings by 0.0068 (−0.0052 × 0.003 × 40), which is slightly smaller than the coefficient of PC04 (0.0076). The coefficients of the interaction variable, PC5AG, indicate that the intrastate and interstate migration rates decline with age at a more rapid rate the higher the level of schooling. Similarly, the rise in earnings with age appears to be more rapid the higher the level of schooling in an occupation.

The effect of licensing variables on mobility and earnings is the major subject, and it turns out that the two licensing variables, licensing with fewer and with more restrictions on reciprocity, have no significant effect on the intrastate migration rate but do have a significant effect on the interstate migration rate. The interstate migration rate of members in licensed occupations is significantly lower than the interstate migration rate of members in unlicensed occupations.[15] The results also indicate that the interstate migration rate is still lower in licensed occupations that place more restrictions on reciprocity than in licensed occupations that place few restrictions on reciprocity. While licensed and unlicensed occupations seem to have quite similar intrastate migration rates, they have appreciably different interstate migration rates. The coefficients of licensing variables are not statistically significant in the earnings equation. (The point estimates of these coefficients indicate that earnings would be about 9 percent higher in licensed than in unlicensed occupations.) All this strongly suggests that licensing erects barriers around state boundaries. The failure to find a significant effect of licensing on earnings is surprising.

Selective comments on the effects of the remaining variables may be appropriate here. Interstate mobility of state and local government workers is lower than the interstate mobility of federal government workers. There is no significant difference between the two groups in intrastate mobility. Interstate mobility for state and local government workers appears to involve higher costs (in lost benefits) than for federal government workers. The pay of federal government workers is no more than expected, given the investment in schooling and job training, while the pay of state and local government workers is less than expected. These findings differ from those reported by Smith.[16]

The results suggest that faster-growing occupations have greater intrastate and interstate mobility and higher average earnings than slower-growing occupations. Occupations with a higher percentage of members living in urbanized areas have higher intrastate and interstate migration rates and higher earnings. Intrastate mobility will be higher for occupations with a large proportion of urbanized workers, because some residence changes will involve a change in county without a change in job. Interstate mobility will be higher if occupations with a higher percentage of urbanized workers are more heavily concentrated in certain areas—as, for example, New York or Washington—than in others. Occupations with a higher percentage of male workers have higher

---

[15] These effects of licensing are quantitatively smaller than those found in a study limited to professional occupations. Licensing appears to be more effectively enforced in professional than in nonprofessional occupations (Pashigian, "Occupational Licensing," p. 13).

[16] Smith, "Government Wage Differentials," p. 263.

migration rates and higher average earnings. These results suggest that male members in occupations where workers are mostly male make larger investments in their jobs.

The reduced-form equations show the net effect, the direct and indirect effects, of each variable on the intrastate and interstate migration rates and on average earnings. As an illustration, the introduction of licensing in an occupation might directly reduce the interstate migration rate in that profession. Yet this change from an unlicensed to a licensed occupation may affect the interstate migration indirectly by raising earnings in the occupation, which might increase interstate migration rates. For some purposes it is useful to measure the size of the direct effects of licensing on mobility and earnings. Tables 5 through 7 show the coefficient estimates of the structural equations described in equations (1), (2), and (3). These estimates measure the direct effects of each variable on each of the three jointly dependent variables. Two different estimating methods have been used. The first two columns in these tables give estimates when ordinary least-squares regression techniques are used.[17] The ordinary least-squares estimates can be deficient (inconsistent) when estimating a system of equations. A more sophisticated estimation procedure may be preferred. This statistical procedure, sometimes referred to as two-stage least-squares, is used here. The last two columns of tables 5 through 7 present the second-stage estimates.

The coefficients of the licensing variables appear to be very stable and not dependent in any important way on the estimation procedure. The second-stage estimates also indicate that licensing reduces interstate mobility but has little direct effect on either the intrastate migration rate or on earnings. For some of the other variables, the second-stage estimates appear to be the less satisfactory. In several instances the coefficient estimates jump around and are sensitive to which variables are included in the three equations. While these estimates have their limitations, several results deserve further comment. The variable LPOC (the log of the intrastate migration rate) is inversely related to earnings and directly related to the interstate migration rate. Occupations with lower intrastate mobility by members have higher earnings and lower interstate mobility. These results suggest that LPOC is serving as a proxy for the absence of place-specific capital. The lower earnings in occupations with greater intrastate mobility by members suggests that the stock of human capital of the representative member is correspondingly lower. Mobility appears to discourage the accumulation of market

---

[17] The differences in the equations reported in tables 5–7, 9, and 10 reflect differences in the estimation methods and in the number and identity of variables included.

TABLE 5

DETERMINANTS OF LPOC

	Ordinary Least-Squares		Two-Stage (second-stage estimates)	
	(1)	(2)	(1)	(2)
Constant	−10.60[c]	−2.73	−5.70	−16.09[c]
Log of growth rate (*LGROW*)	0.167[c]	0.169[c]	0.222[c]	0.109
Five years of college or more (*PC*05)	0.0329[c]	0.0030[a]	0.0220[c]	0.0377[c]
Four years of college (*PC*04)	0.0053[b]	0.0093[c]	0.0134[b]	−0.0012
AGE	−0.0195[c]	−0.0270[c]	−0.0140[b]	−0.0261[c]
Licensed with few reciprocity restrictions (*AL*1)	−0.1361	−0.1344	−0.0820	−0.1818
Licensed with more reciprocity restrictions (*NREC*1)	0.0181	−0.0674	0.0763	−0.0830
Urbanized (*URB*)	0.3189[a]	0.4266[b]	0.6720[b]	0.0089
Union (*U*)	−0.0044[c]	−0.0062[c]	−0.0020	−0.0067[b]
Log of mean hours worked (*LMHW*)	0.7357[b]	1.040[c]	0.9389[b]	0.6950[b]
Full-time (*PWFT*)	−0.5508[b]	−0.9523[c]	−0.2085	−1.027[b]
University (*UN*)	−0.3275[a]	−0.1907	—	−0.4586[b]
Federal (*PFED*)	−0.0019	−0.0022[a]	—	−0.0015
State and local (*PSL*)	0.0013	−0.0011	—	0.0029[a]
Interaction (*PC5AG*)	−0.0008[c]	—	−0.0004[a]	−0.0011[c]
Clergy (*CLE*)	1.689[c]	—	1.044[b]	2.335[c]
Log of earnings (*LMEF*)	0.5230[c]	−0.0571	−0.2531	1.265[b]
Private (*PRI*)	—	0.0048[b]	—	—
Occupational mobility (*LOPIS*)	—	0.7485[c]	—	—
R^2	0.765	0.718	—	—
σ_μ	0.229	0.251	—	—

[a] *t*-statistic between 1.60 and 1.99.
[b] *t*-statistic between 2.00 and 2.99.
[c] *t*-statistic greater than 2.99.

knowledge and on-the-job training. The second-stage results suggest that higher schooling levels raise intrastate and interstate mobility and earnings. Occupations with higher earnings tend to have higher interstate migration rates. Hence the interstate migration rate is related to

TABLE 6

DETERMINANTS OF LMEF

	Ordinary Least-Squares		Two-Stage (second-stage estimates)	
	(1)	(2)	(1)	(2)
Constant	8.23^c	4.51^c	2.34	4.65
Log of growth (*LGROW*)	0.0562^a	0.0762^b	0.2082^b	0.1947^b
Five years of college or more (*PC05*)	0.0084^c	0.0075^c	0.0111^c	−0.0100^c
Four years of college (*PC04*)	0.0049^b	0.0079^c	0.0154^c	0.0119^c
AGE	0.0096	0.0108	−0.009	0.0284
Age squared (*AGE2*)	0.0000	0.0000	—	−0.0003
Licensed with few reciprocity restrictions (*AL1*)	0.0943	−0.0365	−0.0133	0.0563
Licensed with more reciprocity restrictions (*NREC1*)	0.0886	0.0021	0.1045	0.1186
Log of mean hours worked (*LMHW*)	−0.0800	0.5786^c	0.6821^a	0.2204
Urban (*URB*)	0.4431^c	0.6284^c	0.7978^c	0.7429^c
State and local (*PSL*)	−0.0021^c	−0.0021^c	−0.0020^b	−0.0014
Federal (*PFED*)	0.0005	0.0010	—	0.0013
Clergy (*CLE*)	−0.9747^c	−0.9882^c	−0.0833	−0.1976
University (*UN*)	−0.0476	—	0.0500	—
Males (*PMALE*)	0.1693^c	0.1705^c	—	0.2363^b
Union (*U*)	0.0020^b	0.0020^b	0.0011	−0.0001
Full-time (*PWFT*)	0.7131^c	—	0.3638	0.5117^b
Little good will (*LPOC*)	0.1054^b	0.0830^a	−0.6391^b	−0.5111^b
Private (*PRI*)	—	0.0012	—	—
R^2	0.853	0.830	—	—
σ_μ	0.142	0.152	—	—

^{a} *t*-statistic between 1.60 and 1.99.
^{b} *t*-statistic between 2.00 and 2.99.
^{c} *t*-statistic greater than 2.99.

both earnings and educational attainment. The second-stage results suggest a subtle effect of unions on earnings. They show no direct effect of unionization on earnings (table 6). But unionization does reduce intrastate mobility, and intrastate mobility is inversely related to earnings. The effect of unionization on earnings may thus be traced to its indirect effect of reducing the intrastate migration rate.

Grouping the licensed occupations into the two licensing cate-

TABLE 7

Determinants of LOIMR

	Ordinary Least-Squares		Two-Stage (second-stage estimates)	
	(1)	(2)	(1)	(2)
Constant	3.59[a]	0.98	−1.64	−0.026
Log of growth (LGROW)	−0.060	−0.068	−0.139	−0.170[b]
Five years of college or more (PC05)	0.0234[b]	0.0039[b]	0.0271[a]	0.0195[b]
Four years of college (PC04)	−0.0001	0.0016	−0.0073	−0.0076[a]
AGE	−0.0092[b]	−0.0102[b]	−0.0126	−0.0089[a]
Licensed with few reciprocity restrictions (AL1)	−0.3587[c]	−0.4210[c]	−0.4155[c]	−0.3957[c]
Licensed with more reciprocity restrictions (NREC1)	−0.6066[c]	−0.6365[c]	−0.7127[c]	−0.7078[c]
Union (U)	−0.0028[b]	−0.0033[b]	−0.0048[c]	−0.0040[b]
Log of mean hours worked (LMHW)	−1.240[c]	−0.8213[c]	−1.192[c]	−1.203[c]
University (UN)	0.541[c]	0.668[c]	0.406[a]	0.493[b]
Federal (PFED)	0.0007	0.0016	—	0.0018
State and local (PSL)	−0.0053[c]	−0.0049[c]	−0.0040[c]	−0.0043[b]
Clergy (CLE)	−0.086	—	0.354	—
Full-time (PWFT)	0.4291	—	—	0.0086
Interaction term (PC5AG)	−0.0005[b]	—	−0.0007[b]	−0.0005[b]
Log of earnings (LMEF)	0.4928[c]	0.4983[c]	1.123[c]	0.984[c]
Little good will (LPOC)	1.227[c]	1.175[c]	1.301[c]	1.488[c]
Urban (URB)	—	0.3619[a]	—	—
Private (PRI)	—	−0.0016	—	—
Judiciary (JUD)	—	−0.8014[b]	—	—
R^2	0.919	0.920	—	—
σ_μ	0.241	0.239	—	—

[a] t-statistic between 1.60 and 1.99.
[b] t-statistic between 2.00 and 2.99.
[c] t-statistic greater than 2.99.

gories—those with few and more restrictions on reciprocity—is one way to proceed, given that we have only one cross-sectional view. There is interest not only in the average effect of licensing on mobility and earnings but also in the effect of licensing in individual occupations. To obtain precise individual occupation effects, we really need several cross sections. We did, however, proceed by introducing a separate dummy variable for each licensed occupation. The introduction of twenty-three occupational dummy variables to the fourteen other variables with only 157 observations, or about four observations per variable, will inevitably lower the precision of the regression results and seriously limit the reliability of the results. Table 8 shows only the estimated coefficients for the licensed occupations. These coefficients measure the effect of licensing and any specific occupation effects not measured by the other exogenous variables: they show negligible effects of licensing on the intrastate migration rate and more substantial effects on the interstate migration rate and earnings. Many of the t-values are comparatively small, which is not surprising, given the limited number of degrees of freedom. Except for pilots, the t-values tend to be larger for occupations licensed under standard I than for those included under standard II. It is interesting to note that seventeen of the twenty-three coefficients are positive in the earnings equation and seventeen are negative in the interstate mobility equation.

We have found lower interstate migration rates in occupations with lower intrastate migration rates. *LPOC*, the log of the intrastate migration rate, is assumed to be a proxy for the absence of place-specific capital. This assumption can be tested. Occupations do differ in the interstate mobility of older relative to that of younger workers. The decline in the interstate migration rate with age should be even more rapid in those occupations where place-specific capital is more important. The constraints on mobility for older workers who have made few place-specific investments are less important. Other variables may also affect the interstate migration rate–age relationship. Licensing may also affect the mobility of older workers more than it affects that of younger workers. Obtaining a license in another jurisdiction requires an investment of time that is largely independent of age. It takes time to apply for consideration, to pass an examination, and to satisfy residency requirements. The forgone earnings of older workers will be higher than those of younger workers. Licensing can also raise the cost of entry into a new market if certain forms of advertising are prohibited. (Note, however, that the earlier results show licensing reducing only interstate mobility, not all forms of mobility.

The census of population reports the interstate migration rate in each occupation for two age groups: those between twenty-five and forty-four years old and those between forty-five and sixty-four years old. The ratio of the interstate migration rate for the older members to the interstate migration rate for the younger members was formed and is the dependent variable. The ratio will be directly related to *LPOC* (if *LPOC* is serving as a proxy for the absence of place-specific investments) and inversely related to the licensing variables. It will be higher

TABLE 8

REGRESSION COEFFICIENTS FOR OCCUPATIONAL DUMMY VARIABLES

Occupation	LPOC Coef.	t	LMEF Coef.	t	LOIMR Coef.	t
Licensed under standard I						
Architect	−0.297	1.1	0.160	1.2	−0.557	1.4
Optometrist	−0.087	0.3	0.019	0.1	−0.651	1.5
Pharmacist	−0.060	0.2	−0.217	1.6	−1.150	2.8
Physician (including osteopath)	−0.188	0.6	0.567	3.5	0.275	0.6
Elementary, prekindergarten, and kindergarten teacher	−0.158	0.5	−0.162	1.0	−0.837	1.7
Secondary teacher	−0.165	0.5	−0.124	0.8	−0.953	2.0
Insurance agent and broker	0.056	0.2	0.164	1.3	−0.224	0.6
Real estate agent and broker	−0.033	0.1	0.266	2.0	−0.235	0.6
Lawyer	0.047	0.2	0.362	2.4	−0.598	1.3
Dentist	−0.024	0.1	0.411	2.7	−0.303	0.7
Barber	−0.005	0.0	−0.216	1.7	−0.503	1.3
Hairdresser and cosmetologist	0.012	0.1	0.141	1.1	−0.423	1.1
Funeral director	−0.016	0.1	0.222	1.7	−0.727	1.8
Licensed under standard II						
Accountant	−0.025	0.1	−0.109	0.8	−0.550	1.4
Civil engineer	0.122	0.5	−0.005	0.0	−0.055	0.1
Registered nurse, dietician, and therapist	0.206	0.8	0.041	0.3	0.225	0.6
Health technologist and technician	0.148	0.6	0.033	0.3	−0.024	0.1
Psychologist	−0.017	0.1	0.271	1.7	0.048	0.1
Stock and bond salesman	−0.120	0.5	0.342	2.6	−0.569	1.4
Optician, lens grinder, and polisher	−0.034	0.1	0.071	0.6	−0.149	0.4
Electrician	0.186	0.7	0.104	0.8	0.318	0.8
Plumber	0.107	0.4	0.091	0.7	0.073	0.2
Pilot	0.614	2.3	0.575	4.4	1.477	3.7
Number of positive coefficients	9		17		6	
Number of negative coefficients	14		6		17	

NOTE: Only the coefficients of the occupational dummy variables are displayed.

as educational attainment is higher (if educational attainment is directly related to firm-specific or place-specific investments), higher as the degree of unionization is greater (if seniority and job rights are not easily transferred), and higher as the average age of workers is higher (since a larger proportion of workers in the lower age bracket will be closer to the upper boundary of the bracket and less mobile). The results in table 9 show that older workers are comparatively less mobile in those occupations (1) where larger place-specific investments are made, (2) with more highly educated members, (3) with a higher percentage of unionized workers, (4) with licensing, and (5) with older workers. These results suggest that more highly educated workers make more place-specific investments and consequently become comparatively less mobile with age. The significant effect of *LPOC* supports the assumption that *LPOC* serves as a proxy for the absence of local good will. The effects of licensing on the interstate migration rate–age relationship do depend on which standard for licensing is used. They are more pronounced under the stringent standard (standard I) and generally weaker for occupations qualifying under standard II but not under standard I.

Average earnings in licensed occupations have not been found to be significantly higher than in unlicensed occupations. An indirect and

TABLE 9

RATIO OF INTERSTATE MIGRATION RATE OF OLDER WORKERS TO THE INTERSTATE MIGRATION OF YOUNGER WORKERS (*IMROY*)

	(1) Coefficient	(2) Coefficient
Constant	0.503[c]	0.510[c]
Little good will (*LPOC*)	0.0935[c]	0.0966[c]
Five years of college or more (*PC05*)	−0.0016[c]	−0.0017[c]
Four years of college (*PC04*)	−0.0007	−0.0006
State and local (*PSL*)	−0.0001	−0.0001
University (*UN*)	−0.0395	−0.036
AGE	0.0029[b]	0.0030[b]
Licensed with few reciprocity restrictions (*AL1*)	−0.0699[a]	—
Licensed with more reciprocity restrictions (*NREC1*)	−0.09556[b]	—
Private (*PRI*)	0.0004	−0.0001
Union (*U*)	−0.0012[c]	−0.0012[c]
Licensed with few reciprocity restrictions (*AL2*)	—	−0.0465[a]
Licensed with more reciprocity restrictions (*NREC2*)	—	−0.0238
R^2	0.227	0.264
σ_μ	0.084	0.085

[a] *t*-statistic between 1.60 and 1.99.
[b] *t*-statistic between 2.00 and 2.99.
[c] *t*-statistic greater than 2.99.

independent test of the effect of licensing on earnings would be whether the probability of leaving a licensed occupation is lower than the probability of leaving an unlicensed one. If the probability of leaving a licensed occupation is no different from that of leaving an unlicensed occupation, this would support the hypothesis that earnings are not abnormally high in licensed occupations. *LOPIS* (the log of the ratio of the probability of remaining in an occupation to 1 minus this probability) is the dependent variable. The results of the regression analysis are presented in table 10. Occupational turnover is higher in occupations with (1) a larger proportion of young workers, (2) a smaller proportion of self-employed, (3) a greater average number of hours worked per week, (4) a larger proportion of full-time workers, (5) a smaller proportion of workers with five or more years of college, (6) a smaller proportion of unionized workers, and (7) a smaller proportion of state and local government workers. The inverse relationship between hours worked per week and the probability of remaining in an occupation suggests that occupational turnover increases when earnings per hour fall. The direct relationship between the proportion of state and local government workers and the probability of remaining in an occupation is unexplained in view of the comparatively low earnings of state and local government workers. Two new variables are included in this table. The estimated value of the log of mean earnings (abbreviated *EST-LMEF*) and the deviation of the actual from the estimated value (abbreviated *DEV-LMEF*) were obtained from the reduced-form equation and were used in the regression equation to measure the effects of any unmeasured quality component and any occupation-specific effect from licensing. The results in column two show that the probability of remaining in the occupation is directly related to *DEV-LMEF*, but no effect is observed in column four.

The evidence of the effect of licensing on the probability of remaining in the same occupation is mixed. Under standard I only members of licensed occupations with greater restrictions on reciprocity have higher probabilities. Under standard II both categories of licensed occupations have significantly higher probabilities. Evidently the results do not permit unambiguous conclusions about the effect of licensing on the probability of remaining in the same occupations. The evidence is suggestive but not conclusive.

Conclusions

The aim of this study was to identify the major effects of occupational licensing, and it has turned out that the most pronounced effect of licensing is the reduced interstate mobility of members in licensed oc-

TABLE 10

DETERMINANTS OF THE PROBABILITY OF REMAINING IN THE SAME
OCCUPATION DEPENDENT VARIABLE (*LOPIS*)

	(1) Coef.	(2) Coef.	(3) Coef.	(4) Coef.
Constant	-4.23^c	-3.83^b	-4.01^c	-3.37^b
Less than thirty (*YOUTH*)	-0.6981^c	-0.6929^c	-0.7253^c	-0.7354^c
Private (*PRI*)	0.0034^c	0.0032^c	0.0028^c	0.0028^b
Log of mean hours worked (*LMHW*)	-0.2534^a	-0.2680	-0.2897^b	-0.3163^a
Full-time (*PWFT*)	0.7494^c	0.7934^c	0.7604^c	0.8204^c
Federal (*PFED*)	0.0001	0.0000	0.0001	0.0000
State and local (*PSL*)	0.0012^b	0.0011^b	0.0011^b	0.0010^a
Five years of college or more (*PC05*)	0.0014	0.0036^c	0.0023^a	0.0036^c
Four years of college (*PC04*)	0.0002^a	0.0022	0.0001	0.0013
Log of growth (*LGROW*)	0.0538^b	0.0558^b	0.0538^b	0.0589^b
Union (*U*)	0.0040^c	0.0040^c	0.0036^c	0.0037^c
Male (*PMALE*)	0.0657	0.0760	0.0820^a	0.0931^a
Licensed with few reciprocity restrictions (*AL1*)	0.0233	0.0354	—	—
Licensed with more reciprocity restrictions (*NREC1*)	0.1246^a	0.1416^a	—	—
Licensed with few reciprocity restrictions (*AL2*)	—	—	0.1107^b	0.1213^b
Licensed with more reciprocity restrictions (*NREC2*)	—	—	0.1437^b	0.1547^b
Log of earnings estimate (*EST-LMEF*)	—	-0.0393	—	-0.0596
Residual of log of earnings (*DEV-LMEF*)	—	0.1756^b	—	0.1225
R^2	0.752	0.761	0.768	0.772
σ_μ	0.127	0.126	0.123	0.123

[a] *t*-statistic between 1.60 and 1.99.
[b] *t*-statistic between 2.00 and 2.99.
[c] *t*-statistic greater than 2.99.

cupations. Restrictions on the use of reciprocity reduce interstate mobility still more. While licensed occupations have about the same within-state mobility as unlicensed occupations, they have significantly lower interstate migration rates. The evidence suggests that licensing is the primary reason for this difference. Licensing also appears to reduce the interstate mobility rates of older members more than it reduces that of younger workers. The findings on the effect of licensing on earnings are more ambiguous: coefficients in the earnings equation failed to show a significant effect due to licensing. The findings on occupational mobility produced some but not uniform support for the hypothesis that occupational turnover was lower in licensed occupations.

Assuming these findings stand the test of time, one can speculate on the long-run consequences of licensing. Members of licensed occupations make longer-term choices when they select the place and state of employment. The lower interstate mobility resulting from licensing means that the speed of supply adjustment to differential growth rates of states is slower in licensed occupations. The emigration of practitioners from states with slower growth rates will be smaller than it would be without licensing. The reduced interstate mobility encourages a more geographically dispersed distribution of training facilities if licensing raises the benefits of training in the state of planned practice. Finally, one might offer the conjecture that the variability in mean earnings between states is higher under licensing, although this conjecture has not yet been systematically tested.

Unfortunately, the findings do not help explain which groups have benefited from occupational licensing. Members of licensed occupations do not have significantly higher earnings. Hence suppliers in these licensed occupations have apparently not been the primary beneficiaries. Yet it is unclear how consumers have benefited from occupational licensing. If consumers were to benefit from some type of occupational regulation, one would expect more frequent use of certification in place of licensing. It is also unclear how consumers would have benefited from the reduced interstate mobility of members in licensed occupations. It is possible to argue that the state licensing authority knows more about the quality of the training facilities in the state than about the quality of those outside it. If so, the cost of detecting whether an applicant satisfies the minimum qualifications in the state is lower if most applicants are graduates of an in-state licensed training facility. If there is considerable mobility by graduates from the state of training to the state of licensure, it is difficult to accept this argument and to understand how consumers benefit from the reduction in the interstate mobility of established practitioners. In short, the major beneficiaries from occupational licensing have not yet been discovered.

Appendix: List of Occupations in Sample, N = 157

Professional, Technical, and Kindred Workers
  1. Accountants

2. Architects
3. Computer specialists
Engineers:
    4. Aeronautical and astronautical
    5. Chemical
    6. Civil
    7. Electrical and electronic
    8. Industrial
    9. Mechanical
    10. Metallurgical and materials
    11. Sales
12. Judges
13. Lawyers
14. Librarians, archivists, and curators
15. Mathematical specialists
Life and physical scientists:
    16. Agricultural
    17. Biological
    18. Chemists
    19. Geologists
    20. Physicists and astronomers
21. Personnel and labor relations workers
Physicians, dentists, and related practitioners:
    22. Dentists
    23. Optometrists
    24. Pharmacists
    25. Physicians, including osteopaths
26. Registered nurses, dieticians, and therapists
27. Health technologists and technicians
28. Clergymen
Social scientists:
    29. Economists
    30. Psychologists
31. Social and recreation workers
Teachers, college and university:
    32. Biology
    33. Chemistry
    34. Engineering
    35. Mathematics
Teachers, except college and university:
    36. Elementary, prekindergarten, and kindergarten
    37. Secondary school
38. Engineering and science technicians

Technicians, except health and engineering and science:
39. Airplane pilots
40. Air traffic controllers
Writers, artists, and entertainers:
41. Actors, dancers, musicians, and composers
42. Editors and reporters
43. Public relations
44. Radio and television announcers

Managers and Administrators, except Farm
45. Assessors, controllers, and treasurers, local public administration
46. Bank officers and financial managers
47. Buyers, wholesale and retail trade
48. Funeral directors
49. Health administrators
50. Construction inspectors, public administration
51. Inspectors, except construction, public administration
52. Managers and superintendents, building
53. Officials of lodges, societies, and unions
54. Postmasters and mail superintendents
55. Restaurant, cafeteria, and bar managers
56. Sales managers and department heads, retail trade
57. Sales managers, except retail trade
58. School administrators, college
59. School administrators, elementary and secondary

Sales Workers
60. Advertising agents and salesmen
61. Insurance agents, brokers, and underwriters
62. Real estate agents and brokers
63. Stock and bond salesmen

Clerical and Kindred Workers
64. Bank tellers
65. Billing clerks
66. Bookkeepers
67. Cashiers
68. Counter clerks, except food
69. Expediters and production controllers
70. Insurance adjusters, examiners, and investigators
71. Mail carriers, post office
72. Meter readers, utilities
73. Office machine operators

74. Payroll and timekeeping clerks
75. Postal clerks
76. Real estate appraisers
77. Receptionists, secretaries, stenographers, and typists
78. Shipping and receiving clerks
79. Statistical clerks
80. Stock clerks and storekeepers
81. Ticket, station, and express agents

Craftsmen and Kindred Workers
82. Brickmasons and stonemasons
83. Bulldozer operators, cranemen, and road machine operators
84. Cabinetmakers
85. Carpenters
86. Cement and concrete finishers
87. Compositors and typesetters
88. Electricians
89. Floor layers, except tile setters
90. Forgemen and hammermen
91. Heat treaters, annealers, and temperers
92. Jewelers and watchmakers
93. Job and die setters, metal
94. Locomotive engineers and firemen
95. Machinists
Mechanics:
    96. Airconditioning, heating, and refrigeration
    97. Aircraft
    98. Automobile mechanics and body repairmen
    99. Heavy equipment mechanics, including diesel
    100. Radio and television
101. Opticians, lens grinders, and polishers
102. Painters, construction and maintenance
103. Photoengravers and lithographers
104. Plasterers
105. Plumbers and pipe fitters
106. Power station operators
107. Pressmen and place printers, printing
108. Rollers and finishers, metal
109. Sheetmetal workers and tinsmiths
110. Stationary engineers
111. Structural metal craftsmen
112. Tailors
113. Telephone installers, repairmen, linemen, and splicers

114. Tile setters
115. Tool and die makers

Operatives, except Transport
116. Assemblers
117. Bottling and canning operatives
118. Checkers, examiners, and inspectors, manufacturing
119. Clothing ironers and pressers
120. Furnacemen, smeltermen, and pourers
121. Garage workers and gas station attendants
122. Graders and sorters, manufacturing
123. Meat cutters, butchers, and wrappers
124. Oilers and greasers, except auto
125. Precision machine operatives
126. Punch and stamping press operatives
127. Riveters and fasteners
128. Shoemaking machine operatives
129. Solderers
130. Textile operatives
131. Welders and flame cutters

Transport Equipment Operatives
132. Bus drivers
133. Deliverymen and routemen
134. Parking attendants
135. Railroad brakemen and switchmen
136. Taxicab drivers and chauffeurs
137. Truckdrivers

Laborers, except Farm
138. Carpenters' helpers
139. Construction laborers, except carpenters' helpers
140. Freight and material handlers
141. Garbage collectors
142. Longshoremen and stevedores
143. Stock handlers
144. Vehicle washers and equipment cleaners

Farmers and Farm Managers
145. Farmers, owners and tenants
146. Farm managers

Farm Workers
147. Farm foremen
148. Farm laborers, wage workers

Service Workers, Including Private Household
149. Cleaning service workers
150. Food service workers
151. Health service workers
Personal service workers:
      152. Barbers
      153. Hairdressers
Protective service workers:
      154. Crossing guards and bridge tenders
      155. Firemen, fire protection
      156. Guards and watchmen
      157. Policemen, marshals, and sheriffs

Commentary

Stuart Dorsey

Capturing the impact of occupational licensing on market outcomes is a difficult task. The issues here are subtle, and the effects of licensing may not be revealed by a simple regression of licensing dummy variables on mobility and earnings.

Consider the effect of licensing on geographic mobility. Mobility is expected to be reduced if reciprocity is limited. Professor Pashigian also considers other determinants of mobility, including education, age, accumulation of local-specific capital, and union membership. The discussion of the way these variables affect mobility can be simplified by noting that any factor that increases the positive difference between a worker's current earnings and his best alternative wage will reduce mobility. Presence of human or nonhuman specific capital or nontransferable union job rights will increase this wage differential, raising the cost of moving to another location and changing jobs.

Lack of reciprocity, however, raises the cost of moving only if workers in licensed occupations are receiving a positive wage differential. It does not deter mobility if there is no loss in earnings from changing occupations; however, occupation-specific investment and rents created by restrictive licensing imply that workers in occupations where reciprocity is limited will face costs of moving across state lines higher than those in occupations that are unlicensed, have few restrictions on reciprocity, or require little occupation-specific investment. This suggests use of an interaction term between licensing and proxies for occupation-specific investment, such as age and education. Pashigian finds that reciprocity restrictions do reduce mobility, indicating a market differential for licensed occupations. I think, however, that a proper specification would include these interaction terms.

Testing for the effect of licensing on earnings is a more difficult task. Professor Pashigian correctly notes that if supply is restricted by raising educational requirements or training and experience requirements, earnings will rise until new entrants are exactly compensated for their additional investment. Rents will accrue only to existing members ("grandfathers"). After the grandfathers have retired, an earnings regression will reveal no effect of licensing. Higher earnings will be explained by greater education and training.

This result he contrasts with the result of direct control over entry, enforced by limiting the number of places in training schools. We should expect this limitation to raise earnings and increase the number of applicants for available positions in these training schools. Pashigian, however, claims that training schools would not raise tuition or fees. Under this assumption new entrants would earn a greater than competitive rate of return, and an earnings regression would show a positive effect of licensing. I do not understand Professor Pashigian's reasoning here. He states that existing and future members of the occupation have an incentive to limit tuition increases. Yet existing members do not have to pay higher fees, and the incentive for prospective members is to compete for available openings in training schools by bidding up tuition. One should thus expect tuition to increase, especially if the training school is privately owned. Even if tuition and fees did not rise, I would not expect to find new entrants earning rents. The increase in earnings would attract more educated applicants to training schools and eventual entry to the occupation. If tuition were not raised, the school would probably ration available openings to the most highly educated applicants. Once again, new entrants would have greater education and earn a competitive rate of return. As when minimum-education requirements are raised, in this case also a licensing dummy variable would not show any effect.

A common way of directly controlling entry is by a licensing examination. If examinations restricted supply and raised earnings, one still might not find new entrants receiving rents. The rise in earnings would attract workers with greater opportunity wages. In a recent study I found that the better-educated, whites, and those with greater training are more likely to pass licensing examinations.[1] Those applicants admitted under the examination screen have greater opportunity wages and tend to earn a competitive return after entry, even though earnings in the licensed occupation are higher. The effect of licensing on earnings again is captured by variables such as education and race. In general, rents created by direct restrictions on entry are dissipated by competition among prospective entrants. The way that licenses are rationed determines the form of competition and how the rents are dissipated. Thus

---

[1] Stuart Dorsey, "The Occupational Licensing Queue," Working Paper no. 34, Center for the Study of American Business, Washington University, St. Louis, and *The Journal of Human Resources*, in press.

Pashigian's finding that licensing has no effects, given schooling and other attributes, does not support his conclusion that direct entry controls are not commonly used or do not contribute to higher earnings. Neither the effects of raising minimum requirements nor the effects of directly restricting entry may show up in such an analysis.

Given this difficulty, what test could be devised that would allow acceptance or rejection of the hypothesis that licensing raises earnings? One test would involve looking at the older cohorts. If licensing does raise earnings, those who are already in the occupation would receive an above-competitive return. Further, if entry restriction were tightened periodically, which would be likely in order to create rents for late entrants, the rent would rise with the length of the worker's tenure. This would appear as a return to experience or age in an earnings regression. Evidence of a steeper age-earnings profile for licensed than for unlicensed occupations would indicate that licensing raises earnings. Indication that levels of education rise faster in licensed than in unlicensed occupations also would imply a positive effect of licensing on earnings.

Finally there is the problem of testing whether licensing influences the probability that an individual will stay in an occupation. We should uncover such an effect only if licensing raises the rate of return above the rate for other occupational choices. Pashigian correctly concludes that his findings—that licensing has no influence on occupational change—are consistent with licensing's having no impact on earnings. Rents would be created for grandfathers, however, and their job mobility should be reduced. Thus we should find that job changing declines with age in licensed occupations if licensing raises earnings. A test for differences in occupational mobility by age cohort would be required to allow any strong conclusions about the impact of licensing on job changing.

While Pashigian's tests of the effect of licensing on occupational change and earnings are inconclusive, he does report some good results for the relationship of licensing and geographic mobility. The most interesting of these is that licensed workers have less interstate but not less *intrastate* mobility. This would indicate that reciprocity barriers, rather than other characteristics of licensed workers of occupations, are the cause of reduced mobility.

My final comment on this paper concerns the results for unionism. The reduced-form equation indicates a positive effect of union membership, but two-stage estimates show no effect on earnings and a reduction in mobility. Professor Pashigian's interpretation is that unionism raises earnings indirectly—it makes workers less mobile, and less mobility leads to greater earnings. This would explain the statistical results, but it makes very little intuitive sense. Why should reduced mobility lead directly to higher earnings? According to theory, causation runs from unionism to earnings, then to reduced mobility. Trade unions create rents for their members, and these rents limit mobility because the union job rights may not be transferable to the new job. In any event, the implication that unions do not directly affect wages but work indirectly through mobility is suspect, and I would regard this result as extremely fragile.

Janice F. Madden

Professor Pashigian, using data from the 1970 U.S. census, finds that while individuals in licensed occupations do not earn more than those in nonlicensed occupations, they are less likely to move interstate but equally likely to move within state.

I find the first result—that licensing does not affect earnings—surprising. In my own research, a similar characteristic—membership in a labor union—consistently shows a significantly positive effect in earnings equations. Pashigian explains his result by arguing that licensing, which raises requirements, would not affect earnings in the long run because new entrants would receive returns equivalent to their other alternatives. The long run to which Pashigian refers, however, is *very* long because it must at least be longer than the work life of any incumbent at the time the requirement is changed. Because I doubt that there is a licensed occupation in the United States that has not upgraded its requirements within the lifetimes of its present incumbents, I do not find Pashigian's explanation of his earnings results convincing. Pashigian's earnings equation seems to demonstrate that individuals in licensed occupations are not receiving any rents in the form of higher earnings.

Pashigian goes on to argue that individuals in licensed occupations should be less mobile than others, but he never explains why licensing per se should decrease geographic mobility. If one is licensed into a national market, the license should not have a negative effect on mobility. Of course, occupations that are state licensed with no reciprocity would reduce mobility; but it is the lack of reciprocity, not licensing itself, that produces this effect. Nonetheless, Pashigian's empirical work shows evidence of a link between licensing and interstate mobility, although interpretation of his result poses several problems.

First, as Pashigian points out in passing, he is measuring residential mobility, not job mobility. If members of an occupation are disproportionately located in interstate local labor markets such as New York City, Chicago, Philadelphia, or Washington, D.C., the interstate migration rate would in some part indicate residential mobility and would overstate the movement out of jobs. Incidentally, this data problem may very well explain the positive correlation between urbanization and the interstate migration rate, which mystified Pashigian.

Second, factors other than licensing may be decreasing mobility in the licensed occupations. When Pashigian disaggregates and reports the effect on specific occupations, it is apparent that the negative mobility effects are largely centered on two occupations: pharmacy and teaching. In the latter, factors other than licensing clearly account for lower mobility. Because of increased female participation in the labor force with little change in occupation, the supply of teachers has expanded relative to the demand. As a result, teaching jobs are scarce, and incumbents are reluctant to move because of job scarcity, not because of licensing.

Third, Pashigian has not carefully considered differential reciprocity practices, and this complicates any interpretation of his results. For example, he lists "lawyer" as an occupation with restrictions on reciprocity. While such restrictions do exist, lawyers with three to five years of practice are granted reciprocity in nearly every state. Obviously, similar variance in reciprocity practices occurs in other occupations, and it is not clear whether any conclusions can be drawn when such widely differing reciprocity practices are aggregated.

Because of the problems in interpreting the relationship between geographic mobility and licensing in using the 1970 U.S. census data, I am curious why Pashigian did not use the large individual data files—such as the National Longitudinal Survey or the Panel Survey of Income Dynamics—which contain better mobility data, the same occupational information, and information on whether the individual actually is licensed or certified.

Even with the myriad of data problems surrounding Pashigian's empirical results, it is still likely that there is a negative relationship between geographic mobility and occupational licensing. I found this result mystifying until Professor Benham enlightened me. Professor Benham argued that licensing provides members of an occupation with security. If he is correct, occupations that are licensed would attract risk-averse individuals, who are less likely to migrate. Therefore, licensed occupations show lower rates of geographic mobility because risk-averse individuals also choose not to migrate. In this case, licensed occupations do not themselves inhibit migration.

We do need to look harder at the costs of occupational licensing. While we may not observe the expected earnings differentials in licensed occupations, the rents may be earned through nonmonetary returns, or, alternatively, there may be no rents. Licensing may affect the type of individuals attracted to an occupation, and this fact may or may not have real social costs. Furthermore, the costs associated with the fact that licensing increases the requirements for an occupation depend on the extent to which quality of service is increased by increasing the requirements. These matters remain on the research agenda.

Part Seven

Needs and Licenses

Michael Pertschuk

Our culture is dominated by professionals who call us clients and tell us of our needs. Morticians advise us of what is required for a decent burial. Sex therapists counsel us about what is required for intimacy. Professional hypertrichologists diagnose and treat our "excessive and unsightly" facial hair. Our children's educational requirements are determined by professional teams of speech therapists, learning-disability specialists, child psychologists, social workers, school administrators, and guidance counselors.

Our very language has transformed the word "need" from a personal verb, dependent for its content on the one who feels it, into an objective noun. Needs are now somehow separate and apart from people; they have become the objects of professional competence, beyond our private competence to diagnose. We speak of the "delivery" of health care of social services and of the "achievement" of mental health or degrees of educational competence as if we were talking about commodities manufactured in uniform portions for those who lack them.

The increasing ubiquity of the professionals has had an insidious and intimidating effect. We lack confidence in our unprofessional abilities to diagnose our private needs on the basis of our experience. Increasingly, we ask professionals to reveal our needs, not merely to serve them. The professional stockbroker, real estate agent, insurance agent, doctor, dentist, lawyer, pharmacist, auto mechanic, architect, interior decorator, psychiatrist, mortician, family planner, organizational development specialist—all now counsel us about our needs, advise us about what we should want, and then provide the service they have prescribed.

This combination of diagnosis and service is often efficient—how wasteful it would be to require that the diagnosing physician or auto mechanic put the body back together again before offering to repair it—but it is also open to subtle abuse. How can the diagnostician be relied on to understand our unique preferences, our own particular willingness to trade quality against price, our unique aversion to risk? Since it is difficult or impossible for us to know whether the recom-

343

mended services match our personal preferences, how can the diagnostician be relied on not to try to maximize his profits simply by recommending services that will bring him the greatest gain?

To the extent that diagnosticians are conscientious, relying on time-consuming personal interviews and making the effort to listen and explain, they are apt to earn less than they could by sending us off to costly diagnostic centers filled with complex equipment for analyzing our physical, psychological, emotional, or financial needs. To the extent that diagnosticians prescribe changes in personal habits or routines, they are likely to earn less than they could by applying the techniques and remedies for which they have been trained and by which they profit. As a result, we are liable to misdiagnosis and overprescription.

It is estimated that thirty-three cents of every dollar spent last year on auto repair went for unnecessary work. It is also estimated that two million Americans underwent operations last year they did not need, at a cost of 10,000 lives and $4 billion. Personal expenditures for lawyers, physicians, dentists, and other professionals are increasing at a rate faster than the average for all goods and services in the economy.

Licensing is both a response to, and a cause of, this problem. It is a response because—theoretically—it brings to bear the government's comparative advantage in policing against misleading diagnoses and excessive service. If consumers are unable to evaluate bundles of diagnosis and service, then arguably the government should step in and set minimum standards to ensure the competence and integrity of those who offer such bundles. Variations on this argument are expounded to justify most licensing schemes. Indeed, some concerned consumer groups now urge that auto mechanics be licensed in states where they are not and that the licensing of lawyers and physicians be made stricter to guard against the kind of shoddy service that spurs dramatic increases in malpractice suits.

Licensing is, however, also a cause of misdiagnosis and overprescription to the extent that it becomes a vehicle for a profession's legitimizing its monopoly on discovering and remedying needs and enforcing its mystique by limiting access to special knowledge. Generally it is the members of a particular occupation—not the public—that seek licensing (as a means of enhancing prestige and income). At a recent session of one state legislature, occupational groups advanced bills to license themselves as auctioneers, well diggers, home-improvement contractors, pet groomers, electrologists, sex therapists, data processors, appraisers, and television repairers. Hawaii licenses tattoo artists. New Hampshire licenses lightning-rod salespeople.

The evolution of certain occupations from collections of individual sellers to tradesmen to certified professionals and, ultimately, to licensed professionals is well known. Barbers have been transformed into cosmetologists, garbage collectors into sanitary engineers, undertakers into grief counselors. Specialized courses of study are required, displacing apprenticeship and on-the-job training. Qualifying exams, citizenship and residency requirements, and professional fees are imposed on new entrants. Professional journals appear, Washington offices are opened to lobby for favorable legislation, and public relations firms are retained to ensure a favorable image. The profession develops status, political strength, and exclusivity. Each of these attributes reinforces the others.

It is hardly surprising that, once licensed, a profession is in a position to determine how much competition it will tolerate. Licensing boards dominated by members of the profession may act like any other cartel—adjusting entry standards to protect the incomes of established practitioners. It is not unusual for boards to reject higher percentages of applicants during periods of economic downturn when there is less demand for their services. Nor is it unusual for boards to restrict advertising, promotion, and innovative ways of providing services, thereby making it more difficult for new entrants to compete.

Thus, like members of medieval guilds, the licensed professionals can maintain their privileged positions regardless of market forces. Study after study has shown that licensing results in higher direct costs to consumers and that indirect costs, in the form of forgone innovations and experimentation, are higher still.

What about quality? Higher prices might be justified if quality were improved, if there were fewer cases of misdiagnosis and excessive service. Unfortunately, all too often licensing bears little relationship to quality. Several years ago the Federal Trade Commission (FTC) compared the price and quality of television repairs in Louisiana, where repairers were licensed, and the District of Columbia, where no licensing was required. The result: prices were 20 percent higher in Louisiana, and the incidence of unnecessary repairs was virtually the same in both places. Other studies show that uncontested divorces result in the same incidence of legal error whether handled by the parties themselves or by lawyers, and that clinical labs licensed by states have the same incidence of inaccurate clinical test reports as licensed labs.

Indeed, licensing boards rarely monitor quality. Most professionals, once licensed, are licensed for life. One needs periodic reexaminations in most states to drive a car or pilot an airplane but not to continue practicing as a doctor or a lawyer. From 1967 to 1973, the number of doctors disciplined by state boards for incompetence averaged only 1.6 per state per year.

When licensing renders certain services unavailable to those segments of the population that cannot afford to pay for licensed professionals, consumers can end up with poor and dangerous quality of the do-it-yourself variety. One study, for example, shows that states with the most restrictive systems for licensing electricians also have the highest rates of deaths from accidental electrocution.

Are we bound, then, to a closed circle of professionals who identify and adjudicate our needs, professionals admitted to practice by professionals and policed by the same professionals? I do not think so: a rebellion is brewing. Put the blame on a revival of populism, on a resurgence of frontier self-sufficiency, on two decades of economic analysis focusing on occupational licensing, or on increased skepticism about government. Whatever its cause, the barriers to entry and innovation erected by professionals are beginning to fall.

The Supreme Court has struck down state laws prohibiting price advertising by pharmacists and lawyers for routine goods and services—laws passed at the behest of the professionals. Last year the FTC lifted restrictions on price advertising by optometrists, opticians, and ophthalmologists. More recently the commission issued a consent order that bars the American Society of Anesthesiologists from deterring its members from working under contract to hospitals. The FTC staff has recommended a rule requiring funeral directors to disclose the full range of their prices and options. It is also investigating physician control over Blue Shield boards, as well as licensing practices among lawyers, accountants, and dentists.

Private groups and many of the states have also taken steps to open up the professional marketplace. The American Veterinarian Medical Association and the American Psychological Association, after discussions with the FTC, have revised their codes of ethics to permit members to advertise. A committee of the American Bar Association has proposed streamlining its disciplinary procedures. California has placed a majority of public members on most of its licensing boards. Twenty-three states have enacted some form of sunset legislation to enable them to watch over their licensing boards. In Minnesota no group can submit proposed licensing legislation without satisfying the state's Legislative Audit Commission that licensing is necessary.

More and more consumers are discovering that professionals are not markedly different from other sellers who offer their services in trade. Nothing dissolves a mystique faster than seeing lawyers advertise inexpensive legal services just as used-car dealers advertise special deals. Making visible the commercial underpinnings of the professions is therapeutic. It fosters healthy skepticism, and it teaches that, in this area as in all other commerce, vigorous competition coupled with adequate consumer information ensures the optimum range of quality at the lowest possible price.

Certainly it is necessary to be concerned about fraud and deception in these professions, just as it is with door-to-door sellers, but there are means of guarding against fraud and deception that are far less restrictive than licensing. Certification is one alternative. It provides consumers with information about the competence of the seller without creating a barrier to entry. Separation of diagnosis from service—the "second opinion" that allows consumers to do comparison shopping—is another alternative (which is why the FTC eyeglass rule requires eye examiners to provide consumers with a copy of their prescription).

The FTC is committed to finding and remedying vestigial and unjustifiable restrictions on the market for professional services. The remedying is the more difficult part, of course. FTC rule making is a less attractive approach than cooperation with state and local officials and concerned citizen groups—less attractive in part because the FTC may be worse equipped than state and local officials to undertake the difficult trade-offs that are often involved. One area where the FTC can act without arousing substantial concern—indeed, an area where the commission has a major role to play—is the provision of information, designing and funding studies that compare the effects of alternative regulatory systems on price and quality and serving as a clearinghouse for the findings of other studies.

At the same time, the FTC must carry out its congressional mandate to police unfair methods of competition and unfair and deceptive practices in the marketplace. It will continue to act forcefully where professional regulation violates the basic tenets of our laws of competition and consumer protection and where there exists no serious alternative reform possibility.

When enough barriers have been removed so that professionals, disciplined by the market, must rely to a greater extent on their reputations for competence, perhaps we consumers will be more confident of ourselves and less awed by those who tell us of our needs. We will bury the unfair advantages of the morticians, retreat from the intimate queries of the sex therapists, discover that hypertrichologists are excessive (if not unsightly), and require that the teams of educators do in fact educate our kids.

Occupational Licensure for Economists?

George J. Stigler

In keeping with an underlying theme of this conference—the reform of economic institutions—I wish to explore (somewhat tongue-in-cheek) the desirability and feasibility of establishing occupational licensure for economists.

Economics teaches us that there are two ways by which an occupation becomes licensed. The first is that the occupation develops a cohesive and effective political coalition and uses that coalition to bring about change through the political process. Economists lack this requirement: while there are many loose jokes about the diversity of opinion among economists, they are not really a very cohesive (or effective) group.

The second way an occupation becomes licensed is to pay homage to idealistic professional standards and perform tasks that are sometimes extremely complex and difficult. They then counsel their customers that only members of the profession are capable of ensuring "quality" performance, because they, the customers, do not always possess adequate information to make proper judgments. Licensing is thus brought on somewhat indirectly by creating a demand for it on the part of the "public." We economists have not been very successful along this line either: the public is forever saying, "I'm not an economist, *but . . .*"

In trying to design appropriate specifications for a properly organized licensure of the economics profession, I turned for guidance to the first and greatest of all economic reformers, Mr. Adam Smith. Smith says, in widely separated passages, that two things should be guarded against. First, he says: "In Holland the money price of the bread consumed in towns is supposed to be doubled by means of [various excise] taxes. In lieu of a part of them, the people who live in the country pay every year so much a head, according to what sort of bread they are supposed to consume." Smith goes on to say: "These, and some other taxes of the same kind, by raising the price of labour, are said to have ruined the greater part of the manufactures of Holland." Now comes the lesson. "A French author, of some note, has proposed to reform the finances of his country, by substituting in the room of the greater part of other taxes, this most ruinous of all taxes. There is nothing so absurd, says Cicero, which has not sometimes been asserted by some philosophers."[1] Thus we draw from Smith the first lesson: The theorist is a dangerous person to let loose on economic reform.

Now a second passage suggests the opposite problem. Beginning a great chapter in his diatribe against mercantilism, Smith says:

> Mr. Colbert, the famous minister of Louis XIV, was a man of probity, of great industry and of knowledge of detail; of great experience and acuteness in the examination of public accounts, and of abilities, in short, every way fitted for introducing method and good order into the collection and expenditure of the public revenue. That minister had unfortunately embraced all the prejudices of the mercantile system, in its nature and essence a system of restraint and regulation, and such as could scarce fail to be agreeable to a laborious and plodding man of business.[2]

Thus the second lesson deduced from Smith is that a man of wide experience and factual knowledge is equally unequipped to address the problem of economic reform.

These two lessons suggest a first general requirement—that a good economic reformer be a man both of theory and of detail. In practice, this means that the licensed economist have a Ph.D. from a good university. Moreover, to prove the candidate's mastery of institutional detail, as Smith requests, two additional credentials must be present. The first is that the prospective licensed economist must have demonstrated, by a detailed econometric investigation, that a previously unexamined policy has had grievously bad effects or has had no effects at all but is administered at grievously high costs. The second requirement is that this prospective licensee must uncover a serious flaw in the demonstration of grievous effects or grievous costs demonstrated by another economist.

Now, having identified appropriate standards for membership in the economics profession, I would like to describe appropriate behavior for that profession. Here, as elsewhere, I believe Smith's views should be followed. Consider the following lines of great fame and notoriety, which began with the most widely quoted of all passages:

> People of the same trade seldom meet together, even for merriment and diversion, but the conversation ends in a conspiracy against the public, or in some contrivance to raise prices. It

---

[1] Adam Smith, *An Inquiry into the Nature and Causes of the Wealth of Nations*, Cannan ed. (New York: Modern Library, 1937), pp. 826–27.
[2] Ibid., p. 627.

is impossible to prevent such meetings, by any law which either could be executed, or would be consistent with liberty and justice. But though the law cannot hinder people of the same trade from sometimes assembling together, it ought to do nothing to facilitate such assemblies; much less to render them necessary.[3]

He then continues his discussion of corporations by saying: "An incorporation not only renders [assemblies] necessary, but makes the act of the majority binding on the whole."[4] He points out as an evil effect of this that:

The pretense that corporations are necessary for the better government of trade, is without any foundation. The real and effectual discipline which is exercised over a workman, is not that of his corporation, but that of his customers. It is the fear of losing their employment which restrains his frauds and corrects his negligence. An exclusive corporation necessarily weakens the force of this discipline. A particular set of workmen must then be employed, let them behave well or ill. It is upon this account, that in many larger incorporated towns no tolerable workmen are to be found, even in some of the most necessary trades. If you would have your work tolerably executed, it must be done in the suburbs, where the workmen, having no exclusive privilege, have nothing but their character to depend upon, and you must then smuggle it into the town as well as you can.[5]

In contemporary terms, this means that the licensed economist must be in favor of the Sherman Act.[6]

Let me turn now to two of the more important and serious conditions that should be imposed upon members of the licensed economics profession. The first is that the economist should never pass judgment on a problem as a technologist. Economists as a rule know little about technology and are not apt to learn much about it either. To bring this point home, I will again turn to Smith, who also erred in this respect:

It frequently happens that while high wages are given to the workmen in one manufacture, those in another are obliged to content themselves with bare subsistence. The one is in an advancing state, and has, therefore, a continual demand for

---

[3] Ibid., p. 128.

[4] Ibid., p. 129.

[5] Ibid.

[6] When I was younger, I would have left it there, but now I am inclined to accept, as a substitute, the licensed economist's approval of Senator Sherman's brother's march through Georgia.

new hands: The other is in a declining state, and the superabundance of hands is continually increasing. Those two manufactures may sometimes be in the same town, and sometimes in the same neighborhood, without being able to lend the least assistance to one another. The statute of apprenticeship may oppose it in the one case, and both that and an exclusive corporation in the other. In many different manufactures, however, the operations are so much alike, that the workmen could easily change trades with one another, if those absurd laws did not hinder them. The arts of weaving plain linen and plain silk, for example, are almost entirely the same. That of weaving plain wollen is somewhat different; but the difference is so insignificant, that either a linen or a silk weaver might become a tolerable workman in a very few days.[7]

Contrary to what is implied, there is very little evidence that Smith actually knew anything about weaving. He should have restrained himself to being an economist and should have tested the ease of transferability and substitutability of skills by the kinds of measures that an economist has at his disposal—measures of mobility of actual resources. In this regard contemporary economists are no exception. Economic literature is loaded with technological judgments. Here are a few examples.

In what was perhaps one of the most famous doctoral theses ever written in the United States, Milton Friedman assumed that the main difference between a doctor and a dentist is a year or two of medical training. Yet what this technologist was saying is that allowing for two years of additional training, if it were not for the American Medical Association, there would be an absolute equivalence in the rates of pay and in incomes from independent professional practice in these two areas.

In my own writings on scale economies, again, I casually decided that such economies or diseconomies are manifest entirely within the plant and not within the firm—a technological judgment for which there is not the slightest basis whatsoever.

A final, more contemporary example: Analysts at the FTC are convinced that a dulcet voice will make a normally rational child consume presugared cereals in unlimited amounts—a technological judgment I would argue they are incapable of making.

As I mentioned earlier, there is a propensity to license fields in which the task is difficult or the task of the customer in determining whether it is well performed is difficult. It is impossible to come up with a definition of "difficult" in this context, however, at least in economic

---

[7] Smith, *The Wealth of Nations*, pp. 134–35.

terms other than price terms. Yet we surreptitiously say brain surgery must be difficult and making a hamburger must be easy. Actually, on a scientific basis we know nothing of the sort. I would propose, therefore, that we cease making technological judgments. (Had this rule been in effect during the conference's presentations, there would have been long periods of sustained silence.)

My final requirement for a licensed economist is that if one wishes to reform an economic policy, one must first be able to explain why that policy was adopted. The reasons for this fairly strenuous requirement are several. First of all, as reformers, our primary focus is (and should be) on policies that have been adopted by numerous governments or have been adhered to by a government for a long period of time. Thus the accidental, the ephemeral, the transitory, the experimental are, if not eroded, at least overcome by the central focus and drive of the policy in question. Indeed, economists are not really very good at detecting or analyzing reform of short-run policies. We find out about a public policy problem well after it has developed; we seldom predict its oncome.

Second, policies that persist, that is, those that have not been stopped or grossly modified once tried, should be considered purposely chosen. They must have definite beneficiaries, and those beneficiaries know and desire the results of the policies. Most people will say this sounds all right but in their actual behavior will reject that precept. In fact, I believe that if you were to canvass our profession in a skillful way, you would find that the overwhelmingly popular theory that we have for economic policies may be called the theory of mistakes.

If I asked the typical economist why we have the minimum wage laws (when all good economists, and most bad ones, view such laws as "bad"), the answer will be that it is a mistake; the benevolence of the public at large leads them to support what is essentially perverse legislation. If I asked why, over the 200 years since Smith launched his attack on mercantilism, tariffs have, if anything, increased in their protective content, the common answer would be something like: the doctrine of comparative cost is too complex for people, and they are hoodwinked by the short-run transition costs of adopting a policy of free trade. If I asked why it now takes increased training to be an account executive for a brokerage house—and therefore be able to read to the customer over the phone the day's gossip in the *Wall Street Journal*—the answer would be that this is a mistake.

Now, I want to emphasize that this is a wonderful theory in one respect. I defy anyone to name a phenomenon that you ask me to explain to which I cannot answer, "It's a mistake." The theory obviously has enormous explanatory power. This means, however, that it is a vacuous theory. If everything can be explained as a mistake, then nothing can be explained. While I do believe societies make mistakes, I do not think that we ought ever to use that theory, that explanation, until we have an actual theory of mistakes. If we can devise classes of phenomena on which societies systematically make mistakes and can show their mistakes by the fact that, once having committed them, they recognize them as such and withdraw from them, then we would have something to work with. But as long as we say the only reason society does not repeal the minimum wage laws is that Milton Friedman is only writing once every three weeks in *Newsweek*, I have to say that we are in a romantic, self-deluding state.

The other theory, which I prefer, characterizes people as rational utility-maximizers. Yet I want to warn against its misuse, for it could easily become a tautology. Probably no government is skillful enough to invent a law that does not have some beneficiaries and some losers.

We could always say, after suitable research, that we had identified the beneficiaries and that these beneficiaries had clearly been the supporters of the new law. This itself, however, is a tautology; it is not a suitably demanding scientific stance for an economist to assume.

What is required in addition to identifying the beneficiaries of a policy change is to show that the beneficiaries have the characteristics appropriate to the successful achievement of policy change. That is an area in which our progress so far has been extremely small. I would also argue that the way to discover the *intended* effects of a policy is to discover what they actually are. The preambles of most statutes give little clue to the *real* purposes, and congressional hearings, often remarkable for their irrelevance or digressive properties, can usually be relied on to support virtually *any* new legislation. To learn what a law is really doing, one has to study its actual effects.

To emphasize this point, let us return to Mr. Smith. In his marvelous book 4—that splendid, powerful, massive assault on mercantilism—he paints mercantilism as a policy adopted by a clever, deceptive group of merchants and manufacturers who were skilled in the deployment of duplicitous argument, in the deception of their bucolic landlord opponents—rustics who were not skilled in fertile, fast, intellectual combat. Hence, Smith concludes, this 150-year-old policy of mercantilism had been sold to the dominant class of Great Britain by a clever and small, but growing, minority. In other words, he was saying that it was all a mistake.

Now, I find this an absolutely incredible interpretation, although I have done none of the historical work necessary to document my suspicions. Parliament, even as late as George III, was owned lock, stock, and barrel by the landed classes of Great Britain. The landed classes perhaps were better at hunting a fox than a fallacy, but they knew how to hire experts, and they knew how to get fairly promising agents, such as Edmund Burke, to propose and support their interests in the legislature. They were not required to stay home nights and study up on these things for themselves.

I question the common thesis that the main thrust, burden, and purpose of the policy of mercantilism were hostile to the economic interests of Great Britain. It is difficult to believe that a persistent, widespread policy was inimical to the interests of the dominant classes of English society and was kept on the statute books for 150 years only by the sneaky, sniveling, clever deceptions of the merchants and their representatives.

Let me sum up. The two conditions that I have outlined for membership in the economics profession—that you not be a technologist and that you find rational, tested explanations for the adoption of public policies—seem to me to be very promising challenges and, at the same time, enormously discouraging. Our ability to follow this advice, however, will affect greatly the amount of useful advice we will be asked to give over the next 150 years.